GUIDE

Logis
of
Great Britain

*also listing the
hotels in
Logis of Ireland*

Fayrer Garden, Bowness on Windermere

Crossways, Wilmington

Published by Logis (GB) Limited, 20 Church Road, Horspath, Oxford OX9 1RU

Cabra Castle, Kingscourt

Shaftesbury Hotel, Dundee

Text Copyright © 1995 Logis (GB) Ltd.
Illustrations Copyright © 1995 Logis (GB) Ltd.
Map Copyright © 1995 The Ordnance Survey

ISBN 0 9518694 3 4

Text compiled & edited by Jenny Horsley, Juliet Nixey
& Sonia Yeatman
Cover Illustration by Paul Cox
Cover and colour section designed by
Melissa Orrom Swan
Typeset by Gary Millard of QPP and
Getset (BTS) Ltd
Printed & Bound in Great Britain by The Bath Press,
Bath, Avon
Distributed by Springfield Books, Huddersfield, West Yorkshire

David Adams

Eoin Hickey

Welcome to Logis!

As the Presidents of Logis of Great Britain and Logis of Ireland we are delighed to have the opportunity to introduce this, the 1995 guide to the best independent hospitality in Britain and Ireland.

Scanning the pages of this guide you will find many different hotels, varying from country houses to traditional coaching inns and restaurants with rooms. Whatever their individual style you are assured of a genuine warm welcome, good accommodation and excellent regional cuisine wherever you see the yellow and green fireplace sign. It is the beauty of Logis that each of our hotels are individual.

This is why we say that Logis means hospitality with a human face. We hope that you enjoy using this guide to travel through Britain and Ireland and discover the Logis spirit for yourself.

David Adams
President
The Association of
Logis of Great Britain

Eoin Hickey
President
The Association of
Logis of Ireland

Europlogis in 1995

The Logis Associations of Great Britain and Ireland are sisters to the long established Logis de France and recently formed, Logis of Italy. These four individual groups have joined together to create Europlogis, to unite the best in independent hospitality throughout Europe.

Over 5,000 hotels linked by a sign and philosophy. So, wherever you are in Europe, to ensure the best hospitality, look for the fireplace sign.

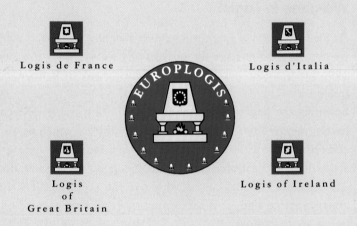

Logis de France

Logis d'Italia

Logis of Great Britain

Logis of Ireland

For further information about Europlogis please contact:–

Logis of Great Britain	or	Logis of Ireland
20 Church Road		Unit 2
Horspath		Sandymount Village Centre
Oxford OX9 1RU		Dublin 4
Tel 01865 875888		Tel 01 668 9688
Fax 01865 875777		Fax 01 668 9727

Reservations for the hotels in Logis of Great Britain and Logis of Ireland can be made either directly with the relevant hotel or through the Logis office. Visitors travelling from the USA might prefer to contact our local agent, Toll Free 800 989 7676, Fax 203 838 5338.

Copies of the individual guides are available from any of the following Logis national offices. Prices quoted are in GB£ sterling and cover postage within Europe. Please add an additional £1 to the cost for postage outside Europe.

If you would prefer to pay by credit card (Visa or Mastercard) please send details of your card number, expiry date and authorised user name. We will then send you the relevant guide(s) and debit your account accordingly.

Federation nationale des Logis de France
83 Avenue d'Italie
75013 Paris, France
tel + 33 1 45 84 70 00
fax + 33 1 45 83 59 66

1995 Guide £9.75

Logis d'Italia
Via Lamarmora 44
1 - 20122, Milano, Italy
tel + 39 2 55 18 79 60
fax + 39 2 55 18 83 49

1995 Guide £4.50

Logis of Ireland
Unit 2, Sandymount Village Centre
Dublin 4, Ireland
tel + 353 1 668 9688
fax + 353 1 668 9727

Details of the Irish hotels are included in the Logis of Great Britain directory.

Logis of Great Britain
20 Church Road, Horspath, Oxford
OX9 1RU England
tel + 44 1865 875888
fax + 44 1865 875777

1995 Guide £7.95

LOGIS OF GREAT BRITAIN
REGIONAL CUISINE AWARDS

Logis hotels are noted for their excellent food, taking pride in the use of the best fresh regional produce.

In 1994 Logis of Great Britain organised a regional cuisine competition to celebrate the wealth of regional fare offered by its hotels. Finalists were picked to represent each of the nine areas of Britain. Flying the flag for their regions were: **Scotland** – Sukie Barber, Old Pines, Spean Bridge; **North** – Chris Davy, Rose & Crown, Barnard Castle; **Midlands** – Jeremy Hall, Portland Hotel, Buxton; **Wales** – Jo Reddicliffe, Dolmelynllyn Hall, Dolgellau; **Heart of England** – Jenny Wratten, Yew Tree Inn, Newbury; **East Anglia** – Mark Deveney, Hill House Hotel, Horndon on the Hill; **South West** – Mark Brimson, Ebford House Hotel, Exeter; **South** – Veronica Colley, Little Barwick House, Yeovil; **South East** – David Stott, Crossways, Wilmington.

On November 1st our judges met for the competition final, a cook off at Westminster College, London. Albert Roux, chairman of the judging panel, Michael Wynn Jones, Editor of The Sainsbury's Magazine and The Earl Howe, Parliamentary Secretary (Lords), Ministry of Agriculture, Fisheries and Food,

Veronica Colley sprinkling on a secret ingredient!

Sukie & Bill Barber preparing fresh vegetable selections.

Jenny Wratten, Albert Roux and the
praiseworthy Ginger Sponge Pudding.

Chris Davy and assistant, Gaynor Edwards.

tasted each of the 27 dishes placed before them – a starter, main
course and sweet from each chef. Among the delicacies they
sampled were Colchester oysters and mussels from East Anglia,
Moorland venison from The Midlands, Bara Brith ice cream
from Wales, lamb from the South and rabbit from the South
East.

After much deliberation it was declared that the standard of all
the entrants had been praiseworthy, but Chris Davy was
awarded first prize, Jo Reddicliffe second and Mark Deveny
third. Then a surprise. Albert Roux was so impressed by Jenny
Wratten's Steamed Ginger Sponge that he rewarded her with a
special prize, the opportunity to spend a week working in one of
his many restaurants world-wide.

For full details of the hotels that cooked in the competition final
please consult the relevant guide entry.

The finalists with Albert Roux

THE MARCHES
Tranquility in the Land of Conflicts Past

From Chester to Chepstow lies a strip of distinctive, yet little known, countryside where the mountains of Wales dissolve into the gentler hills and valleys of England – the Welsh Marches.

Today we view the border as little more than a statement of administrative fact – the boundary between two countries. But the division is no arbitrary line on the map. It has always been border country in every sense. This was the very western edge of the civil Roman empire.

The Stiperstones

In Saxon times, King Offa defined a similar boundary with the dyke that now takes his name; a mighty ditch and rampart running from Prestatyn in North Wales to Chepstow in the south.

Offa's Dyke was probably more a political statement than a defensive rampart; but boundaries always generate conflict and the Marches were no exception. The evidence lives on in the splendid chain of border castles running through the area. These were the fortresses of the Marcher Lords, a semi-autonomous group of barons who were despatched to the border to keep the peace between Welsh and English. Their territories were served by the delightful market and county towns that now offer such a feast of history to the visitor.

The area boasts three great fishing rivers: the Wye, Severn and Welsh Dee. Each has at least one tributary that should be on the itinerary of the Marches' explorer.

Stokesay

Carding Mill Valley, Church Stretton

The Marches is a district to explore leisurely, and for all who can that means on foot. The Shropshire hills around Church Stretton offer variety to suit all tastes from the stroller who may wander up the Cardingmill Valley to the rambler who wants a day over the summits of the dramatic Stiperstones or the rolling Long Mynd. Or why not follow the border itself making sallies along the Offa's Dyke National Trail, but treating yourself to the warmth and comfort of a 'Logis Fireplace' for the evening.

A few minutes with this guide book will reveal a wealth of touring opportunities up and down this undiscovered territory. And though its main attraction is that it offers a haven away from the rush, bustle and stress of the modern world, it is easy to get to. No motorways disturb its peace, but they deliver you right to the doorstep, whether on the M56 to Chester, the M54 to Shropshire or M4 to Chepstow.

One thing is certain – wherever you first choose to visit the Marches you will get a taste for this gem of unspoilt Britain that will bring you back time and again – and there will always be something new to see.

A typical vista of Marches hills

Logis Central Reservations, for all reasons ...
... and all seasons.

If you are interested in a touring holiday travelling between Logis hotels why not contact the Logis central reservations office?

Many Logis hotels, particularly those in the Cotswolds and Wensleydale Valley, work together, offering visitors the opportunity to abandon the car and tour an area of natural beauty on foot or bicycle. Some hotels will offer a luggage transfer service and advise on routes to make the most of your stay whether for a long weekend or two week complete break.

Explore The Dales from Simonstone Hall, Hawes or The Rose & Crown, Barnard Castle.

Enjoy a cookery course, or visit the antique shop at Fosse
Farmhouse, Nettleton.

Cycling through the Cotswolds.

A number of Logis of Great Britain hotels also offer unusual
activity programmes; wine appreciation, adult learn to swim
courses, play the guitar weekends, horse racing programmes
and golfing breaks playing a selection of different courses, to
name but a few.

Of course you could choose to visit a Logis hotel just to relax
and enjoy the good food and excellent individual hospitality!
Whatever you are looking for why not contact our central
reservations team and ask if they can suggest a Logis hotel to
suit your particular requirements?

Use The Steppes, Hereford at the south of the Welsh Marches to
explore the area.

Logis Central Reservations 01865 875888 Fax 01865 875777

Glenfriars Hotel, Jedburgh

Old Manor, Trowbridge

Tottington Manor, Henfield

Duke of Connaught Hotel, York

Ordnance Survey®
MiniScale mapping

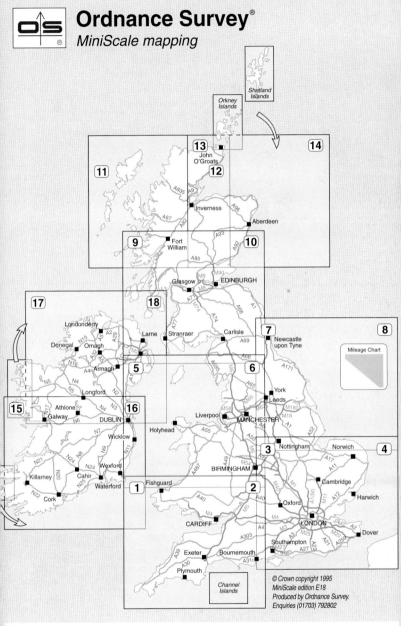

Shetland Islands

Orkney Islands

13 John O'Groats **12**

11

Inverness

Aberdeen

14

9 Fort William **10**

Glasgow EDINBURGH

17 **18**

Londonderry Larne Carlisle **7** Newcastle upon Tyne **8**

Donegal Omagh Stranraer

Armagh **5** **6**

Mileage Chart

Longford York Leeds

Athlone Holyhead Liverpool MANCHESTER

15 Galway **16** DUBLIN Wicklow Nottingham Norwich **4**

Wexford **3**

Killarney Cahir Waterford **1** Fishguard BIRMINGHAM **2** Cambridge Harwich

Cork Oxford

CARDIFF LONDON Dover

Southampton

Exeter Bournemouth

Plymouth

Channel Islands

© Crown copyright 1995
MiniScale edition E18
Produced by Ordnance Survey.
Enquiries (01703) 792802

Key to map pages

▲ **LOGIS** Hotel

M4 S Motorway, service area

Junction, limited access

A31 Primary route

Other main road

County boundary

National boundary

Domestic ferry route

✈ Airport/with Customs

Urban area

○ Primary town

○ Other town

National Parks,
Forest Parks &
Scenic areas

River / Lake

*Northern Ireland based upon the Ordnance Survey map with the sanction
of the controller of H M Stationery Office. Crown copyright reserved. Permit No. 761*

*Ireland based on the Ordnance Survey by permission of the Government
of the Irish Republic. Permit No. 6000*

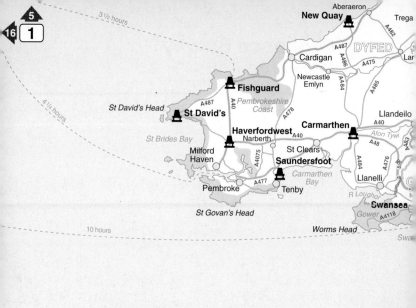

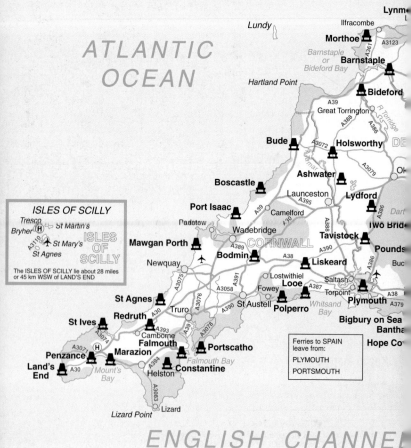

ATLANTIC
OCEAN

ENGLISH CHANNEL

ISLES OF SCILLY

Tresco
Bryher
St Martin's
St Mary's
St Agnes

ISLES
OF
SCILLY

The ISLES OF SCILLY lie about 28 miles
or 45 km WSW of LAND'S END

Ferries to SPAIN
leave from:

PLYMOUTH

PORTSMOUTH

© Crown copyright 1995

Ashbourne
Ripley
A517
Derby
A6
Burton
upon Trent
geley
Lichfield
A444
Tamworth
nwhills
Sutton
Coldfield
Nuneaton
Coventry
M6
A45
A46
M42
Rugby
Leamington
Spa
Warwick
A425
Daventry
Weedon
Stratford-
upon-Avon
A422
Shipston-
on-Stour
A429
esham
Blockley
Chipping
Norton
ow-on-
Wold
Bledington
am
Bourton on the
Water
Burford
A40
Bibury
Witney
Coln St
aldwyns
Lechlade
Oxford
A420
Dorchester
on Thames
Swindon
Wantage
BERKSHIRE
Hungerford
A4
ugh
Newbury
Pewsey
North Wessex
Downs
Basingstoke
Andover
A303
Stockbridge
A30
Salisbury
A3057
ury
Romsey
A31
Eastleigh
Southampton
Hythe
Brockenhurst
Ringwood
Christ-
church
Lymington
Sway
urnemouth
ole Bay
The
Needles
Yarmouth
St Catherine's Point
Ventnor

Nottingham
A52
A1
Sleaford
A607
Boston
A1121
Hunst
THE WASH

Castle
Donington
East
Midlands
Loughborough
A6006
A607
Grantham
A52
A607
A16
A1
A15

Melton
Mowbray
Stretton
A606
Stamford
A16
Bourne
Spalding
A151
A1073
A17
A1101
Wisbech
A1122
March

Leicester
Oakham
A6121
A47
R Nene
A605
Peterborough
A1139
Chatteris
CAMBRIDGESHIRE

Hinckley
Wigston
A6
Market
Harborough
A427
Harringworth
A427
A605
Corby
Oundle
Thrapston
A14
Huntingdon
A141
A142
Ely
Ha

Wellingborough
Northampton
Kettering
A14
ENGLAND
A508
A14
A1123
St Ives
A14
Cambridge

Bedford
Rushden
St Neots
A6
A428
A1198
Sandy
Royston
A505
Ha
Sa
Wa

Banbury
A361
A43
Towcester
A5
A422
A421
Milton
Keynes
Buckingham
Leighton Buzzard
A5
Letchworth
A507
Baldock
A1
Rickling
Green
Hitchin
A602
Stevenage
Bishop's
Stortford
Du

Steeple
Aston
A34
Bicester
BUCKING-
HAMSHIRE
A41
A413
A418
Dunstable
Luton
A505
Luton
Airport
Hemel
Hempstead
Welwyn
A120
Stanste
Airport
Harlow
ESS

Princes
Risborough
Aylesbury
A329
Thame
A413
The Chilterns
High
Wycombe
Amersham
Great
Missenden
St Albans
M1
Hatfield
Hertford
A414
A414

Watford
Beaconsfield
Maidenhead
Slough
A40
LONDON
Brentwood
Ilford
Dagenham

Henley-on-
Thames
A423
A4
Reading
Heathrow
Airport
Bracknell
Staines
Richmond
A205
London
A13
Dartford
Orpington
A225

Woking
Esher
Leatherhead
A24
Sutton
Croydon
A232
Surrey Hills
M26

Pewsey
GREATER LONDON
Harrow

Guildford
Farnham
A287
SURREY
Dorking
Redhill
Reigate
Sevenoaks
A21

Godalming
Gatwick
Airport
Crawley
East
Grinstead
A264
Tunbridge
Wells
A267
Cro
EA

Crawley
Alton
A31
A3
Haslemere
A272
A283
R Arun
Forest Row
Horsham
Haywards
Heath
Uckfie
SU

Winchester
Petersfield
Sussex
Downs
Midhurst
A272
Billingshurst
A272
A23
Ashington
Henfield
Halland
Lewes
A27
Hailsham

Sutton
Southampton
Wickham
Havant
Pulborough
Arundel
WEST SUSSEX
Worthing
A263
Wilmington
A259

Fareham
A32
Gosport
Bosham
Chichester
Littlehampton
Brighton
& Hove
Newhaven
Birling Gap

Cowes
Portsmouth
Hayling Is.
Selsey
Bognor
Regis
Selsey Bill

Newport
A3054
A3020
ISLE OF WIGHT
A3055
Seaview

© Crown copyright 1995

Ferries to ISLE OF WIGHT
leave from:

LYMINGTON

PORTSMOUTH

SOUTHAMPTON

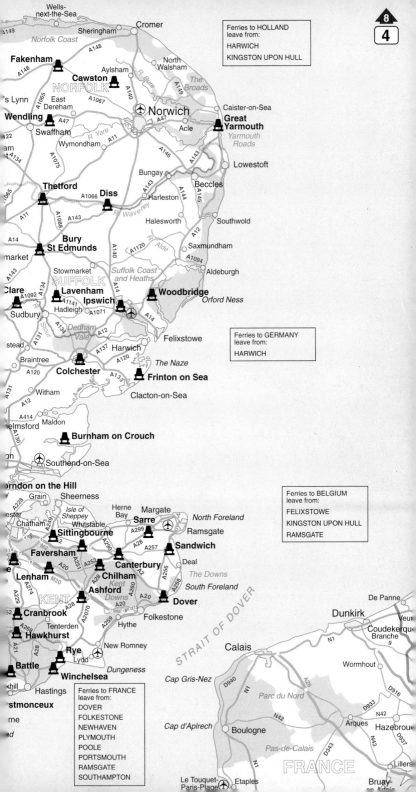

A3
9
18 5
1
A49
A21
A22
A20
A1
A24
A7
DOWN
Downpatrick
A50
A25
Newcastle
Lecale
Newry
A2
Coast
Mourne

Point of Ayre
A10
Ramsey
Bay
ISLE OF MAN
ISLE OF MAN
Ramsey
A3
A14
Peel
A18
A1
A2
Douglas
A27
A25
Port Erin
A7
Castletown

T62
Carlingford

4¾ hours (Seasonal)

IRISH SEA

eda

Balbriggan
Skerries
4¾ hours
(Seasonal)
Rush
Malahide
DUBLIN
UBLIN City
1 hour 10 min
(Seacat)
Dun Laoghaire
Bray
Greystones

Wicklow

w

Amlwch
A5025
ANGLESEY
Holyhead
A5
Menai
Bridge
Ban

Caernarfon
A40
Capel C
Caernarfon Bay
A4085
A4
Beddgelert
A487
Nefyn
A499
Porthmadog
Pwllheli
A497
Criccieth
Lleyn
Harlech
A496
Abersoch

Barmouth
A

Tywyn
Aberdovey
CARDIGAN BAY

Aberystwyth

Llanon

Aberaeron
New Quay
Trega
A482
DYFED
A487
Cardigan
Le

© Crown copyright 1995

Road Distances in Miles

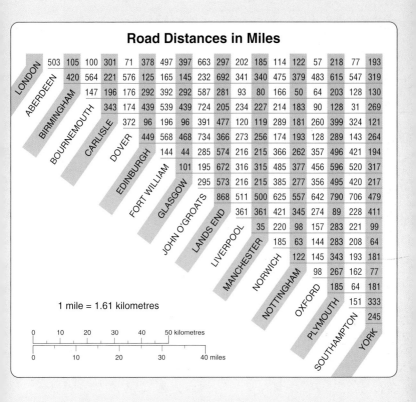

From \ To	ABERDEEN	BIRMINGHAM	BOURNEMOUTH	CARLISLE	DOVER	EDINBURGH	FORT WILLIAM	GLASGOW	JOHN O'GROATS	LANDS END	LIVERPOOL	MANCHESTER	NORWICH	NOTTINGHAM	OXFORD	PLYMOUTH	SOUTHAMPTON	YORK
LONDON	503	105	100	301	71	378	497	397	663	297	202	185	114	122	57	218	77	193
ABERDEEN		420	564	221	576	125	165	145	232	692	341	340	475	379	483	615	547	319
BIRMINGHAM			147	196	176	292	392	292	587	281	93	80	166	50	64	203	128	130
BOURNEMOUTH				343	174	439	539	439	724	205	234	227	214	183	90	128	31	269
CARLISLE					372	96	196	96	391	477	120	119	289	181	260	399	324	121
DOVER						449	568	468	734	366	273	256	174	193	128	289	143	264
EDINBURGH							144	44	285	574	216	215	366	262	357	496	421	194
FORT WILLIAM								101	195	672	316	315	485	377	456	596	520	317
GLASGOW									295	573	216	215	385	277	356	495	420	217
JOHN O'GROATS										868	511	500	625	557	642	790	706	479
LANDS END											361	361	421	345	274	89	228	411
LIVERPOOL												35	220	98	157	283	221	99
MANCHESTER													185	63	144	283	208	64
NORWICH														122	145	343	193	181
NOTTINGHAM															98	267	162	77
OXFORD																185	64	181
PLYMOUTH																	151	333
SOUTHAMPTON																		245

1 mile = 1.61 kilometres

```
0    10    20    30    40    50 kilometres
|----|----|----|----|----|

0         10        20        30        40 miles
|---------|---------|---------|---------|
```

NORTH SEA

Ferries to DENMARK
leave from:
HARWICH
NEWCASTLE UPON TYNE

Wells-
next-the-Sea
49
Cromer
Norfolk Coast   Sheringham
A148
Fakenham
A148   Aylsham   North
Cawston   Walsham
NORFOLK   The

Ferries to HOLLAND
leave from:
HARWICH
KINGSTON UPON HULL

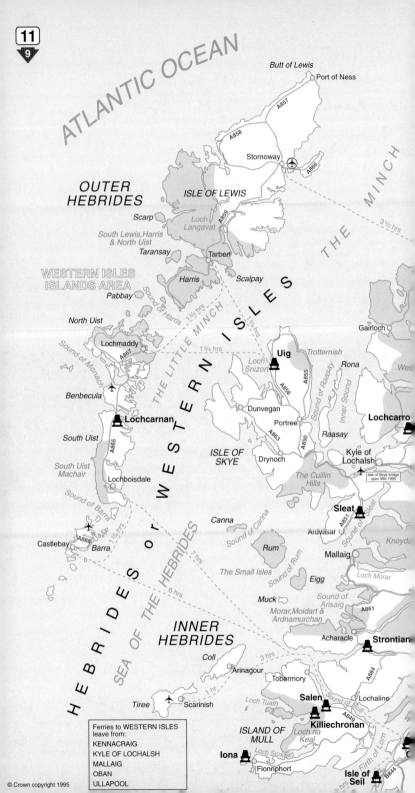

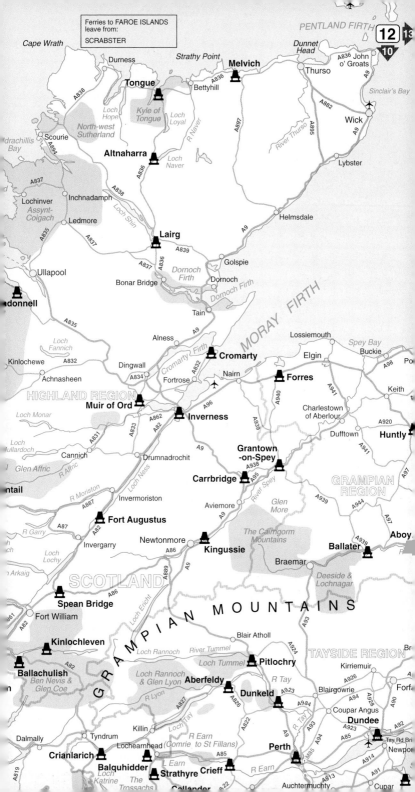

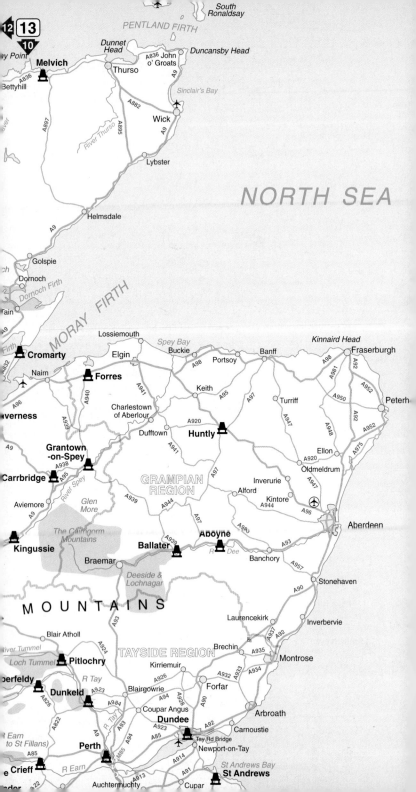

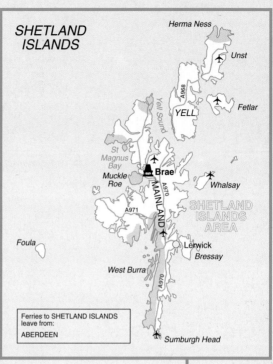

SHETLAND ISLANDS

Herma Ness

Unst

A968

Fetlar

YELL

St Magnus Bay

Muckle Roe

🏠 Brae

MAINLAND

A970

Whalsay

SHETLAND ISLANDS AREA

Yell Sound

A971

Foula

Lerwick

Bressay

West Burra

A970

Ferries to SHETLAND ISLANDS leave from:

ABERDEEN

Sumburgh Head

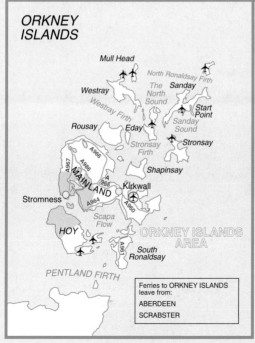

ORKNEY ISLANDS

Mull Head

North Ronaldsay Firth

Sanday

Westray

The North Sound

Start Point

Westray Firth

Sanday Sound

Rousay

Eday

Stronsay

A966

Stronsay Firth

A967

A986

MAINLAND

A965

Shapinsay

Kirkwall

Stromness

A964

A960

ORKNEY ISLANDS AREA

Scapa Flow

HOY

South Ronaldsay

A961

PENTLAND FIRTH

Ferries to ORKNEY ISLANDS leave from:

ABERDEEN

SCRABSTER

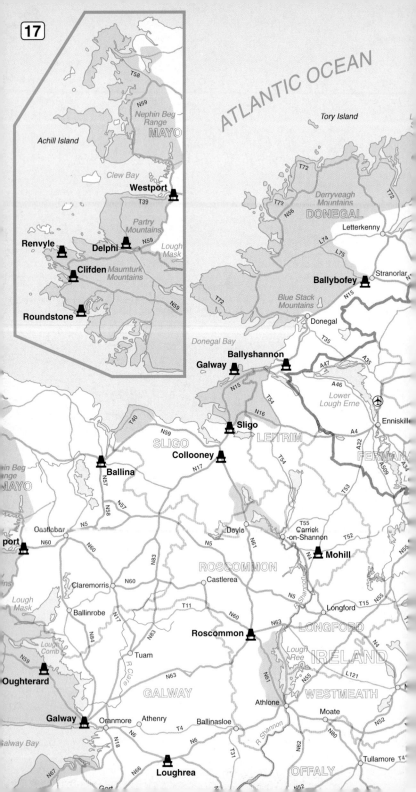

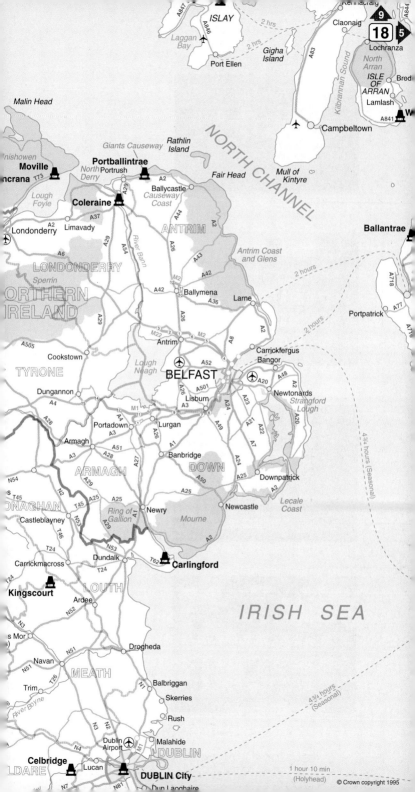

Melvich Hotel, Melvich

Cedar Hotel, Westbury

Kees Hotel, Ballybofey

Winston Manor, Churchill

How to use this Guide

There are five main sections to this guide; this the map and introductory section, the alphabetical list of member hotels in England and Wales, the alphabetical list of member hotels in Scotland, the alphabetical list of member hotels in Ireland, and the indexes which detail entries by town location and hotel name. We suggest that to identify the Logis hotel closest to your desired destination you first refer to the map section, where the location of a Logis hotel has been highlighted by a black fireplace symbol and bold printing of the place name. Then, find the relevant hotel's entry in one of the alphabetical lists of members.

Fireplace grading

While many hotels apply to join the Logis Association, only a few pass our rigorous inspection and are allowed to display the familiar yellow and green fireplace symbol. When an hotel is licensed to display the Logis sign it is a quality endorsement, indicating to the traveller that a certain degree of good hospitality, care, comfort and personal attention will be offered him.

Every member hotel has been graded according to the European Logis standard. On the basis of the score awarded at this grading, linked with the comments of our Inspector, we have awarded each Logis hotel 1, 2 or 3 fireplaces. This grading is shown next to the hotel name on the guide entry. We believe that any hotel that has passed the rigorous Logis inspection and is in this Guide will offer high standards of comfort and service. The fireplace grading, however, can be read as an
indication of the level of facilities and comfort that the hotel offers. Use the fireplace grading as a guide, but read the individual description thoroughly to create a true impression of the type of hotel. A fabulous, secluded, quiet hotel set in the highlands of Scotland may only be a 1 fireplace hotel because it has few 'modern' facilities, yet its restaurant and tranquil setting may be worth travelling miles for.

Children

The majority of hotels listed in this guide are happy to accept children of any age, and many have family rooms, cots, high chairs and baby listening services. However, we recommend that whenever travelling with children under the age of 12, you enquire with the hotel at the time of booking about their ability to accommodate children.

Some British Logis are unable to accept young children due to their antique decor and building style. Where possible we have given this information in the individual guide entry.

Reservations

We recommend that bookings are made as early as possible to avoid disappointment, particularly during the high season of early June to the end of September. Reservations should be made directly with the hotelier, who may request a deposit to secure the booking.

Prices

The prices listed in this Guide were correct at the time of going to press. However, we advise all customers to verify charges with the individual hotel when making a reservation, since some rates may vary with seasonal and economic changes.

Comment utiliser ce guide

Il y a cinq principales sections dans ce guide: la section d'introduction et des cartes, la liste alphabétique des hôtels en Angleterre et au Pays de Galles, la liste alphabétique des hôtels en Ecosse, la liste alphabétique des hôtels en Irlande et, enfin, deux index, des villes d'une part, des noms d'hôtels d'autre part, classés par ordre alphabétique.

Nous vous proposons de choisir l'hôtel Logis le plus proche de votre destination sur la section des cartes sur lesquelles l'emplacement d'un hôtel Logis a été mis en évidence par une cheminée. Ensuite, vous se cherchez l'hôtel dans une des listes alphabétiques.

Classement 'en Cheminée'

Alors que de nombreux établissements postulent pour adhérer à l'Association des Logis, très peu d'entre eux sont admis et habilités à afficher la célèbre cheminée jaune et verte, après avoir fait l'objet de notre rigoureuse inspection. Le label des Logis est un gage de qualité garantissant au voyageur un certain niveau en matière d'accueil, d'hospitalité, de confort.

Chaque hôtel a été classé selon les normes des Logis européens et en tenant compte des appréciations de nos inspecteurs, en 1, 2 ou 3 cheminées. Ce classement est indiqué à côté du nom de l'hôtel.

Dès lors, tout hôtel de ce guide, après l'inspection rigoureuse des Logis, offre une garantie de qualité. Le classement 'en cheminée' précise le niveau du confort et des services. Utilisez ce classement comme un guide, mais lisez minutieusement les descriptions individuelles pour avoir une impression complète sur le type d'hôtel. Ainsi, un hôtel confortable, tranquille et retiré dans la Haute-Ecosse pourra avoir seulement

1 cheminée, étant donné qu'il est équipé de peu d'installations "modernes"; néanmoins, son restaurant et sa localisation très retirée méritent que l'on fasse un détour pour s'y rendre.

Enfants

La majorité des hôtels inscrits dans ce guide y seront très heureux de recevoir les enfants de tout âge, et plusieurs d'entre eux ont des chambres familiales, des lits pour enfants, des chaises hautes. Cependant, chaque fois que vous voyagez avec des enfants de moins de 12 ans, nous vous recommandons, au moment de la réservation, de vérifier avec l'hôtel ses possibilités d'accieilliz les enfants. En effet, quelques Logis de Grande-Bretagne, à cause de leur décoration d'époque et de leur style de construction, n'accepteront pas les jeunes enfants. Cette précision est mentionnée dans le guide, dans la description de chaque hôtel.

Réservation

Pour éviter les déceptions, il est recommandé de faire vos réservations le plus tôt possible, particulièrement durant la haute-saison: de début juin y à fin septembre.

Les réservations doivent être faites directement auprès de l'hôtelier qui peut, le cas échéant, vous demander un acompte à titre de garantie.

Prix

Les prix inscrits dans ce guide ont étés fixés au moment du tirage. Toutefois, nous vous conseillons de vous les faire préciser au moment de la réservation, car les tarifs peuvent varier selon les saisons, et en fonction des changements économiques.

Benutzungshinweise für diesen Führer

Dieser Führer beinhaltet fünf Hauptsektionen; die Karte und die Einführung, das alphabetische Verzeichnis der Mitgliedhotels in England und Wales, das alphabetische Verzeichnis der Mitgliedhotels in Schottland, das alphabetische Verzeichnis der Mitgliedhotels in Irland, und das Inhaltsverzeichnis, welches Eintragungen von Städtelagen und Hotelnamen vermittelt.

Wir schlagen vor, daß Sie, um das Ihrem Reiseziel am nächsten gelegene Logishotel zu finden, Ihre Kartensektion aufschlagen, wo Sie die Lage eines Logishotels durch das Symbol eines schwarzen Kamines und Fettdruck des Ortsnamens hervorgehoben sehen. Schlagen Sie dann dieses bezügliche Hotel in einem der alphabetischen Mitgliedsverzeichnissen nach.

Kaminklassifizierung

Während viele Hotels der Logisassoziation beitreten möchten, bestehen nur wenige unsere rigorose Inspektion und erhalten damit die bekannte gelbe und grüne Kaminplakette. Das Logissymbol ist ein Gütezeichen, das dem Reisenden einen bestimmten Standard von Gastfreundlichkeit, Fürsorge, Komfort und persönlicher Bedienung garantiert.

Jedes Mitgliedhotel wurde entsprechend eines europäischen Logisstandards eingestuft. Wir haben durch ein Punktsystem eine Einstufung ausgearbeitet und in Verbindung mit der Begutachtung unseres Inspektors jedem Logis Hotel 1, 2 oder 3 Kamine verliehen. Diese Einstufung ist neben dem Hotelnamen im Führer angezeigt.

Wir sind der Meinung, daß jedes Hotel, das diese rigorose Logisinspektion bestanden hat und in diesem Führer erscheint, einen hohen Standard an Komfort und Bedienung bietet. Die Einteilung nach Kaminen deutet auch den Einrichtungsgrad und die angebotenen Mahlzeiten an. Bedienen Sie sich der Abstufung nach Kaminen als Anhaltspunkt, aber lesen Sie die einzelne Beschreibung gründlich durch, damit Sie sich ein wahres Bild vom Typ dieses Hotels machen können. Ein fabelhaftes, abgelegenes, ruhiges Hotel im Schottischen Hochland gelegen, ist z.B. nur

ein 1-Kamin Hotel, weil es wenig moderne Einrichtungen hat, jedoch sein Restaurant une seine ruhige Lage sind eine weite Reise wert.

Kinder

Die Mehrzahl der Hotels, die in diesem Führer verzeichnet sind, heißen Kinder jeden Alters willkommen und viele haben Familienzimmer, Kinderbetten, Kinderstühle und Babyruf. Jedoch empfehlen wir, daß Sie sich bei der Anmeldung am Hotel nach den Unterbringungsmöglichkeiten für Kinder erkundigen, falls Sie mit Kindern unter 12 Jahren reisen.

Einige britische Logis können wegen ihrer antiken Ausstattung keine kleinen Kinder aufnehmen. Wo möglich, haben wir diese Information unter der Sektion für die einzelnen Hotels eingetragen.

Zimmerreservierungen

Um Enttäuschungen zu vermeiden, empfehlen wir sobald wie möglich zu buchen, besonders während der Hochsaison von Anfang Juni bis Ende September.

Buchungen sollten direkt an den Hotelier gemacht werden, der Sie um eine Anzahlung ersuchen kann, um so Ihre Bestellung zu garantieren.

Preise

Die in diesem Führer angegebenen Preise waren zu Zeit des Druckes korrekt. Wir enpfehlen jedoch allen Interessenten, bei der Buchung die Preise mit den einzelnen Hotels zu bestätigen, da einige Preise sich nach Saison und wirtschaftlicher Lage verändern.

Come usare questa guida

La guida e'composta da cinque sezioni principali: la sezione introduttiva con carta geografica, l'elenco alfabetico degli hotel membri d'Inghilterra e Galles, l'elenco alfabetico degli hotel membri scozzesi, l'elenco alfabetico degli hotel membri d'Irlanda e l'indice contentente i nomi degli hotel e la posizione delle citta'.

Per identificare l'hotel Logis nella localita' desiderata, vi suggeriamo innanzitutto di consultare la mappa nella sezione introduttiva, dove la localita' degli hotel Logis e' evidenziata in grassetto col simbolo del caminetto. Una volta effettuata la scelta, cercate la descrizione dell'hotel negli elenchi alfabetici degli hotel membri.

Categoria caminetto

Parecchi hotel richiendono l'iscrizione all'Associazione Logis, ma solo quelli che superano il nostro severo esame possono esporre la targa gialla e verde con il tipico caminetto. Questo simbolo sanziona la qualità Logis e segnala al turista che troverà buona ospitalità, trattamento accurato e comfort.

Ogni hotel membro e' stato sottoposto ad ispezione, in conformita' dei requisiti europei Logis, al fine di stabilirne la categoria. A ciascun hotel sono stati assegnati 1, 2 o 3 caminetti, in base al risultato ottenuto con l'ispezione.

Accanto al nome di ciascun hotel elencato nella guida tranerete la relativo categoria assegnata.

Siamo certi che gli hotel sottoposti alla rigorosa ispezione Logis e presenti in questa guida vi offriranno le migliori comodita' ed un ottimo servizio.

La classifica caminetto, comunque, puo' essere interpretata come un'indicazione dei servizi offerti dall'hotel. Usate la classifica caminetto come una guida, ma leggete attentamente la descrizione dell'hotel al fine di averne la giusta impressione. A un favoloso, tranquillo e isolato hotel posto sulle montagne scozzesi potrebbe essere stato assegnato un solo caminetto poiche' dispone di poche "modernita", anche se probabilmente vale la pena di effuttuare un lungo viaggio per raggiungerlo e gustarne la buona cucina e la splendida posizione.

Bambini

Le maggior parte degli hotel elencati nella guida accetta bambini di ogni eta'. Molti di essi dispongono di stanze familiari e ottimi servizi per famiglie con bambini. Nel caso di viaggi con bambini di eta' inferiore ai 12 anni vi consigliamo di informarvi, all'atto della prenotazione, circa le capacita' dell'hotel di accettarli.

Alcuni hotel britannici Logis, a causa delle loro antiche decorazioni e stile dell'edificio, non accettano bambini al di sotto di una certs eta'. Dove possibile, queste informazioni sono state segnalate nella descrizione degli hotel.

Prenotazioni

Vi raccomandiamo di prenotare il piu' presto possibile, soprattutto per i periodi di alta stagione (inizio giugno – fine settembre).

Prezzi

I prezzi contenuti nella guida erano corretti al momento della messa in stampa. Consigliamo comunque ai clienti di verificare i prezzi all'atto della prenotazione, in quanto alcune tariffe possono avere subito dei cambiamenti.

Como usar la guía

Hay cinco secciones esenciales en esta guía: un mapa con la introducción, una lista alfabetica de hoteles Logis en Inglaterra y en Gales, una lista alfabetica en Escocia, una lista alfabetica de hoteles Logis en Irlanda, y por último dos indices el cuál le explica como encontrar los hoteles de acuerdo a la ciudad y al nombre del hotel.

Le sugerimos que si desea encontrar el hotel logis más cercano a la destinación que se dirige, lea la sección del mapa donde la ubicación de un hotel Logis claramente sobresale con el simbolo de una chimenea negra y el nombre del lugar. Luego, busque como llegar al hotel en una de la listas alfabéticas.

Categorias en chimeneas

Mientras muchos hoteles solicitan el ingreso en la Asociación de los Logis, solo unos pocos lo consiguen, tràs una inspección rigorosa, y se pueden distinguir exhibiendo el famoso simbolo de la chimenea verde y amarillo. El sello de los Logis es un compromiso de calidad que garantiza al huesped un cierto nivel de acojida, de hospitalidad y de confort. Cada hotel miembro ha sido categorizado de acuerdo al nivel Europeo de Logis. En base a los puntos otorgados y con los comentarios de nuestro inspector; hemos otorgado a cada hotel Logis 1, 2 o 3 chimeneas. Estas categorias están al lado del nombre del hotel en la guía.

Nosotros creemos que el hotel que haya pasado estas severas inspecciones y que están mencionados en esta guía, le podrán ofrecer alta calidad en comodidad y servicio. Sin embargo, las categorías en chimeneas pueden ser leidas como una indicación del nivel de facilidades y servicios de cocina que el hotel ofrece y también como guía; pero lea la descripción individual con detalle para crear una verdadeva impresión de la clase de hotel en el cuál se hospeda.

Un fabuloso y tranquilo hotel en las montañas de Escocia puede tener solamente 1 chimenea como categoría ya que tiene pocas facilidades "modernas", pero sin embargo su ambiente tranquilo y el restaurante que ofrece hacen que valga la pena viajar unos kilometros.

Niños

La mayor parte de los hoteles mencionados en esta guía estarán encantados de acajer niños de cualquier edad. Diversos de ellos tienen habitaciones para familias y especiales facilidades para personas con bebés. Non obstante, le sugerimos que cuando viaje con niños menores de 12 años, pida información al hotel sobre sus posibilidades de acoger a los niños. Algunos hoteles Logis Británicos no aceptan niños menores debido a la decoration antigua y su estilo de construcción. Esta información esta indicada en la guía.

Reservas

Le recomendamos que haga sus reservas lo más tempranos posible para evitar desilusiones, particularmente durante la temporada alta, en los comienzos de Junio hasta finales de Setiembre.

Las reservas pueden ser directamente hechas con el hotellero quién le solicitará un depósito para asegurar su reserva.

Precios

Los precios listados en esta guía fueron correctos en el momento que se imprentó. Sin embargo le sugerimos que verifiquen con el hotel cuando hagan sus reservas, ya que algunos precios pueden variar según las temporades y los cambios económicos.

Descriptions and Signs

OLD TOWN, Surrey
A picturesque village in the heart of the Surrey Downs.

🔭 **THE RED LION HOTEL**
Main Street, Old Town, Surrey AB1 2CD
📞 (0123) 87654 FAX (0123) 87655
DAVID & JENNY SMITH

🛏 14, 12 en-suite, from £28.00 per person, double occ.
Lunch served. Non-residents welcome. Open all year.
🍴 £13.95, last orders 8pm.
🍷 Fresh fruit and vegetables from the hotels' own garden. Local meats and fish prepared by the chef patron. Beef and Red Bean Casserole. Baked Trout with Roasted Almonds.Old English Sherry Trifle. Apple Pie with Clotted Cream.

A 17th century thatched coaching inn, with comfortable accommodation, open log fires and a warm welcome.

✛ 3 miles north west of Ashlington on City Road.

VISA 🏧 💳 AmEx ⊗ ♿ 🚭 🎾 ✓ 🐕 ⚓ S 🦢 A B C

OLD TOWN, Surrey	A picturesque village
town, county	**local points of interest and beauty**
ville, departement	*lieux d'intérêt touristique*
stadt, bezirk	*örtliche sebenswürdigkeiten*
citta', provincia	*punti di interesse turistico*
civdad,provincia	*puntos locales de interes y belleza*

🔭	DAVID & JENNY SMITH
fireplace grading	**proprietor's name(s)**
classement 'cheminées'	*nom du proprietaire*
einteilung nach 'Kaminen'	*name des inhabers*
classifica 'caminetti'	*nome/i del propietario/i*
clasificación 'chimenea'	*nombre(s) del propietario*

Non-residents welcome	🍴 £13.95
open to non-residents	**average dinner menu price**
(restaurant) ouvert aux non-residents	*prix fixe repas au restaurant*
tagegäste willkommen	*festgesetzler menüpreis*
(ristorante) anche per i non residenti	*prezzo medio del menu*
(restaurante) abierto para los no-residentes	*precio del menu*

🛏14, 12 en-suite

number of bedrooms, number en-suite
nombre de chambres, chambres avec salle de bain
zimmeranzahl, zimmer mit bad
numero di camere, numero di camere con bagno
numero de habitaciones, numero de habitaciones con bano

---

last orders 8pm

restaurant last orders
horaires des dernieres commandes des repas
letzte bestellung für mahlezeiten
orario ultimo di accettazione ordini al ristorante
hora de las últimas pedidas en el restaurante

Lunch served

open for lunch
(restaurant) ouvert pour le dejeuner
mittagstisch
aperto per pranzo
(restaurante) abierto para el almuerzo

VISA ☐ ☐ AmEx

credit cards accepted (Visa, Access, Diners Club, Amex)
cartes de credit acceptees
kreditkarten akzepiert
carte di credito accettate
tarjetas de credito aceptadas

---

from £28.00 per person, double occ.

The guide price per person for B&B based on double occupancy of an ensuite room
a partir de £28 par personne et par nuit, petit déjeuner compris, sur la base de deux personnes par chambre.

bel doppelter Besetzung, ab £28 pro person pro person pro Nacht, Früstück inbegriffen

da £28 per person per notte prima colaxione compresa, in camera doppia (due occupanti)

desde £28 por persona y noche, desayuno incluido, con ocupación doble

---

🎖

cuisine specialities
specialities culinaires
spezialitätch des hauses
specialità culinarie
especialida des culinarias

A 17th century thatched

hotel description
description de l'hotel
hotelheschreibung
descrizione dell'hotel
descriptión del hotel

non smoking rooms available
*chambres pour non-fumeurs
disponibles
nichtraucher zimmer erhältlich
camere per non fumatori
disponibili
habitaciones para no-fumadores
disponibles*

disabled access
*handicapés
gehandicapten
disabili
minusválidos*

swimming pool
*piscine
schwimmbad
piscina
piscina*

directions
*direction
richtung
direccion
direzione*

A B C

tour programme price categories
*categories de prix pour les
programmes de voyage
reiseprogramm preiskategorien
categorie prezzi dei voucher presso
le agenzie di viaggio
categorias de precio en los
programas de viaje*

**tennis in grounds, golf course
nearby**
*tennis, cours de golf
tennisplatz, golfplatz
tennis, compo da golf
tenis, campo de golf*

fishing nearby
*peche
fischen
pesca
pesca*

**safe beach swimming within
200 meters**
*plage à 200 mètres, ou l'on peut
se baigner en securité
sicherer strand innerhalb von
200 metern
spiaggia a 200 metri di distanza
dove si può huotare senza
pericolo
playa cercana a 200 metros de
distancia*

sauna/solarium
*sauna / solarium
sauna / solarium
sauna solarium
sauna / solario*

dogs allowed
*chiens acceptes
mitbringen von hunden untersagt
cani accettati
perros nó acceptados*

ENGLAND
& WALES

ABBOTSBURY, Dorset

Midway between Weymouth and Dorchester. Many houses date back to Tudor times. Enjoy the fine local country walks and wildlife, visit Abbotsbury Swannery, the sub tropical gardens and Chesil Beach.

⌂⌂ MILLMEAD COUNTRY HOTEL

Goose Hill, Portesham, Dorset DT3 4HE
☎ (01305) 871432 FAX (01305) 871884
GRAHAM & KATIE WILLIAMS

🛏 6, 6 en-suite, from £28.00 per person, double occ.
Lunch served. Non-residents welcome. Open all year.
✗ £13.95, last orders 8pm.
🍽 Fresh fruit and vegetables from the hotels' own garden. Local meats and fish prepared by the chef patron. Beef and Red Bean Casserole. Baked Trout with Roasted Almonds. Old English Sherry Trifle. Apple Pie with Clotted Cream.

Millmead is ideally placed for a relaxing holiday amid country scenes, unspoilt villages and the quiet hills of West Dorset.

VISA 🔳 💳 AmEx ✓ **A**

ABERDOVEY, Gwynedd

A small seaside village overlooking the Dyfi Estuary. Set on the edge of the Snowdonia National Park, Aberdovey is a good base for exploring mid Wales and its many attractions. *see also Machynlleth*.

⌂⌂⌂ PENHELIG ARMS HOTEL

Aberdovey, Gwynedd, LL35 0LT
☎ (01654) 767215 FAX (01654) 767690
ROBERT & SALLY HUGHES

🛏 10, 10 en-suite, from £34.00 per person, double occ.
Lunch served. Non-residents welcome. Open all year.
✗ £17.50, last orders 9.30pm.
🍽 Fresh local produce, particularly featuring fish. Pan Fried Skate Wings. Fillet of Halibut, grilled with Prawns, served with Parsley Sauce. White Chocolate Cheesecake.

A delightful traditional inn, which has been totally renovated by the owners to an extremely high standard. Tasteful, individually designed bedrooms. A peaceful restaurant overlooking the harbour, complimented by a public bar full of local life. All the bedrooms are non smoking.

VISA 🔳 ⊗ ♿ ✓ 🍷 🥂 🐾 **B**

ABERGAVENNY, Gwent

A flourishing market town on the edge of the Brecon Beacons National Park. See the castle or visit the leisure centre. Excellent touring base.

ALLT-YR-YNYS

Walterstone, Herefordshire, HR2 0DU
📞 (01873) 890307 FAX (01873) 890539
JANET & JOHN MANIFOLD

🛏 12, 12 en-suite, from £42.50 per person, double occ.
Non-residents welcome. Open all year.
✕ £18.50, last orders 9.30pm.
🍴 Good food prepared from fresh local ingredients. Special diets and functions catered for. Steaks and roasts.

A beautifully furnished 16th century manor house with good accommodation. The all weather clay pigeon range offers everything required to master or practice the sport. Guests can also enjoy the indoor pool and jacuzzi. Conference facilities are available. A peaceful spot on the Herefordshire/Welsh border.

✚ Turn off the A465 at Pandy Pub. To Longtown and Walterstone, next right by Green Barn.

VISA 💳 AmEx 📱 ✓ 🚭 S 🐾 C

APPLEBY-IN-WESTMORELAND, Cumbria

Formerly the county town, Appleby still retains its Norman Castle, rebuilt during the 17th century. An ideal centre for touring the Eden valley, the North Pennines and the Lake District. Visit the Settle-Carlisle railway.

THE ROYAL OAK INN

Bongate, Appleby, Cumbria CA16 6UN
📞 (017683) 51463 FAX (017683) 52300
C. F. & H. K. CHEYNE

🛏 9, 7 en-suite, from £27.50 per person, double occ.
Lunch served. Closed 25th December.
✕ from £10.00 a la carte, last orders 9pm.
🍴 Morecambe Bay Shrimps. Locally reared meats. Vegetarian dishes.

Historic coaching inn with beamed ceilings and oak panelling dating from the 16th century. Traditional ales, roaring log fires and good food provide a warm, welcoming atmosphere.

VISA 💳 AmEx 📱 ⊗ ♿ ✓ 🚭 🐾 A

APPLETON LE MOORS, North Yorkshire

Set in the heart of the North Yorkshire Moors National Park, this is an excellent centre for the coast, Herriot Country, York, the N. York Moors Railway and many places of historical interest. *See also Rosedale Abbey.*

APPLETON HALL COUNTRY HOUSE HOTEL

Appleton le Moors, North Yorkshire, YO6 6TF
☎ (01751) 417227 FAX (01751) 417540
GRAHAM & NORMA DAVIES

🛏 10, 10 en-suite, from £27.50 per person, double occ.
Lunch served. Non-residents welcome. Open all year.
✗ £18.95, last orders 8.30pm.
🍴 Local meat and fresh local produce used wherever possible.

A large Victorian house set in 3 acres of formal gardens with fine plasterwork and original marble fireplaces. The bedrooms have recently been refurbished, are comfortable and offer good value for money.

VISA 🔳 💳 ⊘ ✓ 🐾 B

ARUNDEL, West Sussex

Pleasant town on the River Arun, with a magnificent cathedral and a 12th century castle, home to the Dukes of Norfolk. Visit the Wild Fowl & Wetlands Trust and the Chalk Pits Museum at Amberley.

HOWARD'S HOTEL & RESTAURANT

Crossbush, Arundel, West Sussex BN18 9PQ
☎ (01903) 882655 FAX (01903) 883384
ANTONY WALLACE

🛏 9, 9 en-suite, from £32.50 per person, double occ.
Lunch served. Non-residents welcome. Open all year.
✗ £13.95, last orders 9.30pm.
🍴 Traditional carvery restaurant with fresh fish and Chefs speciality alternatives. Cafe des Amis open for private parties and special theme evenings including Opera, Murder Mystery and Jazz.

On the outskirts of Arundel, Howards Hotel, offers a friendly, comfortable resting place. Staff are welcoming and caring. The bedrooms are attractively furnished in old pine.

⊕ On the A27, east of the town centre.

VISA 🔳 💳 AmEx ✓ 🐾 B

ASHBOURNE, Derbyshire

A market town on the edge of the Peak District National Park, an excellent centre for walking. Visit Chatsworth and Haddon Hall, Alton Towers, Bakewell, Buxton and the Caves at Castleton.

STANSHOPE HALL

Stanshope, Nr Ashbourne, Derbyshire DE6 2AD
✆ (01335) 310278 FAX (01335) 527470
NAOMI CHAMBERS & NICHOLAS LOURIE

▰ 3, 3 en-suite, from £25.00 per person, double occ.
Non-residents welcome. Closed 25th & 26th December.
✖ £16.50, last orders 8pm.
▮ Staffordshire Oatcakes. Home-made crunchy cereal for breakfast. River Dove Trout. Free Range Chicken. Vegetables from the garden.

An 18th century hall which stands on the brow of a hill between the Manifold and the Dove rivers. Stanshope Hall has many original features including an 18th century Hopton stone staircase and Georgian shutters. Local artists have painted murals in many of the rooms.

✛ M1, junction 25, take A52.

⊗ A

ASHBURTON, Devon

At the western edge of Dartmoor National Park and within easy reach of the main south Devon resorts. A busy thriving market town with many medieval and period buildings. Visit Buckfast Abbey. *See also Poundsgate.*

HOLNE CHASE HOTEL

Ashburton, Newton Abbot, Devon TQ13 7NS
✆ (01364) 631471 FAX (01364) 631453
THE BROMAGE FAMILY

▰ 14, 14 en-suite, from £42.50 per person, double occ.
Lunch served. Non-residents welcome. Open all year.
✖ £21.50, last orders 9pm.
▮ Dart salmon. Dartmoor lamb. Devon clotted cream. West Country cheeses.

A 19th century hunting lodge, standing in thirty acres of informal gardens and woodland. The lodge has been tastefully converted into a friendly country house hotel. Accommodation and cuisine standards are excellent. The hotel enjoys its own stretch of the river Dart, with private salmon fishing.

✛ 3 miles north west of Ashburton on Two Bridges Road.

VISA ▰ ▱ AmEx ⊗ ✓ ◺ ⇕ C

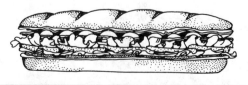

ASHFORD, Kent

In the heart of Wye National Nature Reserve on the North Downs Way.
Close to M20 (Channel Tunnel 20 minutes), Leeds Castle and Canterbury.

THE NEW FLYING HORSE

Wye, Nr Ashford, Kent TN25 5AN
☎ (01233) 812297 FAX (01233) 813487
NORMAN & NITA EVANS

🛏 10, 10 en-suite, from £23.75 per person, double occ.
Lunch served. Non Residents welcome. Open all year.
✗ £12.00 - £15.00, last orders 10pm.
🍽 Freshly prepared food, featuring Kentish regional specialities.

A traditional coaching inn, in a peaceful Kentish village. A warm
welcome and good hospitality are assured. The bedrooms have
recently been refurbished to a high standard and the lively bar is
an ideal place to enjoy some traditional Kentish ale.

✈ 5 minutes drive north east of Ashford, off the main A28 going
towards Canterbury.

VISA 🏧 ⊗ ♿ ✓ 🐕 🦆 A

ASHINGTON, West Sussex

Small village, ten miles north of Worthing. See Arundel castle, Amberley
chalk pits museum, Parham House, Leonardslee gardens. *See also
Pulborough.*

MILL HOUSE HOTEL

Mill Lane, Ashington, West Sussex RH20 3BZ
☎ (01903) 892426 FAX (01903) 892855
YVONNE SHUTE

🛏 10, 9 en-suite, from £38.75 per person, double occ.
Lunch served. Open all year.
✗ £14.95, last orders 9.30pm.
🍽 English cuisine, prepared with French influence. Local fresh
fish used in many dishes. Les Trois Poissons Fume.
Champignons Menage a Trois. Les Langoustines Medina. Le
Carre d'Agneau a la Menthe. Le Chateaubriand Garni.
Macclesfield Pudding.

Delightful 300 year old country house in a very quiet situation just
off the A24. The old world atmosphere and comfortable mix of
antique and modern furnishings complement the reasonably
priced cuisine and personal service.

VISA 🏧 🅿 AmEx ⊗ ✓ 🦆 B

ASHWATER, DEVON

A small village between Launceston and Holdsworthy, within easy reach of the National Trust coastline with its spectacular coves and surfing beaches.

🔱 BLAGDON MANOR COUNTRY HOTEL

Ashwater, Beaworthy, Devon EX21 5DP
☎ (01409) 211224 FAX (01409) 211634
TIM & GILL CASEY

🛌 7, 7 en-suite, from £45.00 per person, double occ.
Closed Christmas.
✕ £20.00, last orders 8pm.
🍴 Spinach and Blue Cheese Soup. Devonshire Pork Fillet with Prunes and Armangac. Rack of Devonshire Lamb with Redcurrant Gravy. Warm Banana Cake with Butterscotch and Walnut Sauce.

17th century listed manor house set in 8 acres with beautiful rural views and peace and tranquility. Log fires coupled with enchanting ensuite rooms. For children under 12 years please contact the hotel direct.

✛ Leave Launceston on A388, Holsworthy Road, turn right at the second sign, then first right. Hotel a few hundred yards further on.

VISA 💳 ⊗ ∿ ⩊ C

ASKRIGG, North Yorkshire

A village in the heart of Wensleydale, famous for its steep narrow streets, three storey 18th century houses and beauty. The town is used as a set for the filming of the BBC's Herriot series. *See also Hawes, Wensleydale.*

🔱 KING'S ARMS HOTEL ✕

Askrigg, Leyburn, North Yorkshire DL8 3HQ
☎ (01969) 650258 FAX (01969) 650635
LIZ & RAY HOPWOOD

🛌 9, 9 en-suite, from £30.00 per person, double occ.
Lunch served. Open all year.
✕ £17.25, last orders 10pm.
🍴 Celestine of Melon with Seasonal Fruits, lacquered by a Lemon Nectar. Roast Mallard with a sauce of Root Ginger and Orange. Boneless Quail filled with a mousseline of Chicken.

An 18th century, Georgian manor house hotel and authentic Dales pub. The public bar has been recorded in film as James Herriot's local! Guests will enjoy excellent food in relaxed surroundings. Most of the bedrooms have four poster or half tester beds. The artist Turner based himself at the King's Arms while he painted the rugged surrounding countryside. Only bar meals served at lunchtimes, except Sunday when full restaurant meals are available.

VISA 💳 ⊗ ♿ ∿ ⩊ ⬧ B

Askrigg continued overleaf...

WINVILLE HOTEL

Main Street, Askrigg, Leyburn, North Yorkshire DL8 3HG
☎ (01969) 650515 FAX (01969) 650594
MR D. BUCKLE

🛏 10, 10 en-suite, from £30.00 per person, double occ.
Lunch served. Non-residents welcome. Open all year.
✕ £15.95 and £17.95, last orders 9pm.
🍴 A four course dinner with a varied menu prepared from fresh local produce. Bar meals also served.

Formerly a 19th century Georgian residence, the hotel has been carefully restored to create a warm and friendly atmosphere. All bedrooms are fully equipped and the public rooms are comfortably furnished, with open fires. The hotel has a private garden and car park.

VISA 🖲 ⌁ ⁄ 🛇 ⁂ A

BADMINTON, Avon

Visit Bath, Bristol, The Cotswolds, Westonbirt Arboretum, and Castle Combe.

BODKIN HOUSE HOTEL & RESTAURANT

A46 Bath/Stroud Road, Badminton, Avon GL9 1AF
☎ (01454) 238310 FAX (01454) 238422
PATRICIA & BRIAN NEVE

🛏 8, 8 en-suite, from £32.50 per person, double occ.
Lunch served. Non-residents welcome. Restaurant closed Sunday evening.
✕ £15.00/£20.00 a la carte, last orders 9pm.
🍴 Good English food with the best of French influences featuring steak, local game, fish and vegetarian dishes.

Restored former 17th century coaching inn surrounded by two and a half acres of grounds, reputedly used by Jane Austen. A comfortable and friendly family atmosphere.

⊹ 6 miles north of junction 18, M4, on A46 Bath/Stroud road.

VISA 🖲 ⚊ AmEx ⊗ ⌖ ⌁ ⁄ 🛇 B

BALA, Gwynedd

At the southern edge of Snowdonia, Bala nestles on the banks of the largest natural lake in Wales, with many opportunities for canoeing, walking, sailing and fishing. There is a narrow gauge railway along the lakeside.

PLAS COCH HOTEL

High Street, Bala, Gwynedd LL23 7AB
☎ (01678) 520309 FAX (01678) 521135
JOHN & MAIR EVANS

🛏 10, 10 en-suite, from £28.00 per person, double occ.
Lunch served. Closed Christmas Day.
✕ £12.00, last orders 8.30pm.
🍴 Traditional roasts and casseroles.

An 18th century building situated in the centre of Bala, furnished in traditional style. Very friendly atmosphere and popular with the locals. The menu is simple and good value for money.

VISA 🖲 ⚊ AmEx ⊗ ⌁ ⁄ 🛇 A

BANBURY, Oxfordshire

This town was founded in Saxon times, see the Cross celebrated in the nursery rhyme and the cattle market. Taste the famous Banbury cakes. A good centre for touring Warwickshire and the Cotswolds.

CROMWELL LODGE HOTEL

North Bar, Banbury, Oxfordshire OX16 0TB
((01295) 259781 FAX (01295) 276619
PAMELA CAMPBELL & JOHN SHELFORD

32, 32 en-suite, from £35.00 per person, double occ.
Lunch served. Non-residents welcome. Closed 25th December to 1st January.
£16.00, last orders 9.30pm.
Table d'hote and Bistro menus available. Skate Wing and Ginger Butter. Mushrooms Stroganoff. Beef Fillet with Orange and Walnuts. Home-made ice cream and desserts.

Situated in the centre of Banbury, this majestic 17th century hotel retains many original beams and traditional character. The hotel has a large car park at the rear, private walled garden and patio area. The service is friendly and professional.

VISA AmEx B

EASINGTON HOUSE HOTEL

50 Oxford Road, Banbury, Oxfordshire OX16 9AN
((01295) 270181 FAX (01295) 269527
MALCOLM & GWYNNETH HEARNE

13, 13 en-suite, from £35.00 per person, double occ.
Lunch served. Restaurant closed Christmas to New Year.
£9.50, last orders 8.30pm.
Freshly prepared seasonal produce.

A former Royal Manor farmhouse (c.1575), built as a wedding present to the great-aunt of George Washington, first President of the USA. During the summer guests are invited to take breakfast or evening barbecues on the patio. Small conferences and functions catered for.

VISA AmEx B

BANTHAM, Devon

A small Devon village with a fine undeveloped beach and sailing on the Avon estuary. Surrounded by the beautiful South Hams with its numerous tourist activities.

THE SLOOP INN

Bantham, Nr Kingsbridge, Devon TQ7 3AJ
((01548) 560489 FAX (01548) 560489
NEIL GIRLING

5, 5 en-suite, from £25.00 per person, double occ.
Lunch served. Closed mid December to end of January.
£11.00 approx, last orders 10pm.
Local seafood, home-made sausages and sweets. Spotted Dick. Treacle Tart.

A 400 year old seaside inn with a colourful history of smuggling and wrecking! Low beams, stone floors and walls create an ancient ambiance. The accommodation is comfortably furnished with most rooms enjoying a sea or river view.

A

BARMOUTH, Gwynedd

On the mouth of the Mawddach estuary with golden sands and miles of mountain and estuary walks. A thriving holiday town with good shops and inns. Visit the nearby medieval castles and 'Great Little Trains' of Wales.

BRYNMELYN HOTEL

Panorama Road, Barmouth, Gwynedd LL42 1DQ
☎ (01341) 280556 FAX (01341) 280276
DAVID & CAROL CLAY

🛏 9, 8 en-suite, from £26.00 per person, double occ.
Closed mid November to mid March.
✕ £12.50, last orders 8.30pm.
🍴 Tuna and Orange Cocktail. Cottage Pears. Mawddach Salmon with Cucumber Sauce. Dyffryn Chicken in Cheese and White Wine. Traditional English Puddings.

Small family run hotel which has been under the same direction for 24 years. Stunning views across the estuary to the Welsh mountains and Cardigan Bay.

VISA 💳 ⊘ ⌇ ⌀ A

BARNARD CASTLE, County Durham

A thriving market town set over the River Tees. Visit Raby Castle, Bowes Museum, High Force waterfall and Rokerby Hall.

THE ROSE & CROWN HOTEL

Romaldkirk, Barnard Castle, County Durham DL12 9EB
☎ (01833) 650213 FAX (01833) 650828
CHRISTOPHER & ALISON DAVY

🛏 11, 11 en-suite, from £37.00 per person, double occ.
Lunch served. Non-residents welcome. Closed 25th & 26th. December.
✕ £22.00, last orders 9pm.
🍴 Terrine of Yorkshire Venison with Cumberland Sauce. Hot Mushroom & Hazlenut Strudel. Imaginative vegetables. Beetroot baked with Tarragon & Cream, Broccoli Spears with Sunflower Seeds, Chinese leaves with Croutons & Smoked Bacon. WINNER OF THE 1994 LOGIS REGIONAL CUISINE COMPETITION.

An 18th century Coaching inn in the picturesque village of Romaldkirk which can trace its history back to Saxon times. The heart of this old inn is still in its kitchen with a menu which reflects the changing seasons.

VISA 💳 ⊘ ⌇ ⌀ ∪

THE RED WELL INN

Harmire Road, Barnard Castle, County Durham DL12 8QJ
☎ (01833) 637002
MIKE & LIZ RUDD, KEN & ANNE THOMPSON

🛏 7, 7 en-suite, from £24.75 per person, double occ.
Lunch served. Open all year.
✕ from £5.00, last orders 9pm.
🍴 English cuisine, featuring local meats. Haunch of Teesdale Venison in a Port and Orange Sauce.

A traditional English country inn, with a warm and friendly welcome. Comfortable surroundings. Families welcome.

VISA 💳 ⊘ ♿ ⌇ A

BARNSTAPLE, Devon

At the head of the Taw estuary, with many attractive period buildings, a modern civic centre and riverside leisure centre. Close to Exmoor National Park.

🏨🏨 LYNWOOD HOUSE HOTEL

Bishops Tawton Road, Barnstaple, Devon EX32 9DZ
☎ (01271) 43695 FAX (01271) 79340
THE ROBERTS FAMILY

🛏 5, 5 en-suite, from £33.75 per person, double occ.
Lunch served. Non-residents welcome. Open all year.
✗ from £25.00 a la carte, last orders 9.30pm.
🍴 Seafood, organic vegetables. Baked Avocado with Vegetables and Nuts in a Citrus Juice with Soy and fresh Ginger Sauce. Home-made Samosas. Local Mussels cooked in White Wine and Parsley.

Lynwood House was originally built as a gentleman's residence. The Robert's Family have lived here for over 25 years and have lovingly converted the building into a comfortable hotel. The kitchens are run by Ruth Roberts with the help of her son Matthew. The hotel is elegantly furnished and enjoys a calm, peaceful atmosphere.

VISA 🖃 AmEx ⊗ ৬ ✓ 🕲 ⊕ B

BASINGSTOKE, Hampshire

Ideally situated between London and Southampton or Portsmouth, within easy reach of Windsor, the Roman remains at Silchester, Highclere Castle and the race courses at Ascot and Newbury.

🏨🏨🏨 THE WELLINGTON ARMS HOTEL

Stratfield Turgis, Nr Basingstoke, Hampshire RG27 0AS
☎ (01256) 882214 FAX (01256) 882934
MOIRA CUNNINGHAM

🛏 33, 33 en-suite, from £37.50 per person, double occ.
Lunch served. Non-residents welcome. Open all year.
✗ £15.95, last orders 9.45pm.
🍴 The best of fresh local produce and a wide range of English cheeses.

Originally a 17th century farmhouse, the Wellington Arms Hotel is now a familiar landmark in Stanfield Turgis between Basingstoke and Reading. The grade II building, which stands at the entrance to Stratfield Saye, the ancestral home of the Duke of Wellington, has been completely refurbished and is furnished in classic English style throughout.

⚜ On the A33 between Reading and Basingstoke.

VISA 🖃 🔜 AmEx ⊗ ৬ ✓ 🕲 ⊕ B

BASSENTHWAITE LAKE, Cumbria

Bassenthwaite Lake nestles below Skiddaw in the heart of Cumbria. The lake is famous for its many varieties of migrating birds.

THE PHEASANT INN

Bassenthwaite Lake, Cockermouth, Cumbria CA13 9YE
✆ (017687) 76234 FAX (017687) 76002
MR & MRS W. E. BARRINGTON WILSON

🛏 20, 20 en-suite, from £46.00 per person, double occ.
Lunch served. Non-residents welcome. Closed Christmas Day.
✗ £23.00, last orders 8.30pm.
🍴 Poached Solway Salmon with Hot Butter Sauce. Smoked Cumberland Trout. Local game in season.

An 18th century farmhouse, which became a coaching inn in 1826 and is now one of Britain's best loved country hotels. The listed building is situated in tranquil countryside, between the Lake and Thornthwaite Forest. The bedrooms are beautifully furnished and the reputation of the Inn's Cumbrian country cooking is excellent.

VISA ⬛ ⊗ ♿ ✓ 🍷 C

BATH, Avon

A Georgian spa city, developed over the top of an important Roman site. Visit the Pump Rooms, Abbey, American Museum or Theatre. Wells and Salisbury, both with famous cathedrals, are easily accessible. *See also Timsbury, Box, Corsham, Frome, Trowbridge, Westbury, Shepton Mallet, Wells.*

DUKES HOTEL

Great Pulteney St., Bath, Avon BA2 4DN
✆ (01225) 463512 FAX (01225) 483733
TIM & ROSALIND FORESTER

🛏 22, 22 en-suite, from £42.50 per person, double occ.
Non-residents welcome. Open all year.
✗ £13.50, last orders 8.30pm.
🍴 Pork and Herb Terrine with Plum Chutney. Poached John Dory with a delicate Saffron Sauce. Best end of English Lamb with Rosemary and White Wine Sauce. Chocolate and Praline Mousse. Bread and Butter Pudding.

Dukes Hotel occupies a Grade I listed building in Great Pulteney Street, Europe's grandest Georgian thoroughfare, just a few minutes walk from the city centre. Children's menu available. The hotel interior has been designed to offer an excellent balance of refined elegance and comfortable relaxation.

⊹ A4 into Bath, turn left onto the A36 Ring Road, over the river, turn right at the roundabout, then right into Great Pulteney Street.

VISA ⬛ 💳 AmEx ⊗ ✓ 🍷 🚗 B

SOMERSET HOUSE HOTEL

35 Bathwick Hill, Bath, Avon BA2 6LD
✆ (01225) 466451 FAX (01225) 317188
JEAN & MALCOLM & JONATHAN SEYMOUR

🛏 10, 10 en-suite, from £31.00 per person, double occ.
Lunch served. Non-residents welcome. Restaurant closed Sunday
evening.
✕ £18.00, last orders 6.30pm.
🍴 Mendip lamb from the family farm. Trout from the River Wylye.
Traditional farmhouse cheese from Somerset. Organically reared
beef & pork. Home-made bread prepared from stone-ground flour.
Free range chicken, duck & eggs. Saturday themed dinners.

Somerset House is an elegant Georgian town house, with fine
views over the city. It is a family run hotel with a good restaurant
where there is a friendly and informal atmosphere, well respected
and loved by visitors who return frequently. Large garden. Car
park in grounds.

⚓ Bathwick Hill is a turning off A36 (Pulteney Road) at St Marys
Church (roundabout) direction Bath University.

VISA 🖃 AmEx ✓ 🌑 ⊕ B

WENTWORTH HOUSE

106 Bloomfield Road, Bath, Avon BA2 2AP
✆ (01225) 339193 FAX (01225) 310460
GEOFF & AVRIL KITCHING

🛏 19, 15 en-suite, from £30.00 per person, double occ.
Closed Christmas & New Year.
✕ £12.50, last orders 8pm.
🍴 Traditional English food.

Wentworth House (built in 1887) is set in its own grounds and
offers guests a quiet, relaxed atmosphere. 15 minutes walk from
the city centre and on a convenient bus route. The hotel's outdoor
pool is open during the summer months. For children under 5
years please contact the hotel direct.

⚓ From Bath, follow the signs for A367 Exeter. Bloomfield Road
is a right hand fork off the A367 hotel is 300 yards on the right.

VISA 🖃 ⟿ ✓ ⊕ A

BATTLE, East Sussex

Built on the site of the Battle of Hastings in 1066. A busy town, with many
old buildings and impressive abbey ruins. An interesting museum.

BURNT WOOD HOUSE HOTEL

Powdermill Lane, Battle, East Sussex TN33 0SU
✆ (01424) 775151
THE HOGGARTH FAMILY

🛏 10, 10 en-suite, from £30.00 to £45.00 per person, double occ.
Lunch served. Open all year.
✕ £15.00, last orders 9.30pm.
🍴 English and continental cuisine. Fresh fish from the south
coast, locally caught game. Smoked Mackerel Pate. Veal Escalope
Holstein. Roast Pheasant.

An elegant Edwardian country house hotel, set in eighteen acres of
beautiful grounds. Tastefully decorated throughout. Croquet
lawn, tennis court and outdoor heated swimming pool. A friendly
relaxed atmosphere.

VISA 🖃 ⟿ AmEx ⟿ 🔍 ✓ 🌑 ⊕ B

BEDDGELERT, Gwynedd

Welsh village at the junction of the rivers Colwyn and Glaslyn in the heart of Snowdonia. Surrounded by spectacular scenery with many opportunities for walking, fishing and climbing. Visit the Sygun copper mine and Cae Du Farm Park. *See also Capel Curig.*

🏛 THE ROYAL GOAT HOTEL ✕✕

Beddgelert, Gwynedd, North Wales LL55 4YE
☎ (0176686) 224 FAX (0176686) 422
EVAN ROBERTS

🛏 34, 34 en-suite, from £34.00 per person, double occ.
Lunch served. Non-residents welcome. Open all year.
✕ £17.50, last orders 9.30pm.
🍽 Traditional Welsh and international dishes.

An imposing hotel, overlooking the heart of the village with spectacular views further to Snowdonia and the National Park. The hotel has recently been fully and tastefully refurbished. All rooms offer every facility. A personal and friendly family hotel.

VISA 💳 💳 AmEx ⊗ ♿ ✓ 🛏 ☂ **B**

BEDFORD, Bedfordshire

Busy county town with interesting buildings and churches near the River Ouse. Pleasant riverside walks. Many associations with John Bunyan including Bunyan Meeting House, museum and statue.

🏛 THE KNIFE & CLEAVER ✕

The Grove, Houghton Conquest, Bedfordshire MK45 3LA
☎ (01234) 740387 FAX (01234) 740900
DAVID & PAULINE LOOM

🛏 9, 9 en-suite, from £33.00 per person, double occ.
Lunch servesidents welcome. Closed 27th to 30th December, & Sunday Evenings.
✕ £16.50, last orders 9.30pm.
🍽 Hot smoked sausages and poultry from Ashwood Smokery. Asparagus from Moulden Farm. Venison from Alcunbury. Turkeys and vegetables from Houghton Conquest.

Converted 16th century inn with dark panelled bar and Victorian style conservatory restaurant. Each bedroom has been tastefully decorated, furnished and overlooks the garden and orchard.

✛ Between A6 and the B530, 5 miles south of Bedford.

VISA 💳 💳 AmEx ♿ ✓ ☂ **A**

BEER, Devon

A small resort near the mouth of the River Axe. A mile long beach extends

🏠 BOVEY HOUSE HOTEL

Beer, Nr Seaton, Devon EX12 3AD
☎ (01297) 680241
PACO & KAY FERNANDEZ-LLORENTE

🛏 9, 8 en-suite, from £30.00 per person, double occ.
Lunch served. Non-residents welcome. Closed end of
January to mid February.
✕ £18.50, last orders 9pm.
🍴 Fan of Melon surrounded by Strawberry Coulis with a Fruit
Sorbet. Shell on Prawns grilled in Garlic Butter. Grilled Salmon
with a spicy Eden Butter. Entrecote Steak Grand Mere. Treacle
Pudding. Chocolate Fudge.

16th century historic manor house, one and a half miles from the
sea, in a peaceful setting. Log fires, fresh flowers and a very warm
welcome.

⚓ Between the villages of Beer and Branscombe.

VISA 🖃 ≜ ⌖/ 🕸 ⊕ A

BELFORD, Northumberland

A small village ideally situated for discovering North Northumberland and
the Scottish Borders. Visit nearby Bamburgh Castle, Lindisfarne and Holy
Island.

🏠 WAREN HOUSE HOTEL

Waren Mill, Belford, Northumberland NE70 7EE
☎ (01668) 214581 FAX (01668) 214484
ANITA & PETER LAVARACK

🛏 7, 7 en-suite, from £52.00 per person, double occ.
Non-residents welcome. Open all year.
✕ £22.50, last orders 8pm.
🍴 A daily changing table d'hote menu using the best of local
produce.

A traditional 18th century country house hotel, beautifully
restored and furnished to the highest standards throughout. A
very peaceful and tranquil setting overlooking Holy Island.

⚓ On southwest courner of Budle Bay on B1342.

VISA 🖃 ≜ AmEx ⊗ ♿ ⌖/ 🖾 ⊕ C

BETWS Y COED, Gwynedd

In the heart of the beautiful Snowdonia National Park, a good base for walking and climbing. Visit Bodnant Gardens, Llechwedd slate quarries, Conwy Castle or Cloglau gold mine which still produces Welsh gold.

THE WHITE HORSE INN

Capel Garmon, Llanrwst, Gwynedd LL26 0RW
☎ (01690) 710271
ROGER & MEGAN BOWER

🛏 6, 6 en-suite, from £22.00 per person, double occ.
Lunch served. Non-residents welcome. Hotel open all year.
Restaurant closed Monday & Tuesday to non-residents.
✕ £8.95, last orders 9pm.
⚘ Traditional Welsh fare, all prepared from fresh locally produced ingredients. Cawl, Welsh soup. Lopsgows, a local hot pot. Fresh local trout when in season. Welsh lamb.

A 17th century inn of character in the heart of Snowdonia. Open log fires, spectacular views and warm, friendly hospitality. Contact the hotel direct if travelling with children under the age of three.

⊹ Follow the A470 from Leanriosk, then follow the sign for Capel Garmon on the left.

⊗ ✓ ⊃ A

BIBURY, Gloucestershire

A picturesque Cotswold riverside village, 30 miles from Stratford upon Avon, Oxford and Bath.

BIBURY COURT HOTEL

Bibury, Gloucestershire, GL7 5NT
☎ (01285740) 337 FAX (01285740) 660
THE COLLIER & JOHNSTON FAMILIES

🛏 20, 17 en-suite, from £37.00 per person, double occ.
Lunch served. Closed 21st to 29th December.
✕ £20.00, last orders 9pm.
⚘ Local game in season. Cotswold Spring Lamb. Bibury Trout.

A Jacobean country house hotel with a wealth of historical character set in seven acres of gardens and parkland by the river Coln. The same family owners for twenty years.

⊹ Behind the church in Bibury village.

VISA ▭ ▭ AmEx ⊗ ✓ ⊃ ⊕ B

BIDEFORD, Devon

A pleasant 17th century seafaring town built on shipbuilding and the cloth industry. Visit nearby Clovelly, Dartington Glass, or the many surrounding stately homes and gardens.

THE OLD RECTORY

Parkham, Bideford, Devon EX39 5PL
☎ (01237) 451443 FAX (01237) 451046
JEAN & JACK LANGTON

🛏 3, 2 en-suite, from £35.00 per person, double occ.
Lunch served. Non-residents welcome. Closed mid December to mid January.
✗ £25.00, last orders 8pm.
🍴 Pork in Cider, Apples and Cream. Fresh local seafish, game in season. Pheasant Breast with Caramalised Apples and a hint of Curry.

A charming, peaceful, small country house set in secluded grounds, tastefully furnished and decorated. Jean, an Elizabeth David devotee, enjoys an excellent reputation for imaginative and interesting cuisine. For children under 12, please contact the hotel direct.

⊹ From Bideford A39 to Horns Cross. Left to Parkham, left at Bell Public House, third right.

⊗ ✓ ⅋ B

YEOLDON HOUSE HOTEL

Durrant Lane, Northam, Bideford, Devon EX39 2LR
☎ (01237) 474400 FAX (01237) 476618
MR & MRS CHEESEWRIGHT

🛏 10, 10 en-suite, from £29.50 per person, double occ.
Non-residents welcome. Open all year.
✗ £17.00, last orders 9pm.
🍴 Melon Frappe. Garlic Prawns. Devilled Whitebait. Salmon Hollandaise. Chicken Provencale. Rack of Lamb.

A Victorian country house set in two acres of garden with relaxing and peaceful surroundings, enjoying magnificent views over the estuary. For children under 7 years please contact the hotel direct.

⊹ A39 to Bideford, turn onto the A386 to Westward Ho and Appledore within quarter of a mile, third turning on right (Durrant Lane).

VISA ▰ ⊗ ⅋ ✓ A B

BIGBURY ON SEA, Devon

A small resort set on Bigbury Bay on the river Avon. Beautiful wide sandy beaches and rugged cliffs. At low tide Burgh Island can be reached on foot.

HENLEY HOTEL

Folly Hill, Bigbury on Sea, Devon TQ7 4AR
☎ (01548) 810240 FAX (01548) 810331
MARTIN SCARTERFIELD

🛏 8, 8 en-suite, from £24.00 per person, double occ.
Lunch served. Open all year.
✕ £14.00, last orders 8.30pm.
🍴 Locally caught fresh fish. Jugged Devon Steak. Devon Apple Cake. Hourglass Cream. Other Devon delights are included on the menu daily.

An Edwardian cottage style hotel, with spectacular sea views, and private steps to the beach. A lovely cosy atmosphere. This establishment is totally non-smoking.

𝗩𝗜𝗦𝗔 🔲 💷 ⊗ ♿ ↙ ⟍ ⟋ ⚐ A

BILSBORROW, Lancashire

This hamlet is neatly tucked away by the side of the Lancaster canal. Close to Preston, Blackpool, Lake District and the Yorkshire Dales. *See also Lytham St Annes.*

GUY'S THATCHED HAMLET

Canalside, St Michael's Road, Bilsborrow, Preston, Lancashire PR3 0RS
☎ (01995) 640849/640010 FAX (01995) 640141
ROY, SEAN & KIRK WILKINSON

🛏 32, 32 en-suite, from £16.00 per person, double occ.
Lunch served. Non-residents welcome. Closed 25th December.
✕ £10.00-£14.00 a la carte, last orders 11.30pm.
🍴 Rack of lamb. Locally caught fish. Morecombe Bay Potted Shrimps. Scotch Sirloin on the bone. Guy's Pot and gamein season. Thatched canalside building, with cobbled square and craft shops.

Olde worlde restaurant, beamed ceilings, flagged floors, fun and friendly atmosphere. The tavern offers a la carte bar meals for around £3.50-£4.00. Mussel Casserole. Hot Beef Sandwiches. Steak and Kidney Pudding. Battered Cod and Mushy Peas.

⊹ From Preston, A6 follow signs to Garstang, take left hand turning for Lancashire College of Agriculture, over the canal, hotel on the right.

𝗩𝗜𝗦𝗔 🔲 AmEx ⊗ ↙ ⟍ ⚐ A

BIRLING GAP, East Sussex

Cliff top area, close to Beachy Head and Eastbourne with all its tourist attractions.

BIRLING GAP HOTEL

Eastdean, Nr Eastbourne, East Sussex BN20 OAB
☎(01323) 423197 FAX (01323) 423030
GRAHAM & JOHN COLLINS

9, 9 en-suite, from £27.50 per person, double occ.
Lunch served. Non-residents welcome. Open all year.
from £8.00, last orders 10pm.
Locally caught fish, lobster and crab. Home-made desserts including Banoffi Pie.

A Victorian colonial style villa built on the Seven Sisters cliffs. Fantastic views of the surrounding sea and countryside. The interior is furnished in 1930's style.

VISA AmEx A

BIRMINGHAM, West Midlands

Britain's second largest city, with many attractions including Cadbury World, International Convention Centre, Symphony Hall, Birmingham Royal Ballet and Botanical Gardens.

COPPERFIELD HOUSE HOTEL

60 Upland Road, Selly Park, Birmingham, West Midlands B29 7JS
☎(0121) 472 8344 FAX (0121) 472 8344
JOHN & JENNY BODYCOTE & LOUISE MARTIN

17, 17 en-suite, from £29.75 per person, double occ.
Lunch served. Non-residents welcome. Open all year.
£15.95-£17.95, last orders 8.30pm.
Louise was trained by Prue Leith and insists on freshly prepared home-made cuisine.

A mid-Victorian red brick building, with a tranquil garden, set in an exclusive residential suburb of Birmingham. Adequate free parking at the front of the hotel. Two miles south west of Birmingham city centre, within easy reach of BBC Pebble Mill Studios, the University and Queen Elizabeth Medical Centre.

M6 junction 4, A38 through city centre. At the second set of traffic lights turn left (Priory), next set of lights turn right (A441), the third right is Upland Road.

VISA AmEx A

BLACKPOOL, Lancashire

Largest fun resort in the North with every entertainment including amusement parks, piers, tram-rides along the promenade, sandy beaches and the famous Tower.

SUNRAY HOTEL

42 Knowle Avenue, Blackpool, Lancashire FY2 9TQ
☎ (01253) 351937
JEAN & JOHN DODGSON

🛏 9, 9 en-suite, from £27.00 per person, double occ.
Non-residents welcome. Closed mid December to mid January.
✕ £10.00, last orders 5.30pm.
Traditional English cooking. Home-made soups. Salmon en Croute. Raspberry Pavlova with Cream and Ice Cream. Banana Split. Lemon Meringue Pie.

Large semi-detached house situated well away from the busy town centre but accessible for all of Blackpool's many varied leisure facilities.

VISA 🔳 ./🐶 A

BLAENAU FFESTINIOG, Gwynedd

In the heart of Snowdonia National Park, famed for its climbing and walking. Visit slate mines, gold mines, copper mines and any one of the eight castles, or the four steam railways in the area. Miles of safe golden beaches.

GRAPES HOTEL ✗ ✗

Maentwrog, Blaenau Ffestiniog, Gwynedd LL41 4HN
☎ (01766) 590365 FAX (01766) 590654
GILL & BRIAN TARBOX

🛏 8, 8 en-suite, from £25.00 per person, double occ.
Lunch served. Non-residents welcome. Open all year.
✕ from £16.50 a la carte, last orders 9.30pm.
Lean fillet of local Venison with a Stilton and Malt Whisky Sauce. Fillet of Saddle of local Lamb chargrilled pink and served on a bed of sour and sweet Red Cabbage. Breast of Pigeon braised in a Red wine, Juniper and Herbs.

A 17th century coaching inn, steeped in history. The inn offers individually furnished and comfortable rooms, an excellent cellar restaurant as well as an extensive bar meal menu. Many rooms enjoy excellent views. The hotel restaurant has a working spit roast.

✢ Just off the A470, Dolgellau to Porthmadog road on A496. Harlech Road 200 yards on right.

VISA 🔳 💳 AmEx ⊗./ 🦢 🐶 A

BLANDFORD FORUM, Dorset

A charming Georgian town in a rich farming area. Visit Corfe Castle, Kingston Lacey, Badbury Rings or use as a base to explore the Dorset countryside.

THE CROWN HOTEL

Blandford Forum, Dorset, DT11 7AJ
✆ (01258) 456626 FAX (01258) 451084
JAMES B. MAYO

🛏 33, 33 en-suite, from £37.00 per person, double occ.
Lunch served. Closed 24th to 28th December.
✗ from £10.00, last orders 9.15pm.
🍽 Classic Anglo/French cuisine, table d'hote and a la carte menus available. Tornedo Rossini. Fillets of Red Bream Grenobloise. Whole Trout Almandine. Venison Chops Diable.

The present hotel was built in 1731, on the site of an older coaching inn. The hotel's imposing Georgian fascade and oak pannelled interior create an elegant atmosphere. The recently completed Sealy Suite offers an excellent, purpose built, conference and function facility.

VISA 💳 💷 AmEx ⊗ ♿ ✓ 🚭 ⊕ C

BLEDINGTON, Oxfordshire

A small village in the heart of the Cotswolds. Easy access to Stratford upon Avon, Cheltenham, Bath and Oxford.

THE KINGSHEAD INN AND RESTAURANT

The Green, Bledington, Oxfordshire OX7 6HD
✆ (01608) 658365 FAX (01608) 658365
MICHAEL & ANNETTE ROYCE

🛏 6, 6 en-suite, from £30.00 per person, double occ.
Lunch served. Non-residents welcome. Closed 25th December.
✗ £10.00-£12.00 a la carte, last orders 9.30pm.
🍽 Jugged hare, local game, roast guinea fowl, pheasant, quail and venison. Fresh market fish.

15th century inn on the village green which retains all its original old world charm. Trestle tables, pews and inglenook fireplaces are in abundance. Pretty, fully equipped rooms are complemented by a cosy restaurant where good food is prepared daily.

⊹ On the village green.

VISA 💳 ⊗ ♿ ✓ 🚭 A

BLOCKLEY, Gloucestershire

This pretty village close to Broadway, Chipping Campden and Moreton in the Marsh is an ideal centre for touring the northern Cotswolds and Stratford. *See also Chipping Campden.*

THE CROWN INN & HOTEL

High Street, Blockley, Gloucestershire GL56 9EX
✆ (01386) 700245 FAX (01386) 700247
JOHN & ELIZABETH CHAMPION

🛏 21, 21 en-suite, from £36.00 per person, double occ.
Lunch served. Open all year.
✗ £16.95, last orders 10pm.
Fresh local fish, pheasant, partridge and venison, in season.

A delightful 16th century coaching inn built in mellow Cotswold stone, with two restaurants, one specialising in fish dishes. The hotel is well appointed, tastefully furnished and offers extremely good value break rates.

VISA AmEx C

BODMIN, Cornwall

County town at the edge of Bodmin moor. Numerous ancient churches and monuments, as well as National Trust houses and gardens. Ideal central base for touring Cornwall.

TREDETHY COUNTRY HOTEL

Helland Bridge, Bodmin, Cornwall PL30 4QS
✆ (01208) 841262 FAX (01208) 841707
BERYL & RICHARD GRAHAM

🛏 11, 11 en-suite, from £30.00 per person, double occ.
Lunch served. Closed 24th to 26th December.
✗ from £13.50, last orders 8.30pm.
Local lamb, seafood, salmon and trout. Cornish ice cream and clotted cream desserts.

Former manor house, set in nine acres of beautiful private grounds, above the river Camel, one of Cornwall's most beautiful valleys. Accommodation is spacious, and the hotel has a friendly, relaxed atmosphere. Lunches are only served from May to September.

VISA AmEx A

BOROUGHBRIDGE, North Yorkshire

Set just off the A1 within 20 minutes of York, Harrogate and 10 minutes of Ripon. The Yorkshire Dales, Herriot Country and Knaresborough are all also within easy reach.

THE CROWN HOTEL

Horsefair, Boroughbridge, North Yorkshire YO5 9EX
✆ (01423) 322328 FAX (01423) 324512
RICHARD STABLES

🛏 42, 42 en-suite, from £32.50 per person, double occ.
Lunch served. Non-residents welcome. Open all year.
✗ £17.95, last orders 9.30pm.
Game.

A historic coaching inn which dates in parts from the 13th century. Old and new have been tastefully and harmoniously combined to create a modern, high standard, hotel which retains the character, welcome and value of a former era.

VISA AmEx A

BOSCASTLE, Cornwall

Attractive Cornish coastal village, which can trace its history back to before the time of the Norman conquest. Area of outstanding natural beauty.

THE WELLINGTON HOTEL ✳✳

The Harbour, Boscastle, Cornwall PL35 OAQ
✆ (01840) 250202 FAX (01840) 250621
SOLANGE & VICTOR TOBUTT

🛏 21, 16 en-suite, from £26.00 per person, double occ.
Lunch served. Closed December & January, but open for Christmas & New Year.
✖ £15.60, last orders 9pm.
🍴 Traditional English fare, mixed with French regional cuisine. Wines from Solange's family vineyard (Madiran). Salmon Aioli. Profiteroles filled with Chicken Livers and Flat Mushrooms. Fillet of Barbary Duck with Ginger, Shallots and Soya Sauce.

A 400 year old coaching inn at the hub of Boscastle harbour. Ten acres of wooded grounds behind the hotel offer a range of walks and a bird watchers paradise. Regular visitors include jays, tits, crested finches, woodpeckers, dippers, wrens and birds of prey. For children under 7 years, please contact the hotel direct.

VISA 🔳 💳 AmEx ⊗ ✓ 🔉 🕲 ⬥ A

BOSHAM, West Sussex

A small village nestling on Chichester Harbour, close to the Roman Villa at Fishbourne. Nearby are miles of unspoilt coastline, nature and wildlife reserves, yet the village is just ten minutes drive from the historic city of Chichester. *See also Chichester, Selsey.*

WHITE BARN

Crede Lane, Bosham, Nr Chichester, West Sussex PO18 8NX
✆ (01243) 573113
SUSAN & ANTONY TROTTMAN

🛏 3, 3 en-suite, from £31.00 per person, double occ.
Non-residents welcome. Open all year.
✖ £18.50, last orders 8pm.
🍴 Traditional dishes prepared from fresh local ingredients.

Modern open plan single storey building with picturesque gardens and patio. Timbered ceilings. A warm and welcoming atmosphere.

✛ Bosham A259, south from roundabout, left a 'T' junction, next left in Crede Lane.

VISA 🔳 ⊗ ♿ ✓ 🕲 A

BOURNEMOUTH, Dorset

Large seaside town set amongst pines at the edge of the New Forest, renowned for its mild climate. Miles of sandy beaches and numerous leisure activities. Close by is Beaulieu Motor Museum and Thomas Hardy country.

HINTON FIRS HOTEL

9 Manor Road, East Cliff, Bournemouth, Dorset BH1 3HB
(01202) 555409 FAX (01202) 299607
GRAHAM ROBINSON

52, 52 en-suite, from £39.00 per person, double occ.
Lunch served. Non-residents welcome. Open all year.
£11.75, last orders 8.30pm.
Traditional English and continental cuisine. Bar snack lunches are available.

A country-like setting in the heart of Bournemouth's East Cliff, renowned for its pine trees and rhododendrons. All rooms are fully equipped and additional amenities include both indoor and outdoor swimming pools, sauna, spa pool, games room and dancing.

VISA 🔲 👆 🏊 ✓ 🔲 🏊 C

BOURTON ON THE WATER, Gloucestershire

The River Windrush flows through this famous Cotswold village with cottages and houses made of local stone. Visit the Model Village, Birdland and the Motor Museum.

BOURTON LODGE HOTEL

Cirencester Road, Bourton on the Water, Gloucestershire GL54 2LE
(01451) 820387 FAX (01451) 821635
THE MILES FAMILY

11, 11 en-suite, from £32.50 per person, double occ.
Lunch served. Non-residents welcome. Open all year.
£15.50, last orders 9.15pm.
Fan of Sweet Galia Melon and Orange Sorbet. Avocado and Ham Salad. Supreme of Chicken A La Creme. Poached Halibut Steak on a Prawn Sauce.

Comfortable accommodation and a pleasant atmosphere created by the family team. The hotel has stunning views over the surrounding Cotswold Hills and is an ideal base for touring the area.

VISA 🔲 AmEx ✓ 🔲 ♿ B

CHESTER HOUSE HOTEL
Victoria Street, Bourton on the Water, Gloucestershire GL54 2BU
☎ (01451) 820286 FAX (01451) 820471
JULIAN & SUSAN DAVIES

◄ 22, 22 en-suite, from £39.25 per person, double occ.
Lunch served. Non-residents welcome. Closed December to 14th
February.
✕ £16.80, last orders 9.30pm.
Lamb Kidneys flavoured with Shallots. Home-made Wild Garlic
and Brandy Pate. Rack of English Lamb. Steamed Cornish Hake.
Banoffi Pie.

A rambling 18th century country house, lovingly restored with a
mix of antique and modern. A quiet relaxed atmosphere prevails
built around comfort and good food.

VISA ◼ ⚏ AmEx ⊗ ✓ ⌇ ⊕ B

BOVEY TRACEY, Devon
Standing by the river, just east of Dartmoor National Park, this old town
has good moorland views and an interesting 12th century church and
tower. There are numerous surrounding NT houses and gardens and the
South Devon coast is within easy reach.

COOMBE CROSS HOTEL
Bovey Tracey, Newton Abbot, South Devon TQ13 9EY
☎ (01626) 832476 FAX (01626) 835298
VERONICA & MALCOLM DAY

◄ 24, 24 en-suite, from £32.00 per person, double occ.
Closed December.
✕ £17.95, last orders 8pm.
Traditional English cuisine. Roasts. Fresh fish. Home cooked
ham and home baked sweets.

An attractive country house, quietly situated at the edge of the
town, enjoying spectacular views across Dartmoor National Park.
The hotel has recently undergone extensive refurbishment to
include a large indoor pool and leisure complex.

✛ Turn off A38 at sign for Bovey Tracy. Hotel is 400 yards past
the Parish Church at the top edge of town.

VISA ◼ ⚏ AmEx ⚷ ⇘ Ⓢ ⊕ A

BOWNESS ON WINDERMERE, Cumbria

Lake side town with a wide range of tourist attractions and water sport opportunities. *See also Windermere.*

FAYRER GARDEN HOUSE HOTEL

Lyth Valley Road, Bowness, Windermere, Cumbria LA23 3JP
☎(015394) 88195 FAX (015394) 45986
IAIN & JACKIE GARSIDE

🛏 9, 9 en-suite, from £16.25 per person, double occ.
Lunch served. Non-residents welcome. Open all year.
✗ £12.95, last orders 8pm.
Herdwick lamb. Cumberland Sausage. Air dried ham, venison and Morecombe Bay shrimps.

A large Victorian country house which has recently been renovated by the owners to provide comfortable, attractive accommodation. The hotel is set in 5 acres of grounds and overlooks Lake Windermere. Greeted by a warm, friendly atmosphere, guests are made to relax and feel `at home'. Guests enjoy free use of the nearby Parklands Leisure Complex, with indoor pool, sauna, steam room, badminton, snooker and squash.

✛ On A5074 1 mile from Bowness Pier.

VISA ▄ AmEx ⊗ ♿ ♣ ✓ 🕿 🦆 A

BOX, Wiltshire

A picturesque small village just four miles east of Bath. An ideal out of town base for visiting Castle Combe, Old Sarum, Stonehenge, The Cheddar Gorge and of course Bath. *See also Bath, Corsham.*

BOX HOUSE HOTEL

Box, Nr Bath, Wiltshire SN14 9NR
☎(01225) 744447 FAX (01225) 743971
TIM & KATHRYN BURNHAM

🛏 9, 9 en-suite, from £32.50 to £42.50 per person, double occ.
Lunch served. Non-residents welcome. Open all year.
✗ £9.95, last orders 9pm.
Anglo/French cooking featuring the best of local seasonal ingredients.

An elegant Georgian mansion house set in 9 acres of beautiful gardens. All the bedrooms are individually furnished with fine antiques and are fully modernised. Nestling in a corner of the sheltered, walled garden is an inviting outdoor swimming pool.

✛ On the outskirts of Bath towards London on the old 'A4'.

VISA ▄ AmEx ⊗ 🏊 ♣ ✓ 🕿 🦆 B

BRAMPTON, Cumbria

A pleasant market town on the Scottish borders. Visit Carlisle, the historic border city, Hadrians Wall and the Eden Valley.

🏠🏠🏠 KIRBY MOOR COUNTRY HOUSE HOTEL ✕✕

Longtown Road, Brampton, Cumbria CA8 2AB
📞 (016977) 3893 FAX (016977) 41847
JOHN & ANNE ROBINSON

🛏 5, 5 en-suite, from £22.00 per person, double occ.
Lunch served. Non-residents welcome. Closed 25th & 26th December.
🍴 £11.95, last orders 9.15pm.
🍲 Hot Shrimps in Butter. Fillet Kirby Moor. Scampi Pernod. Supreme of Chicken in a mild and creamy Madras Sauce.

A detached Victorian country house set in two acres of grounds with outstanding views of open countryside. The hotel is decorated to reflect the age of the building, with antiques and a log fire in winter.

✚ M6, junction 43, follow the A69 to Brampton.
VISA ▧ AmEx ✎/ ⊕ A

BRANDESBURTON, Humberside

An attractive village, 7 miles from the historic town of Beverley, within easy reach of the Yorkshire Wolds and the coast. *See also Tickton.*

🏠🏠 BURTON LODGE HOTEL ✁

Brandesburton, Nr Driffield, North Humberside YO25 8RU
📞 (01964) 542847 FAX (01964) 542847
PETER & ROSE ATKIN

🛏 10, 9 en-suite, from £22.50 per person, double occ.
Closed Christmas.
🍴 £12.00, last orders 9.30pm.
🍲 Local market beef. Rack of Lamb in Yorkshire Sauce. English cooking and carefully selected wines.

Delightfully situated in two acres of grounds and gardens, with a new grass tennis court and an adjoining 18 hole Parkland golf course.

✚ On the southern edge of the village of Brandesburton on the A165 Hull to Bridlington road.

VISA ▧ AmEx ⚲ ✎/ ⎙ ⊕ A

BRECON, Powys

This is the main touring centre for the Brecon Beacons National Park. An attractive old town, with a busy market, castle, cathedral, priory and interesting museums. Lots of outdoor sporting activities. *See also Llyswen.*

THREE COCKS HOTEL & RESTAURANT ✕

Three Cocks, Nr Brecon, Powys LD3 0SL
☎ (01497) 847215
MICHAEL & MARIE - JEANNE WINSTONE

🛏 7, 6 en-suite, from £30.00 per person, double occ.
Lunch served. Non-residents welcome. Closed December to mid February, Sunday lunchtimes & all day Tuesday.
✕ £23.00, last orders 9pm.
🍽 Continental cuisine, featuring selected Belgian dishes, prepared from the freshest available local produce. Served in the elegant dining room.

L-shaped house, beside the Hereford to Brecon road, set in one and a half acres of garden. The inn dates from the fifteenth century and has the distinction of being built around a tree. The cobbled forecourt, mounting blocks, ivy clad walls, cracked doorways, great oak beams and log fires create a charming historical atmosphere.

VISA 🖃 ⊗ 🦢 ✓ A

BRENDON, Devon

A small hamlet, close to Lynton and Lynmouth. Excellent walking opportunities along the coastal path or on Exmoor. *See also Lynmouth.*

STAG HUNTERS HOTEL ✕

Brendon, Lynton, North Devon EX35 6PS
☎ (015987) 222 FAX (015987) 352
P. & P. GREEN, V. THOMAS & G. PHILLIPS

🛏 12, 12 en-suite, from £27.00 per person, double occ.
Lunch served. Non-residents welcome. Open all year.
✕ £12.95, last orders 8.30pm.
🍽 Exmoor lamb, venison and pheasant. Small, daily changing, three course set menu, featuring popular dishes. Mussels in Cider. Fillet of Plaice stuffed with Prawns. Home-made raised Pork Pie.

A traditional ancient coaching inn. The Stag Hunters Hotel is built on the site of an old Abbey, indeed the former chapel is now the hotel lounge. The friendly family atmosphere and local outdoor attractions, including shooting, fishing, horse riding and walking, make this an excellent spot to relax and recuperate from urban life.

⊹ Between Porlock & Lynmouth turn off A39 signposted Brendon. Cross bridge and turn right.

VISA 🖃 💳 AmEx ⊗ ✓ 🦢 🐟 A

BRIDGNORTH, Shropshire

A cliff railway links the old and new parts of Bridgnorth. View the half timbered houses, the Iron Bridge Gorge Museum, the Midland Motor Museum and the Aerospace Museum. *see also Worfield, Telford.*

CROSS LANE HOUSE HOTEL

Astley Abbotts, Bridgnorth, Shropshire WV16 4SJ
✆ (01746) 764887 FAX (01746) 762962
DIANE & ROBERT CLEAL

🛏 8, 8 en-suite, from £23.75 per person, double occ.
Open all year.
✗ £21.50, last orders 8.30pm.
🍽 Fresh local meat and vegetables are used to prepare each day's menu.

A charming Georgian farmhouse. Each room has been individually furnished to provide a warm welcoming atmosphere.

✛ On B4373 1 mile north of Bridgnorth.

VISA 🔜 🈷 ✓ 🛏 🐾 A

BRIDPORT, Dorset

A market town, close to the dramatic Dorset coast. Old broad streets and pleasant gardens, grand arcaded Town Hall and Georgian buildings. Visit the history museum with its Roman relics.

ROUNDHAM HOUSE HOTEL

Roundham Gardens, West Bay Road, Bridport, Dorset DT6 4BD
✆ (01308) 422753 FAX (01308) 421145
PAT & DAVID MOODY

🛏 8, 8 en-suite, from £29.50 per person, double occ.
Non-residents welcome. Closed November to January.
✗ £14.50, last orders 8pm.
🍽 Fresh local sea fish, including crab from West Bay. Traditional dishes. Home-made soups and sweets.

A turn of the century stone residence in a quiet elevated location with country and sea views. Set in one acre of garden. Well appointed and comfortable bedrooms. Renowned for excellent food and service.

✛ From roundabout on A35 south of the town, take sign for West Bay, take 2nd turning left into Roundham Gardens.

VISA 🔜 🈷 🚫 ✓ 🛏 ⚓ A

BRIGHTON & HOVE, East Sussex

Seaside towns developed during the Regency period. See the Royal Pavillion, The Lanes, Brighton Marina or walk along the Pier.

⌂⌂⌂ ## IMPERIAL HOTEL

First Avenue, Hove, East Sussex BN3 2GU
✆ (01273) 777320 FAX (01273) 777310
JOHN GOODCHILD

🛏 75, 75 en-suite, from £31.50 per person, double occ.
Lunch served. Non-residents welcome. Open all year.
✖ from £11.00, last orders 10.30pm.
☞ International cuisine is offered in `Hamilton's Brasserie'. The food is realistically priced and varied in style and appeal. Children and special diets are catered for.

Recent extensive refurbishments have given this Victorian building a high level of comfort. Elegant and beautifully proportioned public rooms lead to well appointed bedrooms, most of which have sea views.

✛ Turn left from the seafront into First Avenue.

VISA 🔳 ⚖ AmEx ⊗ ♿ ✓ 🕭 🚣 🐟 B

⌂⌂ ## ADELAIDE HOTEL

51 Regency Square, Brighton, East Sussex BN1 2FF
✆ (01273) 205286 FAX (01273) 220904
RUTH & CLIVE BUXTON

🛏 12, 12 en-suite, from £32.50 per person, double occ.
Closed 24th to 26th December, restaurant closed Wednesday & Sunday.
✖ £14.50, last orders 8.30pm.
☞ Traditional English food prepared with fresh ingredients.

A Regency town house centrally situated in Brighton's premier seafront square. All rooms are tastefully furnished and the owners offer a warm welcome, friendly service and quiet informality. Parking is available in the square and shops, theatre, historical attractions and conference venues are nearby.

✛ In one of the squares on Brighton seafront.

VISA 🔳 ✓ 🚣 🕭 B

BROCKENHURST, Hampshire

Attractive thatched village in the heart of The New Forest. Beaulieu Motor Museum, Broadlands and Lymington are closeby.

WHITLEY RIDGE COUNTRY HOUSE HOTEL

Beaulieu Road, Brockenhurst, Hampshire SO42 7QL
(01590) 622354 FAX (01590) 622856
RENNIE & SUE LAW

13, 13 en-suite, from £43.00 per person, double occ.
Non-residents welcome. Open all year.
£18.00, last orders 8pm.
Fresh Ravioli Scallops. Saute of Venison with Red Cherries. Tournedos New Forest.

Originally an 18th century royal hunting lodge, this picturesque hotel is set in five acres of secluded gardens and surrounded by the New Forest. Whitley Ridge is noted for its food and wine as well as its warm hospitality. All rooms are beautifully appointed to a very high standard of comfort. Open for lunch on Sundays.

Travelling from Lyndhurst on A337, turn left towards Beaulieu on B3055 for about 1 mile.

VISA AmEx C

BUDE, Cornwall

A resort with charming Georgian cottages, a canal and excellent sandy beaches. A dramatic coastline, with high cliffs and spectacular views. Outdoor activities include golf, cricket, surfing, coarse fishing and boating.

MAER LODGE HOTEL

Crooklets Beach, Bude, Cornwall EX23 8NG
(01288) 353306 FAX (01288) 353306
BERYL & BILL STANLEY

18, 18 en-suite, from £22.50 per person, double occ.
Lunch served. Non-residents welcome. Open all year.
£10.00, last orders 8pm.
Continental and English cuisine.

The hotel is peacefully situated in spacious private grounds overlooking a golf course, close to the beach. A family owned and run establishment.

Proceed from mini-island alongside the river up past the shops to the beach.

VISA AmEx A

BUILTH WELLS, Powys

A small, attractive market town of the upper Wye valley, centrally located for visiting both mid-wales and the Brecon Beacons. *See also Llyswen.*

CAER BERIS MANOR

Garth Road, Builth Wells, Powys LD2 3NP
☎ (01982) 552601 FAX (01982) 552586
PETER & KATHARINE SMITH

🛏 20, 20 en-suite, from £37.50 per person, double occ.
Lunch served. Non-residents welcome. Open all year.
✗ 18.00, last orders 9.30pm.
🍴 Pan fried Mushrooms. Home-made French Onion Soup. Fresh local Trout with Capers. Chargrilled baby Chicken. Chargrilled Swordfish Steak. Tagliatelle with Smoked Salmon and Dill Cream Sauce.

The original part of this hotel was built in 970AD, it was then enlarged and completed in Elizabethan times, set in 27 acres of parkland and woodlands. The oak panelling in the restaurant is dated 1570.

✤ To the west of Builth Wells on the A483 signposted to Llandovery.

VISA 🔳 💳 AmEx ♿ ✓ 🛇 🆂 ⊕ C

BURFORD, Oxfordshire

A small historic village between Oxford and Cheltenham, Burford is known as the gateway to the Cotswolds and has many buildings of architectural interest, its high street offers visitors the chance to browse around many quaint antique and specialist shops.

THE GOLDEN PHEASANT HOTEL

The High Street, Burford, Oxfordshire OX18 4QA
☎ (01993) 823223 FAX (01993) 822621
DANIEL M.HOLMES

🛏 12, 11 en-suite, from £44.00 per person, double occ.
Lunch served. Non-residents welcome. Open all year.
✗ From £16.00, last orders 9.30pm.
🍴 Anglo-french cuisine prepared to order using fresh ingredients. A warm salad of Smoked Duck, Mangetout and orange segments. Baked Salmon en Papi Votle flavoured with wine and tarragon. Tenderloin of Lamb with fresh herbs and grain mustard set on a stir fry of seasonable vegetables.

A former 15th C Coaching Inn which has been tastefully restored into a hotel of charm, character and quality. Twelve individually styled bedrooms which all have private facilities and the restaurant has an excellent local reputation for its cuisine and friendly service.

✤ Half-way down Burford High Street, on the right.

VISA 🔳 AmEx ♿ ✓ 🛇 ⊕ C

BURNHAM ON CROUCH, Essex

Set on the north bank of the river Crouch, six miles from the sea, this town is a popular yachting centre. Visit St. Peters Church and Bramwell Lodge.

YE OLDE WHITE HARTE

The Quay, Burnham-on-Crouch, Essex CM0 8AS
✆ (01621) 782106
MR G. LEWIS

🛏 15, 11 en-suite, from £29.70 per person, double occ.
Lunch served. Non-residents welcome. Closed 25th & 26th December.
✕ £9.50, last orders 9pm.
🍴 Traditional English food. Roasts, grills, casseroles, braised lambs hearts, locally caught fish, gateaux.

A 16th century building, overlooking the estuary. The White Harte is full of old world atmosphere, exposed beams, antiques and open fires.

VISA ◼ ⊗ 🖎 ✓ 🐾 A

BURY ST EDMUNDS, Suffolk

Historic market town with a wealth of interesting sites and places to visit. A good central base to explore Lavenham and Long Melford or the delights of Cambridge.

RAVENWOOD HALL COUNTRY HOTEL & RESTAURANT

Rougham, Bury St Edmunds, Suffolk IP30 9JA
✆ (01359) 270345 FAX (01359) 270788
CRAIG JARVIS

🛏 14, 14 en-suite, from £38.50 per person, double occ.
Lunch served. Non-residents welcome. Open all year.
✕ £16.50, last orders 9.30pm.
🍴 Recipes prepared from the finest local produce. Herbs from the hotel garden and venison from a local game farm. Home pickled fruits and vegetables. Meats and fish smoked on the premises.

A fine Tudor manor house, dating in parts from 1530, set in secluded woodland and gardens two miles east of Bury St Edmunds. The hotel retains its historic atmosphere with beamed ceilings, ornate oak panelling and roaring log fires. There is an outdoor heated swimming pool, tennis court and croquet lawn.

⊹ 2 miles east of Bury St Edmunds off the A14 (formerly A45).

VISA ◼ ♨ AmEx ⊗ 🏊 🔍 ✓ 🖎 🐾 C

BUXTON, Derbyshire

A market town with one of the oldest spas in England. Visit the Opera house and attractive Pavilion gardens. An excellent centre for exploring the Peak District.

PORTLAND HOTEL

32 St Johns Road, Buxton, Derbyshire SK17 6XQ
✆ (01298) 71493 FAX (01298) 27464
BRIAN & LINDA MILLNER

🛏 25, 25 en-suite, from £32.50 per person, double occ.
Lunch served. Non-residents welcome. Closed 1st & 2nd January.
✕ £16.50, last orders 9.30pm.
🍴 Traditional English cuisine. Roast Topside of Beef. Rack of Lamb. Traditional British Breakfasts. FINALIST, REPRESENTING THE MIDLANDS, IN THE 1994 LOGIS REGIONAL CUISINE COMPETITION.

A family run hotel, offering a warm welcome along with courteous, traditional service. The restaurant is housed in an attractive conservatory.

VISA 💳 🔷 AmEx ⊗ ✓ 🔷 B

CAERNARFON, Gwynedd

Town on the wide open plains between Snowdonia and the sea, with the Llanberis Pass and the Isle of Anglesey nearby. Visit Caernarfon Castle, Snowdon, Snowdonia National Park and Bodnant Gardens.

TYN RHOS COUNTRY HOUSE

Llanddeiniolen, Caernarfon, Gwynedd LL55 3AE
✆ (01248) 670489 FAX (01248) 670079
NIGEL & LYNDA KETTLE

🛏 11, 11 en-suite, from £28.00 per person, double occ.
Non-residents welcome. Closed 20th December to 4th January.
✕ £18.50, last orders 8pm.
🍴 Smoked Haddock Rarebit on Tomato Salad. A fan of Honeydew Melon with a Sabayon Glaze. Thai Vegetable Soup. Loin of local Pork served with Apple Fritters. Spiced Bramley Apple and Wild Bramble Cobbler. Special diets and requests can be catered for.

A former farmhouse, now converted into a country house hotel, full of charm and comfort. The bedrooms are all individual in design.

VISA 💳 AmEx ✓ 🔷 A B

CANTERBURY, Kent

The site of Canterbury Cathedral. St Martins, the oldest church in England, the Royal Museum and old Weaver's House are all attractions in this city. *see also Dover, Chilham*

POINTERS HOTEL

1 London Road, Canterbury, Kent CT2 8LR
☎ (01227) 456846 FAX (01227) 831131
CHRISTINE & JACK O' BRIEN

🛏 14, 10 en-suite, from £27.50 per person, double occ.
Non-residents welcome. Closed 23rd December to mid January.
🍴 £12.95, last orders 8.15pm.
Traditional English cooking, using fresh local produce.

An elegant Georgian hotel, offering a warm and friendly atmosphere.

⚓ North of Canterbury's Westgate opposite St Dunstan's Church.

VISA 🏧 AmEx ⊗ ✓ ⚓ A

KING WILLIAM IV

4 High Street, Littlebourne, Canterbury, Kent CT3 1ST
☎ (01227) 721244 FAX (01227) 721244
PAUL & LYNN THURGATE

🛏 4, 4 en-suite, from £20.00 per person, double occ.
Lunch served. Non-residents welcome. Open all year.
🍴 from £10.00, last orders 9.15pm.
Chicken breasts, stuffed with an number of different fillings and wrapped in filo pastry. Fresh fish. Home-made desserts.

A traditional country inn, dating in parts from 1790, with exposed oak beams and open log fires. Heaps of character. Real ales and a relaxed, friendly atmosphere.

⚓ From Canterbury, follow A257 towards Sandwich for 2 miles. Hotel on left side at end of Tilebourne Village.

VISA 🏧 ⊗ ⚓ ✓ A

CAPEL CURIG, Gwynedd

In the heart of the Snowdonia National Park with numerous opportunities for climbing and walking. The castles of north Wales are easily accessible as are Port Meirion, Anglesey and the Lleyn peninsular. *See also Beddgelert.*

COBDEN'S HOTEL & BRASSERIE

Capel Curig, Snowdonia Nat. Park, Gwynedd LL24 0EE
☎ (016904) 243 FAX (016904) 354
CRAIG GOODALL & RUSSELL HONEYMAN

🛏 19, 16 en-suite, from £27.50 per person, double occ.
Lunch served. Non-residents welcome. Open all year.
🍴 approx £14.00 a la carte, last orders 9.30pm.
Local produce a speciality.

An internationally famous walking and climbing hotel, set amidst the splendour of Snowdonia. Cobden's offers an informal and relaxed atmosphere, with extremely comfortable accommodation and healthy, fresh, wholesome food.

⚓ On the A5, 4 miles north of Betws-Y-Coed, on the Bangor/Holyhead road.

VISA 🏧 AmEx ✓ ⚓ A

CARLISLE, Cumbria

At the Western end of Hadrian's Wall, close to Gretna Green, Lanacost Priory, Carlisle Castle and the Tuille House Museum.

THE STRING OF HORSES INN

Faugh, Heads Nook, Carlisle, Cumbria CA4 9EG
*(0122870) 297 FAX (0122870) 675
ERIC & ANNE TASKER

🛏 14, 14 en-suite, from £49.00 per person, double occ.
Lunch served. Non-residents welcome. Open all year.
🍴 £16.95, last orders 10pm.
🍲 Old English Fish Pie. Salmon Elizabeth.

A 17th century country inn full of character, antique fittings and interesting prints. The modern accommodation offers a high level of comfort and includes spa baths, sauna, solarium and a heated outdoor swimming pool. Dogs not allowed in public rooms.

⚓ From M6, follow A69 towards Brampton, turning off for Heads Nook after first garage.

VISA 💳 💳 AmEx ⊗ ⌇ ✓ S ⚑ **B**

HOLMHEAD FARMHOUSE

Hadrian's Wall, Greenhead-in-Northumberland, Cumbria CA6 7HY
*(016977) 47402 FAX (016977) 47402
BRIAN & PAULINE STAFF

🛏 4, 4 en-suite, from £22.50 per person, double occ.
Open all year.
🍴 £16.00, last orders 8pm.
🍲 Local cheeses. Some Roman recipes used. Home-made bread, jam, scones, chutneys. Home grown herbs. Guests eat together 'house party' style.

Holmhead Farm is no longer a working farm but it retains much of the easy going friendliness of a family home is combined with the standards of comfort and cuisine associated with larger hotels. There is a pretty garden with a stream. A totally non-smoking hotel.

⚓ On A69 and B6318, behind the youth hostel in Greenhead village.

VISA 💳 AmEx ⊗ ✓ S **A**

CARMARTHEN, Dyfed

In the hills above the beautiful Towy Valley. Visit local castles, steam railways and beaches.

PANTGWYN FARM

Whitemill, Carmarthen, Dyfed SA32 7ES
☎ (01267) 290247 FAX (01267) 290247
TIM & SUE GILES

🛏 3, 3 en-suite, from £20.00 per person, double occ.
Closed 24th to 27th December.
✗ £14.50, last orders 8pm.
🍴 Farmhouse Tomato Soup with fresh Basil. Blue Cheese and Walnut Salad. Breast of Chicken with Honey and Orange. Welsh Black Beef in Beer. Pantgwyn Lemon Ice Cream. Elderflower Syllabub with Cherries. Walnut Tart.

A 200 year old farmhouse with an inglenook lounge, beamed dining room and traditionally furnished bedrooms. A peaceful and family run hotel in a rural setting.

✢ 4 miles east of Carmarthen on A40 to Llandeilo. Turn to Whitemill and follow signs 1 mile up the hill by the old school.

⊗ ✓ 🦢 A

CASTLE DONNINGTON, Derbyshire

A Norman castle once stood here. The world's largest collection of single-seater racing cars is displayed at Donnington Park alongside the racing circuit.

PARK FARMHOUSE HOTEL

Melbourne Road, Isley Walton, Derbyshire DE74 2RN
☎ (01332) 862409 FAX (01332) 862364
JOHN & LINDA SHIELDS

🛏 9, 9 en-suite, from £32.50 per person, double occ.
Closed Christmas.
✗ £14.95, last orders 8.30pm.
🍴 Garden Pate. Deep Fried Camembert. Grilled Local Trout. New Orleans Chicken (breast marinated in Cajun spices).

Part 17th century half timbered farmhouse. Large, traditionally furnished, public rooms. Bedrooms are in a country farmhouse style.

✢ On the A453 at Isley Walton take the Melbourne turn, hotel is half a mile on the right

VISA 🔳 💳 AmEx ♿ ✓ 🦢 ⊲ A

CAWSTON, Norfolk

A village with one of the finest churches in the country, St Agnes, built in the Perpendicular style, was much patronised by Michael de la Pole, Earl of Suffolk (1414). Visit the Norfolk Broads, Sandringham, Norwich City and Cathedral.

GREY GABLES COUNTRY HOUSE HOTEL
Norwich Road, Cawston, Norfolk NR10 4EY
☎ (01603) 871259
JAMES & ROSALIND SNAITH

🛏 7, 6 en-suite, from £30.00 per person, double occ.
Non-residents welcome. Closed 24th, 25th & 26th December.
✗ £13.00 to £21.00, last orders 8.30pm.
🍽 Local Crab with salad. Melon with Summer Fruits and Sorbet. Roast Spring Lamb with Mint and Redcurrant Jelly. Local Trout served with Almonds. Stilton Parcel (cheese, peppers, celery, onions all roasted in puff pastry).

A former Rectory set in rural surroundings, comfortably furnished with many antiques. A renowned wine cellar with over 300 different wines.

✦ 10 miles north of Norwich, 1 mile south of Cawston Village near Eastgate, off B1149.

VISA 💳 ✎ ✓ 🖎 🦢 A

CHARD, Somerset

Market town in pretty surrounding countryside with lots of history. Chard Museum, The Guildhall, Cricket St Thomas, Crinkley Bottom, Lyme Regis, Yeovilton and Exeter.

BATH HOUSE RESTAURANT & HOTEL ✕
Bath House, Holyrood Street, Chard, Somerset TA20 2ET
☎ (01460) 67575 FAX (01460) 64401
JEAN & ROB HOUWELING

🛏 8, 8 en-suite, from £23.75 per person, double occ.
Non-residents welcome. Open all year.
✗ £15.00, last orders 9.30pm.
🍽 The restaurant offers a variety of local and international dishes including Indonesian food.

Situated in the centre of Chard with ample car parking, Bath House is a Grade II listed building (c. 1650) with good quality accommodation and hospitality. The owners speak French, Dutch, German and Spanish.

✦ In the centre of Chard.

VISA 💳 AmEx ⊗ ✓ 🖎 A

CHARMOUTH, Dorset

A small town, set back from the south Dorset coastline, close to Lyme Regis. An area of safe sandy beaches full of fossils, part of the Heritage Coast, owned by the N.T. There are many local manor houses nearby. Visit Parnham and Forde Abbey.

THE WHITE HOUSE HOTEL ✕ ✕

2 Hillside, The Street, Charmouth, Dorset DT6 6PJ
☎ (01297) 560411 FAX (01297) 560702
THE BALFOUR FAMILY

🛏 10, 10 en-suite, from £36.00 per person, double occ.
Lunch served. Non-residents welcome. Closed December & January.
✕ £18.50, last orders 8.30pm.
West country cooking with emphasis on fresh local fish dishes.

Built in 1827, The White House has many original and unusual regency features including curved walls and doors. All the bedrooms are extremely comfortable, and include a welcoming decanter of sherry.

VISA ⬛ AmEx ⊗ ⬥ B

CHEDINGTON, Dorset

Small village, four miles south east of Crewkerne. An ideal base for touring Thomas Hardy country. Visit Sherborne, Lyme Regis and the Dorset coast. There are a number of National Trust properties. Excellent walking country.

CHEDINGTON COURT HOTEL

Chedington, Beaminster, Dorset DT8 3HY
☎ (01935) 891265 FAX (01935) 891442
HILARY & PHILIP CHAPMAN

🛏 10, 10 en-suite, from £47.50 per person, double occ.
Non-residents welcome. Closed Christmas & 4 weeks from early January.
✕ £26.50 (inc in room rate), last orders 9pm.
Classic English and French cuisine featuring fresh fish from Brixham, local game in season, and pure local meats reared by traditional methods.

A magnificent Jacobean style manor house, set in ten acres of garden, renowned for good food and wine. Spectacular views. The hotel gardens include a sculptured yew hedge, grotto, water garden, ponds and terraces. Inside, the hotel has a welcoming, informal and relaxed atmosphere, decorated with fine Persian rugs, antiques and stone fireplaces. Chedington Court has its own 9 hole par 74 golf course - free mid-week and half price at weekends for guests.

✢ Just off the A356 at Winyards Gap, 4.5 miles south east of Crewhorne.

VISA ⬛ AmEx ⬥ C

CHELTENHAM, Gloucestershire

This spa town has a wealth of Regency architecture and is surrounded by beautiful Cotswold countryside. A good shopping centre and popular local racecourse. *See also Colesbourne.*

HALLERY HOUSE HOTEL

48 Shurdington Road, Cheltenham, Gloucestershire GL53 0JE
☎ (01242) 578450 FAX (01242) 529730
ANGIE PETKOVIC' & STEVE SHORT

🛏 16, 10 en-suite, from £28.00 per person, double occ.
Open all year. Non-residents welcome.
✗ £11.95 to £18.00, last orders 8.30pm.
🍴 English food with Mediterranean and international influences. Aubergine Gateaux layered with Tomatoes, Feta and Basil. Fillets of baby Halibut with Fennel, Shallots and roasted Red Peppers. Amaretti Chocolate Torte. Most diets are catered for. Free range and organic are used wherever possible.

Built around 1824, Hallery House has been fully restored, full of character and has a good restaurant. Angie and Steve are an enthusiastic couple who, together with their chef, enjoy preparing and serving good food and wine. Also available is bicycle hire, together with planned routes, and picnic lunches.

✠ On the A46 Cheltenham to Stroud road on the south side of town. From central Cheltenham take the Bath road, turn right at the roundabout and hotel is 250 yards on the left.

VISA 🔲 💳 AmEx ⊗ ♿ ✓ 🚭 ⬦ **A**

THE CHARLTON KINGS HOTEL

London Road, Charlton Kings, Cheltenham, Gloucestershire GL52 6UU
☎ (01242) 231061 FAX (01242) 241900
TREVOR STUART

🛏 14, 14 en-suite, from £39.50 per person, double occ.
Lunch served. Non-residents welcome. Open all year.
✗ £15.95, last orders 9pm.
🍴 Deep fried Courgette with a Barbecue Sauce. Devilled Whitebait with a Mustard Sauce. Grilled Trout stuffed with seasonal Berries and Hazelnuts. Medallions of Pork Fillet in a Raspberry and Courgette Sauce.

Set alongside the main A40 in an acre of wide lawns, the hotel is surrounded by the Cotswold Hills. Bedrooms are decorated in a style which compliments the pine furniture and creates a warm, comfortable atmosphere.

✠ Arriving from Oxford, the hotel is to the left on the outskirts of town.

VISA 🔲 AmEx ⊗ ♿ ✓ ⬦ **C**

CHEPSTOW, Gwent

Market town at the beginning of the beautiful Wye Valley. Good racecourse and interesting castle ruins. Use as a base for touring south Wales, The Forest of Dean and Wye Valley. *See also Tintern.*

THE FIRST HURDLE HOTEL

9/10 Upper Church St, Chepstow, Gwent NP6 5EX
✆ (01291) 622189
ROS & MALCOLM SLEEMAN

🛏 12, 7 en-suite, from £24.00 per person, double occ.
Lunch served. Non-residents welcome. Closed Christmas to New Year.
✗ from £10.00 a la carte, last orders 9.45pm.
🍴 English and continental cuisine. Grills and roasts.

Very comfortable, small town centre hotel, adjacent to Chepstow Castle. All rooms are tastefully furnished in antique pine and period pieces. The proprietors' horses are available for guests use.

VISA 🔲 ⊗ 🕲 ✓ 🕸 A

CHESTER, Cheshire

A Roman city with medieval shopping rows, noted for its black and white timber framed buildings. Visit the Roman walls, the Wirral peninsula and north Wales.

ROWTON HALL HOTEL

Rowton Lane, Whitchurch Road, Rowton, Cheshire CH3 6AD
✆ (01244) 335262 FAX (01244) 335464
STUART & DIANA BEGBIE

🛏 42, 42 en-suite, from £44.00 per person, double occ.
Lunch served. Non-residents welcome. Closed 25th to 27th December.
✗ £16.50, last orders 9.30pm.
🍴 Fresh Dee Salmon, local game in season, Sea Bass with provencale herbs, fillets of Red Mullet wrapped in Parma Ham, Pan Fried Escalopes of Veal on a bed of noodles with smoked cheese, Veal Kidneys sauteed in forrest mushrooms finished in a mustard sauce.

A Georgian country house, retaining all its original character with many modern facilities and comforts. The extensive amenities include five conference/meeting rooms, and a ballroom. The Hamilton Leisure Club facilities include a swimming pool, multi gym, sauna and solarium. The Langdale Restaurant has full a la carte and table d'hote menus, and also caters for the health conscious! Some half tester beds and a four poster bed.

⊹ South of Chester city, just off the Whitchurch Road.

VISA 🔲 🏧 AmEx ⊗ 🌊 ✎ ✓ S 🕸 C

THE DENE HOTEL

Hoole Road, Chester, Cheshire CH2 3ND
✆ (01244) 321165 FAX (01244) 350277
BILL WOOD & DAVID PICKERING

🛏 49, 47 en-suite, from £22.50 per person, double occ.
Lunch served. Non-residents welcome. Closed Christmas & New Year.
✗ from £10.00 a la carte, last orders 9pm.
🍴 Traditional English cuisine.
A traditional tourism and business hotel which has undergone substantial refurbishment in the last year under the direction of the new owners. The bedrooms are fully appointed, comfortable and offer good value for money.

VISA 🔲 🏧 ⊗ 🕭 ✓ 🕸 A

 Chester continued overleaf...

THE PHEASANT INN

Higher Burwardsley, Tattenhall, Chester, Cheshire CH3 9PF
☎ (01829) 70434 FAX (01829) 71097
DAVID GREENHAUGH

🛏 8, 8 en-suite, from £30.00 per person, double occ.
Lunch served. Open all year.
✗ £12.00 a la carte, last orders 9.30pm.
🍴 A traditional, popular menu featuring grills and roasts.
Pheasant Casserole and Highland Beef.

A 300 year old, half timbered inn nestling on the top of Peckforton
Hills. Magnificent views over the Cheshire plain towards Wales.
Full of old world charm and ambience. Huge log fire in winter and
year-round good food.

VISA 🔲 ⚡ AmEx ⊗ ✓ 🌙 A

CHESTERFIELD, Derbyshire

Famous for the twisted spire on its parish church, Chesterfield has some
fine modern buildings and excellent shopping facilities, including a large,
traditional open-air market. Hardwick Hall and Bolsover Castle are
nearby.

ABBEYDALE HOTEL

Cross Street, Chesterfield, Derbyshire S40 4TD
☎ (01246) 277849 FAX (01246) 558223
P & M BRAMHILL

🛏 11, 9 en-suite, from £18.75 per person, double occ.
Non-residents welcome. Closed Christmas.
✗ £10.00 to £16.00, last orders 8.30pm.
🍴 Giant Prawns. Garlic Mushrooms. Chilli con Carne. Rump
Steak with Stilton and Mango. Peppered Steak with Brandy.

A converted Victorian house with comfortable and well equipped
bedrooms in a quiet location yet close to the town centre.

⊹ From M1 or A61, follow A619 (Bakewell and Buxton) to island
at the end of Queens Park, turn right up Foljambe Road, Compton
Street to 'T' junction, then turn right for 200 metres to hotel on left.

VISA 🔲 ⚡ AmEx ♿ ✓ A

CHICHESTER, West Sussex

The county town of West Sussex can be traced to Roman times through nearby Fishbourne Palace. The town has a Norman Cathedral and many attractive Georgian buildings. Chichester is surrounded by beautiful countryside. *see also Bosham, Selsey.*

CROUCHERS BOTTOM COUNTRY HOTEL

Birdham Road, Apuldram, Chichester, West Sussex PO20 7EH
☏ (01243) 784995 FAX (01243) 539797
RON & PAM FODEN

🛏 6, 6 en-suite, from £33.00 per person, double occ.
Non-residents welcome. Closed 23rd to 31st December.
✗ £18.50, last orders 8.30pm.
🍴 Fresh market produce is used to prepare the daily changing menu. Fresh Selsey Crab Ramekin au Gratin. Breast of Duck with a fresh Mango, Orange & Brandy Sauce. Little Sticky Toffee Puddings.

Crouchers Bottom is situated 2 miles south of Chichester, close to the harbour and excellent sandy beaches. The hotel is a converted 1920's farmhouse with separate converted coach-house for guest bedrooms. Four ground floor rooms - one with full wheelchair access, all rooms are furnished in pine and enjoy a pleasant rural outlook. Log fires create a warm atmosphere in winter.

⊹ South of Chichester on A286 to Birdham and Witterings. Just after Black Horse public house.

VISA 🖲 AmEx ⊗ ♿ ⟋ **B**

WOODSTOCK HOUSE HOTEL

Charlton, Nr Chichester, West Sussex PO18 0HU
☏ (01243) 811666
MR & MRS M. MC GOVERN

🛏 10, 10 en-suite, from £38.00 per person, double occ.
Non-residents welcome. Open all year.
✗ £15.50-£16.95, last orders 8.30pm.
🍴 Home-style cooking, with a fine selection of wines, served in a candlelit restaurant. Woodstock House is a comfortable, traditional hotel. A sun lounge for summer and log fires in the winter, courtyard gardens. An ideal base for a walking holiday. Near to Goodwood racecourse. For children under 12, please contact the hotel direct.

⊹ Off A3 onto A286 Midhurst to Chichester. Turn off at singleton S/P, Charlton 3/4 mile.

VISA 🖲 ⊗ ⟋ **B**

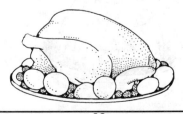

CHILHAM, Kent

Visit nearby Leeds and Dover Castles, the gardens at Sissinghurst, or historic Canterbury. *See also Canterbury, Dover.*

THE WOOLPACK INN

High Street, Chilham, Nr Canterbury, Kent CT4 8DL
☎ (01227) 730208 FAX (01227) 731053
DAVID & JAN ALLSOP

🛏 15, 15 en-suite, from £23.75 per person, double occ.
Lunch served. Non Residents welcome. Open all year.
✕ £12.00 - £15.00, last orders 10pm.
🍴 Freshly prepared food, featuring Kentish regional specialities.

A 15th century coaching inn in the centre of a picturesque village.

⊹ Just off the main A28, in the village centre.

VISA 🖃 ⊗ ♿ ✓ 🌲 ⬦ A

CHIPPING CAMPDEN, Gloucestershire

Charming, Cotswold stone town, within easy travelling distance of Stratford, Broadway and Cheltenham. The famous gardens of Hidcote and Kiftsgate are closeby as are Sudeley and Warwick Castles. *See also Blockley, Stratford.*

THREE WAYS HOTEL

Mickleton, Chipping Campden, Gloucestershire GL55 6SB
☎ (01386) 438429 FAX (01386) 438118
KEITH & JEAN TURNER

🛏 40, 40 en-suite, from £44.00 per person, double occ.
Lunch served. Non-residents welcome. Open all year.
✕ £16.50, last orders 9pm.
🍴 Extensive menus in both the Restaurant and the Bar. Grilled Tuna Steak with Hollandaise Sauce. Whole Baby Poussin with Curry, Honey and Ginger. Braised Venison with Guiness and Orange. Traditional puddings.

A stone built Cotswold coaching inn, with modern additions. Family run, famous for its good food and warm welcome. The hotel has good conference facilities. Enjoy Three Ways for its relaxed and friendly atmosphere and for its ideal location. Three Ways is the home of the Pudding Club, enthusiasts meet on winter evenings to celebrate traditional British puddings - Queen of Puddings, Jam Roly Poly, Spotted Dick etc.

⊹ In the centre of Mickleton village, 2 miles north of Chipping Campden.

VISA 🖃 ⚒ AmEx ♿ ⬦ B

CHURCH STRETTON, Shropshire

In the heart of the border land twixt England and Wales; the historical Marches; where the hills sweep down all around. Ancient town renowned for its views and good walking, excellent local golf and gliding. Ludlow, Shrewsbury and Iron Bridge Gorge are closeby.

MYND HOUSE HOTEL

Little Stretton, Church Stretton, Shropshire SY6 6RB
✆ (01694) 722212 FAX (01694) 724180
ROBERT & JANET HILL

🛏 8, 8 en-suite, from £40.00 per person, double occ.
Lunch served. Non-residents welcome. Closed January & two weeks in Summer.
✖ £24.00, last orders 9.15pm.
☟ Interesting uncontrived dishes produced from the best of the Marches recipes and produce; hoggit, game, fish, oak smoked pork and chicken, Marches cheeses and home-made ice creams and sorbets with goats milk and fruit and berries.

An Edwardian house hotel and restaurant built in 1902, with modern additions and creature comforts, including log fire and warm discreet hospitality. Dinner is an essential ingredient of any stay at Mynd House, booking essential. The wine list is outstanding with over 300 wines in bottles and an impressive 170 in half bottles along with dessert wines and ports by the glass. Innovative, interesting short breaks available all year.

⌖ Half a mile off A49 Shrewsbury to Leominster road, signposted Little Stretton B4370.

VISA ▄ AmEx ⊗ 🐾 ✓ 🐉 🐲 A B C

CHURCHILL, Avon

In the heart of the Mendip Hills, Churchill is just half an hours drive from either Bath, Bristol or Wells, 4 miles from the Cheddar Gorge. *See also Winscombe.*

WINSTON MANOR HOTEL

Bristol Road, Churchill, Avon BS19 5NL
✆ (01934) 852348 FAX (01934) 852033
JILL GREEN & MARION SHERRINGTON

🛏 13, 13 en-suite, from £29.75 per person, double occ.
Non-residents welcome. Closed 25th & 26th December.
✖ £14.75, last orders 8.45pm.
☟ Chicken Breast Somerset Style. Venison Sausages in Redcurrant and Port Wine Sauce. Stilton and Apple Tartlets.

A Victorian manor house set in secluded gardens, offering traditional style and personal service. All the rooms are equipped with modern comforts, the restaurant offers traditional Somerset fare. Sunday lunches served, rest of the week lunch available by prior arrangement. Some bedrooms are available on the ground floor.

⌖ On A38, 5 miles south of Bristol Airport. From M5, junction 21 southbound, junction 22 northbound.

VISA ▄ 🎫 AmEx ✓ 🐉 🐲 A B

CIRENCESTER, Gloucestershire

A historic Roman city in the heart of the Cotswolds, now a thriving market town. Visit Sudeley Castle, Slimbridge Wildfowl Trust, Cotswold Wildlife Park, Cotswold Water Park, Bibury, Cheltenham or Bath. *See also Coln St Aldwyns.*

THE KINGS HEAD HOTEL

Cirencester, Gloucestershire, GL7 2R
☎ (01285) 653322 FAX (01285) 655103
JOHN & HELEN BANNERMAN

🛏 66, 66 en-suite, from £40.00 per person, double occ.
Lunch served. Non-residents welcome. Closed 27th to 30th December.
✕ £14.55
🍽 Traditional English food. Celery & Hazelnut Soup. Honey glazed Leg of Lamb.

Historic, rambling coaching inn, originating in the 16th century. Some four poster bedrooms. Guests can expect a warm welcome and comfortable stay. Situated in the town centre, next door to the Tourist Information Centre.

VISA AmEx C

WILD DUCK INN ✕

Ewen, Cirencester, Gloucestershire GL7 6BY
☎ (01285) 770310 FAX (01285) 770310
BRIAN & TINA MUSSELL

🛏 9, 9 en-suite, from £32.50 to £37.50 per person, double occ.
Lunch served. Non-residents welcome. Open all year.
✕ £8.00-£15.00 a la carte, last orders 9.45pm.
🍽 Frequently changing menu specialising in fresh exotic fish. Parrot Fish, Grouper.

15th century mellow Cotswold stone inn in a delightful village two miles south of Cirencester. Open fires, comfortable accommodation and old world ambiance in a beautiful setting. Bistro style restaurant has a good local reputation.

VISA B

CLARE, Suffolk

Picturesque market town with a ruined Norman castle. A country park now occupies the ruins with extensive nature trails. Local vineyards at Boyton can be visited. Lavenham and Sudbury are closeby.

THE PLOUGH INN

Nr Hundon, Sudbury, Suffolk CO10 8DT
☎ (01440) 786789 FAX (01440) 786710
DAVID & MARION ROWLINSON

🛏 8, 8 en-suite, from £25.00 per person, double occ.
Lunch served. Non-residents welcome. Open all year.
✕ £13.95, last orders 9.30pm.
🍽 Mainly traditional English cuisine. Plenty of fresh seafood available.

A country inn, where exposed beams & soft red brickwork combined with natural soft furnishings create a warm and friendly atmosphere.

VISA A

CLEARWELL, Gloucestershire

Picturesque village in the beautiful Wye valley and Royal Forest of Dean. See Symonds Yat Rock, the Falconry centre, and Clearwell Caves.

🏠🏠🏠 THE WYNDHAM ARMS ✗ ✗

Clearwell, Gloucestershire, GL16 8JT
✆ (01594) 833666 FAX (01594) 836450
JOHN & ROSEMARY STANFORD

🛏 17, 17 en-suite, from £30.00 per person, double occ.
Lunch served. Non-residents welcome. Open all year.
✗ £15.25, last orders 9.30pm.
🍴 English cuisine, with French influence. Fresh salmon, local lamb and pheasant in season. Guinea Fowl Montmorency, casseroled with red wine, cherries, onions and bacon. Mixed Grill. Kidneys Creole. Filet de Boeuf en Croute.

A 14th century village inn, refurbished and modernised to an extremely high standard. The adjoining annex offers luxury accommodation and the busy restaurant has a justified excellent reputation. Bar meals served daily.

✛ On the B4231, in the centre of the village of Clearwell.

VISA 🔲 💳 AmEx ♿ ⬨ A

CLEOBURY MORTIMER, Shropshire

Village close to the Clee Hills with attractive half timbered and Georgian houses and a church with a wooden spire. Visit Clee Hill Gardens with over 400 birds and animals.

🏠🏠 THE REDFERN HOTEL

Cleobury Mortimer, Kidderminster, Shropshire DY14 8AA
✆ (01299) 270395 FAX (01299) 271011
JON & LIZ REDFERN

🛏 11, 11 en-suite, from £34.00 per person, double occ.
Lunch served. Non-residents welcome. Open all year.
✗ from £15.95, last orders 9.30pm.
🍴 English and French cuisine.

An 18th century stone built inn and hotel in a picturesque old market town. A warm welcome and relaxed hospitality.

VISA 🔲 💳 AmEx ✓ ⬨ ⬨ B

COLCHESTER, Essex

Britain's oldest recorded town standing on the River Colne and famous for its oysters. Visit Colchester Castle, Colchester Zoo, Constable Country, numerous historic buildings, ancient remains and museums.

ROSE & CROWN HOTEL

East Gate, Colchester, Essex CO1 2TZ
✆ (01206) 866677 FAX (01206) 866616
SHAROKH BAGHERZADEH

🛏 30, 20 en-suite, from £27.50 per person, double occ.
Lunch served. Non-residents welcome. Open all year.
✗ £14.95, last orders 10pm.
🍴 Deep Fried Whitebait. Hot Pot of Mushrooms with Garlic. Cucumber and Tomato salad. Braised slices of Pork in Orange and Grape Sauce. Poached Lemon Sole Fillet in Mushroom Sauce. Marbled Chocolate Cheesecake. Chocolate Ganache.

A 15th century coaching inn (the oldest in Colchester) elegantly furnished and equipped, offering a warm, friendly atmosphere.

✛ Off A12 or A120 junction (1232), follow Ipswich Road for 2 miles. Cross over the 2 mini roundabouts, hotel on the left.

VISA 💳 💳 AmEx ⊗ ♿ ✓ 🐾 A

COLESBOURNE, Gloucestershire

A picturesque hamlet, mid way between Cheltenham and Gloucester in the heart of the beautiful Cotswolds. *See also Cheltenham, Cirencester.*

COLESBOURNE INN

Colesbourne, Cheltenham, Gloucestershire GL53 9NP
✆ (01242) 870376 FAX (01242) 870397
ERIC & MARY BIRD

🛏 10, 10 en-suite, from £25.00 per person, double occ.
Lunch served. Non-residents welcome. Open all year.
✗ £11.50, last orders 10pm.
🍴 Traditional, old fashioned British cooking. Popular inn food, roasts, grills, casseroles and pies. Daily blackboard specials.

A 200 year old Cotswold stone inn on the Cheltenham to Cirencester road. Heaps of character and rustic charm, open log fires and exposed beams. The accommodation is in a converted stable block adjacent to the inn. An ideal base for touring this beautiful part of the Cotswolds.

VISA 💳 💳 AmEx ⊗ ✓ 🏵 A

COLN ST ALDWYNS, Gloucestershire

A small village situated within the Cotswolds, with walking and riding country right on the doorstep. Visit Burford, Stow on the Wold, Bibury, Bath, Cheltenham and Oxford. *See also Cirencester.*

THE NEW INN

Coln St Aldwyns, Cirencester, Gloucestershire GL7 5AN
((01285) 750651 FAX (01285) 750657
BRIAN & SANDRA EVANS

11, 11 en-suite, from £32.00 per person, double occ.
Lunch served. Non-residents welcome. Open all year.
£17.50, last orders 9.30pm.
Smoked Chicken and Avocado in Puff Pastry with Mushroom Cream Sauce. Spicy Tomato and Red Pepper Soup with a Cheese Crouton. Steamed supreme of Halibut served on buttered Noodles with a Ginger and Rosemary Sauce. Bread and Butter Pudding with Jersey Cream. Poached Pear served on a Puff Pastry disk with Banana Ice Cream.

A 400 year old Cotswold coaching inn which has been restored and refurbished. The thick, creeper-clad walls and open hearths, have warmed and welcomed Cotswold travellers since the time of Elizabeth I.

Coln St Aldwyns is east of Cirencester. Hotel in centre of village.

VISA AmEx B

CONSTANTINE, Cornwall

Small village between Falmouth and Helston. Local beauty spots include the Helford River, Gweek Seal Sanctuary, Glendurgan and Trebah gardens, and The Lizard. *See also Falmouth.*

TRENGILLY WARTHA COUNTRY INN

Nancenoy, Constantine, Falmouth, Cornwall TR11 5RP
((01326) 40332 FAX (01326) 40332
THE MAGUIRE FAMILY & THE LOGAN FAMILY

6, 5 en-suite, from £29.50 per person, double occ.
Lunch served. Non-residents welcome. Open all year.
£19.00, last orders 9.30pm.
Fresh Cornish seafood. Grilled Sea Bass on a Saffron Rice Cake with Watercress Sauce. Speciality Sausages.

A traditional country inn set in an area of outstanding natural beauty. Very comfortable accommodation and an excellent restaurant. Good bar snack menu accompanied by a vast range of real ales. The inn hosts a variety of `special events' throughout the year, including regular gourmet evenings and wine tastings.

VISA AmEx A

CONWY, Gwynedd

One of Wales' most historical locations with it's magnificent 13th century Castle. An ideal centre for touring Snowdonia and the North Wales coast.

BERTHLWYD HALL HOTEL

Llechwedd, Nr Conwy, Gwynedd LL32 8DQ
℡ (01492) 592409 FAX (01492) 572290
JOANNA & BRIAN GRIFFIN

8, 8 en-suite, from From £25.00 per person, double occ.
Non-residents welcome. Open all year.
£18.50, last orders 9pm.
French country cuisine prepared from fresh Welsh ingredients. Welsh lamb and cheeses.

A Victorian manor hotel in Snowdonia National Park. Splendid oak panelling in the entrance hall, a galleried landing and individually furnished bedrooms.The restaurant tables are set around a 140 year old wine press brought back from Bordeaux by the owners to create an atmosphere of rural France.

Enter Conwy (off the A55) over the bridge, past the Castle and into the Centre, turn left before the Castle wall into the Sychnant Pass, after 1 mile look for sign on the left.

VISA AmEx B

THE LODGE

Tal-y-Bont, Nr Conwy, Gwynedd LL32 8YX
℡ (01492) 660766 FAX (01492) 660534
MR & MRS BALDON

10, 10 en-suite, from £17.50 per person, double occ.
Lunch served. Non-residents welcome. Open all year.
£14.95, last orders 9pm.
Welsh lamb. Salmon and Trout.

A modern hotel set back from the road in a small village just South of Conwy. A very friendly and welcoming atmosphere with the emphasis firmly placed on food.

VISA A

CORFE CASTLE, Dorset

A small village nestling under the spectacular ruins of Corfe Castle. The area enjoys the benefit of many attractions including bird and wildlife sanctuaries, country houses and is close to Poole Harbour.

MORTONS HOUSE HOTEL

Corfe Castle, Dorset BH20 5EE
℡ (01929) 480988 FAX (01929) 480820
MR & MRS D. LANGFORD

17, 17 en-suite, from £40.00 per person, double occ.
Lunch served. Non-residents welcome. Open all year.
£22.50, last orders 8.30pm.
Fish. lobster, crab. lamb. strawberries. Dorset Cream Teas.

A 400 year old Elizabethan manor house in this historic fairytale village. Stone floors and fireplaces, oak panelling and fine carvings together with individually furnished bedrooms, some with four posters and spa baths, fill the hotel with character and atmosphere. Afternoon teas are served in the delightful walled gardens.

In the centre of the village.

VISA AmEx C

CORSHAM, Wiltshire

Pleasant small town, 5 miles from Bath, with a wealth of Norman and Elizabethan history.. Visit Castle Combe, Old Sarum, Stonehenge, Cheddar Gorge, and numerous NT houses and gardens. *See also Bath, Box.*

⌂⌂⌂ RUDLOE PARK HOTEL

Leafy Lane, Corsham, Wiltshire SN13 0PA
☎ (01225) 810555 FAX (01225) 811412

🛏 11, 11 en-suite, from £35.00 to £45.00 per person, double occ.
Lunch served. Open all year.
✗ £15.95, last orders 9.30pm.
🍴 Fresh fish from Devon and Cornwall. Scotch beef and veal. Young Welsh lamb. Local game, ducks, chicken and vegetables.

A neo-gothic Victorian mansion, set in 4 acres of lovely gardens. Superb valley views towards the Georgian city of Bath. An hotel with the charm of a bygone era. For children under 10, please contact the hotel direct.

VISA 🖃 ♒ AmEx ⊗ ⇪ C

CRANBORNE, Dorset

Situated on the eastern edge of the Cranborne Chase, just 5 minutes drive from the New Forest, and a short distance from the coast at Bournemouth. Cranborne Chase is a region of magnificent scenery.

⌂⌂ LA FOSSE AT CRANBORNE

London House, The Square, Cranborne, Dorset BH21 5PR
☎ (01725) 517604
MAC & SUE LA FOSSE

🛏 3, 3 en-suite, from £24.00 per person, double occ.
Lunch served. Non-residents welcome. Closed 26th December, Saturday lunchtime & Sunday evening.
✗ £14.95, last orders 9.30pm.
🍴 Fresh local fish and shellfish, local game in season, meat dishes.

A charming country restaurant, with a high standard of accommodation, offering varied and imaginative menus. The La Fosse family have run the restaurant for twelve years, and have built a firm and loyal following with both locals and visitors alike.

VISA 🖃 AmEx ⊗ ⋱ ⤸ 🍴 A

CRANBROOK, Kent

The centre for weaving in the the 15th century. See the three storey windmill, which is still in working order. Visit Royal Tunbridge Wells, Tenterden, Sissinghurst Castle (2 miles) and Bodiam Castle (8 miles).

HARTLEY MOUNT COUNTRY HOUSE HOTEL

Cranbrook, Kent TN17 3QX
☎ (01580) 712230 FAX (01580) 715733
LEE & LIONEL SKILTON

6, 6 en-suite, from £45.00 per person, double occ.
Lunch served. Non-residents welcome. Closed 25th December.
£15.50, last orders 9.30pm.
Traditional English food with fresh seasonal vegetables cooked to order; menu changes daily. Eggs Benedict(us). Veal Smitane and Seafood Saint-Jacques. Home-made Desserts. Extensive vegetarian menu available.

A fine old Edwardian country manor house, with all the grace and ambiance of the period, with open fires and a relaxing atmosphere. Gardens and lawns extend to over two acres, backing onto farmland with Hop Fields and Oast Houses closeby. There are tennis and croquet lawns within the grounds, together with Pitch & Putt and Boule. This is a non-smoking hotel.

✦ Situated on the A229, 1 mile south of Cranbrook.

VISA ▃ AmEx ⊗ ♿ ✎ ✓ ℠ C

CRAWLEY, Hampshire

A delightful, picturesque, small village 4 miles north of Winchester, famous for it's stunning Cathedral. Within easy distance are Stonehenge, Salisbury and Romsey. *See also Winchester.*

THE FOX & HOUNDS

Crawley, Nr Winchester, Hampshire SO21 2PR
☎ (01962) 776285 FAX (01962) 776285
DOREEN & LUIS SANZ

3, 3 en-suite, from £27.50 per person, double occ.
Lunch served. Non-residents welcome. Open all year.
£15.00, last orders 9.30pm.
French and English home cooking.
A traditional village inn built in 1750 in a Tyrolean style which has undergone complete modernisation. The accommodation is excellent with beautifully appointed rooms offering good value for money, whilst the restaurant and bars are extremely popular with both visitors and locals.

✦ Halfway between Winchester and Stockbridge off the A272.

VISA ▃ ⊗ ℠ ✎ ✈ A

CRICKHOWELL, Powys

A small market town in the Brecon Beacons National Park. Ideal for country lovers and walkers. Visit the famous book town of Hay on Wye, Aberdulais Falls, Raglan, Chepstow & Caerphilly Castles, Tintern Abbey & the Wye Valley all within easy reach.

TY CROESO HOTEL ✗

The Dardy, Crickhowell, Powys NP8 1PU
✆ (01873) 810573 FAX (01873) 810573
KATE & PETER JONES

🛏 8, 8 en-suite, from £32.50 per person, double occ.
Lunch served. Non-residents welcome. Open all year.
✗ From £13.95, last orders 9pm.
🍴 'Taste of Wales Menu' includes Laverbread and Cockles, Fresh Gower Crab and Herb Mousse, Welsh Lamb with Rowan and Orange, Usk/Teifi Salmon with Samphire Honey. Lemon and Yoghurt Ice Cream. Full A la Carte menu also available with a good selection of vegetarian dishes.

Ty Croeso - translates to "House of Welcome" is an old stone building in a quiet location. Tastefully refurbished to offer comfortable surroundings without destroying its unique character. Magnificent views are enjoyed from the gardens, terrace and most bedrooms. Log fires in winter, cool and airy in summer. Friendly but efficient service.

⊹ A40 Crickhowell, road opposite Action Garage over River Bridge. Turn right, in half mile first left up hill.

VISA 💳 AmEx ⊗ ♿ ❦ 🐾 ⊕ A

CULLOMPTON, Devon

An old market town, with cobbled pavements and 17th century houses. Interesting 16th century church with fan vaulted aisle.

RULLANDS ✗ ✗

Rull Lane, Cullompton, Devon EX15 1NQ
✆ (01884) 33356 FAX (01884) 35890
GEORGINA CHARTERIS

🛏 5, 5 en-suite, from £22.50 per person, double occ.
Non-residents welcome. Closed Sunday for non-residents.
✗ £15.00, last orders 9.45pm.
🍴 Local country fare, including fresh vegetables, game and fish. The chef's home-made desserts are all served with local clotted cream. Extensive and well balanced wine list.

A 15th century Devon country home, set in its own grounds, with hard tennis court and beautiful countryside. Rullands has an elegant dining room which can seat up to 35.

VISA 💳 ⊗ ♿ 🔑 ❦ 🐾 ⊕ A

DALWOOD, Devon

A small village, 3 miles outside the busy market town of Axminster. Visit Lyme Regis, Honiton, the Beer Caves, Exeter Cathedral, Dartmoor and Exmoor.

🏠 THE TUCKERS ARMS

Dalwood, Axminster, Devon EX13 7EG
☎ (01404) 881342 FAX (01404) 881740
DAVID & KATE BECK

🛏 5, 5 en-suite, from £22.50 per person, double occ.
Lunch served. Non-residents welcome. Open all year.
✕ £12.50, last orders 10pm.
🍽 Fresh fish and seafood including for example John Dory, Sea Bass, fresh Crab, King Prawns and local fresh water fish are featured on a blackboard whilst the a la carte menu offers "Tiddy's" - pillows of pastry with savoury fillings such as Chicken in Cider or Steak & Kidney in Stout.

A typical old Devon inn, set in a quiet village with grounds bordering a small river. Flagstone floors lead into bars and dining areas with a courtyard at the rear. Functions catered for. On Sunday's last orders for food are at 9.30pm.

✛ 2 miles to the north of the A35, half way between Honiton and Axminster.
VISA 🏧 ⊗ 🕭 ✓ A

DARLINGTON, County Durham

Central for touring the Dales or North East coastal regions. Durham City 18 miles.

🏠🏠🏠 HEADLAM HALL HOTEL & RESTAURANT

Headlam, Nr Gainford, County Durham DL2 3HA
☎ (01325) 730238 FAX (01325) 730790
JOHN & CLARE ROBINSON

🛏 26, 26 en-suite, from £35.00 per person, double occ.
Non-residents welcome. Closed December 24th & 25th.
✕ £17.75, last orders last orders 9.30pm.
🍽 Locally reared game and meats. Home grown vegetables and fruit.

Historic Jacobean country house of great charm, set in large formal gardens within its own working farm. All rooms are individually furnished in period style. Other facilities include an indoor heated pool, sauna, tennis court and snooker room.

✛ 1 mile north of A67 Darlington to Barnard Castle road at Gainford.

VISA 🏧 💳 AmEx ⊗ ♿ 🛋 ⚲ ✓ 🕭 🐕 B

DARTFORD, Kent

Town on the edge of London's M25 ring road. Visit Greenwich Observatory, the Maritime Museum and Brands Hatch.

ROWHILL GRANGE

Wilmington, Dartford, Kent DA2 7QH
✆ (01322) 615136 FAX (01322) 615137
DEBORAH MURPHY & PETER HINCHCLIFFE

🛏 7, 7 en-suite, from £40.00 per person, double occ.
Lunch served. Non-residents welcome. Open all year.

✕ £12.95, last orders 9pm.
🍽 Saffron and Potato Soup garnished with Mussels. Tai Cocktail of fresh Crab and Prawns. Best End of Lamb with a fresh Mint and crushed Pepper Crust, with Potato and Aubergine Gateau. Prime Sirloin Steak with Wild Mushrooms and a Madeira Sauce. Fresh Broccoli Bake in a Wild Mushroom, Muscadet, Tarragon, Mustard and Cheese Sauce.

120 year old thatched country house set in eight acres of mature English gardens. All bedrooms are beautifully furnished and all enjoy magnificent views over the grounds and the Kentish countryside.

⊕ 3 miles from M25/M20 junction 3. Follow B2173 Swanley, then B258 to Hextable. Hotel entrance is in Hextable village.

VISA ▬ 💳 AmEx ⊗ ✓ C

DARTMOUTH, Devon

An old port on the river Dart, with many ancient buildings, including a Church, Castle and Naval Museum. A carnival is held in June and a regatta in August.

FINGALS HOTEL

Dittisham, Nr Dartmouth, Devon TQ6 0JA
✆ (01803) 722398 FAX (01803) 722401
RICHARD JOHNSTON

🛏 9, 9 en-suite, from £34.00 per person, double occ.
Lunch served. Closed New Year to Easter.

✕ £25.00, last orders 9.30pm.
🍽 Locally caught fish, particularly Dart salmon, crab and scallops. Unpasteurised cheeses from the area. Organic meats are available if requested. West Country air dried ham.

A very old farmhouse, with a grand Queen Anne facade, of old character. Very relaxed, informal atmosphere. The wooden panelling gives an inviting, cozy feeling and Fingals is decorated with old country furniture and old classic paintings.

VISA ▬ 💳 AmEx ⇗ 🐾 ✓ 🚭 S 🦆 C

DAVENTRY, Northamptonshire

Ancient market town, close to Silverstone, Towcester, Warwick and the site of the battle of Naseby. The town retains some Georgian buildings and the site of an Iron Age encampment. *See also Weedon, Rugby.*

THE WINDMILL AT BADBY

Main Street, Badby, Nr Daventry, Northamptonshire NN11 6AN
☎ (01327) 702363 FAX (01327) 311521
JOHN FREESTONE & CAROL SUTTON

🛏 6, 6 en-suite, from £29.50 per person, double occ.
Lunch served. Non-residents welcome. Open all year.
🍴 from £5.75, last orders 9.30pm.
🍲 Variety of home cooked dishes prepared daily. Badby Mushrooms in Stilton and Garlic. Normandy Chicken. Chargrilled Cajun Chicken. Lamb and Mushroom Curry. Vegetarian Nut Wellington. Range of substantial snack sandwiches and jacket potatoes. Barbecues on the village green in summer.

A 17th century, thatched, stone country pub in the centre of picturesque Badby village, with recently created accommodation, offering a combination of old and new; old world charm with modern facilities. Log fires and flagged floors create traditional warmth and ambiance. The inn offers a programme of special events throughout the year, cycling breaks or a complete 'House Party' package.

✤ Just off the A361, 2 miles south of Daventry.
VISA 💳 💳 AmEx ⊗ ✓ ⬥ A

DENBIGH, Clwyd

Historical town in the fertile Vale of Clwyd. See the castle, friary and museum or enjoy the local pony trekking, riding, fishing, golf, tennis and bowls.

BRYN MORFYDD HOTEL 🎋

Llanrhaeadr, Nr Denbigh, Clwyd LL16 4NP
☎ (0174578) 280 FAX (0174578) 488
DUNCAN & MARIE MUIRHEAD

🛏 29, 29 en-suite, from £25.00 per person, double occ.
Lunch served. Open all year.
🍴 £14.50, last orders 9pm.
🍲 Traditional fare, prepared from fresh ingredients. Harlequin Flan. Crudites with Dolcellate Cheese Dip. Welsh Lamb Cutlets. Salad of Steamed Skate. Fresh Local Trout.

A neo-Edwardian hotel, set on a hill five miles outside Denbigh, in the centre of its own two golf courses. Attractive views from a range of bars and restaurants. The hotel is undergoing extensive refurbishment.

VISA 💳 💳 ⊗ ⚓ 🔍 ✓ 🛶 ⬥ A

DISS, Suffolk

A small market town on the Norfolk/Suffolk borders ideally situated for visiting Thetford Forest, the historic cities of Bury St Edmunds and Norwich, the Norfolk Broads and Snape Maltings.

🛏🛏 SALISBURY HOUSE

Victoria Road, Diss, Norfolk IP22 3JG
☎ (01379) 644738
BARRY & SUE DAVIES

🛏 3, 2 en-suite, from £35.00 per person, double occ.
Non-residents welcome. Closed for Christmas & 2 weeks in summer. Restaurant closed Sunday & Monday.
✕ £22.00, last orders 9.15pm.
French and modern British cuisine using the freshest local ingredients available. Fresh fish from Lowestoft. Cheeses.

An impressive Victorian house in an acre of gardens which has built a considerable reputation for its outstanding cuisine and wine list. The decor is predominantly Victorian and the bedrooms are all comfortably furnished and tastefully decorated to a high standard.

+ Quarter of a mile out of town heading east, turn right before mini roundabout (A1066 is Victoria Road).

VISA 🗠 ⊗ ♿ ✓ A

DOLGELLAU, Gwynedd

An attractive market town, surrounded by mountains. There are interesting shops, pubs and cafes. An excellent base for touring the north Wales coast and countryside.

🛏🛏🛏 DOLMELYNLLYN HALL HOTEL

Ganllwyd, Dolgellau, Gwynedd LL40 2HP
☎ (01341) 440273 FAX (01341) 440273
JON B. BARKWITH

🛏 10, 10 en-suite, from £52.50 per person, double occ.
Lunch served. Non-residents welcome. Closed December to February.
✕ £22.50, last orders 8.30pm.
Inventive modern British cooking using much local Welsh produce whenever possible. Grilled Red Mullet on a Vermouth and Saffron Cream. Roulades of Brenin Venison with Baby Carrots and Chestnuts and a Sloe Gin Gravy. Walnut Stuffed Pears in a Filo Purse. FINALIST, REPRESENTING WALES, IN THE 1994 LOGIS REGIONAL CUISINE COMPETITION.

Dolmelynllyn is a beautiful, tranquil hotel set in magnificent scenery, with a relaxed, friendly aura of a bygone era. The dining room is the centre of the hotel, where five course daily changing dinner is served. Excellent views. For children under 10 years, please contact the hotel direct. This is a non-smoking hotel.

+ Drive entrance is on the A470, 5 miles north of Dolgellan at the southern end of the village of Ganllwyd.

VISA 🗠 ⚊ AmEx ⊗ 🗠 ⤸ C

DONCASTER, South Yorkshire

Ancient Roman town famous for its railway works, heavy industries, butterscotch and race course (Saint Leger). Attractions include 18th century Mansion House, Cusworth Hall Museum, Doncaster Museum of Roman and Saxon relics.

REGENT HOTEL

Regent Square, Doncaster, South Yorkshire DN1 2DS
✆ (01302) 364180 FAX (01302) 322331
MICHAEL LONGWORTH

🛏 50, 50 en-suite, from £34.00 per person, double occ.
Lunch served. Non-residents welcome. Closed 26th December & 1st January.
✖ £9.99, last orders 10pm.
🍽 Deep Fried Camembert. Supreme of Chicken poached in Champagne with Onions and Mushrooms with Cream Sauce. Poussin with a Potato Rosti and Red Wine Sauce.

A Victorian building overlooking Regents Park, with traditional furnishings. A family run hotel with a pleasant, welcoming atmosphere.

⚓ In a central location, overlooking Regents Park.

VISA 🔲 AmEx ♿ ✓ 🐾 B

DORCHESTER, Dorset

An ancient Roman town, founded in AD43. Birthplace of Thomas Hardy, setting of many of his novels. Superb museum, wonderful coastline, ideal base for touring Wessex.

WESTWOOD HOUSE HOTEL

29 High West Street, Dorchester, Dorset DT1 1UP
✆ (01305) 268018 FAX (01305) 250282
PHILIP SEVIER SUMMERS

🛏 7, 6 en-suite, from £28.75 per person, double occ.
Lunch served. Non-residents welcome. Restaurant closed 26th & 27th December, 1st to 3rd January & all day Sunday. Hotel open all year.
✖ from £15.95, last orders 9.30pm.
🍽 A highly rated restaurant, using local produce. Game and fish dishes. Pintadeau Entire, Guinea Fowl filled with Walnuts and Mushrooms with a Madeira Sauce.

A Georgian listed property. The bedrooms are individually decorated and well equipped, two with luxury spa bathrooms. The Mock Turtle restaurant is not open on Sunday.

⚓ In centre of Dorchester.

VISA 🔲 ⊗ ♿ ✓ 🐾 A

YALBURY COTTAGE HOTEL

Lower Bockhampton, Dorchester, Dorset DT2 8PZ
✆ (01305) 262382 FAX (01305) 266412
HEATHER & DEREK FURMINGER

🛏 8, 8 en-suite, from £32.00 per person, double occ.
Non-residents welcome. Open all year.

✕ £17.50, last orders 8.30pm.

🍴 Celery and Stilton Soup. Noisettes of Lamb with a Cassis and Caramelised Shallot Sauce. Medallions of Pork with a Port and Thyme Sauce. Fresh Fruit Platter with Lime Syrup and fresh Ginger Cream.

A thatched hotel dating back around 400 years. The lounge and dining room have large inglenook fireplaces and low, beamed ceilings, giving a warm, welcoming atmosphere. Each bedroom overlooks either the garden or surrounding fields.

✛ From A35 between Dorchester and Puddletown, follow road signposted to Lower Bockhampton for 1 mile.

VISA ▬ AmEx ⊗ ⁄ ▨ A

DORCHESTER ON THAMES, Oxfordshire

A small town situated just a few miles south east of the university city of Oxford. Locally, Dorchester Abbey is worth discovering. Further afield, Blenheim Palace and Henley are within thirty minutes drive.

THE GEORGE HOTEL

High Street, Dorchester on Thames, Oxfordshire OX9 8HH
✆ (01865) 340404 FAX (01865) 341620
MESSRS. NEVILLE & GRIFFIN

🛏 17, 17 en-suite, from £37.50 per person, double occ.
Lunch served. Non-residents welcome. Closed 23rd to 30th December.

✕ £18.00 & £22.00, last orders 9.45pm.

🍴 International style. Mousseline of Cornish Seafood on a Langoustine Sauce. Peach Cheese-cake with White Chocolate and Orange.

Reputedly one of the oldest coaching inns in England, dating from the 15th century, the hotel retains much of its original character and is attractively furnished with many antiques.

VISA ▬ ▪ AmEx ⊗ ⁄ ▨ ⏚ C

DOVER, Kent

The main cross channel ferry port. Historic town and seaside, situated under the famous white cliffs. *See also Canterbury, Chilham.*

THE OLD COACH HOUSE

Dover Road, Barham, Kent CT4 6SA
✆ (01227) 831218 FAX (01227) 831932
JEAN - CLAUDE & ANGELA ROZARD

🛏 5, 5 en-suite, from £31.00 per person, double occ.
Lunch served. Non-residents welcome. Open all year.

✕ £16.50, last orders 9pm.

🍴 Local game in season, fresh fish, bass, grilled lobster, Dover sole, Moules Marinieres.

Originally a coaching inn (c.1815), the hotel is now run along the lines of a French Auberge by Jean Claude, the chef/patron. Comfortable, attractive bedrooms and high quality cuisine. The hotel is half way between Dover and the historic town of Canterbury.

✛ On the A2 southbound, 7 miles south of Canterbury.

VISA ▬ AmEx ⊗ ⏚ ⁄ A   *Dover continued overleaf...*

LODDINGTON HOUSE HOTEL

14 East Cliff, Dover, Kent CT16 1LX
☎ (01304) 201947 FAX (01304) 201947
THE CUPPER FAMILY

🛏 6, 4 en-suite, from £26.00 per person, double occ.
Closed 24th, 25th & 26th December.
✕ £14.00, last orders 7.30pm.
🍽 Grilled Grapefruit with Cinnamon Butter and Cherry. Smoked Trout. Chicken Breasts with Bacon, Onions and Mushrooms in a Wine Sauce. Lemon Sole. Hazelnut Meringue Cake. Baked Apple and Almond pudding.

A Regency style listed building situated on the sea front with panoramic views over the harbour and English Channel.

✦ Hotel overlooking harbour and within 200 yards from main ferry terminal.

VISA 🚗 ⁄ 🦢 🏊 A

DULVERTON, Somerset

Set amongst the woods and hills of south east Exmoor, Dulverton is the headquarters of the National Park with an extensive visitors centre. An interesting 13th century church and many National Trust properties closeby.

CARNARVON ARMS HOTEL ✳

Dulverton, Somerset, TA22 9AE
☎ (01398) 23302 FAX (01398) 24022
MRS TONI JONES

🛏 25, 23 en-suite, from £35.00 per person, double occ.
Lunch served. Non-residents welcome. Open all year.
✕ £21.25, last orders 8.30pm.
🍽 Local salmon and trout from the Barle and Exe rivers. Game, in season, venison and pheasant.

A solid and imposing Victorian hotel built in 1874 by The Earl of Carnarvon to accommodate travellers arriving at the now defunct Dulverton Station. More recently the hotel is renowned for its informal friendly atmosphere, sport, particularly fishing, and excellent food and wine.

VISA 🚗 ⊘ 🛇 ➔ 🎣 ⁄ 🦢 🏌 C

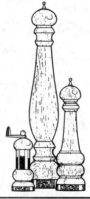

EASINGWOLD, North Yorkshire

Easingwold is 13 miles north of the historic city of York and makes an ideal base for exploring the Moors and Dales. Castle Howard and the castles of Richmond, Helmsley and Pickering are all closeby.

OLD FARMHOUSE COUNTRY HOTEL & RESTAURANT

Raskelf, Nr Easingwold, North Yorkshire YO6 3LF
(01347) 821971 FAX (01347) 822392
BILL & JENNY FROST

10, 10 en-suite, from £25.00 per person, double occ.
Non-residents welcome. Closed 22nd December to 31st January.
£15.00, last orders 8.30pm.
Local game in season. Rabbit with Lavender and Thyme. Home baked bread and preserves.

Originally part of the village farm, the Old Farmhouse has been converted into an award winning comfortable hotel with all modern amenities. The emphasis is firmly on food, where good traditional Yorkshire home cooking, using fresh local ingredients wherever possible, is the rule.

In Raskelf village, 2 miles north of Easingwold.

A

EVERSHOT, Dorset

A village in the heart of Thomas Hardy's Dorset, a mile from the A37, main Yeovil/Dorchester road. The village boasts its own bakery, pub and shop. Many beautiful local walks to be explored.

RECTORY HOUSE

Fore Street, Evershot, Dorset DT2 0JW
(01935) 83273 FAX (01935) 83273
MRS CHRIS WALFORD

6, 6 en-suite, from £30.00 per person, double occ.
Non-residents welcome. Closed December.
£16.00, last orders 7pm.
Home cooking, traditional and exotic dishes using fresh local ingredients. Dorset Lamb, roasted with Wine, Honey and Rosemary. Local Beef. Special Rectory House Bread and Butter Pudding, Chocolate Mousse with Hazlenuts and Rum & Whiskey Ice Cream.

An 18th century listed building, once a Rectory, with great charm, set in a quiet, unspoilt Dorset village. Friendly, homely atmosphere.

VISA A

EVESHAM, Worcestershire

A pleasant market town, many walks along the River Avon.   Close to Stratford-upon-Avon, the Cotswolds and Warwick Castle.

RIVERSIDE HOTEL & RESTAURANT

The Parks, Offenham Road, Evesham, Worcestershire WR11 5JP
☎ (01386) 446200 FAX (01386) 40021
VINCENT & ROSEMARY WILLMOTT

🛏 7, 7 en-suite, from £40.00 per person, double occ.
Lunch served. Non-residents welcome. Open all year.
🍴 £21.95, last orders 9pm.
🍲 Home cooking using only fresh local ingredients.   Marinaded haunch of local venison, local lamb sweetbreads, home-made blackberry and damson ice cream are featured frequently on the daily changing menu.

A 17th century farmhouse, with a personal and elegant   style. Each room is individually designed with exquisite taste and decor. The restaurant is bright and sunny and has a magnificent view over the river.

VISA 🖃 ⊗ ⟋ ✓ A

EXETER, Devon

An historic cathedral city, with excellent shopping facilities only a short drive from the coast or the moors.   Visit the Maritime museum, Royal Albert Memorial museum, Northcott theatre, Killerton House, Powderham Castle, Bicton Gardens and Brunel Atmospheric Railway.

EBFORD HOUSE HOTEL

Exmouth Road, Ebford, Nr Exeter, Devon EX3 0QH
☎ (01392) 877658 FAX (01392) 874424
DONALD & SAMANTHA HORTON

🛏 16, 16 en-suite, from £35.00 per person, double occ.
Lunch served. Non-residents welcome. Open all year.
🍴 from £18.50 a la carte, last orders 9.30pm.
🍲 English & International dishes.   Local Lobster Thermidor. Fresh Local Fillet of Sea Bass, baked in Cider and Coriander Cream Sauce.   All bread, pastas and speciality ice creams are home-made. FINALIST, REPRESENTING THE SOUTH WEST, IN THE 1994 LOGIS REGIONAL CUISINE COMPETITION.

A Georgian country house hotel, which has retained all its friendly, homely atmosphere and character. The hotel has its own indoor gym and fitness centre, and two restaurants, one more formal, the other, a superb cellar wine bar/bistro.

✢ From M5, junction 30 take A376 to Ebford village, hotel is immediately on the left.

VISA 🖃 AmEx ⊗ : Ⓢ ⟋ B

ST. ANDREWS HOTEL
28 Alphington Road, Exeter, Devon EX2 8HN
(01392) 76784 FAX (01392) 50249
DAVID & SALLY BAILEY & MARIE & WALLY NOBBS

16, 16 en-suite, from £28.00 per person, double occ.
Lunch served. Non-residents welcome. Closed 24th December to 2nd January.
£12.50, last orders 8.15pm.
Home cooking, prepared using fresh local produce. Chef/proprietor specialises in unusual soups and grills.

A large Victorian house converted and modernised by the present owners. This family run hotel offers a warm welcome with many modern facilities. St Andrews is located near to the city centre, within a few minutes walk of the Riverside and Leisure Centre, Exeter Cathedral and shopping centre.

From M5 junction 31, follow signs to Marsh Barton, then the city centre. Hotel is on the left.

VISA AmEx A

FAKENHAM, Norfolk
A small market town close to the North Norfolk coast with it's abundant wildlife and Sandringham.

THE CROWN HOTEL
Market Place, Fakenham, Norfolk NR21 9BP
(01328) 851418 FAX (01328) 862433
BERNARD HOUSSIN

11, 11 en-suite, from £26.00 per person, double occ.
Lunch served. Non-residents welcome. Open all year.
£9.95, last orders 9.30pm.
Fresh local produce in season.
A grade II listed town centre coaching inn built in 1752 which has recently been tastefully refurbished under the new proprietor. The bedrooms are pleasantly furnished with pine. The restaurant and bustling bars are popular with both residents and locals alike.

VISA AmEx A

FALMOUTH, Cornwall
A famous seaside resort with many fine sandy beaches within a short distance. Visit Pendennis Castle, Glendurgan Gardens and Trelissick Gardens. *See also Constantine.*

GREEN LAWNS HOTEL
Western Terrace, Falmouth, Cornwall TR11 4QN
(01326) 312734 FAX (01326) 211427
MR R. COLLINGS & MR A. WILLIAMS

40, 40 en-suite, from £32.00 per person, double occ.
Lunch served. Non-residents welcome. Closed 24th December to 30th December.
£17.00, last orders 10pm.
English and French cuisine. Fresh seafood dishes and speciality steaks.

Chateau style hotel situated midway between the town centre and the main beaches. A warm, relaxed, informal atmosphere with a wealth of amenities that one would expect from a first class family hotel.

VISA AmEx B

FAREHAM, Hampshire

Town on a quiet backwater of Portsmouth Harbour. The high street is lined with fine Georgian buildings. Visit Solent Naval Heritage Sites. Napoleonic and Roman Forts and Castles. *See also Portsmouth.*

AVENUE HOUSE HOTEL

221 The Avenue, Fareham, Hampshire PO14 1NS
☎ (01329) 232175 FAX (01329) 232196
STEWART & HILLARY MITCHELL

🛏 17, 17 en-suite, from £24.75 per person, double occ.
Closed Christmas Week.

✗ N/A

🍴 Restaurant is adjacent to hotel. Soupe de poissons. Salade de poissons fumes. Carre d'agneau en Chevreuil (Rack of Lamb marinated in red wine). Tournedos de bouef a la creme d'estragon (medallions of fillet of beef, tarragon sauce and wild mushrooms). Nougatine glacee (home-made nugatine ice cream with a raspberry coulis).

Originally built in 1930 to a rustic design, the small hotel has charm and character. It is set in his own pleasant mature gardens with individually furnished bedrooms. Ample parking.

VISA 🔷 AmEx ⊗ ⼕ ⸴ ⁄ ⼸ A

FAVERSHAM, Kent

An unspoilt market town. Boughton is a small village, surrounded by hop fields and fruit orchards. Ideal for visiting the Canterbury coast.

THE WHITE HORSE INN ✗

The Street, Broughton, Nr Faversham, Kent ME13 9AX
☎ (01227) 751343/751700 FAX (01227) 751090
MARK & URSULA ELLAND

🛏 14, 14 en-suite, from £23.75 per person, double occ.
Lunch served. Non Residents welcome Open all year.

✗ £12.00 - £15.00, last orders 10pm.

🍴 Freshly prepared food, featuring Kentish regional specialities.

A characterful inn, mentioned in Chaucer's Canterbury Tales, which has retained much of its traditional charm. Exposed oak beams and open fires. Good accommodation and a warm welcome. Locally brewed real ales.

✚ In Broughton village, south east of Faversham.

VISA 🔷 ⊗ ⼕ ⸴ ⁄ ⼻ ⼤ ⼸ A

FISHGUARD, Dyfed

A town with a cluster of old wharfs and cottages around a beautiful harbour. Good walks along the Pembrokeshire coastal path. Visit Pentre Ifan, Cilgerran Castle and Trefdraeth Beach.

PENLAU OLEU

Llanychger, Fishguard, Dyfed SA65 9TL
((01348) 881314
RHYS HUGHES & TARNE DURBIN

4, 4 en-suite, from £20.00 per person, double occ.
Non-residents welcome. Open all year.
£12.00 to £15.00, last orders 8pm.
Prawn and Stilton Puffs. Brecon Chicken cooked with Bacon and Shallots. Roast Lamb stuffed with Apricots. Baked Apple with Honey and Orange. Peach and Strawberry Sponge Pudding. Celtic Rice Pudding.

A converted Welsh hill farm, situated in a quiet rural setting, surrounded by wonderful views.

From Fishguard take the B4313 for 3 miles, turn right for Puncheston for approximately half a mile then turn right.

A

FORDINGBRIDGE, Hampshire

On the northern edge of the New Forest, where there has been a bridge over the River Avon since the middle ages, hence the town's name. Visit nearby Salisbury, Bournemouth, Beaulieu Abbey and Motor Museum.

LIONS COURT RESTAURANT & HOTEL

29-31 High Street, Fordingbridge, Hampshire SP6 1AS
((01425) 652006 FAX (01425) 657946
MICHAEL & JENNY EASTICK

6, 6 en-suite, from £22.50 per person, double occ.
Lunch served. Open all year.
£14.00 to £20.00, last orders 10pm.
Warm Bacon and Smoked Chicken Salad. Garlic and Cheese Bundles. Lions Court Prawn Cocktail. Breast of Duck with Port and Blackcurrants. Baked Stuffed Trout. Supreme of Chicken with Orange Sauce.

Lions Court occupies a 300 year old building which has recently been beautifully renovated. A comfortable and pleasant, friendly atmosphere. Inglenook fireplaces and a wealth of exposed beams. Four poster bed. The gardens run down to the River Avon.

In Fordingbridge town centre.

VISA AmEx A

FOREST OF BOWLAND, Lancashire

Superb centre for touring and walking around the Yorkshire Dales, Lake District and Lancashire coast. One hour from Manchester Airport.

BRICKHOUSE COUNTRY HOTEL   ✕

Garstang Road, Chipping, Nr Preston, Lancashire PR3 3QH
✆ (01995) 61316 FAX (01995) 61316
MRS HEATHER CRABTREE

🛏 5, 5 en-suite, from £24.75 per person, double occ.
Lunch served. Closed 25th & 26th December.
✕ £16.95, last orders 9pm.
🍷 The dinner menu offers six courses. `Freshness and flavour, modern with traditional roots'. Breast of Chicken stuffed with Prawns in White Wine Sauce. Slices of Sirloin in a Mustard and Onion Sauce. Bread & Butter Pudding. Pineapple Flambe.

An 18th century former farmhouse, once the only brick built building in the Forest of Bowland. Good food, which can be enjoyed in a friendly environment. Bedrooms are simply but comfortably furnished. There is a large conference/function room.

VISA 🖃 💳 AmEx ⊗ 🎾 ✓ 🥄 A

PARROCK HEAD HOTEL   ✕ ✕

Slaidburn, Clitheroe, Lancashire BB7 3AH
✆ (01200) 446614 FAX (01200) 446313
RICHARD & VICKY UMBERS

🛏 9, 9 en-suite, from £31.00 per person, double occ.
Lunch served. Non-residents welcome. Open all year.
✕ £17.50, last orders 8.30pm.
🍷 Bowland lamb, Lancashire black pudding, Abbeystead grouse in season, home-smoked fish and meats, Yorkshire venison, home-cured gravadlax, all enhanced with fresh garden herbs, Treacle Tart, home-made ice creams, hand-made Dales Farm Cheeses.

An attractive 17th century Dales farmhouse and cottages, converted with a balance of modern facilities and antique furnishings, set in its own gardens. Cosy timbered bar. Upstairs lounges offer panoramic views. Open log fires give a warm atmosphere on chilly winter evenings. An ideal quiet retreat. Good service and standard of comfort. Light lunches available all week. Guests are advised to reserve a table for lunch on Sunday.

VISA 🖃 💳 AmEx ⊗ ♿ ✓ 🥄 ⚓ A

FOREST ROW, East Sussex

Forest Row is on a hillside overlooking the River Medway, this village is a good centre from which to explore the Ashdown Forest.

THE CHEQUERS INN

The Square, Forest Row, Nr East Grinstead, East Sussex RH18 5ES
✆ (0134282) 3333 FAX (0134282) 5454
CLAUDIO PRIORI

🛏 17, 17 en-suite, from £30.00 per person, double occ.
Lunch served. Non-residents welcome. Open all year.
✕ £10.95, last orders 11pm.
🍷 A wide range of Italian, French and English cuisine. Home-made Pate. Fresh Trout.

A 15th century posting inn, where which old world charm has been retained alongside all modern comforts.

✢ In the village.

VISA 🖃 💳 AmEx ⊗ ♿ ✓ 🥄 Ⓢ A

FRINTON-ON-SEA, Essex

A sedate seaside town, developed at the end of the Victorian era. Safe sandy beaches. Within an easy drive of Colchester or the ferry ports of Harwich and Felixstowe.

THE MAPLIN HOTEL ✗

3 The Esplanade, Frinton-on-Sea, Essex CO13 9EL
☎ (01255) 673832
NICK & SUE TURNER

🛏 11, 10 en-suite, from £42.00 per person, double occ.
Lunch served. Non-residents welcome. Open all year.
✗ £18.95, last orders 9pm.
🍽 English and continental cuisine.

Originally a private home (c.1911), this seafront hotel retains many of its original features, including oak panelling and leaded light windows in the public rooms. Most of the bedrooms enjoy sea views.

✦ On the seafront.
VISA 🔲 ⊗ ≥ ✓ 🌂 ⚓ ⚓ C

FROME, Somerset

Old market town, with medieval centre and interesting 18th century wool merchants houses. Longleat, Bath, Wells and Stourhead are closeby.

THE FULL MOON AT RUDGE ✗✗

Rudge, Nr Frome, Somerset BA11 2QF
☎ (01373) 830936 FAX (01373) 831366
PATRICK & CHRISTINE GIFFORD

🛏 5, 5 en-suite, from From £22.50 per person, double occ.
Lunch served. Non-residents welcome. Restaurant closed Monday lunchtime & Sunday evening.
✗ from £13.50 a la carte, last orders 9pm.
🍽 Fresh local produce, Game in season, fresh fish. Fresh Trout with Prawns in Filo with a Dill and Butter Sauce. Rack of English Lamb with an Apricot and Redcurrant Sauce. Pan-fried Escalope of Veal in a Marsala Sauce.

An inn since 1690, strategically placed on the original Salisbury to Bath road which has recently been renovated to provide high standards of hospitality and service in an informal relaxed environment.   The comfortably furnished bedrooms all have panoramic views of the Westbury White Horse. The inn is an ideal centre for the tourist or business customer wishing to visit Salisbury, Bath,Glastonbury or Wells.

✦ 1 mile from A36 Warminster to Bath road, signposted Rudge and Woodland Park.

VISA 🔲 ⊗ 🌂 ✓ ⚓ A

GOATHLAND, North Yorkshire

Spacious village which has several large greens, grazed by sheep. An idea centre for walking the North Yorkshire Moors. Nearby are several waterfalls, among them Mallyan Spout.

WHITFIELD HOUSE HOTEL

Darnholm, Goathland, North Yorkshire YO22 5LA
((01947) 896215
JOHN & PAULINE LUSHER

8, 8 en-suite, from £25.00 per person, double occ.
Closed December & January.
£10.00 to £15.00, last orders 5.30pm.
Chilled Melon with ground Ginger and Orange. Chicken Napoleon, breast of Chicken, stuffed with Apricots and Almonds in a Brandy Sauce. Fillet of Pork in Sherry Sauce with Mushrooms and Herbs. Home-made sweets.

Originally a 17th century farmhouse, Whitfield House has now been carefully modernised to provide every comfort and 'old world' charm. Cottage style furnishings. All bedrooms are non-smoking.

From A169 (Whitby to Pickering) follow signs to Goathland. From village centre follow signs to Darnholm.

VISA ⬛ ⊗ ⬦ A

GODALMING, Surrey

Historic staging post on the London-Portsmouth route. Beautiful surrounding countryside, National Trust properties, and villages. See The Devil's Punch Bowl, Clandon House and Newlands Corner.

SQUIRRELS RESTAURANT & COUNTRY HOTEL

Hurtmore Road, Hurtmore, Godalming, Surrey GU7 2RN
((01483) 860223 FAX (01483) 860592
JORDY & HELEN VASQUEZ

13, 11 en-suite, from £32.50 per person, double occ.
Lunch served. Non-residents welcome. Open all year.
from £10.00-£15.00, last orders 10pm.
Home-cooked pies, marinaded meats and casseroles. Old fashioned English puddings.

A row of 17th cottages full of character and exposed beams have been converted to provide the accommodation at Squirrels. The main building is a little more modern and tastefully decorated, furnished in antique pine.

Just off the A3, take the Hurtmore, Charterhouse slip road.

VISA ⬛ ⬛ AmEx ⊗ ✓ ⬥ S B

GRANTHAM, Lincolnshire

An historic town on the old London to York coaching road with a splendid parish church. Birthplace of Sir Isaac Newton. Visit the local museum, Belvoir Castle, Belton House and 'Middlemarch' country in Stamford.

KINGS HOTEL

North Parade, Grantham, Lincolnshire NG31 8AU
☎ (01476) 590800 FAX (01476) 590800
ROGER & ANNE BLAKEMAN

🛏 23, 22 en-suite, from £27.50 per person, double occ.
Lunch served. Non-residents welcome. Open all year.
✗ £11.50, last orders 10pm.
🍴 Local Lincolnshire meats and vegetables. Stilton cheese. Stilton Pancakes. Lincolnshire Hot Pot.

A refurbished Victorian House which has been extended to include two restaurants, a function suite and a busy bar serving both the local and business communities.

VISA 💳 💳 AmEx ⊗ 🔍 ✓ ⬠ A

GRASMERE, Cumbria

Beautiful Cumbrian village, once the home of Wordsworth who lived at Dove Cottage for nine years. Sample Grasmere Gingerbread which is still made to an ancient secret recipe in the village.

GOLD RILL COUNTRY HOUSE HOTEL

Red Bank Road, Grasmere, Cumbria LA22 9PU
☎ (015394) 35486 FAX (015394) 35486
PAUL & CATHY JEWSBURY

🛏 22, 22 en-suite, from £32.00 to 44.00 per person, double occ.
Lunch served. Open all year.
✗ £18.50, last orders 8.30pm.
🍴 Fresh local produce prepared with modern style. Prawn and Vegetable Stir-Fry. Cream of Lettuce and Chive Soup. Diced Lakeland Lamb in a Rich Rosemary Gravy. Coffee and Walnut Roulade set on a pool of Baileys Irish Cream.

A former country gentleman's residence which has been a hotel since 1948. It is set in two acres of gardens just west of Grasmere village centre and enjoys panoramic uninterupted views. A warm homely atmosphere and attentive service from the young team of staff. There is a croquet lawn, putting green and heated outdoor swimming pool. The hotel offers nursery teas and baby listening.

VISA 💳 ⊗ 🔥 ≈ ✓ 🍲 B

OAK BANK HOTEL

Broadgate, Grasmere, Cumbria LA22 9TA
☎ (015394) 35217 FAX (015394) 35217
SHARON & ATTILIO SAVASI

🛏 14, 14 en-suite, from £26.00 per person, double occ.
Lunch served. Non-residents welcome. Closed January.
✗ £17.00, last orders 8pm.
🍴 Chicken with Tarragon and Cream. Trout. Leg of Lamb with fresh Rosemary and a Redcurrant Glaze. Chocolate Amoretto Cake. Bread and Butter Pudding.

A beautiful stone house, built in 1872, which has been modernised with an Italian influence. All bedrooms are lovingly decorated. Dinner is served in an elegant conservatory. The River Rothay runs past the end of the hotel garden.

⚓ Just outside the village centre.

VISA 💳 🔥 ✓ 🍲 ⬠ A

GREAT MALVERN, Worcestershire

Two miles south of Great Malvern, an historic spa town set amidst the Malvern Hills. Local sites to visit include The Malvern Hills, Eastnor Castle, Worcester, Hereford & Gloucester Cathedrals, Royal Worcester Porcelain. *See also Little Malvern.*

COLWALL PARK HOTEL

Colwall, Nr Malvern, Worcestershire WR13 6QG
✆ (01684) 540206 FAX (01684) 540847
BASIL & ELIZABETH FROST

⊨ 20, 20 en-suite, from £48.00 per person, double occ.
Lunch served. Non-residents welcome. Closed first week of January.
✕ £20.00, last orders 9pm.
Traditional English cuisine. Cream of Mussel Soup. Breast of Guinea Fowl in Madeira Sauce. Filo of Mushrooms and Tomato with a Chive Cream Sauce. Selection of English and Welsh Cheeses.

The hotel was built at the turn of the century and has been modernised by the present owners to retain much of the charm of the old building, while offering the comforts demanded by the visitor of today. Log fires in winter. Wood panelling. Attractive gardens.

✛ M5 junction 7. M50 junction 2. On B4218 between Ledbury and Malvern. On the western slopes of the Malvern Hills in the centre of Colwall.

VISA AmEx ⊗ ✓ ⇦ C

MOUNT PLEASANT HOTEL ✕ ✕ ✕

Belle Vue Terrace, Great Malvern, Worcestershire WR14 4PZ
✆ (01684) 561837 FAX (01684) 569968
GEOF & SOL PAYNE

⊨ 14, 14 en-suite, from £35.00 per person, double occ.
Lunch served. Non-residents welcome. Closed 25th & 26th December.
✕ £15.50, last orders 9.30pm.
English and continental cuisine with Spanish & Vegetarian specialities. Herefordshire Steaks.

An elegant listed Georgian building (c.1730) set in 1.5 acres of terraced gardens ideally located in the centre of Malvern, overlooking the famous Priory Church yet with access to the Malvern Hills. Stunning views over the Severn Valley. An informal hotel with all the facilities of a larger establishment. Emphasis on good food, comfort and relaxation.

✛ On A449 in the centre of town.

VISA AmEx ✓ B

110

GREAT MISSENDEN, Buckinghamshire

Town in the heart of the beautiful Chiltern Hills. Visit nearby Hughenden House and Waddesdon, (both National Trust), Bekonscot Model Village, Chalfont Shire Horse Centre, Ascot Racecourse, Oxford and Windsor. *See also Princes Risborough.*

THE GEORGE INN

94 High Street, Great Missenden, Buckinghamshire HP16 0BG
☎ (01494) 862084 FAX (01494) 865622
GUY & SALLY SMITH

🛏 6, 6 en-suite, from £24.97 per person, double occ.
Lunch served. Non-residents welcome. Closed 25th December (evening only).
✗ £15.00, last orders 9.45pm.
🍽 Oriental Parcels. Deep fried Mushrooms. Noisettes of Lamb, grilled and served with a Port and Stilton Sauce. Scotch Rump Steak. Scampi Tails with Garlic Butter.

15th century coaching inn with oak beams and original fireplaces in the bar and restaurant areas. Recently completely refurbished.

VISA AmEx ⊗ ✓ ⬙ A

GREAT YARMOUTH, Norfolk

A traditional seaside resort, with miles of seafront and every leisure amenity available. A busy harbour and fishing centre. Plenty of museums to visit.

BURLINGTON HOTEL

North Drive, Great Yarmouth, Norfolk NR30 1EG
☎ (01493) 844568 FAX (01493) 331848
RICHARD DELF

🛏 27, 27 en-suite, from £26.00 to £32.00 per person, double occ.
Lunch served. Non-residents welcome. Closed 30th November to 17th February.
✗ £14.00, last orders 8pm.
🍽 Traditional English cooking. The full table d'hote menu offers a variety of dishes, fresh fish from Lowestoft, local meats, home-made deserts and pastries.

The hotel has been run by the same proprietor for the last 25 years. The Burlington offers every family comfort in friendly surroundings. It overlooks the sea, and miles of sandy beaches. A perfect spot for a family holiday.

VISA 🞋 ⊗ ♿ ⬙ ✓ 🛇 Ⓢ A

GUERNSEY, Channel Islands

The second largest Channel Island with many historic sites and leisure activities. The Island is famous for its flower cultivation and duty free status. *See also Jersey, Sark.*

LA COLLINETTE HOTEL ✕✕

St Jacques, St Peter Port, Guernsey, Channel Islands GY1 1SN
☎ (01481) 710331 FAX (01481) 713516
ANDREW CHAMBERS

🛏 24, 24 en-suite, from £22.00 to £37.50 per person, double occ.
Lunch served. Non-residents welcome. Closed January.
✗ £12.50, last orders 9pm.
🍽 Beautiful fresh fish. Crab. Lobster.

A popular family hotel in the centre of town. This white walled hotel has been run by the same family for over 35 years and their relaxed, caring attitude shows. Children are particularly well cared for with a play area, games room and a 6 o'clock high tea.

VISA 🞋 AmEx ♿ ⬙ ✓ 🛇 Ⓢ B   *Guernsey continued overleaf...*

LA FAVORITA

Fermain Bay, Guernsey, Channel Islands GY4 6SD
☎ (01481) 35666 FAX (01481) 35413
MR & MRS SIMON WOOD

🛏 37, 37 en-suite, from £41.00 per person, double occ.
Lunch served. Non-residents welcome. Closed December.
✕ £12.95, last orders 9pm.
🍷 Local fish dishes. Guernsey cream. Home-made patisseries, cakes and desserts.

A former country house which has been carefully converted into a hotel with traditional comforts and modern facilities including an indoor heated swimming pool. Open fires in winter.

VISA 🌐 AmEx ⊗ ♿ ≋ ✓ 🗑 ⚓ Ⓢ C

AUBERGE DU VAL

Sous l'Eglise, St. Saviours, Guernsey, Channel Islands GU7 9EX
☎ (01481) 63862 FAX (01481) 64835
LINDA TWINN

🛏 10, 10 en-suite, from £20.00 to £27.00 per person, double occ.
Lunch served. Non-residents welcome. Open all year.
✕ £15.00, last orders 9.30pm.
🍷 Fresh local fish and shellfish, cooked with Chinese, Indian, French and Creole influences. There is seasonal menu and blackboard `specials'. Duck Auberge, crispy roast breast of duck pan fried with green peppercorns and port. Steak & Oyster Pie.

A friendly, informal hotel which occupies a 150 year old farmhouse. A trout stream runs through the three acres of grounds and an aromatic herb garden. Good accommodation, relaxed surroundings and caring, personal service - excellent value for money.

VISA 🌐 AmEx ⊗ ✓ 🗑 ⚓ Ⓢ 🐾 A

HADLEY HEATH, Worcestershire

Village just off the M5, between junctions 5 & 6. There are a number of good local walks.Well located for visiting The Malvern Hills, Worcester and Stratford upon Avon.

🏨 HADLEY BOWLING GREEN INN

Hadley Heath, Nr Droitwich Spa, Worcestershire WR9 0AR
✆ (01905) 620294 FAX (01905) 620771
TONY & PAULINE RICHARDS

🛏 14, 14 en-suite, from £28.50 per person, double occ.
Lunch served. Non-residents welcome. Open all year.

✕ from £10.00 a la carte, 9.30pm.
🍽 Daily market produce. Fresh fish. Game in season. Baked Brie in Filo Pastry. Gamekeepers Pie, venison, wild boar, pigeon and rabbit, cooked in red wine with a flakey pastry crust. Plum and Apple Lattice Pie.

A 15th century inn in the heart of rural Worcestershire. The inn is beside the bowling green, used by many noted Elizabethan players; the hotel still caters for bowling groups today. A friendly, relaxing place to stay. Two traditional bars with open log fires in winter and a more formal 30 seater dining room.

VISA ⬛ ⊗ ⑂ ✓ 🐾 A

HALIFAX, West Yorkshire

Historic textile town, but now more noted for its building society and toffee! Visit Eureka museum, Piece Hall, Hardcastle Crags, Hebden Bridge and the nearby Bronte country.

🏨 COLLYERS HOTEL

Burnley Road, Luddenden Foot, Halifax, West Yorkshire HX2 6AH
✆ (01422) 882624 FAX (01422) 883897
D. NORTHEY & N. SKELTON

🛏 6, 4 en-suite, from £28.25 per person, double occ.
Lunch served. Non-residents welcome. Open all year.

✕ £15.00, last orders 9pm.
🍽 Modern English a la carte menu, vegetarian selection. Home-made puddings. Good wine list.

Converted mill owners house, renovated and carefully restored, with an elegant dining room, lounge bar and individually styled bedrooms.

⚓ From M62, take exit 22 or 24, then to Sowerby Bridge, Burnley, then A646 to Luddenden Foot.

VISA ⬛ 🔲 AmEx ⊗ ⑂ ✓ 🐾 A

Halifax continued overleaf...

ROCK INN HOTEL ✗ ✗
Holywell Green, Halifax, West Yorkshire HX4 9BS
☎ (01422) 379721 FAX (01422) 379110
ROBERT VINSEN

🛏 18, 18 en-suite, from £25.00 to £34.50 per person, double occ.
Lunch served. Non-Residents welcome. Open all year.
✗ £11.80, last orders 10pm.
🍴 English cooking. Roast Beef and Yorkshire Pudding. Grills. Inn
food is available all day.

A 17th century inn offering high quality accommodation and
traditional fare in rural surroundings. Recently refurbished to
include a large conservatory and patio areas.
VISA 💳 💳 AmEx Ⓟ ✓ Ⓢ ♨ A

HARLECH, Gwynedd
A large village, formerly the chief town of the county of Meirioneth, well
known for its famous castle and song, "Men of Harlech". Visit Snowdonia
National Park, Llechwedd Slate Caverns and Ffestiniog Railway.

ST DAVIDS HOTEL ✗
Harlech, Gwynedd LL46 2PT
☎ (01766) 780366 FAX (01766) 780820
GWYLFA DAVIES

🛏 60, 60 en-suite, from £30.00 per person, double occ.
Non-residents welcome. Open all year.
✗ £13.50, last orders 8.30pm.
🍴 Traditional Welsh fare.
A large Edwardian hotel situated on the coast overlooking Royal
St Davids Golf Course, Cardigan Bay and the Llyn Peninsular. All
bedrooms are ensuite.

VISA 💳 💳 AmEx 🏊 ✓ 🏊 B

HARRINGWORTH, Northamptonshire
Picturesque village in the Welland Valley, close to Uppingham and
Stamford. Rutland Water, Burghley House, Rockingham Castle, and
Kirby Hall are all within a short driving distance.

THE WHITE SWAN
Seaton Road, Harringworth, Northamptonshire NN17 3AF
☎ (01572) 747543 FAX (01572) 747323
CHRISTINE SYKES

🛏 7, 6 en-suite, from £25.00 per person, double occ.
Lunch served. Non-residents welcome. Closed 25th December.
✗ from £6.50 a la carte, last orders 10pm.
🍴 Fillet Steak with Stilton Cheese. Chicken Harringworth.
Asparagus on a Crouton with Mustard Dressing.

16th century coaching inn built in local stone. As well as an oak
bar carved by local craftsmen, the inn is full of agricultural and
building craft memorabilia.

⊹ In centre of village.
VISA 💳 Ⓟ 🐾 ✓ A

HARROGATE, North Yorkshire

A major conference, exhibition and shopping centre renowned for its spa water and floral displays. Within just a short distance are The Yorkshire Dales and Moors, York Minster, the city, and many castles.

THE CROFT HOTEL

42/46 Franklin Road, Harrogate, North Yorkshire HG1 5EE
📞 (01423) 563326 FAX (01423) 530733
FRITZ & VALERIE MAAS

🛏 13, 13 en-suite, from £28.50 per person, double occ.
Non-residents welcome. Open all year.
✗ £13.50, last orders 9.30pm.
🍴 English and continental cuisine. Crofters Pork. Roast Breast of Duck with Cumberland Sauce.

A small family hotel, formerly a Victorian town house, in a tree lined road close to all Harrogate's amenities. Recently refurbished, The Croft offers comfortable accommodation and excellent value for money.

✣ Head for Conference Centre, Strawberry Dale Avenue is opposite, Franklin Road is the first turning on the left.

VISA 💳 AmEx ⊗ 🔄 A

THE DUCHY HOTEL

51 Valley Drive, Harrogate, North Yorkshire HG2 0JH
📞 (01423) 565818
MARILYN BATESON & ALAN DRAKE

🛏 9, 9 en-suite, from £25.00 per person, double occ.
Closed December 23rd to January 4th.
✗ £10.50, last orders 7pm.
🍴 Chicken Goujons with Garlic. Chicken Maryland. Strawberry Cheesecake. Chocolate Nut Sundae. Passion Cake. Fruit Strudel.

Small comfortable hotel of the Victorian era, overlooking Valley Gardens, yet central for Harrogate's delightful floral town centre. Friendly welcoming atmosphere.

✣ A61 into Harrogate. Turn off at main traffic lights, Crescent Road to Valley Gardens entrance. Bear left to Valley Drive.

VISA 💳 ⊗ ✓ Ⓢ A

HARROW, Middlesex

Busy town on the northern edge of London. Very easy access to the capital by rail, underground and bus. Visit Harrow on the Hill, home of the famous school, Woburn Abbey and St. Albans.

HARROW HOTEL

12-22 Pinner Road, Harrow, Middlesex HA1 4HZ
📞 (0181) 427 3435 FAX (0181) 861 1370
IVAN HARTOG

🛏 54, 54 en-suite, from £34.50 per person, double occ.
Lunch served. Non-residents welcome. Open all year.
✗ £16.95, last orders 9.45pm.
🍴 Traditional English roasts and grills, together with a comprehensive French menu. Vegetarian menu available.

A town house hotel, offering personal care and comfort to both business and leisure guests. Friendly staff offer a warm welcome. With it's easy train and tube links into central London, The Harrow Hotel offers an ideal base for visitors wanting to explore the city.

✣ On A404 (Pinner Road) at double roundabout, junction of A312.

VISA 💳 AmEx ⊗ ♿ ✓ 🔄 C

HARTLEPOOL, Cleveland

An ancient industrial centre, with a wealth of local history. See the
Cleveland Hills, the local marina or The Metro Centre.

🏨 RYEDALE MOOR HOTEL

3 Beaconsfield St., Hartlepool, Cleveland TS24 0NX
☎ (01429) 231436 FAX (01429) 863787
ALAN & JEAN SKINNER

🛏 13, 11 en-suite, from £27.00 per person, double occ.
Lunch served. Open all year.
✗ from £4.80-£11.95, last orders 9pm.
🍴 A la carte and table d'hote menus. Vegetarian selection. Spinach
Pate. Deep Fried Corn Rolls. Fruit Curry. Lentil & Cider Loaf.
Potato & Nut Cutlets.

A Victorian seaside hotel on the promenade, offering good
accommodation. There are two dining rooms, one with vegetarian
and a la carte specialities, the other with good value for money
popular food.

VISA 🔲 💳 ⊗ ✓ ⑤ 🍷 A

HAVERFORDWEST, Dyfed

An ancient riverside town, ideal base for exploring the Pembrokeshire
Coastal National Park. Other attractions include Scolton Manor Country
Park, `Mototmania' exhibition, Selvedge Farm Museum and Nant-y-Coy Mill.

🏨 HOTEL MARINERS

Mariners Square, Haverfordwest, Dyfed SA61 2DU
☎ (01437) 763353 FAX (01437) 764258
ANDREW CROMWELL

🛏 30, 30 en-suite, from £31.25 per person, double occ.
Lunch served. Closed 26th & 27th December & 1st January.
✗ £10.00, last orders 9.30pm.
🍴 Local seafood and shellfish. Dressed Crab. Cawl Cenin.

Originally built in 1625, this town centre hotel has been
comfortably modernised and is well known for its relaxed and
informal atmosphere. The hotel has its own short mat bowling
green.

VISA 🔲 💳 AmEx ⊗ ✓ 🐚 B

HAWES, North Yorkshire

A traditional Pennine market town home of Wensleydale cheese. Excellent base for walking or touring. Many waterfalls, historic sites, castles and museums nearby likewise. Good trout fishing and the scenic Settle/Carlisle Railway. see *See also Askrigg, Wensleydale.*

🏛🏛🏛 SIMONSTONE HALL

Hawes, Wensleydale, North Yorkshire DL8 3LY
☎ (01969) 667255 FAX (01969) 667741
JOHN & SHEILA JEFFRYES

🛏 10, 10 en-suite, from £43.00 per person, double occ.
Lunch served. Non-residents welcome. Closed two weeks in January.
✗ from £13.00, last orders 8.30pm.
🍴 Country house menus from local produce including game and fish cooked to order. Traditional home-made puddings. Varied and interesting wine list.

A delightful, 18th century historic building, with all the luxuries of the 20th century, but retaining the grace and aura of a bygone age, with panelled walls, antique furniture and a four poster room. The hotel has a rural hillside location, offering stunning views across Wensleydale. Dogs are always welcome.

⊕ From junction 37, M6 or A1 take A684 to Hawes. 1.5 miles North of Hawes follow directions for Muker.

VISA 🖃 ⊗ 🕄 🖊 ⬦ C

HAWKHURST, Kent

A picturesque village in the heart of the Kent Weald, surrounded by many National Trust houses and gardens and the historic castles of Bodiam, Leeds and Hever.

🏛🏛 THE QUEENS HEAD HOTEL

Rye Road, Hawkhurst, Kent TN18 4EY
☎ (01580) 753577 FAX (01580) 754241
IAN DOE

🛏 8, 8 en-suite, from £27.50 per person, double occ.
Lunch served. Open all year.
✗ £13.25, last orders 9.45pm.
🍴 Local game in season, fresh fish.

Dating back to the 16th century, The Queen's Head is steeped in history and character with oak beams, inglenook fireplaces and creeping ivy, which all enhance the warm, friendly atmosphere. The hotel enjoys a good reputation for its fine food and accommodation.

VISA 🖃 💳 AmEx ⊗ 🖊 🕄 A

HAYLING ISLAND, Hampshire

Quiet, town on an Island close to Portsmouth with its many sites, HMS Victory, Warrior & Mary Rose. Chichester, Midhurst, Arundel and the Isle of Wight are all within a short distance.

COCKLE WARREN COTTAGE HOTEL

36 Seafront, Hayling Island, Hampshire PO11 9HL
☎ (01705) 464961 FAX (01705) 464838
DAVID & DIANE SKELTON

🛏 5, 5 en-suite, from £34.50 per person, double occ.
Open all year.
✕ £24.50, last orders 8pm.
🍴 French and English country cooking using fresh local fish, seafood, poultry, South Down's lamb and game. Five varieties of home-made bread and very naughty puddings!

Traditional farmhouse style cottage hotel, with antiques and period furniture, set in a pretty garden. Diane's exceptional cooking can be tasted at the set daily dinner, which must be ordered in advance. The hotel is renowned for it's food, ambiance and comfort. For young children, please enquire directly with the hotel.

✛ At the seafront, turn left. After approximately 1 mile, hotel on left.

VISA 🟦 ⊗ 🗝 ✎ 🌊 ⚓ ⟲ C

HEBDEN BRIDGE, West Yorkshire

Originally small town on packhorse route, Hebden Bridge grew into booming Mill town in 18th century. Interesting rows of "up-and-down" houses of several storeys built against hillsides.

REDACRE MILL ✕✕

Mytholmroyd, Hebden Bridge, West Yorkshire HX7 5DQ
☎ (01422) 885563
JOHN & JUDITH CLEGG

🛏 5, 5 en-suite, from £25.00 per person, double occ.
Open all year.
✕ £10.50, last orders 8pm.
🍴 Pork Chop a la Vallee d'Auage (grilled Pork Chop dressed with Parsley and Spring Onion served with a Cider Sauce). Panfried Lamb Chops served with a Mint and Ginger Sauce. Home-made Treacle Sponge. Lemon Torte. Selection of Yorkshire Dales Ice-Creams.

Elegant converted Victorian mill in peaceful waterside location and individual furnished rooms all en-suite with a relaxed atmosphere.
VISA 🟦 ⊗ ✎ 🌊 A

HELMSLEY, North Yorkshire

Pretty town with cobbled market square and the ruins of a 12th century castle. Harome, where the Pheasant Hotel is situated, is a village 3 miles south east of Helmsley.

🏠🏠 PHEASANT HOTEL ✗

Harome, Helmsley, North Yorkshire YO6 5JG
☎ (01439) 771241
MR & MRS K. BINKS

🛏 12, 12 en-suite, from £29.97 per person, double occ.
Lunch served. Non-residents welcome. Closed 25th December to February.
✗ £18.50, last orders 8pm.
🍽 Traditional English food.

Overlooking the village pond, this family run hotel occupies a former blacksmith's shop. Its quiet, peaceful location makes it ideal for a relaxing break. Guests are invited to enjoy the new indoor heated pool. All rates quoted are for dinner, bed and breakfast. For children under 12, please enquire directly with the hotel.

✤ Hotel near church in Harome village.

⊗ ♿ ⌇ ✓ 🎣 C

HENFIELD, West Sussex

Small Sussex village, set in rolling countryside, within easy travelling distance of Brighton and the other south coast resorts.

🏠🏠🏠 TOTTINGTON MANOR HOTEL ✗✗

Edburton, Nr Henfield, West Sussex BN5 9LJ
☎ (01903) 815757 FAX (01903) 879331
DAVID & KATE MILLER

🛏 6, 6 en-suite, from £30.00 per person, double occ.
Lunch served. Non-residents welcome. Open all year.
✗ £20.00 inc half bt. wine, last orders 9.15pm.
🍽 English and international cuisine. Seasonal dishes, local Game and produce featured on menu throughout the year. Selection of fresh fish and shellfish on offer daily. Home-made desserts and puddings. Continental and English cheeses.

A 16th century Sussex manor house, in a peaceful setting, at the foot of the South Downs. The settlement at Tottington was mentioned in the Doomsday Book. The chef patron takes great pride in the standard of his food.

✤ Going South on M23/A23 take A281 to Henfield then follow signs for Poynings, Fulking and then Edburton.

VISA 💳 💳 AmEx ⊗ ✓ 🐕 A

HENLEY ON THAMES, Oxfordshire

Prosperous, attractive town on the banks of the River Thames, famed as the home of the annual rowing regatta in July. The town has many Georgian buildings and old coaching inns.

HERNES

Henley on Thames, Oxfordshire RG9 4NT
☎ (01491) 573245 FAX (01491) 574645
RICHARD & GILLIAN OVEY

🛏 3, 2 en-suite, from £30.00 per person, double occ.
Non-residents welcome. Closed mid December to mid January.
✕ £22.50, (Evening meals by prior arrangement only.)
🍽 Traditional English cooking.

This privately owned country house, part Elizabethan, is surrounded by spacious gardens and lawns and overlooks acres of farm and parkland. A totally non-smoking establishment. For children under the age of 12 please contract the hotel direct.

⊹ From the traffic lights in the centre of Henley, turn south onto A4155 (Duke Street), first right into Greys Road, continue for 1 3/4 miles, Hernes is on the right, 200 yards past end of 30 mph area.

⊗ ⩙ ✓ B

SHEPHERDS

Rotherfield Greys, Henley on Thames, Oxfordshire RG9 4QL
☎ (01491) 628413
SUE FULFORD-DOBSON

🛏 4, 4 en-suite, from £24.00 per person, double occ.
Closed 23rd December to 25th January.
✕ £12.00 (Evening meals by prior arrangement only.)
🍽 Traditional English cooking. Country home in an idyllic peaceful setting on the edge of the village green. A hotel with a warm welcome and every comfort. For children under the age of 12 please contract the hotel direct.

⊹ Out of Henley take Peppard Road, after 3 miles turn right to Shepherds Green, Shepherds is 0.3 miles on right.

⊗ ✓ A

HEREFORD, Herefordshire

Many attractions including a splendid cathedral and a cider museum! Visit the birthplace of Elgar, or simply enjoy walking through the surrounding hills and mountains.

THE STEPPES COUNTRY HOUSE HOTEL

Ullingswick, Nr Hereford, Herefordshire HR1 3JG
☎ (01432) 820424 FAX (01432) 820042
HENRY & TRICIA HOWLAND

🛏 6, 6 en-suite, from £38.00 per person, double occ.
Non-residents welcome. Closed 10th to 23rd December & January.
✗ £22.50, last orders 7.30/9pm.
🍽 A five course set gourmet dinner, including many original specialities. Chicken Liver Mousse with Port Sauce. Breast of Duck with Fresh Coriander, Ginger & Mango.

A 17th century country hotel in the peaceful hamlet of Ullingswick, abounding in antiques, oak beams and inglenook fireplaces. The flagged floor dining room and cobbled bar create a Dickensian atmosphere. The restored timber-framed barn and stable offer six large luxurious bedrooms. For children under 12, please enquire directly with the hotel.

⚓ Off the main A417 Gloucester to Leominster road.

VISA 🔲 AmEx ♿ ✓ 🚭 ✈ C

CASTLE POOL HOTEL

Castle Street, Hereford, Herefordshire HR1 2NR
☎ (01432) 356321 FAX (01432) 356321
JOHN & LISA RICHARDSON

🛏 26, 26 en-suite, from £35.00 per person, double occ.
Lunch served. Non-residents welcome. Open all year.
✗ £15.00, last orders 9.30pm.
🍽 Local snails. Duck, Wye salmon and Black Mountain trout.

A white walled house, dating from 1850, which was once the home of the Bishop of Hereford and has now been carefully converted into a country style hotel. The hotel takes its name from the moat in the garden to the rear of the building. During the summer, guests can enjoy barbecues and lunchtime salads in the garden, served from the Castle Bar.

⚓ Reaching Hereford on A438 turn left at first traffic lights, right at 'T'Junction, then left.

VISA 🔲 💳 AmEx ✓ 🚭 ✈ B

HERSTMONCEUX, East Sussex

Picturesque Sussex village dominated by a 15th century castle and gardens. Closeby are Battle Abbey, Pevensey Castle and Eastbourne.

🏠🏠🏠 WHITEFRIARS HOTEL

Boreham Street, Nr Herstmonceux, East Sussex BN27 4SE
☎ (01323) 832355 FAX (01323) 833882
TONY WILLIAMS

🛏 20, 20 en-suite, from £30.00 per person, double occ.
Lunch served. Open all year.
🍴 £17.95, last orders 9.30pm.
🍽 Fresh Sussex produce.

A 16th century, Grade II listed country hotel, formerly the home of the Sherrif of Sussex. The hotel is extremely comfortable and clean with charming furnishings and decor. The hotel's cuisine has an excellent reputation.

VISA 🔳 ⊗ ✓ 🕥 ⊕ A

HINCKLEY, Leicestershire

Delightful country hotel nestling in lovely gardens in the Saxon frontier town of Hinckley.

🏠🏠 KINGS HOTEL & RESTAURANT

13/19 Mount Road, Hinckley, Leicestershire LE10 1AD
☎ (01455) 637193 FAX (01455) 636201
ISTVAN & KAY KEMENY

🛏 7, 7 en-suite, from £27.50 per person, double occ.
Lunch served. Non-residents welcome. Open all year.
🍴 £12.50, last orders 10pm.
🍽 English, Colonial and Hungarian.

The view from the terraces behold the 14th century parish church. Historic battle sites where in 1485 Richard III lost his crown and his life to the future Henry VII is near. Close to Birmingham Airport, Warwick Castle and Mallory Park race circuit.

VISA 🔳 🔳 AmEx ⊗ ♿ ✓ ⊕ A

HINDON, Wiltshire

Attractive, unspoilt Wiltshire village. Visit Stonehenge, Salisbury, Bath, Avebury & Wilton House. *See also Salisbury.*

🏠🏠🏠 THE LAMB AT HINDON

Hindon, Salisbury, Wiltshire SP3 6DP
☎ (01747) 820573 FAX (01747) 820605
JOHN & PAUL CROFT

🛏 12, 12 en-suite, from £27.50 per person, double occ.
Lunch served. Non-residents welcome. Open all year.
🍴 £18.95, last orders 9.30pm.
🍽 Hot Pigeon Breast Salad with Redcurrant Tartlets. Pan fried Sirloin of Beef with Whole Grain Mustard Sauce. Chocolate Caramel Mousse. Cider Apple Cake. Lemon Bakewell Tart.

An historic 17th century village inn noted for its friendly welcome and traditional atmosphere.

✈ 1 mile from the A303 on the B3089, 15 miles west of Salisbury, 15 miles east of Stonehenge.

VISA 🔳 AmEx ✓ 🕥 ⊕ A

HITCHIN, Hertfordshire

Easy access to Stevenage, Letchworth or Luton. Amongst the tourist attractions in the area are Knebworth House, Woburn Abbey, Shuttleworth Museum and Duxford.

REDCOATS FARMHOUSE HOTEL

Redcoats Green, Hitchin, Hertfordshire SG4 7JR
(01438) 729500 FAX (01438) 723322
THE BUTTERFIELD FAMILY

14, 11 en-suite, from £34.50 per person, double occ.
Lunch served. Closed Bank Holidays.
from £15.00 to £25.00, last orders 9.30pm.
English cuisine. Roast Rack of Lamb. Gressingham Duckling with a Honey and Apricot stuffing. Game in season. Quail Roasted and served on a Crouton with Chicken Livers and Brandy.

A 15th century farmhouse liberally furnished with antiques. High standard accommodation complimented by an excellent restaurant with a good local reputation.

VISA AmEx ⊗ ✓ ⊕ B

HOLMFIRTH, West Yorkshire

This village has become famous as the location for the TV series Last of the Summer Wine. It is on the edge of the Peak District National Park. Visit the Pennine Way & Yorkshire Sculpture Park. *See also Stocksbridge.*

HOLME CASTLE COUNTRY HOTEL

Holme Village, Nr Holmfirth, West Yorkshire HD7 1QG
(01484) 686764 FAX (01484) 687775
JILL HAYFIELD & JOHN SANDFORD

8, 5 en-suite, from £32.50 per person, double occ.
Non-residents welcome. Open all year.
£10.00 & £19.00, last orders 9pm.
Cream of Watercress Soup with home-made bread rolls. Asparagus and Mange Tout with Sauce Maltaise. Pan fried Scottish Salmon Tapenade, on a bed on Onions cooked in Balsamic Vinegar. Breast of Chicken with Mustard and Tarragon Sauce. Vanilla Ice Cream with Orange Caramel Sauce.

Unusual Victorian stone residence in a quiet village location with panoramic views over the surrounding countryside.

A6024, 2.5 miles south west of Holmfirth.

VISA AmEx ⊗ ✓ ⦸ A

HOLSWORTHY, Devon

Busy market and farming town on the north Devon/Cornwall border. Within easy reach of the national trust coastline with its spectacular coves and surfing beaches. Many historic houses and gardens. Cycle and ramble trails locally.

COURT BARN HOTEL

Clawton, Holsworthy, Devon EX22 6PS
☎ (01409) 271219 FAX (01409) 271309
ROBERT & SUSAN WOOD

🛏 8, 8 en-suite, from £40.00 per person, double occ.
Lunch served. Non-residents welcome. Closed first week of January.
✕ £16.00 & £19.00, last orders 9.15pm.
🍴 Local trout and fish. Tournedos Court Barn. Chicken and Stilton Roulade. Pork in Pineapple and Wine. Salmon en Croute. Beef Wellington. Delicious home-made sweets.

Originally a 15th century manor house, Court Barn was rebuilt in 1853 and now provides a peaceful homely atmosphere with antique furnishings and pictures. Excellent cuisine and a spectacular wine list of over 300 bins. Croquet lawn, lawn tennis and badminton court, 9 hole putting green and chip & putt.

✤ In village of Crawton.

VISA 🌑 🍷 AmEx ⊗ ♿ 🌂 ✓ ⚓ B

HOLYHEAD, Anglesey

The ferry port to Ireland, an attractive holiday town in itself, is surrounded by low cliffs and sandy beaches. Lots of outdoor activities, including golf, fishing, sailing, walking and swimming.

TRE-ARDDUR BAY HOTEL

Holyhead, Anglesey, Gwynedd LL65 2UN
☎ (01407) 860301 FAX (01407) 861181
IAN & SUSAN MURDOCH

🛏 30, 30 en-suite, from £48.00 per person, double occ.
Lunch served. Non-residents welcome. Open all year.
✕ £17.95, last orders 9.30pm.
🍴 Traditional Welsh and international cuisine, prepared using fresh ingredients, particularly locally caught fish. Extensive table d'hote and a la carte menus, complimented by an extensive wine list.

The hotel is set in its own grounds with views of the bay. The amenities are of a high standard, cocktail bar, heated indoor swimming pool, conference facilities and a pleasant conservatory. Nearby outdoor pursuits include sailing, tennis, golf and horse riding.

✤ The hotel is a short drive from the Holyhead ferry terminal.

VISA 🌑 🍷 AmEx ⊗ 🌊 ✓ 🌂 🏊 S ⚓ C

HOPE COVE, Devon

A crab and lobster fishing village with fisherman's cottages nestling under Bolt Tail. Many safe and sandy beaches. Golf, horse-riding, fishing and sailing are available in the area.

HOPE COVE HOTEL

Hope Cove, Devon TQ7 3HH
☎ (01548) 561233 FAX (01548) 561233
LEO & EMILY CLARKE

🛏 7, 7 en-suite, from £22.50 per person, double occ.
Non-residents welcome. Closed 31st October to 1st February.
✕ £12.50, last orders 8pm.
🍲 Crab & Avocado Salad. Pancakes stuffed with Spinach & Melted Cheese. Seafood Mornay. Pan fried Cod served with a White Wine Sauce. Chicken Provencale in a sauce of Tomatoes and Peppers. Stir fried Beef and Black Beans. Banoffie Pie. Treacle Tart. Creme Caramel & Kiwi Fruit.

Standing two hundred feet above sea level, set in its own grounds, this hotel enjoys magnificent sea views. Comfortable furnishings and a warm atmosphere prevail.

⊹ From Exeter A38, turn off to Salcombe, Hope Cove signed, turn to Inner Hope, hotel on top of hill.

VISA 🖾 ✓ ⚓ 🌊 A

HORNDON ON THE HILL, Essex

Hill-top village, 27 miles east of London. Visit Lakeside Shopping Centre and Southend-on-Sea.

BELL INN & HILL HOUSE

Horndon on the Hill, Essex SS17 8LD
☎ (01375) 642463 FAX (01375) 361611
J & C VEREKER

🛏 10, 10 en-suite, from £29.00 per person, double occ.
Lunch served. Non-residents welcome. Closed Christmas & New Year. Restaurant closed Sunday & Monday (all day).
✕ £17.95, last orders 9.45pm.
🍲 Fresh shellfish from nearby Leigh on Sea. Chicken and Basil Mousse. Goats' Cheese Samosa. Fillet of Plaice, with Chive and Sole Mousse, baked in Filo. Breast of Duck with Pink Peppercorn Sauce. Supreme of Salmon, poached with Ginger. FINALIST, REPRESENTING EAST ANGLIA, IN THE 1994 LOGIS REGIONAL CUISINE COMPETITION.

Georgian town house, brightly furnished with chintzy, individually styled bedrooms. Pretty restaurant with a justified good local reputation for its food and 15th century village inn.

⊹ In the centre of Horndon on the Hill.

VISA 🖾 💷 ⊘ ✓ 🌊 A

HORSHAM, West Sussex

Busy town, with much modern development, but situated close to Gatwick Airport and within easy reach of the south coast.

YE OLDE KINGS HEAD HOTEL

Carfax, Horsham, West Sussex RH12 1EG
☎ (01403) 253126 FAX (01403) 242291
IAN KEMP

🛏 42, 41 en-suite, from £42.50 per person, double occ.
Lunch served. Non-residents welcome. Open all year.
✗ From £12.50, last orders 9pm.
🍽 Light lunches available in the wine cellar buttery, or full traditional English restaurant meals in the panelled dining room. There is also a coffee shop for morning coffee, snack lunches and afternoon teas.

VISA 🔲 💳 AmEx ⊗ ♿ ✓ B

HUDDERSFIELD, West Yorkshire

Originally founded on wool and cloth, Huddersfield has now been largely redeveloped but retains several outstanding Victorian buildings. Easy access to Holmfirth (Summer Wine Country) York and the Dales.

THREE ACRES INN & RESTAURANT ✗

Roydhouse, Shelley, Huddersfield, West Yorkshire HD8 8LR
☎ (01484) 602606 FAX (01484) 608411
MR N. F. TRUELOVE & MR B. A. ORME

🛏 20, 19 en-suite, from £20.00 to £28.75 per person, double occ.
Lunch served. Non-residents welcome. Restaurant closed Saturday lunchtime.
✗ from £12.00 a la carte, last orders 9.30pm
🍽 Good Yorkshire cooking using only local produce. Crispy Lunesdale Duckling. Fresh Black Pudding. Home-made Steak, Kidney and Mushroom Pies.

A privately owned country inn and restaurant with a good reputation for food and accommodation. All the bedrooms are comfortably furnished. Ten rooms are situated in the inn itself, the remainder in an adjacent annexe.

VISA 🔲 💳 ⊗ ✓ A

ELM CREST GUEST HOTEL

2 Queen's Road, Edgerton, Huddersfield, West Yorkshire HD2 2AG
☎ (01484) 530990 FAX (01494) 516227
DEREK GEE & HILARY BIRKS

🛏 8, 5 en-suite, from £29.00 per person, double occ.
Lunch served. Non-residents welcome. Open all year.
✗ £15.00, last orders 9pm.
🍽 English cooking.

A Victorian house, built in 1866, set in delightful gardens.

✦ 1.5 miles from Huddersfield on A629 Halifax road turn right, 150 yards past garage.

VISA 🔲 AmEx ⊗ A

ILKLEY, West Yorkshire

A popular tourist spa town set in the River Wharfe Valley. Excellent walking country. Visit the local museum in the former manor house, Bolton Abbey and the Cow and Calf Rocks.

THE COW & CALF HOTEL

Ilkley Moor, Ilkley, West Yorkshire LS29 8BT
✆ (01943) 607335 FAX (01943) 816022
THE NORFOLK FAMILY

🛏 17, 17 en-suite, from £32.50 per person, double occ.
Lunch served. Non-residents welcome. Open all year.
✗ £13.75, last orders 9pm.
🍷 Panorama Restaurant named for the view. Traditional English local roast joints. Jumbo Yorkshire Pudding. Hot Treacle Tart.

In a spectacular location, high on Ilkley Moor, this old Victorian, family run, coaching inn enjoys incredible views over Wharfedale below. Guests rooms are fully equipped, and one offers a four poster bed. Beautifully restored large Rhododendron garden featuring Victorian Tarn. Conference facilities available.

⊹ Follow the signs for Cow & Calf Rocks from A65.
VISA 💳 AmEx 🚫 ✓ 🐕 B

ILMINSTER, Somerset

Former wool town with a fine market square of mellow ham stone. Some Elizabethan buildings. The surrounding area includes many interesting National Trust properties.

THE SHRUBBERY HOTEL

Ilminster, Somerset TA19 9AR
✆ (01460) 52108 FAX (01460) 53660
STUART SHEPHERD

🛏 12, 12 en-suite, from £45.00 per person, double occ.
Lunch served. Closed Christmas Day.
✗ £12.50, last orders 9.30pm.
🍷 Traditional English cuisine. Roast Rack of Lamb. Slices of Fillet Steak in Brandy and Cream.

A former Victorian gentleman's residence, The Shrubbery stands in two acres of terraced lawns and landscaped gardens. Excellent facilities and accommodation have made the hotel an important conference and meetings venue. For children, please contact the hotel direct.

VISA 💳 AmEx 🚫 🏊 ✓ 🦢 C

IPSWICH, Suffolk

A county town and major port on the River Orwell, birthplace of Cardinal Wolsey.

🏠🏠 THE GOLDEN LION HOTEL

Cornhill, Ipswich, Suffolk IP1 1DP
✆ (01473) 233211 FAX (01473) 233868
JAMES & KAYCE HARDING

🛏 24, 24 en-suite, from £22.25 per person, double occ.
Lunch served. Non-residents welcome. Closed 25th December.
✗ £15.00, last orders 9.30pm.
🍴 Branade of Smoked Mackerel. Spaghetti Al Gambero. Country Baked Gammon with Pineapple Gravy. Beef Casserole with Walnuts and Celery. Summer Fruit Cheesecake. Trio of Ice Cream in a Brandy Snap Basket. Hot Chocolate Fudge Cake.

There was a business on the hotel site in 1250, but it only became known as The Golden Lion in 1543. The hotel, situated in historic Cornhill, is now a busy and bustling town centre hostellry which has lost none of it's original charm.

✢ In the centre of Ipswich.

VISA 💳 AmEx ✓ 🦮 A

JERSEY, Channel Islands

The largest of the five Channel Islands with a wealth of activities and historical sites. A beautiful coastline, sleepy country lanes and lots of variety and local life. *See also Guernsey, Sark.*

🏠🏠🏠 THE OLD COURT HOUSE INN

St Aubin's Harbour, Jersey, Channel Islands.
✆ (01534) 46433 FAX (01534) 45103
JONTY SHARP

🛏 9, 9 en-suite, from £32.50 to £40.00 per person, double occ.
Lunch served. Non-residents welcome. Closed Christmas Day.
✗ £16.50, last orders 10.30pm.
🍴 Steeped in history and full of nooks and crannies, the Old Court House dates in parts back to 1450.

The property has recently undergone a major refurbishment with particular attention given to the individually furnished bedrooms. Housed in the original, 'judges chambers, the restaurant has a cosmopolitan flavour where local fresh fish and shellfood are considered the major specialities.

VISA 💳 AmEx ♿ 🐾 🦮 S 🏌 A

KESWICK, Cumbria

Attractive town, nestling on the shores of Derwentwater beneath Skiddaw Mountain. A good central location for touring the Lake District.

SKIDDAW HOTEL

Main Street, Keswick, Cumbria CA12 5BN
✆ (017687) 72071 FAX (017687) 74850
MICHAEL ATKINSON

🛏 40, 40 en-suite, from £36.50 per person, double occ.
Lunch served. Non-residents welcome. Open all year.

✗ £13.00 approx, last orders 9pm.
🍴 Smoked Herdwick Lamb with a Macon and Gooseberry Sauce. Beef, Mushroom and Cumberland Ale Pie. Cumberland Sausages with Apple Sauce.

Overlooking Keswick's market square, the hotel caters for both business and tourist customers. All bedrooms are comfortably furnished and the hotel is only five minutes from the new Keswick Spa Leisure Centre.

VISA ▨ AmEx ⊗ ✓ Ⓢ ⊕ B

KIELDER WATER, Northumberland

Twenty five miles north west of Hexham and Hadrian's Wall country. Many water sports activities. Explore Cragside House and Wallington Hall (N.T), the Scottish borders or the beautiful Northumberland coast.

PHEASANT INN HOTEL

Falstone, Stannersburn, Northumberland NE48 1DD
✆ (01434) 240382
THE KERSHAW FAMILY

🛏 8, 8 en-suite, from £26.00 per person, double occ.
Lunch served. Non-residents welcome. Closed 25th December & Monday during January & February.

✗ from £14.00, last orders 9pm.
🍴 Oven baked Kielder Trout filled with Garlic Prawns. Cider baked Gammon with a Cumberland Sauce. Noisette of Lamb with Apricot and Ginger Sauce.

A 360 year old country inn, bursting with character and traditional charm. Beamed ceilings, exposed walls and open fires. All the food is prepared from fresh local ingredients, under the direction of the owners. The inn has recently undergone sympathetic refurbishment to provide comfortable accommodation.

⊗ ♿ ✓ ⑄ ⊕ A

KINGSBRIDGE, South Devon

Kingsbridge nestles at the head of the beautiful Kingsbridge estuary, which extends down to the sailing centre of Salcombe. Visit the National Park of Dartmoor, Slapton Nature Reserve, National Trust Land and Houses.

CRABSHELL MOTOR LODGE

Embankment Road, Kingsbridge, South Devon TQ7 1JZ
✆ (01548) 853301 FAX (01548) 856283
LEO & EMILY CLARKE

🛏 24, 20 en-suite, from £19.75 per person, double occ.
Lunch served. Non-residents welcome. Open all year.

✗ £10.10, last orders 9pm.
🍴 Local seafood specialities.

Modern purpose built motor lodge in water's edge location. Maritime decor in the bar and restaurant.

VISA ▨ ▨ AmEx ✓ ⑄ ⊕ A

KIRKBY STEPHEN, Cumbria

A market town situated midway between the Lake District and Yorkshire Dales National Parks, both half an hour's drive.

THE FAT LAMB

Crossbank, Ravenstonedale, Kirkby Stephen, Cumbria CA17 4LL
✆ (015396) 23242
PAUL & HELEN BONSALL

🛏 12, 12 en-suite, from £28.00 per person, double occ.
Lunch served. Non-residents welcome. Open all year.
✗ £17.00, last orders 9pm.
🍴 Mussels with Garlic and White Wine. Citrus Cocktail. Braised Pheasant Forestiere. Poached Salmon with Herb Butter. Trout with Oranges and Almonds. Grilled Sirloin Steak with Pate Crouton. A selection of home-made sweets.

Former 17th century stone built farmhouse with a warm and welcoming atmosphere, converted to combine modern amenities with good old fashioned comfort.

✚ On A683 between the towns of Sedbergh and Kirkby Stephen.
⊗ ♿ ✓ 🚭 ♉ A

THE TOWN HEAD HOUSE

Kirkby Stephen, Cumbria, CA17 4SH
✆ (017683) 71044 FAX (017683) 72128
DAVID MACRAE

🛏 6, 6 en-suite, from £28.25 per person, double occ.
Open all year.
✗ £16.00, last orders 8pm.
🍴 Locally reared meat or game, fresh fruit and vegetables. Vegetarian dish always available.

Dating from the 18th century, Town Head House is now a comfortable, large, warm and friendly hotel. Three of the bedrooms offer four poster or half tester beds. There are open fires in the public rooms on all but the warmest days. The owner takes justified pride in the fact that most of his customers return for more than one visit. An unspoilt area of Cumbria, well worth exploring.

VISA 🔲 ⊗ ♿ 🚭 A

KNIGHTON, Powys

In the heart of the Welsh Marches, an ideal base for touring and activity holidays. Visit the medieval castles of Powys, Clun and Stokesay.

MILEBROOK HOUSE HOTEL

Ludlow Road, Milebrook, Knighton, Powys LD7 1LT
✆ (01547) 528632 FAX (01547) 520509
RODNEY & BERYL MARSDEN

🛏 6, 6 en-suite, from £32.00 per person, double occ.
Lunch served. Closed 25th December & Monday lunchtime
✗ £16.50 and £19.50, last orders 8.30pm
🍴 The productive hotel kitchen garden provides virtually all the vegetables served in the restaurant and the menus feature fresh local produce throughout.

A mature grey stone building set in three acres of gardens and grounds amidst the spectacular scenery of the Welsh Marches. The hotel offers excellent accommodation and an interesting and comfortable restaurant.

VISA 🔲 ⊗ 🚭 ✓ B

KNUTSFORD, Cheshire

Cheshire market town, minutes from junction 19, M6. Visit closeby Tatton Mansion and Park along with a wealth of other historic country houses, Jodrell Bank and Cheshire Peaks.

THE LONGVIEW HOTEL & RESTAURANT

Manchester Road, Knutsford, Cheshire WA16 0LX
☎ (01565) 632119 FAX (01565) 652402
PAULINE & STEPHEN WEST

🛏 23, 23 en-suite, from £35.00 per person, double occ.
Non-residents welcome. Closed 24th December to 3rd January.
✗ £16.00, last orders 9pm.
🍴 Roasted Welsh Spring Lamb with a sweet home grown Rosemary, Mint and Port glaze. Wild Rabbit Casseroled with Cider. Vegetarian dishes. Home-made ice creams.

Formerly the home of a Victorian merchant, the Longview has been lovingly restored to its former elegance with antiques and period furnishings. A friendly, informal hotel, always offering a warm welcome.

⚜ Overlooking the common.

VISA ⬛ 🔟⊘ ⬗ A

LANDS END, Cornwall

The south west tip of Great Britain is rugged and wild with much spectacular scenery. The market town of Penzance, St Michaels Mount, the ancient monuments and the cliff coastal path are all nearby. *See also Penzance, Marazion.*

THE OLD MANOR HOTEL

Sennen, Nr Lands End, Cornwall TR19 7AD
☎ (01736) 871280 FAX (01736) 871280
DENIS & BARBARA SEDGWICK

🛏 7, 4 en-suite, from £22.00 per person, double occ.
Lunch served. Closed 23rd to 28th December.
✗ £8.50, last orders 8pm.
🍴 Freshly caught local fish. Fillets of Fish poached in Orange Juice. Grilled Flat Fish. Prime Sirloin Steaks.

Originally built in 1790, a small granite manor house. Bedrooms are simply furnished, en-suite showers only. Very casual friendly atmosphere, good honest Cornish cooking and excellent value for money.

VISA ⬛ 🔟⊘ ⬗ 〰 🦆 A

LAVENHAM, Suffolk

A mediaeval village built on the prosperity of the local wool trade. The cathedral-like church is stunning, the market place and Guildhall date from the 13th century. The village is surrounded by Constable country.

THE GREAT HOUSE

Market Place, Lavenham, Suffolk CO10 9QZ
✆ (01787) 247431 FAX (01787) 248007
REGIS & MARTINE CREPY

🛏 4, 4 en-suite, from £39.00 per person, double occ.
Lunch served. Non-residents welcome. Closed Sunday evenings & all day Monday.
✗ £15.95, last orders 9.30pm.
🍴 Classic French cuisine.

A Georgian frontage was added to the original 14th century building to create the facade as we see it today. The bedrooms are all beautifully furnished, and consist of mini-suites of 3 to 4 rooms each. There is a pleasant patio for alfresco dining in summer. The award winning cuisine offers quite unbelievable value for money.

⊹ In the market place.

VISA 💳 AmEx Ⓧ 🕭 🖑 C

THE ANGEL HOTEL

Market Place, Lavenham, Suffolk CO10 9QZ
✆ (01787) 247388 FAX (01787) 247057
ROY & ANNE WHITWORTH, JOHN & VAL BARRY

🛏 8, 8 en-suite, from £30.00 per person, double occ.
Lunch served. Non-residents welcome. Closed Christmas Day
✗ £12.00-£15.00 a la carte, last orders 9.15pm
🍴 Imaginative menu is based on fresh local produce. Menu changed daily to include game in season, fresh fish, home-made pies, casseroles and vegetarian dishes.

The Angel has been licensed since 1420 and combines the qualities of a busy local with those of a popular restaurant. The building has a wealth of exposed beams and inglenook fireplaces and provides an informal, friendly atmosphere. Five real ales, good selection of malt Whisky and extensive wine list.

⊹ In the market place.

VISA 💳 🕭 🖑 A

LEAMINGTON SPA, Warwickshire

Georgian and Regency 18th century spa town. Visit the Pump Room, or walk through the Jephson Gardens alongside the river. There is also a museum and an art gallery. Warwick Castle, the finest Medieval Castle in England is only 10 minutes drive away. NEC Birmingham 30 minutes; NAC Kenilworth 10 minutes.

LANSDOWNE HOTEL

87 Clarendon Street, Leamington Spa, Warwickshire CV32 4PF
☎ (01926) 450505 FAX (01926) 421313
DAVID & GILLIAN ALLEN

🛏 15, 12 en-suite, from £29.95 per person, double occ.
Non-residents welcome. Open all year.
✕ £16.95, last orders 8.30pm.
🍽 Daily changing menu. Freshly prepared dishes including seasonal produce. Fresh Cotswold Rainbow Trout topped with Prawns and Capers. Aberdeen Angus Beef Steaks.

A Regency property situated in the centre of town. A warm and personal welcome is extended to all guests. The Lansdowne offers a relaxed, tranquil atmosphere. The personal selection of good quality wines complements the excellent cuisine of this hotel.

✣ In town centre, Warwick Street/Clarendon Street junction.

VISA 🖻 ♿ ✓ A

THE ADAMS HOTEL

22 Avenue Road, Leamington Spa, Warwickshire CV31 3PQ
☎ (01926) 450742 FAX (01926) 313110
J. VAN DEN ENDE

🛏 10, 10 en-suite, from £29.75 per person, double occ.
Open all year.
✕ £16.50, last orders 8pm.
🍽 Fresh local produce.

A 19th century Georgian grade II listed building, originally built in 1827 and retaining much of it's original splendour with modern and tastefully furnished bedrooms.

✣ On the A452, near town centre library.

VISA 🖻 ♿ AmEx 🐾 ✓ A

133

LEDBURY, Herefordshire

Historic 17th century market town retains its cobbled streets and timbered houses. Nearby is Eastnor Castle. The Malvern Hills, Wye valley, Black Mountains and the towns of Hereford and Gloucester.

THE FEATHERS HOTEL

High Street, Ledbury, Herefordshire HR8 1DS
✆ (01531) 635266/7 FAX (01531) 632001
MR D. M. ELLISTON

🛏 11, 11 en-suite, from £39.25 per person, double occ.
Lunch served. Non-residents welcome. Open all year.
✗ from £12.00, last orders 9.30pm.
🍴 Local Roast Pork with an Apple and Westons Cider Sauce. Hereford Braised Beef with Wye Valley Beer and Onions. Smoked Haddock and Spinach bake with Nutmeg Cream Glaze. Fresh Salmon Escalope grilled, topped with Brie on Watercress Sauce. Walnut coated Welsh Lamb Cutlets with Mushrooms.

The Feathers is a half timbered Elizabethan coaching inn, one of Britain's most impressive buildings, renowned for its beauty and charm. All the bedrooms retain their original character yet are equipped to the highest modern standards. A well deserved reputation for cuisine.

VISA 🔳 💳 AmEx ⊗ ✓ 🕲 ⊕ C

LEEK, Staffordshire

An old silk town, with buildings dating from the 17th century. Interesting art gallery and museum. Close to Alton Towers.

THREE HORSESHOES INN

Buxton Road, Blackshaw Moor, Leek, Staffordshire ST13 8TW
✆ (01538) 300296 FAX (01538) 300320
BILL & JILL KIRK

🛏 6, 6 en-suite, from £23.00 per person, double occ.
Lunch served. Closed 24th December to 2nd January.
✗ £14.95, last orders 9pm.
🍴 Traditional English cuisine, home cooking using fresh local produce. The hotel offers both a bar carvery and traditional restaurant. There is a dinner dance on Saturday evenings for the more energetic!

A cottage, farmhouse style inn, set in pretty gardens. The inn is furnished in oak and pine, with open log fires and is close to plenty of country walks.

VISA 🔳 ⊗ ♿ ✓ 🕲 ⊕ A

LEEMING BAR, North Yorkshire

Immediately adjacent to the A1 service area and an ideal stopover whilst travelling North or South. Nearby is Richmond Castle and Wensleydale.

MOTEL LEEMING

Great North Road, Leeming Bar, North Yorkshire DL8 1DT
☎ (01677) 422122 FAX (01677) 424507
CARL LES

🛏 40, 40 en-suite, from £24.50 per person, double occ.
Lunch served. Non-residents welcome. Open all year.
✕ £12.95, last orders 10pm.
🍴 Grilled Black Pudding with Apple Compote. Home cured Salmon. Chicken in Elderberry Wine. Free range Pork with Prunes. Cheeseboard.

Modern family run motor hotel with traditional ideas about innkeeping and hospitality. The rooms are compact but well furnished. Service is welcoming and friendly.
VISA ◼ ⒉ AmEx ⊗ ♿ ✓ ⊕ A

LENHAM, Kent

A picturesque village, centred around an attractive square. 5 minutes drive from Leeds Castle and 10 minutes from the villages around Pluckley, where 'The Darling Buds of May' was filmed. Close to Canterbury.

THE DOG & BEAR HOTEL ✕

The Square, Lenham, Nr Maidstone, Kent ME17 2PG
☎ (01622) 858219 FAX (01622) 859415
BOB & SHEILA HEDGES

🛏 24, 24 en-suite, from £23.75 per person, double occ.
Lunch served. Non-residents welcome. Open all year
✕ £12.00-£15.00, last orders 10pm
🍴 Locally made sausages. Home-made pies. Kentish Cheeses, shellfish, fresh fruit and vegetables and Romney Marsh Lamb.

A traditional coaching inn, built in 1602. The coat of arms above the front door date from 1704, when Queen Anne was a guest. Today's visitors can expect a warm welcome and comfortable stay at this historic hotel. Dogs may be allowed by prior arrangement.

✢ In the centre of Lenham village.
VISA ◼ ⊗ ♿ ✓ ⊗ A

LINCOLN, Lincolnshire

An ancient city, dominated by the 11th century cathedral and Norman castle. See the Lincolnshire life museum, toy museum, historic Bailgate area and Usher art gallery.

HILLCREST HOTEL ✕

15 Lindum Terrace, Lincoln, Lincolnshire LN2 5RT
☎ (01522) 510182 FAX (01522) 510182
JENNIFER BENNETT

🛏 17, 17 en-suite, from £32.50 per person, double occ.
Lunch served. Non-residents welcome. Closed 20th December to 2nd January.
✕ £13.00-£15.00 a la carte, last orders 8.30pm.
🍴 Local Lincolnshire fresh produce. Lincolnshire sausages for breakfast.

A former Victorian rectory, Hillcrest is a quiet friendly hotel, 5 minutes walk from the cathedral and city centre. There are pleasant views over gardens and parkland from the conservatory and restaurant.
VISA ◼ AmEx ⊗ ✓ ⊕ A   *Lincoln continued overleaf...*

WASHINGBOROUGH HALL COUNTRY HOUSE HOTEL

Church Hill, Washingborough, Lincolnshire LN4 1BE
(01522) 790340 FAX (01522) 792936
BRIAN SHILLAKER

12, 12 en-suite, from £44.00 per person, double occ.
Non-residents welcome. Open all year.
From £15.00, last orders 8.30pm.
English and French cuisine.

A listed Georgian manor house set in three acres of quiet, secluded gardens and woodland,three miles outside the cathedral city of Lincoln.The Wedgewood dining room has an original Adam fireplace and a warm atmosphere is created by the open log fire in the lounge. Four poster rooms are available one with corner spa bath en-suite. Guests can enjoy the hotel's outdoor heated pool. Pre-booked parties catered for at lunchtime, Sunday lunches available.

VISA AmEx C

LISKEARD, Cornwall

Small market town built on the prosperity of the mining industry. Four surrounding National Trust properties, Bodmin Moor and the fishing villages of Looe and Polperro are easily accesible.

COUNTRY CASTLE HOTEL

Liskeard, Cornwall PL14 4EB
(01579) 342694/1
MRS ROSEMARY WILMOTT

10, 10 en-suite, from £35.00 per person, double occ.
Non-residents welcome. Closed November.
£16.00, last orders 7.45pm.
Local Cornish seafood and shellfish. Home-made soups.

Victorian country house hotel set in peaceful surroundings and gardens. All rooms are individually furnished with modern amenities. Lunches are available by prior arrangement.

Follow Park & Ride signs on all junctions, past Station Road bend, sign on right.

VISA AmEx A

THE OLD RECTORY COUNTRY HOUSE HOTEL

Duloe Road, St Keyne, Liskeard, Cornwall PL14 4RL
☎ (01579) 342617
MR & MRS R.G. WOLFE

🛏 8, 8 en-suite, from £30.00 per person, double occ.
Closed Christmas.
✕ from £12.60, last orders 8pm.

🍷 Hot Tipsy Sherry Grapefruit. Stuffed Mushrooms with Stilton. Pork Fillet with Cream, Mushrooms and Brandy. Sirloin Steak pan fried with Mushrooms.

A country house built in the 1800's, situated in three acres of grounds and surrounded by farmland with beautiful views of the countryside .

⊹ A38 to Liskeard, pick up signs to St Keyne (B3254). In St Keyne drive to end of village passing church on the left. The hotel is down the hill, 500 yards on the left.

VISA 🖅 ♿ ✓ 🐕 🐾 A

LITTLE MALVERN, Worcestershire

Two miles south of Great Malvern, an historic spa town set amidst the Malvern Hills. Local sites to visit include Ledbury, Worcester, The Severn Valley, Tewkesbury, Hereford and Gloucester. *See also Great Malvern*.

HOLDFAST COTTAGE HOTEL

Little Malvern, Nr Malvern, Worcestershire WR13 6NA
☎ (01684) 310288 FAX (01684) 311117
STEPHEN & JANE KNOWLES

🛏 8, 8 en-suite, from £40.00 per person, double occ.
Non-residents welcome. Open all year.
✕ £16.00 - £18.00, last orders 9pm.
🍷 Three course, daily changing dinner menu, using the best local and seasonal produce. Innovative dishes with an eye for tradition. Home-baked bread. Salmon and Dill Mousse with Lemon Mayonnaise. Escalope of Pork with fresh Sage served with Cumberland Sauce. Brown Sugar Meringues with mixed berry puree.

A 17th century oak beamed country house set in two acres under The Malvern Hills. Relaxing informal atmosphere, excellent cuisine and beautifully decorated accommodation.

VISA 🖅 ♿ ✓ 🐕 🐾 C

LLANDRINDOD WELLS, Powys

A popular resort town, developed in the Victorian era as a spa. The waters can still be taken at Rock Park gardens. Excellent touring centre for visiting mid-Wales.

THE BELL COUNTRY INN

Llanyre, Llandrindod Wells, Powys LD1 6DY
☎ (01597) 823959 FAX (01597) 825899
CHRISTINE PRICE

9, 9 en-suite, from £28.75 to £32.50 per person, double occ.
Lunch served. Non-residents welcome. Open all year.
£14.50, last orders 9.30pm.
Welsh Lamb Steak Llewellyn. Welsh Venison. Game Creole, acombination of game and poultry casseroled with nutmeg, thyme, tomato, mushrooms and real ale. Vegetarian menu.

A friendly country inn, named because it was sited in the same field as the bell tower belonging to the local parish church. The Bell Inn once offered refreshment to the drovers taking stock from west Wales to the markets of Gloucester and Hereford and now is popular with locals and visitors alike. Attractive, well equipped bedrooms and good food.

VISA AmEx ⊗ ⤳ ✓ S ⟡ A

LLANDUDNO, Gwynedd

A popular seaside resort, developed during the Victorian era. Today there is still a Pier, Donkey rides and Punch & Judy display, together with a dry ski slope, motorcycle museum and excellent shopping.

DUNOON HOTEL

Gloddaeth Avenue, Llandudno, Gwynedd LL30 2DW
☎ (01492) 860787 FAX (01492) 860031
MICHAEL CHADDERTON

56, 56 en-suite, from £35.00 per person, double occ.
Lunch served. Non-residents welcome. Closed November to mid March.
£11.00, last orders 7.30pm.
Traditional and continental food. Conway Salmon in a Dill Sauce. Roast Rack of Welsh Lamb.

A handsome Victorian building which has been run as a hotel by the same family for over 40 years. The Dunoon is operated with personal care and attention, offering customers a comfortable base for a relaxed family holiday.

⤷ From the Promenade turn left at cenotaph, over the roundabout, hotel is 200 yards on the right.

VISA ⊗ ✓ ⪬ S ⟡ A

LLANNEFYDD, Clwyd

The Clwyd valley is full of beautiful rolling hills and attractive villages. Close to the beaches on the north Wales coast. Lots of outdoor activities, including pony trekking, riding, golf and walking.

THE HAWK AND BUCKLE INN

Llannefydd, Nr Denbigh, Clwyd LL16 5ED
☎ (01745) 79249 FAX (01745) 79316
BOB & BARBARA PEARSON

🛏 10, 10 en-suite, from £25.00 per person, double occ.
Lunch served. Non-residents welcome. Closed October to April 30th.
✗ £15.50, last orders 9pm.
🍽 A menu featuring popular dishes, prepared from fresh ingredients. Grills and casseroles. Beef Bourgignonne. Chicken Chasseur. Sirloin or Fillet Steaks served either plain or with Sauce Robert or Mustard Cream Sauce.

A stone built, 17th century coaching inn situated high on the Denbigh Hills, well off the beaten track in the middle of beautiful countryside. The Hawk and Buckle is still the local pub for the tiny hamlet of Llannefydd, making it an important centre of the community. The guest bedrooms are in an attractive modern extension. For children under 8 years please contact the inn direct.

✠ A55 to St Asaph take Denbigh Road turn off to Henllan then Llannefydd.

VISA 🔳 ⊗ ⌇ ✓ A

LLANON, Dyfed

A tiny hamlet on the west Wales coast. Beautiful safe beaches and plenty of walking opportunities. *See also New Quay.*

PLAS MORFA

Llanon, Aberaeron, Dyfed SY23 5HT
☎ (01974) 202415
G. K. PEARSALL

🛏 8, 8 en-suite, from £25.00 per person, double occ.
Non-residents welcome. Open all year.
✗ from £12.00 a la carte, last orders 10pm.

🍽 Welsh dishes. Lobster and fish prepared with an Asian flavour. Menu changes monthly. Flambeed foods. Locally made farm ice cream. Thai style Fish Kebabs wrapped in Bacon. Hot Brie Cheese with Morello Cherry Sauce. Louisiana Spiced Prawns.

The hotel has panoramic views across the bay from the restaurant and every bedroom. A secluded spot, and an ideal base for exploring the delights of beautiful Ceredigion. The nearby golf club offers 18 holes at reasonable fees. Lunches are available on Sunday.

✠ First turning right out of Llanon heading south. First on left coming in from the north.

VISA 🔳 ⊗ ✓ ⌇ 💰 ⊕ A

LLYSWEN, Powys

Nine miles north east of Brecon, in the heart of the Black Mountains. Close to Hay on Wye, famous for its second hand bookshops. *See also Brecon.*

GRIFFIN INN

Llyswen, Brecon, Powys LB3 0UR
☎ (01874) 754241 FAX (01874) 754592
RICHARD & DI STOCKTON & FAMILY

🛏 8, 7 en-suite, from £25.00 per person, double occ.
Lunch served. Non-residents welcome. Open all year, dinner for residents only on Sunday.
✗ from £15.00 a la carte, last orders 9pm.
🍴 Fresh salmon and local game. Traditional farmhouse food.

A long established sporting inn, which features a huge inglenook fireplace, low beams and timeless charm. Sporting facilities are arranged by Richard Stockton and the inn's full-time ghillie and keeper. The bedrooms are simply, but comfortably, furnished.

VISA ◤ ♒ AmEx ⊗ 🚬 ✓ 🖄 ⊕ A

LONDON, (Bloomsbury)

Close to the British Museum. Easy access to both the City and the West End. A good base for shopping, visiting the theatres and the capital's tourist attractions.

THE BONNINGTON IN BLOOMSBURY

92 Southampton Row, London WC1B 4BH
☎ (0171) 242 2828 FAX (0171) 831 9170
ALAN BOSTOCK

🛏 215, 215 en-suite, from £50.00 per person, double occ.
Lunch served. Non-residents welcome. Open all year.
✗ £16.75, last orders 10.30pm.
🍴 Traditional cuisine with modern influence.
A large hotel which manages to retain a high standard of personal care and level of service. Guests will enjoy the friendly, informal surroundings, whether visiting The Bonnington for business or leisure.

✈ From Euston Road (opp. station) turn south into Upper Woburn Place, continue past Russell Square into Southampton Row.

VISA ◤ ♒ AmEx ⊗ 🚬 ⊕ C

LONDON, (Earls Court)

Just 15 minutes from the city centre by tube, this popular cosmopolitan area is close to the main exhibition centres of Earl's Court and Olympia, the museums of South Kensington and the shopping and night life of Knightsbridge and the West End.

THE RUSHMORE HOTEL

11 Trebovir Road, Earls Court, London SW5 9LS
☎ (0171) 370 6505 FAX (0171) 370 0274
SADIK SALOOJEE

🛏 22, 22 en-suite, from £29.50 per person, double occ.
Open all year
✗ No evening meal.

A Victorian town house hotel with 22 individually themed and decorated bedrooms, all with en suite facilities. A warm, friendly, family run hotel in the heart of London. For interesting cuisine, the surrounding area contains literally hundreds of restaurants, of every type, including many of the best of their kind in London.

VISA ◤ ♒ AmEx 🚬 🖄 A

LONDON (Little Venice)

The fashionable residential area of north west London, only ten minutes by bus or tube from the West End and equally handy for the main line stations of Paddington, Euston, Kings Cross and Victoria.

COLONNADE HOTEL

2 Warrington Crescent, London W9 1ER
☎ (0171) 286 1052 FAX (0171) 286 1057
ROBIN RICHARDS

🛏 48, 48 en-suite, from £45.00 per person, double occ.
Non-residents welcome. Restaurant closed Sundays & the month of August.
✗ £12.50, last orders last orders 10pm.
🍴 Duck Liver Mousse. Spaghetti with Broccoli, Garlic and Olive Oil. Panfried Trout Fillets with a Caper Sauce. Lamb Casserole.

A Victorian grade two listed building retaining all it's original elegance while offering every modern convenience.

✦ Just off Edgeware Road.

VISA 🏧 💳 AmEx ⊗ ⟡ C

LONG SUTTON, Somerset

In the heart of the Somerset countryside, Long Sutton is equidistant from Taunton, Yeovil and Glastonbury. Bath, Wells and Wincanton races are within easy reach

THE DEVONSHIRE ARMS HOTEL

Long Sutton, Langport, Somerset TA10 9LP
☎ (01458) 241271 FAX (01458) 241037
DAVID & PAM NAISH

🛏 7, 6 en-suite, from £27.50 per person, double occ.
Lunch served. Non-residents welcome. Open all year.
✗ from £10.95 a la carte, last orders 10pm.
🍴 International and Australasian cuisine.

Originally built as a private house by the Duke of Devonshire in 1787, The Devonshire Arms is now a small hotel with a fine reputation for good food and hospitality.

✦ M3, junction 8, A303, at the Podimore roundabout onto the A372. 3 miles to Long Sutton.

VISA 🏧 💳 ⊗ ✓ 🌀 Ⓢ A

LOOE, Cornwall

A small resort, developed around a former fishing and smuggling port, with narrow winding streets and medieval buildings. Shark fishing centre, boat trips, Lanhydrock House (N.T.). *See also Polperro.*

PUNCH BOWL INN

Lanreath, Nr Looe, Cornwall PL13 2NX
☎ (01503) 220218
H. G. & S. FRITH

🛏 11, 11 en-suite, from £30.00 per person, double occ.
Lunch served. Open all year.
✗ £9.95, last orders 9pm.
🍴 Local seafood and shellfish.

16th century coaching inn with modern facilities. Some four poster bedrooms are available.

VISA 🏧 ⊗ ♿ ✓ 🌀 ⟡ A

LUDLOW, Shropshire

Historical market town of the Welsh Marches with many fine Elizabethan buildings. Visit also Ironbridge Gorge and the many local museums.

DINHAM WEIR HOTEL ✗

Dinham Bridge, Ludlow, Shropshire SY8 1EH
☎ (01584) 874431
MR J. JUKES

🛏 8, 8 en-suite, from £35.00 per person, double occ.
Lunch served. Non-residents welcome. Closed during January.
✕ £12.50, last orders 8.30pm.
🍴 Traditional English cuisine.

Dinham Weir Hotel is quietly situated on the banks of the River Teme surrounded by rolling Shropshire countryside yet within just a couple of minutes walk of Ludlow town centre. All the rooms are fully equipped and enjoy views across the landscaped gardens to the river. The candlelit restaurant is adjacent to the main hotel, immediately on the river bank and large picture windows provide a lovely setting for dinner.

⊹ From Ludlow Castle Square turn left in Dinham, turn right before river bridge, hotel on left hand side.

VISA 🖃 💴 AmEx ⊘ ♿ ✓ 🐕 B

NUMBER TWENTY EIGHT

28 Lower Broad Street, Ludlow, Shropshire SY8 1PQ
☎ (01584) 876996 FAX (01584) 876996
PATRICIA ELMS ROSS

🛏 4, 4 en-suite, from £25.00 per person, double occ.
Non-residents welcome. Open all year.
✕ £14.00, last orders 8.15pm.
🍴 Garlic Mushrooms in Red Wine with Smoked Bacon. Smoked Salmon Mousse with a dusting of Nutmeg. Pork in Hereford Cider and Herb Sauce. Chicken Breasts filled with Pineapple and Ham. Venison casserolled with Red Wine and Mushroom Sauce.

A listed half timbered house, centrally situated below the Broad Gate, close to Ludford Bridge and the River Teme. A warm welcome and comfortably furnished accommodation.

⊹ In the centre of Ludlow town.

VISA 🖃 AmEx ✓ 🐕 🐾 A

LYDFORD, Devon

Historic Saxon village on the western edge of Dartmoor. See the spectacular gorge with its 100ft waterfall (NT) and the ancient castle next to the church with the famous Watchmaker's Tomb. *See also Tavistock.*

♙♙ LYDFORD HOUSE HOTEL ✗

Lydford, Okehampton, Devon EX20 4AU
☎(01822) 820347 FAX (01822) 820442
THE BOULTER FAMILY

🛏 13, 11 en-suite, from £33.00 per person, double occ.
Lunch served. Non-residents welcome. Closed 24th December to 2nd January.
✗£14.50, last orders 8pm.
🍴 English cooking prepared by the resident proprietors using fresh, local produce. Menus change daily and offer a wide choice, always featuring fish and vegetarian dishes, local cheeses and traditional puddings with Devon Clotted Cream.

A Victorian country house peacefully situated in award winning gardens and surrounded by pasture land, just outside the village of Lydford and overlooking Dartmoor National Park. An excellent family-run hotel with delightfully appointed bedrooms, a spacious lounge (log fires in Winter) and a cosy bar. The hotel has its own riding stables in the grounds.

➕ 500 yards off the A386, midway between Okehampton and Tavistock.

VISA ⬛ ⊗ ♿ ⁝/ ⬥ ⚘ B

LYDNEY, Gloucestershire

A small town in the Forest of Dean close to the River Severn where Roman remains have been found. Superb local forest walks. Visit Symonds Yat Rock, Tintern Abbey, steam railway and the Wye Valley.

♙ EDALE HOUSE ✗

Folly Road, Parkend, Nr Lydney, Gloucstershire GL15 4JF
☎(01594) 562835 FAX (01594) 564488
JAMES & SHEILA REID

🛏 5, 5 en-suite, from £25.00 per person, double occ.
Open all year.
✗£15.00, last orders 8pm.
🍴 The set dinner menu changes daily and is creatively prepared by the chef/proprietor. Fresh local salmon, lamb and game in season.

A fine Georgian house (built in 1850) facing the cricket green in Parkend village in the heart of the Royal Forest of Dean. All bedrooms have been tastefully furnished to a high standard. For children under 12 years please contact the hotel direct.

➕ From Lydney turn onto B4234 signposted Parkgate, hotel beside cricket green.

VISA ⬛ ⊗ ⬥ ⁝/ A

LYMINGTON, Hampshire

Town within the New Forest National Park, steeped in history with many major attractions. Within easy reach are Salisbury and Winchester Cathedrals, Stonehenge, Beaulieu and Romsey. *See also Sway.*

⌂⌂⌂ GORDLETON MILL HOTEL

Hordle, Nr Lymington, Hampshire SO41 6DJ
☎ (01590) 682219 FAX (01590) 683073
WILLIAM STONE

🛏 7, 7 en-suite, from £40.00 per person, double occ.
Non-residents welcome. Open all year.
✗ £25.00 to £36.00, last orders 9.30pm.
🍷 Bold and modern French cuisine.

A delightful 17th century water mill house standing in 5 acres on the banks of the Avon Water has recently been extended and refurbished into a stunning country house hotel.

VISA 💳 💳 AmEx ⊗ ♿ ✓ 🚭 🏊 ⊕ C

LYNMOUTH, Devon

Resort set below high cliffs on which the adjoining town of Lynton is sited. Many local dramatic walks, particularly through the Valley of the Rocks to the west. *See also Brendon.*

⌂⌂⌂ THE RISING SUN HOTEL

Harbourside, Lynmouth, Devon EX35 6EQ
☎ (01598) 753223 FAX (01598) 753480
HUGO JEUNE

🛏 16, 16 en-suite, from £39.50 per person, double occ.
Lunch served. Non-residents welcome. Open all year.
✗ £19.95, last orders 9pm.
🍷 Local seafood, lobster, sea bass, salmon, Exmoor game in season, venison, pheasant and duck.

A romantic 14th century thatched smugglers inn, overlooking the small picturesque harbour. All the bedrooms have been recently refurbished without losing any of their old charm. A very friendly and efficient hotel with a good local reputation for its cuisine and well balanced wine list.

⊹ On the seafront.

VISA 💳 💳 AmEx ⊗ ♿ ✓ 🚭 🏊 C

LYTHAM ST ANNES, Lancashire

Fine sandy beaches and attractive gardens. Famous for its championship golf courses. A pleasant resort town. *See also Bilsborrow.*

CHADWICK HOTEL ⚔️✕

South Promenade, Lytham St Annes, Lancashire FY8 1NP
☎ (01253) 720061 FAX (01253) 714455
MILES CORBETT

🛏 72, 72 en-suite, from £24.00 per person, double occ.
Lunch served. Non-residents welcome. Open all year.
✕ £14.00, last orders 8.30pm.
🍽 Set price menus. Gourmet dinner menu and 24 hour food service menu. The hotel prepares locally produced fresh ingredients, particularly fish and shellfish from Fleetwood.

A large family run hotel with a health complex, designed on a Grecian theme with swimming pool, jacuzzi, solarium, sauna, soft play adventure area and games room. Some of the rooms have spa baths and four poster beds.

⊹ On the seafront.
VISA 💳 💷 AmEx ⊗ ⟂ ✓ ⬙ S A

LINDUM HOTEL

63/7 South Promenade, Lytham St Annes, Lancashire FY8 1LZ
☎ (01253) 721534 FAX (01253) 721364
THE ROWLEY FAMILY

🛏 80, 80 en-suite, from £24.00 per person, double occ.
Lunch served. Non-residents welcome. Open all year.
✕ £10.00, last orders 7pm.
🍽 Traditional English cooking. Local fish and Lancashire dishes. Rollmop Herrings. Roast Beef and Yorkshire Pudding. Sticky Toffee Pudding.

Located on the sea front, a family run hotel with every amenity for a traditional family holiday. Live entertainment April to November.

⊹ On the main promenade.
VISA 💳 💷 ⊕ ✓ ⬙ S A

MACHYNLLETH, Powys

Situated on the edge of the Snowdonia National Park, looking over the River Dyfi. Visit Harlech Castle, Tal-yllyn Railway & Aberdovey Golf Course. *See also Aberdovey.*

LLUGWY HALL COUNTRY HOUSE HOTEL

Pennal, Machynlleth, Powys SY20 9JX
☎ (01654) 791228 FAX (01654) 791231
PAUL DAVIS

🛏 15, 14 en-suite, from £19.50 per person, double occ.
Lunch served. Non-residents welcome. Open all year.
✕ £15.95, last orders 9pm.
🍽 Home-made Broccoli and Cumin Soup. Deep fried Squid served on a Tomato and Oregano Sauce. Breaded Welsh Rack of Lamb. Darne of Salmon. Medallions of Beef.

A country house situated in 40 acres of gardens and woodlands overlooking the River Dovey. All bedrooms are decorated and comfortably furnished.

⊹ Take the road from Machynlleth to Aberdovey, turn left before Pennal signed Llugwy Hall Hotel.
VISA 💳 💷 AmEx ⊗ ✓ ⬙ ♻ A   *Machynlleth continued over*...

THE WYNNSTAY ARMS HOTEL

Heol Maengwyn, Machynlleth, Powys SY20 8AE
☎ (01654) 702941 FAX (01654) 703884
LESLEY & PHILIP DAVIES

🛏 20, 20 en-suite, from £26.25 per person, double occ.
Lunch served. Non-residents welcome. Open all year.
✕ £14.95, last orders 11pm.
🍽 Traditional fare, prepared from fresh ingredients.

This handsome town house was once the home of the wealthy
Wynn family. It is now a friendly hotel, offering all modern
comforts, while retaining much of its traditional character. The
hotel bar has an intimate atmosphere and is now the centre of the
local Welsh speaking community. Carvery lunches are served on
Wednesday and Sunday, bar meals available lunch times and
evenings all week.

⊕ In the centre of Machynlleth on A489.

VISA ⬛ 🔁 AmEx ⊗ ♿ ✓ 🕭 ⊕ A

MAIDSTONE, Kent

A busy town set on the River Medway. An excellent centre for excursions,
visit Leeds Castle, Allington Castle, Aylesford Friary or Boughton
Monchelsea Place.

BOXLEY HOUSE HOTEL

Boxley Village, Maidstone, Kent ME14 3DZ
☎ (01622) 692269 FAX (01622) 683536
MR & MRS FOX

🛏 18, 18 en-suite, from £27.50 per person, double occ.
Lunch served. Non-residents welcome.   Open all year.
✕ £16.95, last orders 9.15pm.
🍽 Modern English cuisine.

A 17th century country house, set in 20 acres of parkland, with
modest traditional-style bedrooms.

⊕ Next to the church in Boxley village.

VISA ⬛ 🔁 AmEx ⊗ ♿ 🏊 ✓ ⊕ A

MALTON, North Yorkshire

A thriving farming town on the River Derwent with large livestock market. Famous for racehorse training. Local museum has Roman remains and World War II relics from the "Eden" prisoner of war camp on site in the town.

NEWSTEAD GRANGE

Beverley Road, Norton, Malton, North Yorkshire YO17 9PG
✆ (01653) 692502 FAX (01653) 696951
PAUL & PAT WILLIAMS

🛏 8, 8 en-suite, from £29.50 per person, double occ.
Closed December & January.
✗ £14.00, last orders 8pm.
▪ Traditional English and some French cuisine with fresh local meat and produce from the organic kitchen garden.

Elegant Georgian country house built of stone (1830) set in two and a half acres of grounds and gardens. Furnished with antiques and beautifully decorated bedrooms. This is a totally non-smoking hotel. For children under 12 years please contact the hotel direct.

⊹ Follow Beverley signs out of Malton and Norton-on-Derwent. Newstead Grange is on the left half a mile beyond the last houses and at the junction with the Settrington Road.

VISA 🖃 ⊗ 🔖 ✓ B

THE TALBOT HOTEL

Malton, North Yorkshire, YO17 0AA
✆ (01653) 694031 FAX (01653) 693355
MR SKINNER

🛏 27, 27 en-suite, from £34.50 per person, double occ.
Lunch served. Open all year.
✗ from £12.50, last orders 9pm.
▪ Traditional Yorkshire fare and popular dishes. Yorkshire Pudding with Onion Gravy. Grilled Rainbow Trout with Prawns and Capers. Steak and Kidney Pie.

Attractive, 18th century coaching inn in the town centre. Furnished with antiques, creating a comfortable, relaxed atmosphere. The wine list contains some 70 bins. Fabulous views from the restaurant.

VISA 🖃 ⚋ ⊗ ♿ ⸰ 🔖 🐕 B

MANCHESTER, Greater Manchester

The industrial and cultural capital of the north, with a wealth of Victorian architecture, churches, museums and art gallerys. 15th century cathedral.

CRESCENT GATE HOTEL

Park Crescent, Victoria Park, Manchester M14 5RE
✆ (0161) 224 0672 FAX (0161) 257 2822
TERRY HUGHES

🛏 26, 18 en-suite, from £24.00 per person, double occ.
Closed Christmas to New Year.
✗ £10.00, last orders 8pm.
▪ Traditional English cooking.

A pleasant, comfortable and friendly family run hotel in a quiet, residential area of the city, ideally located for access to both the commercial centre and Manchester airport, both minutes by car.

VISA 🖃 ⚋ AmEx ✓ 🐕 A

MARAZION, Cornwall

Four miles from Penzance, with direct access to St Michaels Mount. Lands End and The Lizard. *See also Penzance, Lands End.*

MOUNT HAVEN HOTEL & RESTAURANT

Turnpike Road, Marazion, Cornwall TR17 0DQ
✆ (01736) 710249 FAX (01736) 711658
JOHN & DELYTH JAMES

🛏 17, 17 en-suite, from £35.00 per person, double occ
Lunch served. Non-residents welcome. Open all year.
✕ £17.50, last orders 9pm.
🍽 Local fish and shellfish, particularly crab and lobster.

Family run hotel in a quiet position overlooking St Michaels Mount and the sea. Parts of the building date from the mid 18th century, particularly the interesting dining room. The remainder of the hotel is more recent, comfortably furnished and has a friendly relaxed atmosphere. Lunches are only available from April to October.

VISA 💳 AmEx ⊗ ✓ 🕭 🏊 🐾 A

MARLBOROUGH, Wiltshire

Historic market town, with broad main street and colonnade shopping. Visit nearby Avebury, Stonehenge, Salisbury, Silbury Hill, the Kennet and Avon Canal and the Savernake Forrest.

THE ROYAL OAK

Wootton Rivers, Nr Marlborough, Wiltshire SN8 4NQ
✆ (01672) 810322
MR & MRS JOHN JONES

🛏 6, 4 en-suite, from £20.00 per person, double occ.
Lunch served. Non-residents welcome. Closed 25th & 26th December.
✕ from £6.00 a la carte, last orders 9.30pm.
🍽 Full a la carte, home-made soups, casseroles, pies and fresh fish. A selection of unusual desserts. A wide selection of spirits, beers and real ales from the wood. An extensive wine list.

A 16th century thatched free house with a wealth of exposed beams situated in the centre of a picturesque Wiltshire village. 13th century village church with very unusual clock. Seasonal Sunday and bank holiday barge cruises along the canal from the lock.

VISA 💳 ⊗ 🕭 ✓ 🐾 A

MAWGAN PORTH, Cornwall

Halfway between Newquay and Padstow, the village of Mawgan Porth is ideally situated as touring centre for Cornwall. Walk the Cornish Coastal Footpath spectacular views in every direction.

TREDRAGON HOTEL ✕

Tredragon Road, Mawgan Porth, Newquay, Cornwall TR8 4DQ
☎ (01637) 860213 FAX (01637) 860269
MR & MRS D. N. BROWN

🛏 27, 27 en-suite, from £25.00 to £30.50 per person, double occ.
Lunch served. Non-residents welcome. Open all year.
✕ £14.00, last orders 8pm.
🍽 Fresh Seafood from the local fishing boats in Padstow. Darne of Fresh Padstow Hake gently poached in White Wine and Butter. Coquille St Jacques Mornay. Scallops served with a Creamy Cheese and Parsley Sauce, sprinkled with Parmesan and garnished with Duchess Potatoes and Watercress. Tredragon's own Lobster Bisque laced with fresh Cornish Cream.

The hotel has been owned and managed by the Brown family since 1964. It offers modern amenities, together with traditional hospitality. The owners show attention to detail and a genuine interest in their guests. There is no single supplement and the hotel is also ideally situated for family holidays.

VISA ▨ ⊗ ⑆ ⌂ ✓ ⌇ ⌅ Ⓢ ⟜ A

MELTON MOWBRAY, Leicestershire

The home of Britain's famous pork pies and Stilton cheese. The town has a traditional market and local museum, and is within a short distance of Belvoir Castle and Rutland Water.

SYSONBY KNOLL HOTEL ✕✕

Asfordby Road, Melton Mowbray, Leicestershire LE13 0HP
☎ (01664) 63563 FAX (01664) 410364
MR & MRS BOOTH

🛏 25, 25 en-suite, from £24.50 per person, double occ.
Lunch served. Non-residents welcome. Closed 25th December to 1st January.
✕ £9.50, last orders 9pm.
🍽 Melton Mowbray Pork Pies and Stilton Cheese. Bar snacks, table d'hote and a la carte menus are available.

A friendly family run hotel operated by professional caring staff. The dining room overlooks the swimming pool and well kept gardens.

VISA ▨ ⌂ ✓ ⟜ A

MERE, Wiltshire

Small town with a grand church surrounded by Georgian houses, old inns and a 15th century chantry house. On the chalk downs overlooking the town is a iron age fort.

♨ CHETCOMBE HOUSE HOTEL

Chetcombe Road, Mere, Wiltshire BA12 6AZ
✆ (01747) 860219
COLIN & SUE ROSS

🛏 5, 5 en-suite, from £25.00 per person, double occ.
Lunch served. Non-residents welcome. Open all year.
✖ £12.50 to £15.00, last orders 8pm.
🍽 Smoked Rainbow Trout Terrine. Beef Casserole with Red Wine and Olives. Chicken Breast with Tarragon Sauce. Roast Chicken with Fennel and Lime. Gooseberry Fool. Meringue Nest with Raspberries.

A 1930's country house with one acre of garden. Bedrooms are individually furnished. The main rooms face south, with outstanding views to Shaftesbury and Blackmore Vale.

⊕ Approach by A303, westbound leaving A303, hotel on left.

VISA 💳 AmEx ⊗ ✓ ⇩ A

MILTON KEYNES, Buckinghamshire

Stoney Stratford is an attractive and historic town forming the Northern part of the New City of Milton Keynes. The High Street contains a picturesque selection of old buildings offering the visitor the opportunity to visit the many specialists shops, public houses, hotels and restaurants.

♨♨ THE DIFFERENT DRUMMER HOTEL

94 High Street, Stony Stratford, Milton Keynes,
Buckinghamshire MK11 1AH
✆ (01908) 564733 FAX (01908) 260646
MRS KESWANI

🛏 13, 13 en-suite, from £49.00 per person, double occ.
Lunch served. Non-residents welcome. Open all year.
✖ £15.95, last orders 10.30pm.
🍽 A specialist Italian Restaurant also serving English and French Cuisine, complimented by an extensive wine cellar.

An historic coaching inn built in 1470 and recently refurbished to provide guests with attractive bedrooms, a delightful wood panelled dining room and well furnished lounge with its own bar.

⊕ Close to the northern end of the A5 dual carriageway running through Milton Keynes.

VISA 💳 💳 AmEx 👤 ⟋ ⇩ B

MINEHEAD, Somerset

On the edge of Exmoor National Park. Dunster Castle and gardens are closeby, as is Knightshayes, Arlington Court and Rosemoor Gardens. Further afield, Taunton, Bath and Glastonbury are accessible.

🏛🏛🏛 PERITON PARK HOTEL

Middlecombe, Nr Minehead, Somerset TA24 8SW
☎ (01643) 706885 FAX (01643) 706885
RICHARD & ANGELA HUNT

🛏 8, 8 en-suite, from £45.00 per person, double occ.
Non-residents welcome. Open all year.
✕ £20.00, last orders 9pm.

🍴 Potted Smokie. Cheese Souffle. Halibut with Lime and Coriander Vinaigrette. Exmoor Venison with Port and Redcurrant Sauce. Vegetarian dishes always available. Somerset cheeses and wine.

This secluded Victorian country house hotel (c.1875) has retained all of its original character and elegance with spacious and light rooms. All bedrooms are individually furnished to the highest standard, whilst the cuisine has a deserved excellent reputation. There are riding stables adjacent to the hotel.

✢ Located on south side of A39 Dunster to Porlock Road, in Middlecombe village.

VISA 💳 AmEx ⊗ ♿ ✒/ 🚭 ⚓ C

MONMOUTH, Gwent

A historic market town in the Wye Valley. Visit the local museum with its collection of Nelson memorabilia. Ruined castle close to the town centre.

🏛🏛🏛 CROWN AT WHITEBROOK HOTEL

Whitebrook, Monmouth, Gwent NP5 4TX
☎ (01600) 860254 FAX (01600) 860607
ROGER & SANDRA BATES

🛏 12, 12 en-suite, from £40.00 per person, double occ.
Lunch served. Non-residents welcome. Closed Sunday evening and Monday lunchtime to non-residents.
✕ £24.00, last orders 8.30pm.
🍴 Welsh lamb, Wye salmon in season, local game and poultry. Moules et Champignons. Souffle de Fromage Chevre. Mousse de Brochet et Homard. Crepes Flambees a la Liquer au Choix. WINNER OF THE 1993 LOGIS REGIONAL CUISINE COMPETITION.

Formerly a 17th century inn, situated in the idyllic Whitebrook valley, 5 miles south of Monmouth, just off the Wye Valley. Relaxed friendly atmosphere.

VISA 💳 💳 AmEx ⊗ ✒/ 🚭 ⚓ C

MORETONHAMPSTEAD, Devon

A small 17th century Dartmoor town. The surrounding moorland is scattered with old farmhouses and prehistoric sites.

WHITE HART HOTEL & RESTAURANT

The Square, Moretonhampstead, Newton Abbot, Devon TQ13 8NF
✆ (01647) 440406 FAX (01647) 440565
PETER MORGAN & CLIFFORD CHUDLEY

🛏 20, 20 en-suite, from £31.50 per person, double occ.
Lunch served. Non-residents welcome. Closed 25th & 26th December.
✕£16.95, last orders 8.30pm.
🍽 Traditional food. Local dishes include Roast Devonshire Beef, Tavistock Trout, Teign Salmon. The home-made desserts include Dartmoor Apple Pie, Old English Bread Pudding, served with Devon Clotted Cream.

An historic inn furnished with antiques, with a comfortable, cozy atmosphere.

⚓ In the town centre.

VISA 💳 AmEx ⊗ ♿ ∕ 🚬 🐾 A

MORTEHOE, Devon

Old coastal village with small Norman church. Visit Exmoor National Park, Barnstaple and the heritage coastal path.

SUNNYCLIFFE HOTEL

Chapel Hill, Mortehoe, Devon EX34 7EB
✆ (01271) 870597
BETTY & VICTOR BASSETT

🛏 8, 8 en-suite, from £32.50 per person, double occ.
Closed November to January.
✕£15.00, last orders 6pm.
🍽 Traditional English cooking.

A quiet hotel enjoying a unique hillside position, surrounded by thousands of acres of open moorland and coastal walks. All bedrooms have sea views. For children under 12 years please contact the hotel direct.

⊗ ∕ 🚬 A

MUCH WENLOCK, Shropshire

A small town close to Wenlock Edge in beautiful scenery and full of interest. In particular there are the remains of the 11th century Priory with fine carving and the black and white 16th century Guildhall.

THE RAVEN HOTEL

Much Wenlock, Nr Shrewsbury, Shropshire TF13 6EN
✆ (01952) 727251 FAX (01952) 728416
KIRK HEYWOOD

🛏 8, 8 en-suite, from £29.00 per person, double occ.
Lunch served. Non-residents welcome. Closed 25th December.
✕£12.00 to £15.00, last orders 9.30pm.
🍽 Venison with Pears. Leicestershire Chicken. Mushroom Stroganoff.

A fine coaching inn established in 1700 (in part 15th century), with open fires, beamed rooms and individually decorated bedrooms.

⚓ Telford to Much Wenlock from Junction 4 or Junction 5 of the M54. Take A442 southbound, merges with A4169 follow to Much Wenlock.

VISA 💳 AmEx ⊗ ∕ A

MUNGRISDALE, Cumbria

An unspoilt Lakeland village. Wide range of local activities, including fell walking, rock climbing, pony trekking, sailing and fishing. Visit the Lake District National Park near Ullswater Lake, Castlerigg Stone Circle and Hadrians Wall. *See also Penrith.*

THE MILL HOTEL ✗

Mungrisdale, Penrith, Cumbria CA11 0XR
✆ (017687) 79659
RICHARD & ELEANOR QUINLAN

🛏 9, 7 en-suite, from £25.00 to £35.00 per person, double occ.
Non-residents welcome. Closed 1st November to 25th
February.
✗ £21.00, last orders 8pm.
🍽 Local Venison braised in Red Wine with Wild Mushrooms and Juniper Berries. Roast Derwent Water Duckling with Cumberland Sauce. Damson and Apple Tansy. Hot sticky Gingerbread with Cumberland Rum Butter.

Mill Cottage (built in 1651) has a beamed lounge with a log fire. All bedrooms are bright and cheerfully decorated. The hotel offers a warm, relaxed atmosphere.

⚓ Next door to Mill Inn public house in village centre.
✓ ⌇ ⚓ ⚓ B

NETTLETON, Wiltshire

Tour the beautiful Cotswolds from this rustic village. Badminton House is two miles away, Bath 12 miles. Visit picturesque Castle Combe village where Dr. Doolittle was filmed.

FOSSE FARM HOUSE COUNTRY HOTEL

Nettleton, Nr Chippenham, Wiltshire SN14 7NJ
✆ (01249) 782286 FAX (01249) 783066
CARON COOPER

🛏 5, 5 en-suite, from £47.50 per person, double occ.
Lunch served. Non-residents welcome. Open all year.
✗ £21.50, last orders 9pm.
🍽 A mix of English and French country cooking, prepared from fresh ingredients. The owners interest in the Dordogne area of France is reflected in the cuisine.

Built in 1750, Fosse Farm is a Cotswold stone farmhouse and stable block, furnished attractively with French and English country antiques. Guests are assured of a warm and friendly welcome. There is a pleasant garden in which to relax during the summer. Afternoon teas are a speciality.

⚓ From M4 junction 17, follow directions to Castle Coombe Race Circuit. Continue on the B4039 for a mile until you enter a village called "The Gib", take first left turn, hotel is one mile on the right.

VISA 💳 🔔 ⊗ ♿ ✓ ⚓ C

NEW QUAY, Dyfed

A picturesque fishing village overlooking the heritage coastal path. *See also Llanon.*

🏨 TY HEN FARM HOTEL

Llwyndafydd, New Quay, Dyfed SA44 6BZ
✆ (01545) 560346
MR & MRS KELLY

🛏 4, 4 en-suite, from £29.00 per person, double occ.
Lunch served. Non-residents welcome. Open mid February to mid November.

✗ from £5.00 a la carte, last orders 6pm.
🍽 Welsh dishes. Courgette & Tomato Pots. Pan fried Trout. Curried Welsh Lamb.

A working farm hotel (a non smoking hotel) with some self catering cottages and an excellent leisure centre with a large indoor heated pool, well equipped fitness room, sauna, sunbed, skittle alley, pool, table tennis etc. Out of season speciality - private swimming lessons for adults.

✢ Hotel is situated at Llwyndafydd 4 miles south of New Quay.

VISA 🅰 ⊗ ♿ ⚓ ✓ 🥢 ⚔ Ⓢ 🍴 A

NEWBURY, Berkshire

Ancient town surrounded by the Downs, half way between the New Forest and the Cotswolds. Visit the 17th century Cloth Hall, now a museum, and the nearby famous racecourse.

🏨 THE YEW TREE INN

Hollington Cross, Andover Rd., Highclere, Berkshire RG15 9SE
✆ (01635) 253360 FAX (01635) 254977
JENNY WRATTEN

🛏 6, 6 en-suite, from £27.50 per person, double occ.
Lunch served. Non-residents Welcome. Open all year.

✗ from £16.00 a la carte, last orders 10pm
🍽 A wide selection of freshly prepared continental and English dishes. Potted Shrimps. Boiled Cornish Crabs. Salmon Fishcakes. Crock of Pheasant and other seasonal and local dishes. Wholemeal walnut Bread. Home-made marmalade, jellies and chutneys. FINALIST, REPRESENTING THE HEART OF ENGLAND, IN THE 1994 LOGIS REGIONAL CUISINE COMPETITION.

The Yew Tree Inn was built some 350 years ago in local brick and tile, with sturdy oak framing. It retains all of its original character today and offers a warm, friendly, informal atmosphere. Restaurant has a good local reputation. Last orders for dinner on Sunday, 9.30pm.

VISA 🅰 AmEx ⊗ ✓ 🥢 A

NEWBY BRIDGE, Cumbria

At the southern end of Windermere on the River Leven, this village has an unusual stone bridge with arches of unequal size. Visit the Lake District, Holker Hall and Stott Park.

SWAN HOTEL ✕ ✕

Newby Bridge, Nr Ulverston, Cumbria LA12 8NB
✆ (015395) 31681 FAX (015395) 31917
JAMES BERTLIN

⊨ 36, 36 en-suite, from £28.00 per person, double occ.
Lunch served. Non-residents welcome. Open all year.
✕ £17.50, last orders 9pm.
▤ Potted Morecambe Bay Shrimps. Air Dried Cumbrian Ham. Fillet of Seabass. Oven Baked Swordfish Steak.

Originally a coaching inn, The Swan is located at the southern end of Lake Windermere. Each of the spacious, fully equipped bedrooms has its own distinctive decor. Public rooms are all attractively decorated and consist of bars, T.V. room, conference room and shop.

⊹ Leave the M6 Motorway at Junction 36. Following the A590 towards Barrow-in-Furness for 16 miles and turn right over Newby Bridge. Hotel immediately ahead.

VISA ◤ AmEx ✒ ◌ C

NEWENT, Gloucestershire

Close to the Forest of Dean and the Wye Valley and within easy reach of Cheltenham. Visit the largest Falconry centre in the northern hemisphere & local vineyards.

THE OLD COURT HOTEL

Church Street, Newent, Gloucestershire GL18 1AB
✆ (01531) 820522
RON & SUE WOOD

⊨ 6, 4 en-suite, from £24.75 per person, double occ.
Non-residents welcome. Open all year.
✕ £11.00, last orders 8.30pm.
▤ English and French influence, using local produce whenever possible. Courgettes stuffed with Walnuts and Sage. Strips of Beef in Drambuie. Lemon Sole with White Wine.

A William and Mary manor house set in large and mature gardens. Elegant period style in a relaxed peaceful atmosphere.

⊹ 3 miles from M50, junction 3. Outskirts of Newent next to St Mary's Church.

VISA ◤ AmEx ⊗ ✒ ◅ A

NEWPORT, Gwent

Historic market town, nestling beneath the Brecon Beacons. Ideally situated for visiting the Usk and Wye valleys, and Cardiff.

NEWPORT LODGE HOTEL
Bryn Bevan, Newport, Gwent NP9 5QN
✆ (01633) 821818 FAX (01633) 856360
CHRIS & LINDA ROBBINS

🛏 27, 27 en-suite, from £27.75 per person, double occ.
Non-residents welcome. Restaurant closed Sunday evening.
✖ £12.50, last orders 10pm.
🍴 Welsh lamb and beef, local vegetables and fresh fish.

A modern hotel, situated high above the town, with well appointed bedrooms. There is a Victorian style restaurant and bar offering a good selection of traditional food. Sunday lunches available.

VISA 💳 💳 AmEx ⊗ ♿ ⚲ ⟋ ⇩ A

NEWTON ABBOT, Devon

Bustling market town at the head of the Teign estuary, ideally situated for both moorland and seaside activities. Interesting old houses include Bradley Manor (15th century) and Forde House (17th century).

THE BARN OWL INN
Aller Mills, Kingskerswell, Newton Abbot, Devon TQ12 5AN
✆ (01803) 872130
DEREK & MARGARET WARNER

🛏 6, 6 en-suite, from £30.00 per person, double occ.
Lunch served. Non-residents welcome. Closed 25th to 27th December.
✖ from £15.50 a la carte, last orders 9.45pm.
🍴 French cuisine. Local farm produce, fresh fish and shellfish from Brixham.

16th century farmhouse inn, featuring beamed ceilings and inglenook fireplaces. The restaurant is set in a converted barn, decorated with antique farming implements. A warm friendly atmosphere.

✛ A380, direction Torquay at Penn Inn Roundabout, continue along A380, turn first right signposted Aller Mills.

VISA 💳 💳 AmEx ⊗ 🌊 A

NEWTON LE WILLOWS, Merseyside

Small market town, adjacent to the M6, within easy reach of both Liverpool and Manchester. Newton is an ideal resting point for visitors travelling to the Lake District or Scotland.

THE KIRKFIELD HOTEL
2/4 Church Street, Newton le Willows, Merseyside WA12 9SU
✆ (01925) 228196 FAX (01925) 291540
MR D. HIRST

🛏 14, 14 en-suite, from £23.00 per person, double occ.
Lunch served. Open all year.
✖ from £12.00 a la carte, last orders 9.30pm.
🍴 A range of European and French regional dishes.

An 18th century converted coaching house, directly opposite St Peter's Church, which has recently undergone complete interior refurbishment. The original oak beams remain to give character to this warm and friendly hotel.

VISA 💳 ⊗ ⚲ ⟋ A

NORTON FITZWARREN, Somerset

Small village 3 miles to the west of Taunton. Visit the Quantock and Brendon hills, Taunton Cider museum and shop, Somerset wetlands and the Mendips. *See also Taunton.*

THE OLD MANOR FARMHOUSE

Norton Fitzwarren, Taunton, Somerset TA2 6RZ
☎ (01823) 289801 FAX (01823) 289801
ERIC & VERA FOLEY

🛏 7, 7 en-suite, from £24.00 per person, double occ.
Open all year.
✗ £15.00, last orders 7pm.
🍽 Grilled Lamb Cutlets in Taunton Cider with Orange Sauce. Somerset venison. Trout poached in Taunton Cider with a Cucumber and Butter Sauce. Vegetarian dishes.

Formerly an Edwardian farmhouse, just 3 miles from the centre of Taunton, the Old Manor is now a comfortable hotel with a good reputation for food in its pleasant log fired restaurant.

⚓ On B3227, 3 miles west of Taunton.

VISA 💳 💳 AmEx ✓ A

NOTTINGHAM, Nottinghamshire

A modern city with a wide range of industries including famous Nottingham lace. It's castle is now a museum and art gallery. Many attractions including "The Tales of Robin Hood" and the "Flight to Sherwood" experience.

PEACOCK FARM & RESTAURANT

Redmile, Nr Nottingham, Nottinghamshire NG13 0GQ
☎ (01949) 842475 FAX (01949) 843127
PETER, MARJORIE & NICKY NEED

🛏 6, 6 en-suite, from £22.00 per person, double occ.
Lunch served. Non-residents welcome. Open all year.
✗ £13.50, last orders 9pm.
🍽 Local mushrooms. Sweet Herring. Lamb Fillet wrapped in a crispy Potato Jacket, Beef Wellington with Madeira Sauce. Turkey Schnitzel with Crab Apple Jelly. Summer Fruit Pancakes topped with Cream.

A 280 year old family run farmhouse. The bedrooms are all entered through doors from outside. Some of the rooms are in converted outbuildings of the original farm. Good service combined with old fashioned hospitality.

⚓ Follow signs to Belvoir Castle, hotel is half a mile out of Redmile.

VISA 💳 AmEx 🐾 🏊 ✓ 🐕 🦆 A

NYMPSFIELD, Gloucestershire

A pretty village high up in the Cotswolds, with a simple mid-Victorian church and prehistoric long barrow nearby.

THE ROSE & CROWN INN

Nympsfield, Gloucestershire GL10 3TO
☎ (01453) 860240 FAX (01453) 860240
ROBERT WOODMAN

🛏 4, 3 en-suite, from £24.00 per person, double occ.
Lunch served. Non-residents welcome. Open all year.
✕ £11.00, last orders 9.30pm.
🍴 Pancake Rolls. Southern Style Wedges (spicy potato pieces served with a garlic dip). Home-made Welsh Faggots wrapped in Bacon. Chicken with Prawn and Lobster. Sticky Toffee Pudding. Chocolate Sponge Pudding.

A 300 year old inn situated in a quiet Cotswold village. Bedrooms are tastefully furnished in country style.

VISA ⬛ AmEx ✓ A

OXFORD, Oxfordshire

A bustling city, home to the famed university, in the heart of England. Visitors can tour the city's colleges and parks, try punting on the river, or visit the Ashmolean museum and nearby Blenheim Palace.

FOXCOMBE LODGE HOTEL

Fox Lane, Boars Hill, Oxford, Oxfordshire OX1 5DP
☎ (01865) 730746 FAX (01865) 730628
JILL HICKS

🛏 20, 20 en-suite, from £32.75 per person, double occ.
Lunch served. Non-residents welcome. Closed 26th December to 1st January.
✕ £15.00, last orders 9.30pm.
🍴 Traditional English Cuisine using fresh local ingredients.

A traditional country hotel located in a pleasant rural location, just three miles south of Oxford city centre. The bedrooms are all fully appointed and comfortable. The restaurant prepares traditional dishes with flair.

VISA ⬛ 💳 AmEx ⊗ ✓ Ⓢ A

WESTWOOD COUNTRY HOTEL

Hinksey Hill Top, Oxford, Oxfordshire OX1 5BG
☎ (01865) 735408 FAX (01865) 736536
TONY & MAY PARKER

🛏 22, 22 en-suite, from £40.00 per person, double occ.
Lunch served. Non-residents welcome. Closed 22nd December to 5th January.
✕ £16.00, last orders 8.30pm.
🍴 Cream teas with home-made jam and scones. Pyreneen Chicken, chicken, pan fried and served with a sauce of fresh oranges with Grand Marnier. Home-made desserts.

A country house hotel, dating from 1923, set in four acres of garden. Westwood Country Hotel is situated south of Oxford in the tranquil 'Boars Hill' area. It is a comfortable, family run hotel. Sauna and jacuzzi available for guests' use.

VISA ⬛ 💳 AmEx ⊗ ♿ ✓ 🍷 Ⓢ B

FALLOWFIELDS

Faringdon Road, Kingston Bagpuize, Oxfordshire OX13 5BH
☎ (01865) 820416 FAX (01865) 821275
PETA & ANTHONY LLOYD

🛏 3, 3 en-suite, from £34.50 per person, double occ.
Non-residents welcome.   Open all year.
✕ £22.00, last orders 8.30pm.

🍴 Imaginative home cooking prepared on a traditional Aga range.
Many ingredients are grown in the hotel garden. A selection of
home-made puddings and cheeses from the British Isles.

An elegant country house dating back 300 years, set in 12 acres of
gardens, once home to the Begun Aga Khan and Sir Robert
Boothby's family. The hotel is totally non-smoking.

⊹ Turn off A420 Oxford to Swindon road at Kingston Bagpuize.
Right at the roundabout, drive on through Southmoor. Hotel drive
is on the left by the last street lamp.

VISA 💳 AmEx ⊗ ⚲ 🔍 / 🕮 ⊲ C

THE BAT & BALL INN

High Street, Cuddesdon, Oxfordshire OX44 9HJ
☎ (01865) 874379
DAVID SYKES

🛏 6, 6 en-suite, from £22.50 per person, double occ.
Lunch served. Non-residents welcome. Open all year.
✕ from £10.00 a la carte, last orders 9pm.
🍴 Freshly prepared meals.

A popular country inn with cricketing themes and memorabilia in
a delightful Oxfordshire village just five miles from the city centre.
The rooms, which are in a separate part of the inn, have all been
recently refurbished and although simply furnished, are
comfortable.

VISA 💳 ⊗ A

PENRITH, Cumbria

An ancient market town at the northern gateway to the Lakes. The ruins
of Penrith Castle stand in the public park.   Hadrian's Wall and the
Scottish border are closeby, as are the numerous outdoor pursuits of
Cumbria. *See also Mungrisdale.*

THE GEORGE HOTEL

Penrith, Cumbria CA11 7SU
☎ (01768) 62696 FAX (01768) 68223
TOMAS & ROSALIND NIEDT

🛏 30, 30 en-suite, from £27.50 per person, double occ.
Lunch served. Non-residents welcome. Closed 25th, 26th
December & 1st January.
✕ £12.50, last orders 9pm.
🍴 Traditional English cooking.

Privately owned 17th century town centre coaching inn, with oak
beams, log fires and a warm and friendly atmosphere. The hotel
is furnished with antiques. The bedrooms are modern and well
equipped.

⊹ In town centre, car park at rear of hotel.

VISA 💳 ⊗ / ⊲ A

Penrith continued overleaf...

BECKFOOT HOTEL

Helton, Nr Penrith, Cumbria CA10 2QB
☎ (01931) 713241 FAX (01931) 713391
LESLEY & DAVID WHITE

🛏 6, 6 en-suite, from £26.00 per person, double occ.
Non-residents welcome. Closed mid November to March.
✕ £12.50, last orders 8pm.

🍴 Home-made Soups. Toasted Camembert with Salad. Home-made Steak Pie. Local Cumberland Pheasant with home-made Cumberland Sauce. St Clements Cheesecake.

Beautiful country house set in three acres of garden with many hidden aspects to discover. To the rear of the house the ground rises to reveal a small paddock behind which lies the Lakeland Fells. All bedrooms are invitingly different.

✠ Leave M6 at Junction 39 and join the A6 northbound to Shap. Follow the sign to Bampton. Beckfoot lies two miles further along the road towards Helton village.

⁘ / 🦢 🐦 A

PENSFORD, Avon

This small village is equidistant between Bath, Wells, Bristol and Weston super Mare with all their heritage and attractions. Visit also Longleat and Wookey Hole. *See also Timsbury.*

THE CARPENTERS ARMS

Stanton Wick, Nr Pensford, Avon BS18 4BX
☎ (01761) 490202 FAX (01761) 490763
NIGEL PUSHMAN

🛏 12, 12 en-suite, from £29.75 per person, double occ.
Lunch served. Non-residents welcome. Open all year.
✕ Bar snacks and a la carte, last orders 10pm.
🍴 Roast Somerset Duckling in Black Cherry Sauce. Mussels in Cider, Shallots and Cream. Mendip Snails in Garlic Butter.

A delightful country inn, formerly a row of miner's cottages, offering very pretty, cottage style, accommodation. Two restaurants, the less formal Cooper's Parlour" or the more formal beamed dining"

✠ Turn off A37 or A368 to Stanton Wick, hotel in village centre.

🍴 AmEx ⊗ 🅂 🐦 A

PENZANCE, Cornwall

Historic market and seaside town of south west Cornwall, ideal for touring the Penwith peninsular, Lands End, The Lizard and nearby St Michael's Mount. *See also Lands End, Marazion.*

TARBERT HOTEL

Clarence Street, Penzance, Cornwall TR18 2NU
(01736) 63758 FAX (01736) 331336
PATTI & JULIAN EVANS

12, 12 en-suite, from £27.50 per person, double occ.
Non-residents welcome. Closed 15th December to 15th January.
£13.00, last orders 8pm.
Fresh fish and seafood from nearby Newlyn. Cornish Crab Soup. Game in season. Rack of Cornish Lamb.

Town centre Georgian listed building (c.1830) with a country house atmosphere. The Tarbert Hotel has a candlelit restaurant, open fires and exposed granite walls which create a warm and welcoming atmosphere.

Follow town by-pass to second roundabout. Take direction 'Hospital/Harbour'. 50 metres after hospital right turn into Clarence Street.

VISA AmEx A

PETERBOROUGH, Cambridgeshire

Rapidly expanding cathedral city on the edge of The Fens. Visit Burghley House, Tallington Lakes, Spalding, The Deepings, and Rutland Water.

CAUDLE HOUSE

43 High Street, Market Deeping, Peterborough, Cambridgeshire PE6 8ED
(01778) 347595 FAX (01778) 348529
CHRIS BOARDMAN & SUE JACKSON

2, 2 en-suite, from £22.50 per person, double occ.
Lunch served. Non-residents welcome. Closed Mondays.
£14.75, last orders 9pm.
Venison. Steak, Kidney and Mushroom Pie. Home-made Desserts.

A listed Georgian town house offering all the comforts of a family home but with every facility and the emphasis firmly on service.

On the A16, Stamford to Spalding road, on the outskirts of Market Deeping.

VISA A

PEWSEY, Wiltshire

On the edge of the Vale of Pewsey and the Wiltshire Downs. Stonehenge and Avebury are closeby as well as many historic houses and gardens.

THE WOODBRIDGE INN

North Newnton, Nr Pewsey, Wiltshire SN9 6JZ
☎ (01980) 630266 FAX (01980) 630266
LOUIS & TERRY VERTESSY

🛏 2, 1 en-suite, from £17.50 per person, double occ.
Lunch served. Non-residents welcome. Closed 25th December.
✗ from £9.50 a la carte, last orders 10.30pm.
🍽 Home cooking, Wiltshire Gammon Ham. Steak and Ale Pie.
Mexican, Indonesian and international dishes.

A 17th century country inn set in four acres of riverside meadow. The inn has an intimate, small restaurant and simple homely accommodation. Good range of bar snacks and excellent reputation for interesting food. Last orders for meals on Sunday evening is 10pm. Pleasant outdoor children's play area. Small meeting room and private dining room available.

✣ 3 miles south of Pewsey on the A345.

VISA 💳 💳 AmEx ⊗ ✓ 🍷 A

PLYMOUTH, Devon

Devon's largest city is also a naval base, shopping and tourist centre. Superb coastal views over Plymouth Sound from The Hoe.

ERMEWOOD HOUSE

Ermington, Ivybridge, Devon PL21 9NS
☎ (01548) 830741
JACK & JENNIFER MELLOR

🛏 12, 12 en-suite, from £30.00 per person, double occ.
Non-residents welcome. Closed Christmas & New Year.
✗ £17.50, last orders 8.30pm.
🍽 Fresh trout from one of the two farms in Ermington village. Range of seafood and shellfish. Devon Lamb. The cooking is prepared by the chef patron.

A grade two listed, Georgian country house hotel, set in open countryside, just outside the village of Ermington, about 8 miles north of Plymouth. The hotel is 20 minutes drive from the ferry terminals. Bedrooms are comfortable but Ermewood House is mostly visited for its welcoming atmosphere and food.

VISA 💳 ⊗ ♿ ✓ ⚓ A

THE DRAKE HOTEL

1/2 Windsor Villas, Lockyer Street, Plymouth, Devon PL1 2QD
☎ (01752) 229730 FAX (01752) 255092
DOUGLAS TILLER

🛏 36, 28 en-suite, from £24.50 per person, double occ.
Lunch served. Non-residents welcome. Closed 22nd December to 1st January.
✗ £12.00, last orders 8pm.
🍽 Fresh seafood.

Two solid Victorian houses, linked to form the hotel, in a quiet yet central location. Good value for money. Weekday last orders are at 9pm.

✣ To Plymouth city centre, left at Theatre Royal, left at traffic lights and then first right.

VISA 💳 💳 AmEx A

POLPERRO, Cornwall

Small, picturesque fishing village close to Looe, historically associated with smuggling. Activities in the surrounding area include shark fishing and visiting National Trust houses. *See also Looe.*

THE CLAREMONT HOTEL

Fore Street, Polperro, Nr Looe, Cornwall PL13 2RG
✆ (01503) 72241 FAX (01503) 72241
G. COUTURIER & N. PEYRIN

🛏 11, 10 en-suite, from £21.50 per person, double occ.
Lunch served. Non-residents welcome. Restaurant closed 6th October to 27th March.
✕ £11.50, last orders 8.30pm.
🍽 French cuisine. Cheese Soup. Steak au Poivre. Duck with Green Pepper Sauce. Scallops Persillees.

A unique, small village hotel with a friendly welcome, fresh and intimate accommodation and a comfortable lounge and restaurant. Good reputation for French cuisine.
VISA ⬛ 🄬 ⊗ ⦂ / 🏊 ⚓ A

PONTYPRIDD, Mid Glamorgan

The fourth largest retail centre in South Wales. An ideal base for business or exploring South Wales.

THE MARKET TAVERN HOTEL

Market Street, Pontypridd, Mid Glamorgan CF37 2ST
✆ (01443) 485331 FAX (01443) 402806
MRS D HOLT

🛏 11, 11 en-suite, from £24.00 per person, double occ.
Lunch served. Non-residents welcome. Closed 26th December to 1st January. Restaurant closed Sunday evening, Monday & Tuesday.
✕ £7.45, last orders 9pm.
🍽 Fresh regional produce.

A traditional Victorian 'pub' exterior. Inside the building was completely renovated in the 1980's to create a comfortable hotel and hostellerie. Pretty bedrooms, attractive first floor formal dining room and busy ground floor bar, offering snacks, light meals and a wide selection of draft beers. Visitors should note that Market Street is pedestrianised between 11am and 4pm, but there is a large public car park only 100 yards from the hotel.

VISA ⬛ ⊗ 🤚 ⦂ / ⚓ A

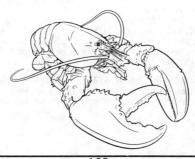

POOLE, Dorset

Poole has a large natural harbour, which has made the town into the boating centre of the south. A perfect base from which to explore Beaulieu Motor Museum, The Lions of Longleat and Hardy's Wessex

🏨 SANDBANKS HOTEL

Banks Road, Sandbanks, Poole, Dorset BH13 7PS
☎ (01202) 707377 FAX (01202) 708885
MR J. G. J. BUTTERWORTH

🛏 105, 105 en-suite, from £45.00 to £52.00 per person, double occ.
Lunch served. Non-residents welcome. Open all year.
🍴 £17.00, last orders 9pm.
🍲 Fresh, locally caught seafood.

Large, family hotel in an excellent location backing onto a sandy beach. All rooms enjoy open sea or harbour views. The hotel offers the complete family holiday service with extensive leisure and relaxation facilities.

VISA 💳 AmEx ⊘ ⌇ / 🍸 🐟 ⑤ C

PORT ISAAC, Cornwall

Picturesque old fishing port, featuring white-washed cottages and narrow alleyways. Visit Tintagel Castle, Lanhydrock House with its famous gardens or any of the magnificent beaches and hidden coves in the area

🏨 HEADLANDS HOTEL

Port Gaverne, Port Isaac, Cornwall PL29 3SH
☎ (01208) 880260 FAX (01208) 880885
CHRIS & ANNA HARRIS

🛏 11, 11 en-suite, from £30.00 per person, double occ.
Lunch served. Non-residents welcome. Open all year.
🍴 £14.50, last orders 9.30pm.
🍲 Local fish and seafood specialities. Grilled Megrim Sole. Chicken with Lobster and Brandy sauce. Locally farmed meat.

One of the most spectacular locations in Cornwall with magnificent sea views from all rooms, overlooking Port Gaverne Cove, only 10 minutes walk from the busy fishing village of Port Isaac. Comfortable, individually styled bedrooms and a cosy lounge with log fire. Guests are assured of a warm cheerful welcome and excellent hospitality.

✤ On cliff top overlooking Port Gaverne, half a mile east of Port Isaac.

VISA 💳 AmEx ⌇ / 🍸 🐟 ⑤ 🦆 A

🏨 OLD SCHOOL HOTEL & RESTAURANT

Port Isaac, Cornwall PL29 3RB
☎ (01208) 880721
MICHAEL WARNER

🛏 14, 14 en-suite, from £16.00 to £39.00 per person, double occ.
Lunch served. Open all year.
🍴 from £15.00 a la carte, last orders 9pm.
🍲 All types of shellfish and seafood. Crab Soup. Grilled King Prawns. Smoked Haddock Pancakes. Grilled Lobster with Garlic Butter. Seafood Omelette. Mariner's Fish Pie.

A sympathetically converted Victorian school house, with a wealth of old beams, standing in the centre of Port Isaac, on the cliff edge, overlooking the harbour. Medieval banquets are offered by the hotel.

VISA 💳 ⊘ ⌇ / 🍸 🐟 🦆 C

THE CORNISH ARMS

Pendoggett, Port Isaac, Cornwall PL30 3HH
☎ (01208) 880263 FAX (01208) 880335
JOHN ROBINSON

🛏 7, 5 en-suite, from £24.00 to £37.00 per person, double occ.
Lunch served. Open all year.
✕ £15.00, last orders 9.30pm.
🍽 Fish and shellfish. Locally caught lobster, scallops and sole.
Tiger Prawns in Garlic Butter. Roast Duck in Brandy. Fillet
Steak stuffed with Smoked Oysters. Cornish Cream Teas.

A sixteenth century, traditional coaching inn. Flagstone floors, log
fires, beamed ceilings and several nooks and crannies give the inn
original atmosphere. The bedrooms are attractively decorated in
pastel shades and chintz fabrics, offering modern comforts,
including satellite television. The bar serves a number of real ales
including the renowned Pendoggett Special Bitter.

VISA 🖃 🔜 AmEx ⊗ ♿ ✓ 🐦 B

PORTSCATHO, Cornwall

Coastal village spreading along the low cliffs of the Roseland peninsula.
Visit the many National Trust properties or walk the south Cornwall
coastal path. Tresillick Gardens and Pendennis Castle are nearby.

ROSELAND HOUSE HOTEL

Rose Vine, Portscatho, Cornwall TR2 5EW
☎ (01872) 580644 FAX (01872) 580801
MR & MRS A. HINDLEY

🛏 16, 16 en-suite, from £25.00 per person, double occ.
Lunch served. Non-residents welcome. Open all year.
✕ £15.50, last orders 8pm.
🍽 Rendezvous of Local Seafish. Scallops in Cream and Mead.
Clotted Cream Pavlova. Local fruits, home-made rolls and cream
teas.

Peaceful and quiet country house hotel, nestling on the cliffs,
above its own private beach in six acres of National Trust gardens.
Superb views across the bay. Very comfortable accommodation
and a friendly warm atmosphere.

VISA 🖃 ⊗ ♿ ✓ 🕏 🏊 A

PORTSMOUTH, Hampshire

The historical centre of Britain's maritime heritage. Visit HMS Victory,
the Mary Rose or the D. Day museum.

THE BEAUFORT HOTEL

71 Festing Road, Southsea, Portsmouth PO4 0NR
☎ (01705) 823707 FAX (01705) 870270
MR & MRS FREEMANTLE

🛏 20, 20 en-suite, from £20.00 to £30.00 per person,
double occ.
Open all year.
✕ from £10.90, last orders 8.30pm.
🍽 Traditional English cooking using fresh local produce.

Beautifully furnished hotel, quietly situated close to the
promenade and canoe lake. Bedrooms offer a high standard of
comfort. Licensed bar and restaurant overlooking garden.
Residents car park.

VISA 🖃 ♿ 🕏 🏊 A

THE WESTFIELD HALL HOTEL
65 Festing Road, Southsea, Portsmouth PO4 0NQ
✆(01705) 826971 FAX (01705) 870200
JOHN & MARGARET DANIELS

🛏 16, 16 en-suite, from £30.00 per person, double occ.
Non-residents welcome. Open all year.
✗ £10.95 to £15.00, last orders 11.30pm.
🍴 Deep Fried Japanese Prawns. Scottish Salmon in Asparagus Sauce. Chicken Breasts in Leek and Stilton Sauce. Hot Chocolate Fudge Cake with Cream. White Ice Cream Bombe. Hot Sticky Banana Gateau with Cream.

A large Victorian detached hotel with comfortably furnished rooms, in a quiet residential area close to the Canoe Lake Rose Gardens.

✢ Follow signs for South Parade Pier, left into St Helens Parade. Festing Road is the 4th road on the left. Westfield Hall is a 100 yards on the right.

VISA 💳 AmEx 🌊 A

POUNDSGATE, Devon
A small Dartmoor village. Superb walking for all ages. Riding. Golf. Racing at Newton Abbot and Haldon. Fishing on the Webburn and Dart. Many archeological remains, gardens and country houses in the region. *See also Ashburton.*

LEUSDON LODGE
Poundsgate, Nr Ashburton, Devon TQ13 7PE
✆(01364) 631304 FAX (01364) 631599
IVOR & MIRANDA RUSSELL

🛏 7, 7 en-suite, from £35.00 per person, double occ.
Non-residents welcome. Closed Christmas.
✗ £21.00, last orders 8.30pm.
🍴 The menu changes daily and is prepared by Miranda Russell using local produce.

150 year old granite house built by Victorian philanthropist and country lover 250 metres above the Dart Valley with stunning views. Totally rural, peaceful and quiet. The hotel is comfortably furnished and has recently been refurbished.

VISA 💳 🚫 🌊 B

PRINCES RISBOROUGH, Buckinghamshire

An old market town with many ancient buildings. Visit nearby Hughenden Manor, West Wycombe House, Cliveden and Waddesdon Manor, alternatively there are many country walks, including The Ridgeway Path. *See also Great Missenden.*

ROSE & CROWN HOTEL

Saunderton, Princes Risborough, Buckinghamshire HP27 9NP
☎ (01844) 345299 FAX (01844) 343140
ROBERT & JOHN WATSON

🛏 17, 14 en-suite, from £28.98 per person, double occ.
Lunch served. Non-residents welcome. Closed 25th to 28th December.
✗ £17.50, last orders 9.15pm.
🍴 Seafood dishes and local game in season. Restaurant menu and bar food available.

A family run Georgian-style country inn, located in the Chiltern Hills. Log fires give a warm welcome in the winter and attractive gardens make it a pleasant summer venue.

✛ Saunderton is 3 miles from Princes Risborough, on the Aylesbury/High Wycombe road, A4010.

VISA 🔳 ⚖ AmEx ⊗ ✓ **B**

PULBOROUGH, West Sussex

A picturesque village overlooking the South Downs. Petworth House (N.T.), Goodwood House and racecourse, Arundel Castle and Pulborough R.S.P.B. reserve are all closeby. The south coast is twenty minutes drive. *See also Ashington, Sutton.*

CHEQUERS HOTEL

Church Place, Pulborough, West Sussex RH20 1AD
☎ (01798) 872486 FAX (01798) 872715
JOHN & ANN SEARANCKE

🛏 11, 10 en-suite, from £36.00 per person, double occ.
Lunch served. Non-residents welcome. Open all year.
✗ £16.50, last orders 8.30pm
🍴 English cooking using fresh local market produce. Home-made soups. Southdown Lamb. Local Seafood. Home-made puddings and desserts. The hotel coffee shop is open all day for light lunches, home-made cakes and biscuits.

Period Queen Anne country house hotel, which has been gracefully refurbished to include a new garden conservatory restaurant. All bedrooms are individually furnished, with modern amenities carefully blended with old world charm and character.

✛ North of the village centre, opposite the church.

VISA 🔳 ⚖ AmEx ⊗ ✓ 🔖 🔖 **B**

REDRUTH, Cornwall

Originally the major tin mining town in Cornwall, Redruth has retained its
heritage. At the heart of Cornwall's tourist industry, there are numerous
activities for everyone.

AVIARY COURT HOTEL

Mary's Well, Illogan, Redruth, Cornwall TR16 4QZ
☎ (01209) 842256 FAX (01209) 843744
THE STUDLEY FAMILY

🛏 6, 6 en-suite, from £29.00 per person, double occ.
Non-residents welcome. Open all year.
✕ £12.00, last orders 8.30pm.
🍴 Local fish and game in season. Cornish dishes, prepared using
local produce.

Aviary Court is a charming 300 year old Cornish country house,
set in two acres of grounds, on the edge of Illogan Woods. Very
friendly, family atmosphere, with a high standard of comfortable
accommodation. For children under 3, please contact the hotel
direct. Lunch served on Sunday.

⊹ From A30 between Redruth & Camborne follow Portreath/Illogan
signs to Alexandra Road and Mary's Well.

VISA 💳 🏧 AmEx ✓ B

REIGATE, Surrey

Old town on the edge of the North Downs, surrounded by beautiful
National Trust countryside. Within easy distance of both Gatwick (20
mins) and Heathrow (40 mins).

BRIDGE HOUSE HOTEL

Reigate Hill, Reigate, Surrey RH2 9RP
☎ (01737) 246801 FAX (01737) 223756
MR O. LANNI

🛏 37, 37 en-suite, from £39.00 per person, double occ.
Lunch served. Non-residents welcome. Open all year.
✕ £19.00, last orders 10.30pm.
🍴 English and French cuisine.

A modern hotel, most rooms have balconies with splendid views
across Surrey and Sussex. A dinner dance is held every Friday
and Saturday night. Conference facilities available.

VISA 💳 🏧 AmEx ⊗ C

CRANLEIGH HOTEL

41 West Street, Reigate, Surrey RH2 9BL
☎ (01737) 223417 FAX (01737) 223734
MR & MRS G. BUSSANDRI

🛏 10, 8 en-suite, from £36.00 per person, double occ.
Closed 24th to 31st December.
✕ £15.00, last orders 9pm.
🍴 International cuisine.

Victorian family run hotel constructed around 1870. Comfortable
accommodation and a quiet, homely atmosphere.

VISA 💳 🏧 AmEx ⊗ 🏊 ✓ B

RICHMOND, North Yorkshire

Interesting market town on the banks of the river Swale. There is a Norman castle, started in 1071 by Alan Rufus, a nephew of William the Conqueror, which boasts one of the best preserved Norman keeps in Britain.

🏠🏠 THE KINGS HEAD HOTEL

Market Place, Richmond, North Yorkshire DL10 4HS
☎ (01748) 850220 FAX (01748) 850635
LESLEY & PHILIP DAVIES

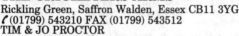

🛏 28, 28 en-suite, from £41.00 per person, double occ.
Lunch served. Non-residents welcome. Open all year.
✗ £17.95, last orders 9.15pm.
🍽 Imaginative traditional Yorkshire cooking using the best of local produce.

This Georgian hotel dominates Richmond's cobbled market square and although originally built as a private house, has been trading as a coaching inn since the early 1700's. Furnished with antiques, the hotel has now been completely refurbished and offers a sympathetic blend of old and new.

✛ Take A6108 from Scotch Corner, through Skelby village for 4 miles.
VISA 💳 💷 AmEx ⊗ ♿ ✓ 🕓 ⚜ C

RICKLING GREEN, Essex

Picturesque village on the Herts/Essex border. Close to Stansted Airport and Cambridge. Visit Audley End House or the Imperial War Museum at Duxford. *See also Saffron Walden.*

🏠🏠 THE CRICKETERS ARMS

Rickling Green, Saffron Walden, Essex CB11 3YG
☎ (01799) 543210 FAX (01799) 543512
TIM & JO PROCTOR

🛏 7, 7 en-suite, from £25.00 per person, double occ.
Lunch served. Non-residents Welcome. Open all year
✗ from £15.50-£17.50, last orders 10pm
🍽 Mussels and offal dishes. Braised Hearts. Liver and Bacon. Kidneys. Ox-Tail.

Large village inn, standing beside the cricket green where the highest innings was recorded for a single day's play. Comfortable accommodation in a tranquil setting. Real ales are served in the both Victorian style public bar and in the traditional, oak beamed saloon bar which is warmed by a roaring log fire. Functions and dinner dances catered for. Dogs by prior arrangement only. On Sunday's last orders for food are at 9.30pm.

✛ 2 miles north of Stansted Mount Fitchet, just off the B1383 at Quendon.

VISA 💳 💷 ⊗ ✓ 🕓 ⚜ A

RINGWOOD, Hampshire

On the edge of the New Forest, the market town of Ringwood is a good centre for riding and walking holidays. Visit Broadlands, Beaulieu Abbey and Museum, Bournemouth and Southampton.

MOORTOWN LODGE HOTEL AND RESTAURANT

244 Christchurch Rd., Ringwood, Hampshire BH24 3AS
✆ (01425) 471404 FAX (01425) 476052
JILLY & BOB BURROWS - JONES

🛏 6, 5 en-suite, from £32.50 per person, double occ.
Non-residents welcome. Closed 24th December to mid January.
✕ from £14.95, last orders 8.15pm.
🍽 A gourmet menu of three or four courses, prepared by the chef patronne, is served nightly. High quality, fresh ingredients are prepared with French influence. Lamb in a Pastry Case. Fillet of Pork in Plum Sauce.

Moortown Lodge is a charming Georgian house dating back to the 1760's and was originally the fishing lodge which formed part of the Gladstone family estate. Each room, including the four poster, is individually decorated to a high standard. The restaurant has a justified high reputation for its food. Moortown Lodge offers a friendly and relaxed atmosphere. French and Spanish spoken.

✛ Approximately 1.5 miles south of Ringwood town centre on the B3347.
VISA 💳 AmEx ⊗ ♿ ✓ 🚭 B

RIPON, North Yorkshire

Attractive Dales market town. The Bull Inn is situated in West Tanfield, a village 6 miles north of Ripon, which dates from the 10th century. Visit the Marmion Tower, riverside gardens or explore one of the nearby historic houses and gardens.

THE BULL INN & RESTAURANT

Church Street, West Tanfield, Ripon, North Yorkshire HG4 5JQ
✆ (01677) 470678 FAX (01677) 470678
MR ALLARD

🛏 5, 5 en-suite, from £27.50 per person, double occ.
Lunch served.Non-residents welcome. Open all year.
✕ £13.95, last orders 10pm.
🍽 Regional Yorkshire fare. Fresh estate game and crayfish when in season. Yorkshire cheeseboard. Both bar snack and restaurant menus are available.

The Bull Inn dates from the 17th century and was originally a ferryman's cottage on the Ure, part of the Tanfield Estate. It has been recently modernised. The bar offers a selection of hand pulled beers. Fishing breaks can be arranged. Dogs will only be accommodated by prior arrangement.

VISA 💳 AmEx ⊗ 🎱 ✓ 🚭 🐕 A

ROSEDALE ABBEY, North Yorkshire

A picturesque village built around the Cistecian nunnery dating from the reign of Henry II. Also visit nearby Rievaulx Abbey, Castle Howard, York and Whitby. *See also Appleton le Moors.*

THE MILBURN ARMS HOTEL

Rosedale Abbey, Pickering, North Yorkshire YO18 8RA
✆ (01751) 417312 FAX (01751) 417312
TERRY & JOAN BENTLEY

🛏 11, 11 en-suite, from £35.00 per person, double occ.
Lunch served. Non-residents welcome. Closed 25th December.
✗ from £17.50 a la carte, last orders 9.15pm.
🍽 Local game and fish in season.

Historic 17th century inn, full of character, nestling in a conservation village in the heart of the North Yorkshire National Park.

✢ Take A170 west from Pickering, after 3 miles turn right and follow signs to Rosedale.
VISA 🔳 ⒉ ⊘ ✓ 🚭 ⚓ **B**

ROSS ON WYE, Herefordshire

Attractive market town close to the Royal Forest of Dean, Wye Valley and Hereford.

GLEWSTONE COURT

Glewstone, Ross on Wye, Herefordshire HR9 6AW
✆ (01989) 770367 FAX (01989) 770282
WILLIAM & CHRISTINE REEVE - TUCKER

🛏 7, 7 en-suite, from £39.00 per person, double occ.
Lunch served. Non-residents welcome. Closed 25th to 27th December.
✗ £20.00, last orders 9.30pm.
🍽 Wye salmon, Herefordshire beef, fruit and vegetables from the Golden Valley. Vegetarians always catered for.

A listed Georgian hotel set amongst fruit orchards and three acres of grounds. The hotel offers a relaxed friendly atmosphere in warm but elegant surroundings.

VISA 🔳 ⊘ ♿ ✓ 🚭 ⚓ **C**

PETERSTOW COUNTRY HOUSE

Peterstow, Ross on Wye, Herefordshire HR9 6LB
✆ (01989) 562826 FAX (01989) 567264
JEANNE & MIKE DENNE

🛏 9, 9 en-suite, from £25.00 per person, double occ.
Lunch served. Non-residents welcome. Open all year.
✗ from £19.50, last orders 9pm.
🍽 Local wild game, Welsh lamb, Welsh cheese and Herefordshire beef. Scallops and Wild Mushrooms scented with Thyme and Rosemary. Fillet of Brill on Tarragon Vinegar Butter. Chocolate Harlequin, a light and dark chocolate mousse on nutmeg cream.

Peterstow Country House stands in twenty eight acres of woodlands and pastures. It has a warm and friendly atmosphere and all rooms are decorated in an individual style. This Georgian rectory was opened as an hotel in 1989 following loving restoration by its owners. For children, please contact the hotel directly.

VISA 🔳 ⒉ AmEx ⊘ ♿ ✓ 🚭 **A**

Ross on Wye continued overleaf...

SUNNYMOUNT HOTEL

Ryefield Road, Ross on Wye, Herefordshire HR9 5LU
☎ (01989) 563880
GEOFF & PEGGY WILLIAMS

🛏 6, 6 en-suite, from £25.00 per person, double occ.
Closed 25th & 26th December.
✗ £15.00, last orders 8pm.
🍽 Home-made Cream of Mushroom Soup. Pork Chops in Cider with Prunes and Apricots. Welsh Lamb. Herefordshire Beef. Chocolate Meringue Glace. Home-grown and local vegetables.

A turreted Edwardian house, built in 1908, which is simply furnished but very comfortable. A welcoming friendly atmosphere.

✦ On A40 from Gloucester go straight ahead at roundabout, first turning right after garage.

VISA 🔲 AmEx ⌁ ⑤ A

ROWSLEY, Derbyshire

Situated in the narrow valley of the river Derwent, an ideal base for exploring Derbyshire's beautiful countryside and scenery. Chatsworth House, Haddon Hall and Hardwick Hall.

EAST LODGE COUNTRY HOUSE HOTEL

Rowsley, Matlock, Derbyshire DE4 2EF
☎ (01629) 734474 FAX (01629) 733949
JOHN & ANGELA BEECROFT

🛏 14, 14 en-suite, from £45.00 per person, double occ.
Lunch served. Non-residents welcome. Open all year.
✗ £19.50, last orders 8.30pm.
🍽 Fresh local game in season. Derbyshire lamb, local trout. Bakewell Tart. Garden produce and herbs.

Formerly a lodge to Haddon Hall, East Lodge has been converted into a warm and friendly country house hotel. Individual decor in each bedroom and a wealth of period furnishings and antiques.

VISA 🔲 AmEx ⌁ ⑤ C

RUGBY, Warwickshire

The busy market town of Rugby is home to the famous boys school. Ashby St Ledgers, four miles away, was the home of the gunpowder plot. Close to Althorp and Stanford Hall. *See also Daventry, Weedon.*

THE OLDE COACH HOUSE INN

Ashby St Ledgers, Nr Rugby, Warwickshire CV23 8UN
☎ (01788) 890349 FAX (01788) 891922
BRIAN & PHILIPPA MC CABE

🛏 6, 6 en-suite, from £26.00 per person, double occ.
Lunch served. Non-residents welcome. Closed 25th December.
✗ from £4.00 a la carte, last orders 9.30pm.
🍴 English and French style cuisine. Wide selection of traditional real ales and wines are available to compliment the home cooking. Daily specials.

This is a traditional English coaching inn with a large garden, car park and meeting facilities. Barbecues in the summer and a large open fire in the winter. A homely atmosphere.

✤ On the A361 Daventry to Rugby road, 3 miles from junction 18 of the M1.
VISA 💳 AmEx ⊗ ✓ ⟁ A

RYE, East Sussex

Picturesque town with winding cobbled streets noted for its church and antique shops. Sissinghurst Castle, Bodiam Castle and Camber Sands are close by. *See also Winchelsea.*

FLACKLEY ASH HOTEL

London Road, Rye, East Sussex TN31 6YH
☎ (01797) 230651 FAX (01797) 230510
CLIVE & JEANIE BENNETT

🛏 34, 34 en-suite, from £49.00 per person, double occ.
Lunch served. Non-residents welcome. Open all year.
✗ £18.95, last orders 9.30pm.
🍴 Fresh Rye Bay fish and seafood, Scotch beef, Romney lamb, fresh vegetables and herbs.

A Georgian country house hotel (c.1770) set in five acres of beautiful grounds. Indoor swimming pool and leisure centre. Exceptional standard of bedroom comfort and furnishings.

VISA 💳 🏊 AmEx ⊗ ≋ ✓ Ⓢ ⟁ C

THE OLD VICARAGE HOTEL

15 East Street, Rye, East Sussex TN31 7JY
☎ (01797) 225131 FAX (01797) 225131
MRS SARAH FOSTER

🛏 4, 4 en-suite, from £32.00 per person, double occ.
Non-residents welcome. Closed January.
✗ £12.50, last orders 9pm.
🍴 Feuilletes of Seafood. Rye Bay Plaice with Prawns. Escalope of Pork in a Honey and Ginger Sauce.

Traditional Queen Anne town house hotel, attractively furnished in period style. The restaurant enjoys outstanding views over the river Rother and Romney Marsh. Very spacious bedrooms, each with their own personality and style.

VISA 💳 AmEx ✓ ⟁ B

SAFFRON WALDEN, Essex

A market town with stunning local church, St. Marys, noted for its large carvings, roof and brasses. There is a maze on the common and, just outside the town, is Audley End House. Close to the Imperial War Museum at Duxford, Linton Zoo and Stansted. *See also Rickling Green.*

QUEENS HEAD INN

Littlebury, Nr Saffron Walden, Essex CB11 4TD
✆ (01799) 522251 FAX (01799) 513522
JEREMY & DEBORAH O' GORMAN

6, 6 en-suite, from £17.00 per person, double occ.
Lunch served. Non-residents welcome. Room only service over the Christmas period.
✗ from £9.75, last orders 9pm.
A daily changing menu, prepared from fresh ingredients. Avocado baked with Stilton Butter. Melon served on a Garden Damson Coulis. Home-made soups. Pike baked with Herbs from the Garden. Salmon in Leek and Green Peppercorn. Pork with Apples and Cider.

This 600 year old coaching inn has bags of character and charm, exposed original beams, inglenook fireplaces and quarry tiles. Some of the bedroom furniture came from the New York Waldorf Astoria. There is an enclosed childrens' play area and walled beer garden, overlooking a small paddock where a lugubrious wolfhound pretends to be a horse!

In centre of Littlebury village.

VISA A

SALISBURY, Wiltshire

A beautiful medieval city, dominated by the cathedral which boasts the tallest spire in England. Visit Old Sarum and Stonehenge. *See also Shaftesbury, Hindon.*

STRATFORD LODGE HOTEL

4 Park Lane, Castle Road, Salisbury, Wiltshire SP1 3NP
✆ (01722) 325177 FAX (01722) 412699
JILL BAYLY

8, 8 en-suite, from £25.00 per person, double occ.
Lunch served. Non-residents welcome. Closed Christmas.
✗ £16.00, last orders 9.00pm.
Imaginative, daily changing menu prepared from fresh ingredients. Dinner commences with a welcome glass of sherry. Poole Crab Cakes with Herb Mayonnaise. Leek and Applewood Cheddar Roulade. Guinea Fowl Supreme with Peach Brandy. Local Game Casserolled with Port and Orange.

An elegant Victorian town house that has been stylishly furnished with antiques, attractive fabrics and flowers. A friendly, small hotel at the end of a quiet lane overlooking a large park, yet conveniently situated only a few minutes from the centre of Salisbury.

VISA A

THE COACH & HORSES

39 Winchester Street, Salisbury, Wiltshire SP1 1HG
☎ (01722) 336254 FAX (01722) 414319
MARTIN & ANGIE COOPER

🛏 2, 2 en-suite, from £24.75 per person, double occ.
Lunch served. Non-residents welcome. Closed Christmas Day.
✗ £10.00-£17.00 a la carte, last orders 10pm.
🍽 Fresh and preserved salmon, local goats' cheese and ham.
Stuffed Mushrooms in Pastry. 'Bakes', Chicken breasts in a
selection of sauces. Home-made desserts.

This is the oldest inn in Salisbury. The building has been totally
refurbished with modern facilities and comforts. A friendly
hostelry. Close to local fitness centre and facilities for tennis,
swimming, gliding and flying.

VISA 🆑 ⊗ ₺ ✓ 🕭 **A**

SANDWICH, Kent

An ancient estuary port between Deal and Ramsgate, ideally located for
the cross channel ferrys. Dover, Richborough and Walmer Castles are
closeby as well as many local vineyards and historic houses.

THE BELL HOTEL

The Quay, Sandwich, Kent CT13 9EF
☎ (01304) 613388 FAX (01304) 615308
MICHAEL TURNER

🛏 29, 29 en-suite, from £42.50 per person, double occ.
Lunch served. Non-residents welcome. Open all year.
✗ £15.00, last orders 9.15pm.
🍽 Local fresh fish, Sussex and Romney lamb. International
speciality nights. Magret de Canard.

A 17th century listed building with Victorian additions which
overlooks the ancient quay. The hotel has been traditionally
refurbished with many antiques to provide a relaxing and friendly
atmosphere. The hotel owns its own 27 hole golf course and offers
access to the two nearby championship links.

VISA 🆑 ⊗ ₺ ✓ 🕭 ⊲ **C**

SARK, Channel Islands

An ancient, feudal and traffic free island untouched by the 20th century.
Spectacular scenery. *See also Jersey,Guernsey.*

DIXCART HOTEL

Isle of Sark, Channel Islands GY9 0SD
☎ (01481) 832015 FAX (01481) 832164
JONATHAN & JACQUELINE BRANNAM

🛏 15, 15 en-suite, from £30.00 to £48.00 per person, double occ.
Lunch served. Non-residents welcome. Open all year.
✗ £14.00 (inc in room rate), last orders 9.30pm.
🍽 Fresh fish and shellfish, lobster, crab, Sark lamb. Local Queen
Scallops with Basil in Puff Pastry and a Pernod Sauce. Noisettes
of Sark Lamb in Kidney and Sherry Sauce. Trio of Poultry, Duck,
Pheasant and Guinea Fowl with Ginger & Orange Sauce.

Sark's oldest hotel, built mainly out of stone. Some parts of the
building date back to the 16th century. Gentle hospitality,
comfortable, quite, relaxing environment.

VISA 🆑 ⚊ AmEx ⊗ ₺ ≋ 🕭 ⊲ **B**

SARRE, Kent

Beautiful Kent village, midway between Margate, Ramsgate, Broadstairs and Canterbury. Several excellent local golf courses.

THE CROWN INN

Sarre, Nr Birchington, Thanet, Kent CT7 0LF
✆ (01843) 847808 FAX (01843) 847914
HENRIQUE & ANNA DA SILVA

🛏 12, 12 en-suite, from £28.25 per person, double occ.
Lunch served. Non-residents welcome. Open all year.
✗ £12.00 - £15.00, last orders 10pm.
🍴 Freshly prepared food, featuring Kentish regional specialities.

This ancient traditional inn has accommodated many famous customers, including Charles Dickens and Rudyard Kipling. Known as 'The Cherry Brandy House' as it still blends a unique cherry brandy, prepared to a secret 17th century recipe. Guests can expect comfortable, accommodation, a warm welcome and an excellent selection of locally brewed ales.

VISA 🔲 ⊗&. / 🐟 🐟 A

SAUNDERSFOOT, Dyfed

Popular seaside resort inside the Pembrokeshire Coast National Park. Picturesque harbour and safe sandy beach. Good sailing and sea fishing.

ST BRIDES HOTEL

Saundersfoot, Dyfed, SA69 9NH
✆ (01834) 812304 FAX (01834) 813303
IAN BELL

🛏 45, 45 en-suite, from £45.00 per person, double occ.
Lunch served. Non-residents welcome. Closed 1st to 14th January.
✗ £17.50, last orders 9.15pm.
🍴 Locally caught fish. Sewin, local crabs and lobsters.

Tudor style hotel with stunning views across Saundersfoot Bay from the panoramic restaurant. Extremely high level of comfort in the hotel and well maintained gardens.

✛ 300 yards from centre of Saundersfoot, on Tenby road.

VISA 🔲 🔳 AmEx ⊗& / 🐟 🐟 C

SCARBOROUGH, North Yorkshire

Popular east coast seaside resort, formerly a spa town. Fine sandy beaches and town gardens. See the castle ruins which date back to 1100.

WREA HEAD COUNTRY HOUSE

Scalby, Scarborough, North Yorkshire YO13 0PB
✆ (01723) 378211 FAX (01723) 371780
THE TURNER FAMILY

🛏 21, 21 en-suite, from £47.50 per person, double occ.
Lunch served. Non-residents welcome. Open all year.
✗ £19.95, last orders 9.30pm.
🍴 International cuisine. Local fish and game in season.

An elegant Victorian country house, set in fourteen acres of gardens and woodland, with a welcoming, friendly atmosphere. The whole house is beautifully decorated and furnished. Guests can relax in the Oak panelled lounge and library. The house is home to a fine collection of Russel Flint paintings. Dogs are welcome by prior arrangement.

VISA 🔲 🔳 AmEx ⊗& ✎ / 🐟 C

SCOTCH CORNER, North Yorkshire

A famous milestone at the junction of the A1 and A66 near Richmond. Good central location for visiting the Yorkshire Dales and surrounding areas.

🏨🏨 VINTAGE HOTEL & RESTAURANT

Scotch Corner, Richmond, North Yorkshire DL10 6NP
☎ (01748) 824424
PETER & NANCY FOTHERGILL

🛏 8, 5 en-suite, from £25.00 per person, double occ.
Lunch served. Non-residents welcome. Open all year.
✗ from £15.00 a la carte, last orders 9.15pm.
🍽 English and international cuisine with a French influence. Duckling in Orange Sauce. Bar lunches and suppers available.

A comfortable roadside hotel, with excellent accommodation, overlooking the open countryside. A rustic bar with a friendly atmosphere. A good stop off point if travelling north or when visiting the Dales.

✢ Leave A1 at Scotch Corner, take A66 towards Penrith, hotel 200 metres on the left.
VISA 🔲 AmEx ⊗ ✓ A

SEAVIEW, Isle of Wight

A small, unspoilt fishing and sailing village four miles East of Ryde, within easy distance of all the island's historical monuments, Osborne House, Carisbrooke Castle, Tennyson Down. *See also Ventnor.*

🏨🏨🏨 THE SEAVIEW HOTEL

Seaview, Isle of Wight PO34 5EX
☎ (01983) 612711 FAX (01983) 613729
NICK & NICOLA HAYWARD

🛏 16, 16 en-suite, from £30.00 per person, double occ.
Lunch served. Non-residents welcome. Open all year.
✗ £17.85, last orders 9.30pm.
🍽 Local island produce, especially shellfish, fish, garlic, vegetables, asparagus, fruit and wine. Warm Pigeon Breast and Mushroom Salad with Pine Kernels and Walnut Oil Dressing. Hot Crab Ramekin. Fillet of Beef stuffed with Braised Chicory.

A bayfronted Victorian hotel retaining all of its original charm and character. The Seaview has been tastefully refurbished and decorated. Each room is individually furnished with antiques. The reputation of the restaurant is outstanding.

VISA 🔲 💳 AmEx ⊗ ♿ ✓ 🍷🥂🐟 C

SELSEY, West Sussex

Set on unspoilt coastline, amidst nature and wildlife reserves, yet just ten minutes from the bustling, historic city of Chichester.

ST ANDREWS LODGE

Chichester Road, Selsey, West Sussex PO20 0LX
☎ (01243) 606899 FAX (01243) 606899
VALMA KENNEDY

🛏 8, 8 en-suite, from £20.00 per person, double occ.
Non-residents welcome. Closed Christmas.
✗ From £7.50, last orders 8pm.
🍴 Traditional English home cooking.

A friendly, relaxed atmosphere at this family run hotel. Comfortable furnishings, a large lounge and gardens.

⊹ 7 miles south of Chichester. Entrance of Selsey Village on right hand side just before the Church.
⊗ ♿ ✓ 🄂 🔄 A

SHAFTESBURY, Dorset

Shaftesbury is a hilltop town. The ancient and cobbled Gold Hill is one of the most attractive in Dorset. Visit the small museum, with it's famous collection of buttons and Stonehenge. *See also Salisbury.*

THE COPPLERIDGE INN ✗

Motcombe, Shaftesbury, Dorset SP7 9HW
☎ (01747) 851980 FAX (01747) 851858
CHRIS GOODINGS

🛏 10, 10 en-suite, from £29.50 per person, double occ.
Lunch served. Non-residents welcome. Open all year.
✗ £9.00 - £20.00, last orders 10.30pm.
🍴 Game dishes. Poole fish and shellfish. Chicken dishes.

A converted 17th century stone farmhouse set in 15 acres of meadow and woodland. All rooms overlook the countryside.

⊹ From Shaftesbury follow the road to Gillingham. Fifty yards after passing under the flyover turn-right to Motcombe. Drive through village. At the top of hill turn left to Mere, then left after hotel sign, hotel twenty five yards on the left.
VISA 🄂 AmEx ⊗ ♿ ✎ ✓ 🄂 🄂 🔄 A

THE SUNRIDGE HOTEL

Bleke Street, Shaftsbury, Dorset SP7 8AW
☎ (01747) 853130
PAUL & JENNY WHITEMAN

🛏 10, 10 en-suite, from £27.50 per person, double occ.
Non-residents welcome. Open all year.
✗ from £12.00 a la carte, last orders 9pm.
🍴 Traditional home cooked favourites together with unusual dishes, served with fresh vegetables.

A friendly, family run hotel with a comfortable and cosy atmosphere. All the rooms are tastefully furnished including the elegant restaurant and bar. The hotel also offers a heated indoor swimming pool and sauna. Car parking available.

VISA 🄂 🄂 AmEx ⊗ ♿ 🏊 ✓ A

SHEPTON MALLET, Somerset

An historic market town nestling beneath the Mendips, originally thrived on the wool trade but is now famous for its cider. Wells, Bath, Glastonbury, Cheddar Gorge, Longleat and Stourhead are all closeby.

🔖🔖 BOWLISH HOUSE RESTAURANT

Wells Road, Shepton Mallet, Somerset BA4 5JD
☎ (01749) 342022 FAX (01749) 342022
BOB & LINDA MORLEY

🛏 3, 3 en-suite, from £27.50 per person, double occ.
Open all year.
✕ £22.50, last orders 9.30pm.
🍴 A menu with a strong emphasis on regional dishes using fresh local ingredients and herbs. Local game in season, fresh seafood and river fish as available.

An elegant Georgian building on the edge of the Mendip Hills, Bowlish House is an excellent restaurant with three bedrooms. Lunches are available by prior appointment.

VISA 💳 ⊗ ✓ ⬠ A

SHERBORNE, Dorset

Historic country town dating from Roman times now famous for the fine Abbey, two castles and several "Public" schools. A wealth of National Trust properties are nearby Yeovilton Fleet Air Arm Museum and Wincanton Race Course are closeby.

🔖🔖 THE PHEASANTS RESTAURANT WITH ROOMS

24 Greenhill, Sherborne, Dorset DT9 4EW
☎ (01935) 815252 FAX (01935) 815252
ANDREW & MICHELLE OVERHILL

🛏 4, 4 en-suite, from £25.00 per person, double occ.
Lunch served. Non-residents welcome. Closed two weeks in January. Restaurant closed on Monday, except for residents.
✕ £20.00, last orders 9.45pm.
🍴 Pigeon with Foie Gras. Smoked Pork with an Apple Confit. Calves Liver with Maderia Mango. Turbot with a Herb Crust. Banana and Coconut Russe.

An attractively refurbished, substantial stone building, offering comfortable accommodation and excellent cuisine. Functions and small meetings catered for. Special Cuisine evenings occur monthly.

✤ On the A30 Salisbury to Exeter road, at the top of the town's High Street.

VISA 💳 ⊗ ✓ A

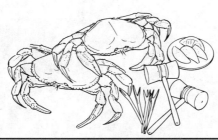

SHIPSTON-ON-STOUR, Warwickshire

A small village situated on the edge of the Ilmington Hills. Visit Upton House, Stratford-upon-Avon, Warwick Castle, Hidcote, Kiftsgate, Batsford, Brook Cottage, Sezincote, Whichford Pottery and Blenheim Palace.

☖ BLACKWELL GRANGE

Blackwell, Shipston-on-Stour, Warwickshire CV36 4PF
✆ (01608) 682357 FAX (01608) 682357
THE VERNON-MILLER FAMILY

🛏 3, 3 en-suite, from £26.00 per person, double occ.
Non-residents welcome. Open all year.
✕ £15.50, last orders 9pm.
🍴 Traditional English cooking using fresh local produce. Leg of Lamb. Home-grown vegetables. Damson Ice-cream. Meringues. Guests are welcome to bring their own wine.

Early 17th century stone farmhouse on the edge of the village, overlooking an attractive garden and surrounding countryside. Stone-flagged dining-room with inglenook fireplace. The sitting-room has a log fire and deep sofas to sink into and relax.

✛ Entering Blackwell village (from Stratford) take right fork, through village, entrance is just beyond thatched barn (on right).

⊗ � ✓ ⇪ A

SHREWSBURY, Shropshire

A fine example of a Medieval and Tudor town with strong historical links. In the beautiful county of Shropshire, with rolling hills, picturesque valleys and the Shropshire Plain.

☖☖ SYDNEY HOUSE HOTEL

Coton Crescent, Coton Hill, Shrewsbury, Shropshire SY1 2LJ
✆ (01743) 354681 FAX (01743) 354681
TERENCE & PAULINE HYDE

🛏 7, 4 en-suite, from from £21.00 to £30.00 per person, double occ.
Non-residents welcome. Closed 24th December to 1st January.
✕ £8.50 to £12.00, last orders 8pm.
🍴 Melon with Parma Ham. Herrings in a light Mustard Sauce. Lamb Shrewsbury. Fillet of Salmon with Cucumber and Dill. Chicken Breast in Orange and Cream. Italian Stuffed Peach. Pauline's Bread and Butter Pudding.

A traditional Edwardian town house which enjoys all the comforts of a family home.

VISA 🔳 AmEx � ✓ 🌑 Ⓢ A

SITTINGBOURNE, Kent

The centre of the paper making industry. Surrounded by delightful villages and orchards. Close to Canterbury, Leeds Castle, Hever Castle and coastal towns and ports. Only 1 hour by train to London.

HEMPSTEAD HOUSE   ✗ ✗ ✗

London Road, Bapchild, Sittingbourne, Kent ME9 9PP
☎ (01795) 428020 FAX (01795) 428020
MANDY & HENRY HOLDSTOCK

🛏 7, 7 en-suite, from £31.00 per person, double occ.
Lunch served. Non-residents Welcome. Open all year.
✗ £15.00, last orders 9pm.
▯ English and continental cuisine, using fresh meat and fish. Home-grown vegetables feature here, and special diets are catered for. Private functions, including conferences, weddings and parties of all sizes take place within the spacious reception rooms and grounds.

An exclusive, private, Victorian country house hotel set in three acres of beautifully landscaped gardens. The accommodation is spacious and luxurious. A friendly atmosphere and exceptionally warm hospitality, extended to all.

✦ 1.5 miles east of Sittingbourne on the A2 towards Canterbury.

VISA 💳 💳 AmEx ⊗ ⇘ ≏ ⬡ A

SKIPTON, Yorkshire

A pleasant market town with a farming community atmosphere at the gateway to the Dales. Visit Harewood House, Skipton Castle, Castle Howard and York.

THE RED LION HOTEL   ✗

Burnsall, Nr Skipton, Yorkshire BD23 6BU
☎ (01756) 720204 FAX (01756) 720292
ELIZABETH GRAYSHON

🛏 11, 11 en-suite, from £34.00 per person, double occ.
Lunch served. Non-residents welcome. Open all year.
✗ £16.95, last orders 9.30pm.
▯ Home-made Soup. Locally made Black Pudding coated in Breadcrumbs, deep-fried and served with Mustard Sauce. Local Chicken Breast stuffed with Blue Wensleydale Cheese with a Leek and Tomato Sauce. Sticky Toffee Pudding with Caramel Sauce. A Light Lemon Tarte with Raspberry Coulis.

A 16th century ferryman's inn on the banks of the River Wharfe with beamed ceilings, log fires and antiques. Bedrooms are traditionally furnished, many with antiques and most have wonderful views of the river and fells.

✦ On the B6160 between Bolton Abbey and Grassington.

VISA 💳 ⊗ ⇘ ✓ ⬡ B

SOUTHAMPTON, Hampshire

One of Britain's leading seaports. Visit Beaulieu Motor Museum at Broadlands the home of Lord Mountbatten.

NIRVANA HOTEL

384-386 Winchester Road, Bassett, Southampton, Hampshire SO16 7DH
☎ (01703) 790087 FAX (01703) 790575
EILEEN & DOUGLAS DAWSON

🛏 10, 7 en-suite, from £22.00 per person, double occ.
Lunch served. Open all year.
✕ £11.95, last orders 8.45pm.
🍴 King Prawns in a Garlic Dip. Home-made Pate. Chicken in Marsala, Tomatoes and Brandy. Venison. Boeuf Bourguinonne. Local Rainbow Trout. Home-made sweets.

A superior town house with attractive Tudor bar and excellent decor with a warm friendly atmosphere. Good parking facilities.

⚜ Follow M3 to A33, keep in right hand lane and take slip road to A33 proceed for about half a mile to a mile, straight over the roundabout and at the next roundabout turn right and Nirvana Hotel will be half a mile on the right hand side.

VISA ▨ AmEx ✓ ⊕ A

SOUTHPORT, Merseyside

A resort noted for its gardens and long sandy beaches. Visit Atkinson Art Gallery and the Transport Museum or play one of the six local championship golf courses.

CRIMOND HOTEL

28 Knowsley Road, Southport, Merseyside PR9 0HN
☎ (01704) 536456 FAX (01704) 548643
GEOFF & PAT RANDLE

🛏 12, 12 en-suite, from £29.50 per person, double occ.
Lunch served. Non-residents welcome. Open all year.
✕ £12.00, last orders 8.30pm.
🍴 Melon in Port. Mushrooms sauted in Garlic Butter and Cream. Poached Halibut in a Prawn Sauce. Northern Lamb Chops glazed with a Redcurrant Sauce. Pork Chops casseroled in Cider. Aunty Needy's Special Fruit Meringue Nests.

A Victorian property set in the residential district of Southport. The bedrooms are comfortably furnished. There is an indoor swimming pool, jacuzzi, and sauna.

⚜ Knowsley Road runs parallel to the Promenade, close to the golf course.

VISA ▨ 💷 AmEx ⌇ ✓ 🥄🍴 Ⓢ⊕ B

ST AGNES, Cornwall

Small town on the north Cornish coast surrounded by magnificent coastal scenery and superb walks. Wide sandy beaches and coves, many NT houses and gardens. Good central base for exploring all Cornwall.

ROSE-IN-VALE COUNTRY HOUSE HOTEL

Mithian, St Agnes, Cornwall TR5 0QD
((01872) 552202 FAX (01872) 552700
TONY & VANDA ARTHUR

🛏 17, 17 en-suite, from £43.00 per person, double occ.
Lunch served. Non-residents welcome. Closed January & February.
✗ from £15.95, last orders 8.30pm
🍴 Fresh Cornish produce, prepared with a French influence. Vegetables from the family farm. Local seafood. Gratin de Crabe au Pamplemousse. Langoustines. Fish from Newlyn, Cornish beef, vegetarian dishes.

A Georgian country house, set in its own secluded valley and 11 acres of gardens, woods and pasture. The house has recently been upgraded and refurbished. A peaceful, relaxing atmosphere.

✦ Take B3284 to Perranporth off A30. Cross A3075, hotel is third turning on the left.

VISA 💳 💳 AmEx ⊗ ♿ 🏊 ✓ 🚭 ⟡ C

ST ALBANS, Hertfordshire

A town dating from Roman times, just 15 minutes from central London by train.

ARDMORE HOUSE HOTEL

54 Lemsford Road, St Albans, Hertfordshire AL1 3PR
((01727) 859313 FAX (01727) 859313
TOM McGORRIAN

🛏 23, 23 en-suite, from £28.20 per person, double occ.
Open all year.
✗ from £9.00, last orders 8.30pm.
🍴 Traditional English cuisine. Pork Olde Worcester, pork marinated in cider with apple slices and nut dumplings.

Large Edwardian building close to the centre of St Albans which has recently been completely refurbished.

VISA 💳 💳 ⊗ ✓ ⟡ A B

ST DAVIDS, Pembrokeshire

Historic cathedral city in the heart of the Pembrokeshire National Park. Many beaches and coastal walks, as well as interesting ancient monuments to be discovered.

WARPOOL COURT HOTEL

St Davids, Pembrokeshire, SA62 6BN
✆ (01437) 720300 FAX (01437) 720676
PETER TRIER

🛏 25, 25 en-suite, from £60.00 per person, double occ.
Lunch served. Non-residents Welcome. Closed January.
✖ £22.00, last orders 9.15pm.
🍽 Local produce is used wherever possible. Welsh lamb and beef. Fresh seafood daily, including crab, lobster, sewin and sea bass. Welsh cheeses are purchased from local farms. Salmon is smoked on the premises.

Victorian country house hotel in secluded peaceful gardens, with spectacular sea views. Chef, Mark Strangward, makes a particular feature of his reliance on local suppliers, his cuisine has become an integral part of any stay at Warpool Court.

✚ From Cross Square in St Davids, bear left between Cartref Restaurant and Midland Bank. Follow hotel signs.

VISA ◼ 💳 AmEx ⬦ 🔍 S ⬦ C

ST IVES, Cornwall

A charming old fishing port, popular with artists for its scenery, light and picturesque cottages. Visit the Tate Gallery in St Ives, Barbara Hepworth Museum, RSPB bird sanctuary or Gweek seal sanctuary.

THE GARRACK HOTEL

Burthallan Lane, St Ives, Cornwall TR26 3AA
✆ (01736) 796199 FAX (01736) 798955
THE KILBY FAMILY

🛏 18, 18 en-suite, from £47.50 per person, double occ.
Lunch served. Non-residents welcome. Open all year.
✖ £14.50, last orders 8.30pm.
🍽 Hot Mussels in Garlic and White Wine. Petit Fillet of Chicken Barbados. Entrecote Steak with Brandy and Mushroom Sauce. Steamed Supreme of Salmon with Lemon Hollandaise. Hot Bread and Butter Pudding. Hot Beignets Souffles.

Vine covered granite hotel set in two acres of grounds. Fabulous coastal views overlooking Porthmeor Beach, St Ives Tate Gallery and old St Ives.

VISA ◼ 💳 AmEx ⬦ 🏊 ✓ S 🏊 ⬦ C

SKIDDEN HOUSE HOTEL

Skidden Hill, St Ives, Cornwall TR26 2DU
✆ (01736) 796899 FAX (01736) 798619
MICHAEL HOOK & DENNIS STOAKES

🛏 6, 6 en-suite, from £36.00 per person, double occ.
Lunch served. Non-residents welcome. Closed December.
✖ £19.00, last orders 8.30pm.
🍽 Fresh local fish. Items imported from Britanny, Poached Halibut Steaks with Asparagus Spears and Hollandaise. Butter braised Monkfish with Onion, Tomato and Capsicums.

A coaching inn, dating from 1540, with a long and varied past. Now, tastefully converted into a small, comfortable hotel, with an intimate restaurant. The chef patron can be seen at work by guests drinking in the bar. Skidden House is conveniently situated in the centre of St. Ives, close to the harbour. Parking is limited.

✚ Entering St Ives at "Y" junction, bear right, first right past railway and coach station.

VISA ◼ 💳 AmEx ⊘ ⬦ ✓ S 🏊 ⬦ B

ST IVES, Cambridgeshire

Picturesque market town with a narrow six-arched bridge spanning the River Ouse on which stands a bridge chapel. There are numerous Georgian and Victorian buildings. The Norris Museum has a good local collection.

▦▦▦ OLIVER'S LODGE

Needingworth Road, St Ives, Cambridgeshire PE17 4JD
☎ (01480) 463252 FAX (01480) 461150
CHRISTOPHER & ELIZABETH LANGLEY

🛏 16, 16 en-suite, from £30.00 per person, double occ.
Lunch served. Non-residents welcome. Closed 25th December.
✗ £15.00 to £17.00, last orders 9.30pm.
🍴 Tropical Fruit Cocktail. Deep Fried King Prawns with Marie Rose Sauce. Seafood Tagliatelle. Roast Loin of Pork.

Originally a Victorian building, sympathetically extended in 1990/91. All rooms have been refurbished and have private bathrooms.

✛ Off A604 signposted to St Ives, straight across first roundabout, left at next roundabout and then first right. Hotel two hundred yards on right.

VISA 🔳 AmEx ✓ 🖎 ⏚ B

STAFFORD, Staffordshire

A town with much history. Several half-timbered buildings, most notably the 16th century High House. Several local museums, including the former cottage of Izaak Walton, the famous angler.

▦▦▦ THE OLD PARSONAGE

High Offley, Woodseaves, Staffordshire ST20 0NE
☎ (01785) 284446 FAX (01785) 284446
JEFF & NORMA WILKINSON

🛏 4, 4 en-suite, from £20.00 per person, double occ.
Lunch served. Non-residents welcome. Open all year.
✗ £12.50 to £18.50, last orders 9pm.
🍴 Fresh smoked salmon. Chowder. Grilled Fillet of Beef served on Oyster Mushrooms. Crisp Brandy Snap Basket.

The hotel provides a warm welcome and is surrounded by terraced lawns. Comfortably furnished bedrooms.

✛ Off the A519 Eccleshall to Newport road.

VISA 🔳 🔳 AmEx ⊗ ✓ 🖎 ⏚ A

STEEPLE ASTON, Oxfordshire

On the fringe of the Cotswolds. Visit the Cotswold Wildlife Park, the ancient marketing town of Burford and Bourton on the Water with its famous model village.

WESTFIELD FARM HOTEL

The Fenway, Steeple Aston, Bicester, Oxfordshire OX6 3SS
✆ (01869) 340591
GRAHAM HILLIER & JULIE WAIN

🛏 6, 6 en-suite, from £24.00 per person, double occ.
Open all year.
✗ £11.50, last orders 7.30pm.
🍴 Good home cooking with locally grown vegetables and locally produced meats. A converted stable block surrounded by beautiful gardens in a small valley, with it's own natural spring and stream.

✛ 2 minutes drive from the A4260, halfway between Oxford and Banbury.

VISA 🔳 ⋰/⬥ A

STOCKSBRIDGE, South Yorkshire

Town on the edge of the Peak District National Park. *See also Holmfirth.*

ALDERMANS HEAD MANOR

Hartcliffe Hill Road, Stocksbridge, Sheffield, South Yorkshire S30 5GY
✆ (01226) 766209
ANN UNITT

🛏 4, 3 en-suite, from £30.00 per person, double occ.
Lunch served. Closed Christmas and New Year.
✗ £15.00, last orders 8pm.
🍴 Creamed Prawns. Fresh Fruit and Mint Vinaigrette. Pheasant with Cream and Apples. Poached Salmon with Parsley Sauce. Gooseberry Fool. Chocolate Meringue Ice Cream.

A manor house farmed by monks over seven centuries ago. In 1290 the Lord of the Manor was granted permission by Edward I to hold a regular Tuesday market and fair. This medieval fare was said to be held under a great yew tree at Aldermans House. A totally non-smoking establishment. For children under 12 years please contact the hotel direct.

✛ On A616, at Langsett turn onto Gilbert Hill. At next crossroads turn right and continue for 1 mile.

⊗ ⬥ A

STOGUMBER, Somerset

Small, farming hamlet, two miles south east of Williton, in the beautiful Quantock Hills. Visit Dunster Castle, Hestercombe House, Rosemoor Gardens or the West Somerset Steam Railway. *See also Williton.*

CURDON MILL

Lower Vellow, Stogumber, Williton, Somerset TA4 4LS
✆ (01984) 656522 FAX (01984) 656197
RICHARD & DAPHNE CRIDDLE

🛏 6, 6 en-suite, from £25.00 per person, double occ.
Open all year.
✗ £16.50, last orders 8pm.
🍴 Choice on arrival. Suggestions include: Salmon Mousse. Fried Brie. Seasoned Racks of Lamb. Braised Pigeon. Pork in Calvados.

Pleasant conversion of an old sandstone water mill, set in two hundred acres of farmland. Rooms are furnished in country chintz style, creating a comfortable relaxed atmosphere. There is an outdoor heated pool, croquet lawn and stabling is available for guests' horses. Lunches served on Sunday. For dogs and children, please contact the hotel directly.

⊹ A358 from Taunton 12 miles - left for Vellow, hotel 1 mile on left.

VISA 💳 ⊗ ⌇ 🗲 ∕ 🐾 A

STRATFORD UPON AVON, Warwickshire

One of Britain's most popular tourist destinations, through its connections with Shakespeare. Visit his birthplace, Anne Hathaway's cottage, Holy Trinity church where he was buried and the town's theatre. *See also Chipping Campden.*

DUKES HOTEL

Payton Street, Stratford upon Avon, Warwickshire CV37 6UA
✆ (01789) 269300 FAX (01789) 414700
ALAN POWER

🛏 22, 22 en-suite, from £34.75 per person, double occ.
Non-residents welcome. Closed mid December to mid January.
✗ from £17.50 a la carte, last orders 9.30pm.
🍴 Pre and apres theatre light snacks and suppers by arrangement.

Listed Georgian town centre hotel in a quiet residential street. Excellent accommodation and ambiance, the hotel is furnished with antiques. Complimentary guest parking. For children under 12 years, please contact the hotel direct.

VISA 💳 💳 AmEx ⊗ ⌇∕ C

COACH HOUSE HOTEL

16-17 Warwick Road, Stratford upon Avon, Warwickshire CV37 6YW
✆ (01789) 204109 FAX (01789) 415916
JUDY & GEOFF HARDEN

🛏 23, 19 en-suite, from £32.50 per person, double occ.
Lunch served. Non-residents welcome. Open all year.
✗ £15.00, last orders 10pm.
🍴 Fish and vegetarian dishes.

A comfortable family run hotel just five minutes walk from the centre of Stratford. The building is Victorian, the annexe Georgian. The vaulted restaurant is situated in the cellar.

⊹ Entering Stratford on A439 road, hotel on the right before the one-way system.

VISA 💳 💳 AmEx ⊗ ♿ ⌇∕ B

STRETTON, Leicestershire

An ideal overnight or meal stop whilst travelling north or south on the A1. Visit nearby historic Stamford, Burleigh House, Belton House or Grantham.

THE RAM JAM INN

Great North Road, Stretton, Oakham, Leicestershire LE15 7QX
✆ (01780) 410776 FAX (01780) 410361
TIM HART

🛏 8, 8 en-suite, from £24.50 per person, double occ.
Lunch served. Non-residents welcome. Closed Christmas.
✗ approx £15.00 a la carte, last orders 10pm.
🍽 Traditional English cooking. Grilled Rutland Sausage. Blackberry and Apple Pie. Stilton Cheese.

A roadside inn with exceptional stylish interior, concentrating on good food and friendly service.

VISA 🖭 💳 AmEx ⊗ 🚻 ⚬/ ⊕ A

STURMINSTER NEWTON, Dorset

A livestock market held every Monday in this small town. One of the bridges over the River Stour is a fine medieval example and bears a plaque declaring that anyone "injuring" it will be deported!

STOURCASTLE LODGE

Goughs Close, Sturminster Newton, Dorset DT10 1BU
✆ (01258) 472320 FAX (01258) 473381
JILL & KEN HOOKHAM BASSET

🛏 5, 4 en-suite, from £34.00 per person, double occ.
Open all year.
✗ £15.00, last orders 9pm.
🍽 A Mousse of Mange Tout with Basil Scones. Crab Cakes. Pork cooked in Tomatoes, Peppers, Garlic and Coconut. Breast of Chicken.

An 18th century oak beamed house with well equipped rooms, a relaxing atmosphere and a delightful garden.

⊹ Arriving from London M3 - A303 - Mere exit 3095 Gillingham 3092 - Sturminster Newton first turning on right from market square.

VISA 🖭 ⊗ 🌊 ⚬/ A

SUTTON, West Sussex

Small village nestling under the South Downs between Pulborough and Chichester. A good base for exploring this pretty area of West Sussex including Goodwood House and racecourse and Arundel Castle. *See also Pulborough.*

THE WHITE HORSE INN

Sutton, Nr Pulborough, West Sussex RH20 1PS
*(*01798) 869221 FAX (01798) 869291
HOWARD & SUSIE MACNAMARA

5, 5 en-suite, from £27.00 per person, double occ.
Lunch served. Open all year.
£12.00, last orders 9.30pm.
Fresh local fish and game. Casseroles. Freshly prepared meat and poultry dishes.

Charming Georgian country inn (c.1746) set well off the beaten track in a picturesque village in the heart of Sussex. The inn offers daily blackboard specials to supplement a good a la carte and fixed price menu. Facilities for children are limited, please enquire directly before arrival.

VISA A ⊗ ℘ ✓ ⊕ A

SUTTON COLDFIELD, Warwickshire

An old market town now part of the conurbation of Birmingham. The nearby 2400 acre Sutton Park has facilities for golf, fishing and riding with walks around the woodlands and lakes.

MOXHULL HALL HOTEL

Holly Lane, Wishaw, Sutton Coldfield, Warwickshire B76 9PE
*(*0121) 329 2056 FAX (0121) 311 1980
JOHN BODEN

20, 20 en-suite, from £28.25 per person, double occ.
Lunch served. Non-residents welcome. Open all year.
£10.95, Last orders 10pm.
French and English cuisine.

A country house hotel in eight acres of gardens and woodlands. The hotel offers 20 individually decorated bedrooms, all of which overlook the gardens or the surrounding woodlands.

 Just off the A446 1 mile north of the Belfry golf course.

VISA A ₂ AmEx & ✓ ⊕ B

SWANSEA, West Glamorgan

Visit the Gower peninsula, Swansea Leisure Centre, Swansea Museum, the shopping centre and theatre. Dry ski slope nearby.

WINDSOR LODGE HOTEL

Mount Pleasant, Swansea, West Glamorgan SA1 6EG
*(*01792) 642158 FAX (01792) 648996
MR & MRS R. RUMBLE

18, 18 en-suite, from £28.00 per person, double occ.
Lunch served. Closed Christmas Day.
£13.00, last orders 9.30pm.
Welsh fare, prepared from fresh local ingredients. Welsh Lamb with Wine and Rosemary. Laverbread Mousse. Local sewin and salmon. Leek Tarts.

An attractive Georgian style building close to the centre of the city, furnished with an individual combination of antique and modern furniture.

VISA A ₂ AmEx ⊗ ⊕ A

SWAY, Hampshire

Small village on the south western edge of the New Forest, noted for its 220ft tower, Peterson's Folly, built in the 1870's by a retired Indian judge. Visit Lymington, Beaulieu Motor Museum and the New Forest. *See also Lymingtom.*

🏠🏠🏠 STRING OF HORSES HOTEL

Mead End Road, Sway, Lymington, Hampshire SO41 6EH
☎ (01590) 682631
GILL REARDON

🛏 7, 7 en-suite, from £45.00 per person, double occ.
Lunch served. Non-residents welcome. Open all year.
✗ £17.95, last orders 9pm.
🍽 Sauted Mushrooms with Ham and Stilton. Beef Stroganoff. Supreme of Chicken with Vermouth and Cream Sauce. Iced Lemon Souffle in a White Chocolate Sauce. Caramel Cream with Strawberries.

Cottage style old world hotel with every modern convenience including spa baths in most bedrooms and a relaxed, peaceful atmosphere. For children under 12 years please contact the hotel direct.

⊹ A337 from Lyndhurst to Brockenhurst, turn right onto the B3055 to Sway, second left after station, Mead End Road is 350 yards on left.

VISA 🔲 AmEx 🏊 ✓ 🦮 **C**

TAUNTON, Somerset

Many fine period buildings in this attractive county town. The home of Somerset cider. *See also Norton Fitzwarren.*

🏠🏠 FARTHINGS HOTEL & RESTAURANT ✗

Hatch Beauchamp, Taunton, Somerset TA3 6SG
☎ (01823) 480664 FAX (01823) 481118
DAVID & MARIE BARKER

🛏 8, 8 en-suite, from £32.50 per person, double occ.
Lunch served. Non-residents welcome. Open all year.
✗ £15.00, last orders 9pm.
🍽 Pigeon Breast coated with a Tarragon and Hazelnut Dressing. Lobster and Mussel Ragout on a light Coriander Sauce. Maize fed Breast of Chicken on a bed of Forest Mushrooms and Asparagus. Quenelles of Dark and White Chocolate.

A Georgian country hotel which has recently been completely renovated and refurbished.

⊹ 5 miles south east of Taunton, off A358.

VISA 🔲 AmEx ⊘ ✓ 🦮 🛏 **B**

TAVISTOCK, Devon

Pretty market town on the western edge of Dartmoor, and only 10 miles north of Plymouth and the south Devon and Cornwall coastline. *See also Lydford.*

🏠 ## MOORLAND HALL HOTEL ✗ ✗

Brentor Road, Mary Tavy, Nr Tavistock, Devon PL19 9PY
☎ (01822) 810466
MR & MRS A. R. FARR

🛏 7, 7 en-suite, from £29.00 per person, double occ.
Non-residents welcome. Open all year.
✗ £15.00, last orders 8pm.
🍴 English cooking with French influence. River Tavy Trout stuffed with Smoked Mackerel and Cream Cheese. Noisettes of Lamb with Herb Crust and Cumberland Sauce. Bread & Butter Pudding. Summer Pudding. Creme Brulee.

Moorland Hall is a delightful Victorian country house in 5 acres of secluded gardens and paddocks, with direct access onto Dartmoor. Golf, fishing, and riding nearby, excellent base for touring and walking. Non-residents are advised to reserve a table for dinner before arrival.

✦ Take A386, 4 miles north of Tavistock. Hotel signposted from centre of Mary Tavy, along Brentor road.
VISA 🔳 ⊗ 🖊 🐕 A

TELFORD, Shropshire

A new town, named after Thomas Telford, engineer of canals, bridges and viaducts. Visit nearby Ironbridge Gorge with monuments and museums to the industrial revolution and fine 18th century buildings. *See also Worfield, Bridgnorth.*

🏠 ## THE HUNDRED HOUSE HOTEL

Norton, Nr Shifnal, Shropshire TF11 9EE
☎ (01952) 730353 FAX (01952) 730355
THE PHILLIPS FAMILY

🛏 9, 9 en-suite, from £34.50 per person, double occ.
Lunch served. Non-residents welcome. Closed evening of 26th December.
✗ £12.00 to £25.00, last orders 10pm.

🍴 Modern British and European cooking. Local game in traditional style. Severn Salmon. Shellfish from Welsh coast. Herbs from the kitchen garden.

18th century inn set in a superb large garden with many interesting items of antiquity. Excellent accommodation. Every room is designed to a very high standard on a patchwork theme, some rooms even provide a matching swing.

✦ Exit M54 at junction 4. Follow signs to Kidderminster/Bridgnorth (A442).Norton village is halfway between Telford and Bridgnorth.

VISA 🔳 AmEx ⊗ 🖊 🐕 🐕 B

TETBURY, Gloucestershire

A small market town with 18th century houses and an interesting 17th century Town Hall. Local sites include Berkeley Castle, Slimbridge Wildfowl Trust, Westonbirt Arboretum and Badminton Estate.

HUNTERS HALL INN

Kingscote, Nr Tetbury, Gloucestershire GL8 8XZ
☎ (01453) 860393 FAX (01453) 860707
DAVID ROBERTS

🛏 12, 12 en-suite, from £29.00 per person, double occ.
Lunch served. Non-residents welcome. Open all year.
✗ £15.50, last orders 9.30pm.
🍴 Tenderloin of Pork with Brie and Smoked Bacon. Roast Rack of Lamb with a Rhubarb and Ginger Sauce.Vegetarian and other regional dishes.

Five miles north west of Tetbury, a 16th century coaching inn with a wealth of original charm including beams, antique furniture and roaring log fires in winter.

✤ On the A4135 4 miles west of Tetbury.

VISA 💳 AmEx ⊗ ♿ ✦ ／ 🐾 A

TEWKESBURY, Gloucestershire

A market town at the confluence of the Avon and the severn rivers, in the fertile vale of Evesham, sheltered by the Malvern and Cotswold hills. The area is full of history and fascinating to explore.

JESSOP HOUSE HOTEL

65 Church Street, Tewkesbury, Gloucestershire GL20 5RZ
☎ (01684) 292017 FAX (01684) 273076
RON & SUE JAMES

🛏 8, 8 en-suite, from £37.50 per person, double occ.
Non-residents welcome. Closed 24th December until 2nd January.
✗ from £15.00 a la carte, last orders 8.45pm.
🍴 English cuisine prepared from local produce. Evesham asparagus and Severn salmon.

A 250 year old, Grade II, listed building, which was once part of Tewkesbury's grammar school. Jessop House has been furnished in period style creating a quiet and peaceful atmosphere.

✤ From town centre, take A38 towards Gloucester.

VISA 💳 ⊗ 🔍 ✦ ／ 🐾 A

THETFORD, Norfolk

Small medieval market town with numerous reminders of its long history. The ruins of the 12th century Priory, iron age earthworks at Castle Hill and Norman castle mound. The timber-framed Ancient House is now a museum.

WEREHAM HOUSE HOTEL

24 White Hart Street, Thetford, Norfolk IP24 1AD
☎ (01842) 761956
COLIN & JILL ROGERS

🛏 8, 8 en-suite, from £23.50 per person, double occ.
Non-residents welcome. Open all year.
✗ from £10.00, last orders 9.30pm.
🍴 Mushroom Stroganoff. Pork with Cider. Peppered Steak. Rainbow Trout. Spring Garden Lamb. Spinach and Mushroom Lasagne.

Small family run, Georgian style hotel in the town centre. All rooms are well furnished and comfortable.

VISA 💳 A

THORNE, South Yorkshire

A quiet market town, with easy access to Doncaster, Goole, York, Lincoln, Leeds, Sheffield Rotherham, Humberside and the east coast resorts.

BELMONT HOTEL
Horsefair Green, Thorne, Nr Doncaster, South Yorkshire DN8 5EE
☎ (01405) 812320 FAX (01405) 740508
MURRAY & ROSEMARY STEWART

🛏 23, 23 en-suite, from £40.00 per person, double occ.
Lunch served. Non-residents welcome. Open all year.
✗ £10.95, last orders 9.30pm.
▤ Table d'hote and a la carte menus. Giant Yorkshire puddings with a variety of fillings. Venison with Mushrooms and Red Wine. Grilled Sword fish with Apple and Tarragon Sauce. Supreme of Duck with fresh orange and cointreau sauce. Belmont Kebab with fillet of Beef, Prawns, Salmon and Vegetables.

Fully referbished the Belmont Hotel offers very comfortable accommodation and friendly personal service. Ideal location for conferences with a fully equipped conference room. Easy access to racecourses at Doncaster, York, Beverley, Pontefract and Doncaster Exhibition Centre.

VISA 🏧 AmEx ⊗ ♿ ✎ ⌲ B

TICKTON, Humberside

Two miles north east of the historic town of Beverley with its medieval Minster. Easy drive to York, the Yorkshire Wolds and coastline. *See also Brandesburton.*

TICKTON GRANGE HOTEL
Tickton, Humberside HU17 9SH
☎ (01964) 543666 FAX (01964) 542556
THE WHYMANT FAMILY

🛏 16, 16 en-suite, from £28.20 per person, double occ.
Non-residents welcome. Open all year.
✗ £14.95, last orders 9.30pm.
▤ Fish, game in season, hand-made chocolate desserts and truffles.

A Georgian country house hotel set in four acres of rose gardens. Each bedroom has its own individual character and has been furnished and equipped to a very high standard.

VISA 🏧 AmEx ⊗ 🔍 ✎ ⌲ A

TIMSBURY, Avon

Tiny village half way between Bath and Wells. Visit Radford Farm and Shire Horses or Priston Mill. *See also Bath, Box, Wells, Corsham, Pensford.*

⌂⌂ ## THE OLD MALT HOUSE HOTEL ✗

Radford, Timsbury, Nr Bath, Avon BA3 1QF
☎ (01761) 470106 FAX (01761) 472726
MARGUERITE & MIKE HORLER

🛏 10, 10 en-suite, from £33.00 per person, double occ.
Lunch served. Non-residents welcome. Closed 24th December to 2nd January.
✕ £16.00, last orders 8.30pm.
🍴 English country cooking. Steak and Kidney Pie. Jugged Hare. West Country Duck. Vegetarian dishes available.

Formerly an old brewery malt house, built in 1835 and converted into an hotel 20 years ago. An informal, comfortable hotel, furnished with antiques and interesting pictures.

✢ From the A367 take the B3115 and follow the 'Radford Farm' signs.
VISA 💳 AmEx A

TINTERN, Gwent

At the southern end of the beautiful Wye Valley. See Tintern Abbey, Chepstow castle, Raglan castle, Offa's Dyke, Caerleon Roman Barracks. *See also Chepstow.*

⌂⌂ ## PARVA FARMHOUSE HOTEL

Tintern, Gwent NP6 6SQ
☎ (01291) 689411 FAX (01291) 689557
DERECK & VICKIE STUBBS

🛏 9, 9 en-suite, from £29.50 per person, double occ.
Non-residents welcome. Open all year.
✕ £16.50, last orders 8.30pm.
🍴 Welsh and international dishes. Small, four course fixed price menu, prepared daily, with choices at each course. Mushrooms Tumerlin (raw mushrooms in a curried yoghurt dressing). Rack of Welsh Lamb. Crispy Duck with a Brandy and Black Cherry Sauce.

A 17th century farmhouse hotel, nestling on the banks of the river Wye. The restaurant has an inglenook fireplace and the lounge is furnished with plump leather Chesterfield sofas. Food is prepared by the chef proprietor and guests are assured of a warm welcome.

✢ Located on the A466.

VISA 💳 ⊗ 🍷 ✓ 🐕 A

TISBURY, Wiltshire

Near a small market town in the heart of the Wiltshire Downs which makes an ideal base for exploring Salisbury, Stonehenge and Stourhead. Also visit Longleat, Shaftesbury and Wardour Castle. In area of outstanding natural beauty.

THE BECKFORD ARMS

Fonthill Gifford, Nr Tisbury, Wiltshire SP3 6PX
☎ (01747) 870385 FAX (01747) 851496
GWYNETH MILES & RON GAFFNEY

🛏 7, 7 en-suite, from £24.75 per person, double occ.
Lunch served. Non-residents welcome. Open all year.
✗ from £11.00 a la carte or bar meals, last orders 10pm.
🍽 Leek and Ham Bake. Local Duck with butter orange and maple sauce. Specialising in traditional and fresh fish dishes.

An 18th century traditional inn, with superb views over the surrounding countryside. The bedrooms have all been recently refurbished in Laura Ashley style fabrics, some four poster beds available. Downstairs, the inn retains all of its original character with roaring log fires, many real ales and excellent food.

✦ Halfway between Tisbury and Hindon. 2 miles from A303 (signposted Fonthill Bishop).
VISA 🔲 AmEx ⊘ ⋰ 🔲 ⊕ A

TORQUAY, Devon

The South West's most famous resort, in sheltered Torbay, known for its mild climate, palm-lined promenades, elegant Victorian terraces and glorious coastline.

FAIRMOUNT HOUSE HOTEL

Herbert Road, Chelston, Torquay, Devon TQ2 6RW
☎ (01803) 605446 FAX (01803) 605446
NOEL & MAGGIE TOLKIEN

🛏 8, 8 en-suite, from £29.00 per person, double occ.
Lunch served. Closed November to February.
✗ £11.00, last orders 7.30pm.
🍽 Fresh Brixham fish and local specialities. Devon Clucker (breast of chicken in a creamy cider and tarragon sauce) and Beef Blackawton (casseroled in local real ale). Fresh garden produce in season.

Set above the picturesque Cockington Village, Fairmount is a peaceful holiday setting, with its mature gardens and sunfilled patios overlooking Chelston's quiet residential valley and distant views toward the Bay. During Summer, no Sunday evening meal is served, but lunch is available.

✦ Approaching Torquay on A3022, follow signs to Cockington. At top of St Matthews Road turn right.

VISA 🔲 ⊘ ⅙ 🔱 ⊕ A

TOTNES, Devon

Old market town at the head of the Dart estuary. Remains of medieval gateways, churches and 16th century Guildhall worth visiting. Surrounded by some of Devon's most beautiful countryside.

GABRIEL COURT HOTEL

Stoke Gabriel, Totnes, Devon TQ9 6SF
☎ (01803782) 206 FAX (01803782) 333
MICHAEL & ERYL BEACOM

🛏 19, 19 en-suite, from £39.50 per person, double occ.
Non-residents welcome. Open all year.
✕ £22.00, last orders 8.30pm.
🍴 English country cooking with game dishes in season. Roast Devon Pheasant. Fresh fish, landed at Brixham.

Quiet, comfortable country manor house set in three acres of terraced Elizabethan gardens in village on the banks of the river Dart. The house has origins going back to 1487, but was reconstructed during the 17th century.

✢ 3 miles southwest of Totnes. Take A385 from either Totnes or Paignton, turn towards Stoke Gabriel at Parkers Arms.
VISA 🔳 💳 AmEx ⊗ ✓ 🔌 🦢 🐧 C

TROWBRIDGE, Wiltshire

Wealthy Wiltshire market town with many attractive buildings. Close to Bath, Longleat, Wells, Stonehenge, Avebury, Bristol and the Mendip Hills. *See also Bath, Westbury.*

OLD MANOR HOTEL

Trowle, Trowbridge, Wiltshire BA14 9BL
☎ (01225) 777393 FAX (01225) 765443
DIANE & BARRY HUMPHREYS

🛏 14, 14 en-suite, from £33.00 per person, double occ.
Open all year.
✕ from £18.00 a la carte, last orders 8pm.
🍴 Traditional menu. Fresh vegetables, fish and poultry.

A Grade II*, part mediaeval, part Queen Anne manor farmhouse, set in 4 acres. All the bedrooms are individually and tastefully decorated with antiques, pine and chintz. There are several half tester and four poster beds available. New bedrooms have been created by converting the hotel's stable block and barns. All bedrooms offer an extremely high standard of accommodation, with fine lounges in the main house.

✢ On the A363 between Trowbridge and Bradford on Avon.

VISA 🔳 💳 AmEx ⊗ ♿ A

TUNBRIDGE WELLS, Kent

A famous spa town dating from the 17th century, much of its charm has been retained. The Pantiles are a delightful walk lined with elegant shops. Many parks and gardens.

RUSSELL HOTEL ✗

80 London Road, Tunbridge Wells, Kent TN1 1DZ
✆ (01892) 544833 FAX (01892) 515846
KEVIN & TONI WILKINSON

🛏 26, 26 en-suite, from £41.00 per person, double occ.
Lunch served. Non-residents welcome. Open all year.
✗ £17.00, last orders 9.30pm.
▣ Traditional English and international cuisine. Roast Sirloin Henry VIII. Mild Vegetable Curry. Escalope of Veal with White Wine, Herbs and Cream. Home-made Fruit Pies.

A traditional Victorian building overlooking Tunbridge Wells common. The adjacent house has been converted into the hotel annexe. Recently refurbished, very comfortable. A family run hotel with an assured warm welcome.

✛ On A26, 200 metres north of intersection of A264.

VISA ▪ 🔁 AmEx ⊘ ♿ ✓ 🚭 C

THE DANEHURST HOTEL

41 Lower Green Road, Rusthall, Tunbridge Wells, Kent TN4 8TW
✆ (01892) 527739 FAX (01892) 514804
ANGELA GOBBOLD

🛏 5, 4 en-suite, from £24.75 per person, double occ.
Closed two weeks in August.
✗ £18.95, last orders 8pm.
▣ Freshly prepared, home cooked fare. Country Mushroom Starter. Lamb and Cherry Casserole. Apple Crumble.

A large Victorian family home, a couple of miles west of Tunbridge Wells. Guests are offered individual attention, in a relaxed environment. Breakfast is served in the conservatory, dinner in the more formal dining room. Vegetarian and other special diets catered for with advance notice. A non-smoking hotel.

VISA ▪ ♿ ✓ A

TWO BRIDGES, Devon

In the centre of Dartmoor National Park, superb views of West Dartmoor and open moorland. Visit Plymouth (13 miles) or any of the many National Trust houses and gardens that surround the moor.

PRINCE HALL HOTEL ✗ ✗ ✗

Two Bridges, Yelverton, Devon PL20 6SA
✆ (01822) 890403/4 FAX (01822) 890676
MR & MRS J.C. DENAT

🛏 8, 8 en-suite, from £30.00 per person, double occ.
Non-residents welcome. Closed approximately mid December to mid January.
✗ £19.95 (inc in room rate), last orders 8.30pm.
▣ Local Dartmoor beef and lamb. Salmon and trout from the river Dart.

A small, homely, peaceful country house hotel in five acres of grounds. An ideal base for walking, dogs are welcomed. Cuisine is attentively prepared by the French owner/chef and there is a superb wine list. For children under 8, please enquire directly with the hotel. The rate quoted is per person, per day for dinner, bed and breakfast.

VISA ▪ 🔁 AmEx ⊘ ♿ ✓ 🚭 ⇪ B *Two Bridges continued over...*

TWO BRIDGES HOTEL

Two Bridges, Dartmoor, Devon PL20 6SW
☎ (01822) 890581 FAX (01822) 890575 ✗
LESLEY & PHILIP DAVIES

🛏 25, 20 en-suite, from £32.00 per person, double occ.
Lunch served. Non-residents welcome. Open all year.
✗ £14.50, last orders 9pm.
🍴 Dartmoor beef and lamb. Fresh fish from Brixham. Carvery lunches served on Sundays.

Old world inn, situated by the river Dart, right in the centre of the moor. Huge log fires, antiques and the gleam of copper create an instant feeling of history and warmth.

✠ At the centre of Dartmoor, where the B3367 and B3212 meet.

VISA 💳 AmEx ⊗ ♿ ✓ 🛏 ⊕ A

TYNEMOUTH, Tyne & Wear

Seaside town. See Tynemouth Priory and Castle, Hadrian's Wall and visit The Metro Centre, Europe's largest shopping complex. A short Metro ride to Newcastle City Centre.

HOPE HOUSE

47 Percy Gardens, Tynemouth, Tyne & Wear NE30 4HH
☎ (0191) 257 1989 FAX (0191) 257 1989
ANNA & PASCAL DELIN

🛏 3, 2 en-suite, from £24.75 per person, double occ.
Open all year.
✗ £14.50, last orders 9pm.
🍴 Anglo-French cuisine prepared by the French chef proprietor. Fresh fish and shellfish bought daily from the local fish quay. Northumberland game. Wild Duck in Port. Pheasant a la Normande.

A double fronted Victorian house with sea views from most rooms. Period furnishings, in immaculate order. Guests dine from Japanese porcelain and silverware from a single Regency dining room table. The quality of decor and cuisine offered at this hotel represents outstanding value for money.

✠ A1058 from Newcastle to Tynemouth sea front. At roundabout facing sea turn right. Keep sea to left and hotel is half a mile to the right facing the sea.

VISA 💳 ✓ 🛏 A

UCKFIELD, East Sussex

An attractive, unspoiled village just 20 miles north of Eastbourne. Visit nearby Sheffield Park, the Bluebell Steam Railway, Glyndebourne, Charleston Manor and the Ashdown Forest.

HALLAND FORGE HOTEL & RESTAURANT

Halland, Nr Lewes, East Sussex BN8 6PW
✆ (01825) 840456 FAX (01825) 840773
JEAN & MAX HOWELL

🛏 20, 20 en-suite, from £37.00 per person, double occ.
Lunch served. Non-residents welcome. Open all year.
✕ £16.55, last orders 9.30pm.
🍴 Traditional English cooking.

This family run hotel is situated amongst attractive gardens and natural woodlands in the heart of Sussex and is an ideal base for exploring the beautiful surrounding countryside.

⚓ Situated in the hamlet of Halland on A22 London to Eastbourne road at the junction of the B2192, 4 miles south of Uckfield.

VISA ▬ AmEx 🐾 🕊 🦆 C

THE GRIFFIN INN

Fletching, Uckfield, East Sussex TN22 6SS
✆ (01825) 722890
BRIDGET & NIGEL PULLAN

🛏 4, 4 en-suite, from £25.00 per person, double occ.
Lunch served. Non-residents welcome. Closed 25th December.
✕ from £12.00 a la carte, last orders 9.30pm.
🍴 Traditional Sussex dishes. Strong Mediterranean influences, particularly Italian and Southern French.

16th century village inn with heaps of character, style and traditional furnishings. Bedrooms are more cottagey in style. Three rooms have four poster beds.

⚓ 1 mile to the north of A272, turning marked Fletching. 2 miles east of Newick.

VISA ▬ AmEx 👶 ⊗ 🕊 🦆 A

UPTON-UPON-SEVERN, Worcestershire

Attractive country town on the banks of the Severn. A good river cruising centre.

WHITE LION HOTEL

High Street, Upton-upon-Severn, Worcestershire WR8 0HJ
✆ (01684) 592551 FAX (01684) 592551
ROBERT & BRIDGET WITHEY

🛏 10, 10 en-suite, from £37.00 per person, double occ.
Lunch served. Non-residents welcome. Closed 25th & 26th December.
✕ £14.95, last orders 9pm.
🍴 Mediterranean Prawns. Crab and Stilton Tartlets. Supreme of Chicken. Fillet Steak with Stilton Butter and a Cream, Mushroom and Port Sauce.

A former 16th century coaching inn which retains most all of it's old world charm and character. All rooms are individually furnished.

⚓ 5 miles from M5/M50. Leave the A38 onto the A4104 over the bridge into town.

VISA ▬ AmEx 🕊 🦆 B

VENTNOR, Isle of Wight

Victorian seaside resort, renowned for its mild climate. Visit Blackgang Chine, Hay Monument, Osbourne House, (the summer residence of Queen Victoria), St Catherines Down and The Needles. *See also Seaview.*

VENTNOR TOWERS HOTEL

Madeira Road, Ventnor, Isle of Wight PO38 1QT
☎ (01983) 852277 FAX (01983) 855536
THE JANZEN FAMILY

🛏 27, 26 en-suite, from £41.00 per person, double occ.
Non-residents welcome. Open all year.
✕ £14.50, last orders 8.30pm.
🍴 A mixture of English and continental cuisine, using fresh fish and seafood wherever possible.

A quiet, Victorian seaside hotel with extensive facilities, set in four acres of gardens, overlooking the sea. There is an excellent wine list featuring 81 bins and the hotel has its own pitch n' putt golf course.

✛ A3055 (ring road) to Ventnor, hotel is situated in Maderia Road, on Bonchurch side of town, near Trinity Church.

VISA 🔲 AmEx 🔲 🌊 ⚓ : / 🔲 ⚓ **C**

WARKWORTH, Northumberland

A pretty village overlooked by a medieval castle, with a 14th century fortified bridge.

WARKWORTH HOUSE HOTEL ✗ ✗

16 Bridge Street, Warkworth, Northumberland NE65 OXB
☎ (01665) 711276 FAX (01665) 713323
DUNCAN & JOAN OLIVER

🛏 14, 14 en-suite, from £37.50 per person, double occ.
Lunch served. Non-residents welcome. Open all year.
✕ £15.95, last orders 8.45pm.
🍴 Chinese Dimsum. Pork Stroganoff with Pilau Rice. Halibut Steak with a White Wine and Grape Sauce. Chicken Breast with Cream and Lemon Sauce. Rack of Lamb with Tikka Sauce. Honey baked Gammon with Parsley Sauce.

Built in 1830, the hotel is unspoilt while offering all modern comforts. Individually designed bedrooms compliment the period feeling.

✛ 8 miles east of the A1 on the Coastal Road 1068, 7 miles south of Alnwick.

VISA 🔲 AmEx 🚫 ♿ : / 🔲 ⚓ **B**

WATFORD, Hertfordshire

Town on the edge of London, with good rail and underground lines into the city, yet with its own commercial and shopping centre.

THE WHITE HOUSE HOTEL

27-31 Upton Road, Watford, Hertfordshire WD1 2EL
✆ (01923) 237316 FAX (01923) 233109
IVAN HARTOG

🛏 50, 50 en-suite, from £39.50 per person, double occ.
Lunch served. Non-residents welcome. Open all year
✗ £16.95, last orders 9.30pm
🍴 Extensive choice of freshly prepared English and International dishes.

A privately owned, professionally run hotel, meeting the needs of both business and leisure guests. A warm friendly welcome and efficient courteous service.

VISA ⬛ ⚎ AmEx ⊗ ♿ ✓ ⬨ C

WEEDON, Northants

Situated close to the M1, three miles west of junction 16, this small village is at the centre of England and is surrounded by Civil War battlefields and ancestral homes. *See also Daventry, Rugby.*

THE GLOBE HOTEL

Watling Street, Weedon, Northamptonshire NN7 4QD
✆ (01327) 340336 FAX (01327) 349058
PETER & PENNY WALTON

🛏 18, 18 en-suite, from £19.50 to £24.75 per person, double occ.
Lunch served. Open all year
✗ from £9.50, last orders 9.30pm
🍴 Brixworth Pat. Beef and Pedigree Ale Pie. Aunt Cindy's Apple Pie.

An 18th century posting house which has been modernised into a friendly, family run country inn offering simple but good value accommodation.

VISA ⬛ ⚎ AmEx ⊗ ♿ Ⓢ A

WELLINGBOROUGH, Northamptonshire

Close to the M1, A1 and A45, this small Northamptonshire market town is well situated for exploring the many stately homes and other historical places of interest in the East Midlands.

THE COLUMBIA HOTEL & RESTAURANT

Northampton Road, Wellingborough, Northamptonshire NN8 3HG
✆ (01933) 229333 FAX (01933) 440418
BARRIE & CAROLINE FOGERTY

🛏 29, 29 en-suite, from £32.50 per person, double occ.
Lunch served. Non-residents welcome. Closed Christmas.
✗ £12.95, last orders 9.30pm.
🍴 English Cuisine.

A very friendly, family run commercial hotel in this small Northamptonshire market town which has undergone substantial interior refurbishment. All the rooms are comfortably furnished and the public areas are tastefully decorated and functional.

VISA ⬛ AmEx ✓ B

WELLS, Somerset

Small city, set beneath the Mendips, dominated by one of Britain's most magnificent cathedrals. Wookey Hole Caves, Cheddar Gorge, Bath, Longleat and Stourhead are all closeby. *See also Chelwood, Bath, Timsbury.*

GLENCOT HOUSE HOTEL ✕✕✕

Glencot Lane, Wookey Hole, Wells, Somerset BA5 1BH
✆ (01749) 677160 FAX (01749) 670210
MRS M. J. ATTIA

🛏 10, 10 en-suite, from £30.00 per person, double occ.
Non-residents welcome. Open all year.
✕ £16.50 & £21.50, last orders 8.45pm.
🍴 English cuisine. Traditional Gravalax with Dill and Brandy Dressing. Fillets of Brill on an Orange and Ginger Sauce. Roast Rack of English Lamb with a Herb Crust.

Elegant country house hotel, set in eighteen acres of gardens with river frontage. High class accommodation, excellent cuisine and friendly service.

VISA 💳 ⊗ ⌇ ✓ 🕲 🆂 🐧 B

WHITE HART HOTEL

Sadler Street, Wells, Somerset BA45 2RR
✆ (01749) 672056 FAX (01749) 672056
PETER AYTON

🛏 12, 12 en-suite, from £29.50 per person, double occ.
Lunch served. Non-residents welcome. Open all year.
✕ £12.00, last orders 9.30pm.
🍴 Crisp winter salad with Avocado and Smoked Chicken. Smoked Fish, Cream and Cheese Ramekin. Pan fried Sirloin Steak flamed with Whisky and a Red Peppercorn Sauce. Slices of Pork Tenderloin served in a Stilton Cream Sauce, garnished with Chives.

A 15th century coaching inn, recently refurbished and modenised in the centre of historic Wells.

VISA 💳 AmEx ⌇ ✓ 🕲 🍴 🆂 🐧 A

WELSHPOOL, Powys

Borders market town full of life, many half-timbered buildings and old inns. A pretty canalside. Powis Castle, Clive of India museum, Offas Dyke all closeby.

EDDERTON HALL ✕

Forden, Nr Welshpool, Powys SY21 8RZ
✆ (01938) 580339 FAX (01938) 580452
MR & MRS W. HAWKSLEY

🛏 8, 8 en-suite, from £27.50 per person, double occ.
Lunch served. Open all year.
✕ £18.95, last orders 9.30pm.
🍴 Welsh regional cuisine. Welsh lamb, local game in season.

A listed Georgian building. Superb views looking over the Severn Valley and Powis Castle. Still used as a working farm.

VISA 💳 💲 AmEx ⊗ ✓ 🕲 🐧 A

WELWYN, Hertfordshire

One of the first garden city developments. Close to Stevenage, Hertford and the Roman City of St Albans. Excellent shopping facilities.

🏠🏠 TEWIN BURY FARMHOUSE

Tewin Bury Farm, Nr Welwyn, Hertfordshire AL6 0JB
☎ (01438) 717793 FAX (01438) 840440
THE WILLIAMS FAMILY

🛏 16, 16 en-suite, from £27.50 per person, double occ.
Lunch served. Non-residets welcome. Restaurant closed from Christmas to New Year.
✖ from £11.50 a la carte, last orders 9pm.
🍷 Good farmhouse cooking. Fresh local trout. Steak in Madeira Sauce.

A 19th century farmhouse on the banks of the river Mimram halfway between Welwyn and Hertford. All rooms have been individually furnished in pine. The atmosphere is friendly and informal, as is the restaurant where fresh farm produce is used in the preparation of all the meals.

✛ Junction 6, A1 (M). B1000 signposted Hertford.
VISA 💳 AmEx ⊗ ✓ ⏚ A

WENDLING, Norfolk

Small village five miles west of East Dereham. Visit nearby Norwich, Sandringham, or the East Anglian coast.

🏠🏠 GREENBANKS COUNTRY HOTEL ✗

Swaffham Road, Wendling, Norfolk NR19 2AR
☎ (01362) 687742
ALEX & JENNIE LOCK

🛏 4, 4 en-suite, from £24.00 per person, double occ.
Lunch served. Non-residents welcome. Open all year.
✖ £16.50, last orders 9.30pm.
🍷 Crisp Apple and Walnut Coleslaw Salad in light Curry Mayonnaise. Local Rabbit. Chicken Hymettus. Fresh Banana and Peach Sundae.

Charming 18th century hotel with peaceful gardens, meadows and private fishing lake. Ideal for short breaks. All bedrooms are decorated with pine furniture.

✛ Midway between Kings Lynn/Norwich on A47 turn off at Wendling.
VISA 💳 ♿ ✓ 🖥🅂 ⏚ A

WENSLEYDALE, North Yorkshire

In the heart of Herriot country, Wensleydale provides historical and scenic countryside for everyone. Castle Bolton, Richmond town and castle, Reeth, Askrigg and Leyburn are well worth a visit. *See also Askrigg, Hawes.*

MILLERS HOUSE HOTEL

Middleham, North Yorkshire, DL8 4NR
((01969) 622630 FAX (01969) 623570
JUDITH & CROSSLEY SUNDERLAND

7, 6 en-suite, from £34.50 to £38.25 per person, double occ.
Closed 3rd to 31st January.
£19.50, last orders 8.30pm.
Daily changing four course menu, made with fresh local produce, featuring imaginative dishes, prepared with a French influence. Mussels with Pistou. Kidneys Creole. Asparagus Pots. Duck with Blueberries and Port. Apricot Meringue Swans.

A peaceful Georgian property in the quiet village of Middleham. The tasteful period decorations are kept immaculately clean. The hotel offers a variety of activity weekends, including wine tasting, racing, romantic, Christmas and New Year. For children please contact the hotel direct.

VISA C

THE WENSLEYDALE HEIFER

West Witton, Wensleydale, North Yorkshire DL8 4LS
((01969) 622322 FAX (01969) 624183
JOHN & ANNE SHARP

19, 19 en-suite, from £35.00 per person, double occ.
Lunch served. Non-residents welcome. Open all year.
£22.50, last orders 9.30pm.
Traditional Yorkshire home cooking. Menus change to reflect the seasons. Fresh fish and seafood a speciality.

A coaching inn which dates back to 1631. Accommodation is provided in the main building and two adjacent houses. Open fires, antiques and original beams provide the traditional ambience of a country inn. In the heart of the tranquil Yorkshire Dales National Park.

⊹ 4 miles west of Leyburn on A684 road to Hawes.

VISA AmEx B

WEST BEXINGTON, Dorset

Close to Chesil beach and surrounded by the beautiful Dorset countryside, visit the Swannery, Abbotsbury Gardens, Parnham House, Cricket St Thomas, Hardy's Monument, Athelhampton House and Thomas Hardy's cottage.

THE MANOR HOTEL

Beach Road, West Bexington, Dorset DT2 9DF
((01308) 897616 FAX (01308) 897035
RICHARD & JANE CHILDS

13, 13 en-suite, from £38.00 per person, double occ.
Lunch served. Non-residents welcome. Open all year.
£14.95 & £18.95, last orders 9.30pm.
Fresh local seafood and game in season.

A 16th century manor house situated just five hundred yards from Chesil Beach. Jacobean oak panelling and flagstone floors create an impressive atmosphere and most of the bedrooms enjoy views of the Dorset coast and Lyme Bay.

VISA AmEx B

WESTBURY, Wiltshire

A market town centrally situated for visiting Bath, Stonehenge, and Salisbury Plain. Longleat Safari Park is closeby. *See also Trowbridge.*

THE CEDAR HOTEL

Warminster Road, Westbury, Wiltshire BA13 3PR
((01373) 822753 FAX (01373) 858423
LYN & TERRY FROST

 16, 16 en-suite, from £25.00 per person, double occ.
Lunch served. Non-residents welcome. Closed 27th December to 30th December.
 £15.00, last orders 9pm.
 British and continental dishes using the best of local available produce.

An 18th century house which was converted into a hotel in the 1940's. The rooms are all tastefully and individually furnished in a traditional style such that the hotel retains much of the character of a country home.

VISA ⊗ ✓ A

WETHERBY, West Yorkshire

A prosperous market town, built on the banks of the River Wharfe. Linton Springs is a couple of miles west of Wetherby, within 20 minutes drive of Leeds and York.

LINTON SPRINGS

Sicklinghall Road, Wetherby, West Yorkshire LS22 4AF
((01937) 585353 FAX (01937) 587579
NIGEL GRAHAM

 12, 12 en-suite, from £37.50 per person, double occ.
Lunch served. Non-residents welcome. Open all year.
 from £13.00 a la carte, last orders 9.30pm.
 Fresh ingredients, classically prepared with French and modern influences. Seafood Crepe with Prawn, Salmon and Crab. Roast loin of Lamb served with a Tarragon and Blueberry Sauce. Mushroom Risotto with Chargrilled Winter Vegetables and Truffle Oil.

A beautiful Georgian building, recently totally refurbished to excellent standards, set in 14 acres of private parkland. The restaurant is a casual bistro, decorated in a country style. There is also an oak panelled dining room which is used for special functions and Sunday lunches.

 From Wetherby, take the Harrogate road, turn left for Sicklinghall, the hotel is 2 miles on the left.

VISA AmEx ✓ C

WEYMOUTH, Dorset

Ancient port and one of Britain's oldest seaside resorts. Chesil beach, Abbotsbury Swannery and Dorchester are all nearby.

🏛🏛🏛 MOONFLEET MANOR HOTEL & SPORTS RESORT

Fleet Road, Weymouth, Dorset DT3 4ED
☎ (01305) 786948 FAX (01305) 774395
BRUCE & JAN HEMINGWAY

🛏 37, 37 en-suite, from £36.00 per person, double occ.
Lunch served. Non-residents welcome. Open all year.
✗ from £15.00, last orders 9.30pm.
🍴 English and continental cuisine.

A hotel, leisure and sporting complex built around an original Georgian House overlooking Chesil beach and nature reserve.

VISA 💳 💳 AmEx ⊗ 🏊 🎣 ✓ 🐕 Ⓢ 🕊 B

🏛 THE STREAMSIDE HOTEL

29 Preston Road, Overcombe, Weymouth, Dorset DT3 6PX
☎ (01305) 833121 FAX (01305) 832043
JOHN ALDERMAN

🛏 15, 9 en-suite, from £32.00 to £36.00 per person, double occ.
Lunch served. Non-residents Welcome. Closed 26th to 30th December
✗ £10.75, last orders 9pm
🍴 Local seafood, Dorset lamb, and a wide choice of vegetarian food.

Mock Tudor style building. A family restaurant with rooms, where a warm welcome can be assured. The hotel is set in an award winning garden. Ample parking.

VISA 💳 💳 AmEx ⊗ ✓ 🏊 🕊 A

WHITBY, North Yorkshire

A town with a nautical heritage, on the banks of the river Esk, once the home of Captain Cook. Whitby is dominated by the ruins of an Abbey founded by St. Hilda in AD 657 which can be reached by climbing 199 steps.

🏛🏛🏛 LARPOOL HALL

Larpool Lane, Whitby, North Yorkshire YO22 4ND
☎ (01947) 602737 FAX (01947) 602737
KEITH & ELECTRA ROBINSON

🛏 12, 12 en-suite, from £40.00 per person, double occ.
Lunch served. Open all year.
✗ from £15.95, last orders 9.30pm.
🍴 Local game, shellfish and fish, grouse, pheasant, venison, mussels, brill and turbot. Deep fried Clams, served on a bed of Salad and sharp dressing. Baked Trout filled with Celery and Walnut stuffing. Larpool Mixed Grill Special.

Larpool Hall is an elegant, stone built, 18th century country house mansion set in ten acres of grounds overlooking the Esk valley and the North Yorkshire Moors. The personal service and calm atmosphere of Larpool Hall make it a suitable venue for both tourist and commercial guests.

VISA 💳 ⊗ ♿ ✓ 🐕 C

WICKHAM, Hampshire

Lying to the south end of the Meon valley, this attractive town, still noted for its annual horse fair, is centered on its Georgian market square. *See also Winchester.*

THE OLD HOUSE HOTEL

Wickham, Hampshire, PO17 5JG
☎ (01329) 833049 FAX (01329) 833672
MR & MRS R. P. SKIPWITH

🛏 9, 9 en-suite, from £42.50 per person, double occ.
Lunch served. Non-residents welcome. Closed 2 weeks Christmas, 2 weeks August.
✕ £25.00, last orders 9.30pm.
🍴 Classic regional French cuisine. Le Filet de Boeuf a la Creme d'Ail. Le Pintadeau aux Deux Poivres. Le Foie de Veau au Citron Vert.

A classic Georgian town house hotel (c.1705), noted for its superb French food and private house atmosphere. Bedrooms are furnished to an extremely high standard. Lunches are served from Tuesday's to Friday's.

VISA 🔲 💳 AmEx ⊗ ∴ **C**

WILLITON, Somerset

On the north edge of Exmoor, close to the sea and the north Devon coastal path. Visit Dunster Castle, Exmoor, Cleeve Abbey and the Quantock Hills. *See also Stogumber.*

THE WHITE HOUSE HOTEL

Williton, Taunton, Somerset TA4 4QW
☎ (01984) 632306
DICK & KAY SMITH

🛏 12, 9 en-suite, from £42.50 per person, double occ.
Non-residents welcome. Closed 1st November to mid May.
✕ £26.00, last orders 8.30pm.
🍴 Souffle Suissesse. Exmoor Venison and Game. Grilled Breast of Wood Pigeon with Warm Beetroot Salad. Stuffed Pork Tenderloin with Caramelised Apples and Apple Brandy. Sticky Toffee Pudding. Mrs Smiths' Chocolate Pudding.

A late Georgian Hotel noted for it's cuisine and good wine list, run by owner-chef"s in a relaxed atmosphere. Stylishly furnished with antiques, paintings, prints and ceramics.

⊗ ♿ ∴ 🚭 🐾 **B**

WILMINGTON, East Sussex

A small village between Eastbourne and Lewes and an ideal base for touring this beautiful area of Sussex. Visit The Long Man of Wilmington, Wilmington Priory, Michelham Priory and Glyndebourne Opera House.

CROSSWAYS HOTEL ✕✕

Lewes Road, Wilmington, East Sussex BN26 5SG
((01323) 482455 FAX (01323) 487811
D. STOTT & C. JAMES

🛏 7, 7 en-suite, from £34.00 per person, double occ.
Non-residents welcome. Closed 24th December to 24th January, Restaurant closed Sunday & Monday.
✕ £22.95, last orders 8.45pm.
🍽 Southdown lamb, local seafood and shellfish, game in season.
FINALIST, REPRESENTING THE SOUTH EAST, IN THE 1994 LOGIS REGIONAL CUISINE COMPETITION.

A delightful Georgian Hotel standing in two acres of grounds. A very high standard of accommodation and food. For children under 12, please contact the hotel direct.

✣ On A27 2 miles west of Polegate, 8 miles from Brighton.

VISA 🏧 💳 AmEx ✓ B

WINCHELSEA, East Sussex

A hilltop town established by Edward I in the 13th century to replace the ancient Cinque Port which was eventually engulfed by the sea. *See also Rye.*

THE COUNTRY HOUSE AT WINCHELSEA ✕✕

Hastings Road, Winchelsea, East Sussex TN36 4AD
((01797) 226669
IAN & MARY CARMICHAEL

🛏 3, 3 en-suite, from £25.00 per person, double occ.
Closed December & January.
✕ £15.00, last orders 8.30pm.
🍽 All dishes are home-made using local produce. Soups, pate, lamb, beef, poultry, fish, shellfish & ice cream. Sticky Toffee Pudding.

A delightful 17th century listed former Sussex farmhouse, surrounded by N.T. countryside, fully restored to offer guests a comfortable and relaxing stay. For children under 9 years please contact the hotel direct.

✣ Set back from the A259 on the Hastings side of Winchelsea.

VISA 🏧 AmEx ⊗ ✓ A

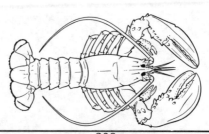

WINCHESTER, Hampshire

A fine city that was once the capital of Saxon England and is still home to a Norman cathedral, with one of the longest naves in Europe. Visit the New Forest, Portsmouth or Marwell Zoo. *See also Wickham, Crawley.*

THE WYKEHAM ARMS

75 Kingsgate Street, Winchester, Hampshire SO23 9PE
((01962) 853834 FAX (01962) 854411
GRAEME JAMESON

7, 7 en-suite, from £37.50 per person, double occ.
Lunch served. Non-residents welcome. Open all year, no food served on Sunday.
£15.00, last orders 8.30pm.
Wholesome traditional fare, prepared from fresh ingredients.

An 18th century coaching inn situated in the oldest and quietest part of the city, close to the cathedral. This friendly inn is decorated with antique pine and many interesting prints. For children under the age of 14, please contact the hotel direct.

South of the Cathedral by Kingsgate, next to Winchester College. Junction Cannon Street/Kingsgate Street.
VISA AmEx C

WINDERMERE, Cumbria

A lakeside town which has long been one of Britain's most popular holiday destinations. Visit Dove Cottage, Rydal Mount and Tarn Hows, Hilltop "Beatrix Potter", boat trip, or simply enjoy the fabulous scenery. *See also Bowness, Grasmere.*

HOLBECK GHYLL COUNTRY HOUSE HOTEL

Holbeck Lane, Windermere, Cumbria LA23 1LU
((015394) 32375 FAX (015394) 34743
DAVID & PATRICIA NICHOLSON

14, 14 en-suite, from £60.00 per person, double occ.
Lunch served. Non-residents welcome. Open all year.
From £27.50 (inc in room rate), last orders 8.45pm.
Menu changes daily; specialities include Herdwick Lamb, Windermere Char, Cumberland Sausages.

The standard room rate at this spectacularly appointed country house hotel is inclusive of the five course evening meal which is served in an oak panelled restaurant. (Please note that this does not extend to customers travelling with Logis vouchers). Magnificent views over the Lake. The hotel occupies the former home of Lord Lonsdale and offers the highest standards of comfort and hospitality. Free use of nearby swimming pool, putting green, billiard room, sauna and full leisure facilities.

From Windermere towards Ambleside, pass Brockhole. Turn right for Troutbeck. Hotel drive half a mile.

VISA AmEx C

Windermere continued overleaf...

QUARRY GARTH COUNTRY HOUSE HOTEL

Troutbeck Bridge, Windermere, Cumbria LA23 1LF
☎ (015394) 88282 FAX (015394) 46584
HUW & LYNNE PHILLIPS

🛏 10, 10 en-suite, from £45.00 per person, double occ.
Lunch served. Non-residents welcome. Open all year.
✕ £19.50, last orders 9pm.
🍴 Specially selected salmon and hams, locally smoked. Rack of
Herdwick Lamb, roasted in garden herbs and arran mustard crust
presented on honey roasted Mediterranean vegetables. Supreme
of chicken filled with mango and banana in creamy curry sauce.
Traditional hot puddings.

This gracious and mellow Edwardian country house is set in acres
of peaceful Lakeland gardens and woodland near Lake
Windermere. Five course dinners can be taken by candlelight in
the restaurant where the rich oak panelling and log fires
underline the unique ambience of a true country house hotel.

VISA 🔲 💳 AmEx ⊗ ∵/ 🖎 ⊕ C

BRAEMOUNT HOUSE HOTEL

Sunny Bank Road, Windermere, Cumbria LA23 2EN
☎ (015394) 45967 FAX (015394) 45967
IAN & ANNE HILL

🛏 5, 5 en-suite, from £27.00 per person, double occ.
Non-residents welcome. Open all year.
✕ £15.50, last orders 8.30pm.
🍴 Daily changing menu. Wild Scotch Salmon. Lakeland Lamb.
Cucumber and Three Mints Sorbet. Double Chocolate Truffle
Torte.

An attractive, peaceful, detached Victorian house, built in 1879,
which retains much of its original charm and character. For
children under 10 years please contact the hotel direct.

VISA 🔲 ⊗🖎∵/ A

WINSCOMBE, Somerset

Village six miles inland from Weston-super-Mare just off A38. Visit
Cheddar, Wells, Bath or Bristol. Near to Bristol Airport. Closest
Motorway Junction 21 M5. *See also Churchill.*

DANESWOOD HOUSE HOTEL

Cuck Hill, Shipham, Nr Winscombe, Somerset BS25 1RD
☎ (01934) 84 3145 FAX (01934) 84 3824
MR D. E. & MRS E. HODGES

🛏 12, 12 en-suite, from £32.50 per person, double occ.
Lunch served. Non-residents welcome. Open all year.
✕ from £17.95 a la carte, last orders 9.30pm.
🍴 A daily changing menu offers only the freshest of seasonally
available produce. The style of the cuisine is best described as
"New English".

An Edwardian country house hotel, which has been tastefully
restored. The rooms offer excellent standard of accommodation,
and the restaurant is attractively furnished in the period style.

✛ Shipham signposted from A38 Bristol - Bridgwater road. Go
through village towards Cheddar. Hotel on left leaving village.

VISA 🔲 💳 AmEx ⊗ ∵/ 🖎 C

WITHERIDGE, Devon

Small village in the centre of Devon, a good base from which to visit any of the county's attractions.

THELBRIDGE CROSS INN ✗ ✗ ✗

Thelbridge, Nr Witheridge, Devon EX17 4SQ
✆ (01884) 860316 FAX (01884) 860316
BILL & RIA BALL

🛏 8, 8 en-suite, from £26.00 per person, double occ.
Lunch served. Non-residents welcome. Open all year.
✗ £10.00, last orders 9pm.
🍴 Home-made pies, lasagnes and speciality dishes prepared from fresh local ingredients. Breaded Brie. Prawn Cocktail. Rack of Lamb Almondine. Chicken Leoni, chicken breast in a lemon cream sauce with asparagus. Grills.

A personally owned and run, typical Devon inn, offering a warm welcome, attentive staff and comfortable, individually furnished accommodation. Our inspector classed this as `a real gem' offering blazing log fires, two dining rooms, two bar areas and an immaculate kitchen presided over by the chef patronne. There is a family suite with its own sitting room and kitchen facilities.

VISA 💳 AmEx ⊗ ✓ 🚭 A

WITHYPOOL, Somerset

A small village in the heart of Exmoor National Park, on the banks of the river Barle. Breathtaking local scenery. Close to many historic sites and ten miles from the coast.

ROYAL OAK INN ✗

Withypool, Somerset TA24 7QP
✆ (0164383) 506/7 FAX (0164383) 659
MICHAEL BRADLEY

🛏 8, 7 en-suite, from £33.00 per person, double occ.
Lunch served. Non-residents welcome. Closed 25th & 26th December.
✗ £18.50, last orders 9pm.
🍴 Salmon, local game in season and English cheeses. Carefully selected wine list.

A 17th century inn, featuring exposed beams and log fires. Guests can enjoy a calm, relaxing atmosphere, in comfortable surroundings. The beautiful village of Withypool is an ideal base from which to ride, hunt, shoot, fish or simply walk over the moors.

✙ M5 exit junction 27. A361 to South Molton, turn right for North Molton then Withypool.

VISA 💳 AmEx ⊗ 🚭 🐕 B

WITNEY, Oxfordshire

Small Oxfordshire market town built around a medieval square and green, surrounded by merchants houses. Within easy reach of Oxford, Blenheim Palace and the Cotswolds.

THE BIRD IN HAND ✗✗

Hailey, Nr Witney, Oxfordshire OX8 5XP
✆ (01993) 868321 FAX (01993) 868702
PAUL DAVIDSON

🛏 16, 16 en-suite, from £29.75 per person, double occ.
Lunch served. Non-residents welcome. Open all year.
✗ approx £16.50 a la carte, last orders 9.30pm.
🍴 A la carte menu of mainly English cooking is supplemented by fresh fish and seafood from the chalkboard, reflecting the days fish market.

Originally, a Cotswold coaching house and farm, The Bird In Hand has recently undergone major renovation and restoration to develop a spacious residential inn. The cottage style, high standard accommodation is built around a quiet grass courtyard, set in peaceful open countryside.

VISA 🔷 ⊗ ♿ ⌣ / 🐾 A

WOODBRIDGE, Suffolk

Once a major sea port, Woodbridge is now a sailing centre. Visit Minsmere bird sanctuary, Orford and Framlingham castles or Aldeburgh.

THE OLD RECTORY

Campsea Ashe, Woodbridge, Suffolk IP13 0PU
✆ (01728) 746524
STEWART BASSETT

🛏 6, 6 en-suite, from £24.00 per person, double occ.
Non-residents welcome. Closed 25th & 26th December.
✗ £15.50, last orders 8.45pm.
🍴 Anglo-French cuisine prepared from fresh local ingredients. Parcel of Salmon, Fennel and Halibut in Filo Pastry. Haunch of Venison marinaded in Burgundy. Upside down Ginger and Pear Cake with Cream.

A 17th century rectory set in four acres of mature garden. A peaceful location, offering unpretentious comfortable surroundings. In summer dinner is taken in an attractive conservatory. Comprehensive fine wine list.

VISA 🔷 AmEx ⊗ ⌣ / A

WORFIELD, Shropshire

A small village between Bridgnorth and Wolverhampton. See the Severn Valley Railway, Ironbridge Gorge and the aerospace museums. *See also Bridgnorth, Telford.*

THE OLD VICARAGE HOTEL

Worfield, Bridgnorth, Shropshire WV15 5JZ
☎(01746) 716497 FAX (01746) 716552
PETER & CHRISTINE ILES

🛏 14, 14 en-suite, from £44.00 per person, double occ.
Lunch served. Non-residents welcome. Open all year.
✕£21.50 & £26.50, last orders 9pm.
🍴 Seafish and shellfish from the West Country, wild salmon from the Severn and Wye, Welsh lamb, local game, traditionally reared pork, beef and poultry. Home-made bread, ice cream, sorbet, jams and preserves.

An Edwardian country house set in two acres of grounds overlooking fields and farmland. The hotel offers an air of efficient informality set amidst period furnishings and decor.

VISA 🖃 💳 AmEx 🚫 🚫 ✓ 🐾 C

YEOVIL, Somerset

A pretty market town beside the river Yeo. See the interesting Parish church and the Museum of south Somerset at Hendford Manor.

LITTLE BARWICK HOUSE HOTEL

Barwick, Yeovil, Somerset BA22 9TD
☎(01935) 23902 FAX (01935) 20908
CHRISTOPHER & VERONICA COLLEY

🛏 6, 6 en-suite, from £36.00 per person, double occ.
Non-residents welcome. Closed from 24th December for three weeks.
✕£21.90, last orders 9pm.
🍴 English and continental cuisine, made from local produce. Roast Rack of Somerset Lamb. Wild Duck in Plum Sauce. Breast of Pheasant with Chestnut Stuffing and Game Sauce. Marinaded Salmon in Dill, Garlic and Olive Oil. Steamed Treacle Pudding. FINALIST, REPRESENTING THE SOUTH, IN THE 1994 LOGIS REGIONAL CUISINE COMPETITION.

A small Georgian Dower House, in the countryside, 1 mile from Yeovil. Set in three and a half acres of lovely garden, comfortably furnished with a relaxed atmosphere.

⊹ Turn off A37 Yeovil/Dorchester road opposite Red House Inn. Hotel 500metres on the left.

VISA 🖃 💳 AmEx 🚫 ✓ 🖎 🐾 B

YORK, Yorkshire

A Roman walled city. Visit York Minster, The Shambles, Stonegate as well as numerous other attractions. The North Yorkshire countryside is amongst the most varied and spectacular in Britain.

KNAVESMIRE MANOR HOTEL

302 Tadcaster Road, York, North Yorkshire YO2 2HE
☎ (01904) 702941 FAX (01904) 709274
MR & MRS I. C. SENIOR

🛏 21, 21 en-suite, from £34.50 per person, double occ.
Non-residents welcome. Open all year.
✕ £13.75, last orders 9pm.
English and continental cuisine, prepared from local Yorkshire produce wherever possible.

A late Georgian house, built in 1833, formerly a Rowntree family home. The hotel overlooks York racecourse and is close to the city centre. In a sunny corner of the walled garden there is a tropical pool and spa in a Victorian conservatory.

⚓ From south take A1036; or from city centre take Leeds/Racecourse route.

VISA ⬛ AmEx ⊗ ⚓ ✓ ⑤ ⬧ B

THE HOTEL FAIRMOUNT

230 Tadcaster Road, York, North Yorkshire YO2 2ES
☎ (01904) 638298 FAX (01904) 639724
LESLEY LOCKWOOD

🛏 12, 10 en-suite, from £27.00 per person, double occ.
Non-residents welcome. Open all year
✕ £14.00, last orders 8pm
Roast Beef and Yorkshire Pudding. Home Baked York Ham. Yorkshire Curd Tart. Local sausages. Fresh locally caught fish. Yorkshire Dales Lamb and North York Moors Pheasants when in Season. Home-made fruit cake and Yorkshire Dales Cheeses, Yorkshire Cream Teas.

A mid-terrace, Victorian villa built in 1881 and now tastefully restored to provide comfortable accommodation. A few minutes walk from the ancient city walls, station and overlooking York's famous Knavesmire Racecourse.

⚓ From south take A1036; or from city centre take Leeds/Racecourse route.

VISA ⬛ ⊗ ♿ ✓ ⬧ A

THE DUKE OF CONNAUGHT HOTEL

Copmanthorpe Grange, York, North Yorkshire YO2 3TN
☎ (01904) 744318
JACK HUGHES

🛏 9, 9 en-suite, from £27.50 per person, double occ.
Closed Christmas & New Year.
✕ £12.00 to £14.00, last orders 11pm.
🍽 Smoked Mackerel. Rainbow Trout braised with Butter and Almonds. Venison in Red Wine Sauce. Chicken Breast in Leek and Stilton Sauce. Chocolate Fudge Cake. Treacle Sponge.

Formerly a famous stud farm, the hotel is set in woods and farmland 4 miles from York. It retains all the character of the original tack room and farm buildings. Relaxed friendly atmosphere.

VISA ▰ AmEx ⊗ ♿ ⌖ ⅃ ⊕ A

The Old Vicarage Hotel, Worfield

Somerset House, Bath

Salisbury House, Diss

SCOTLAND

ABERFELDY, Perthshire

A picturesque town situated at the geographic centre of Scotland. Ideal base for sight seeing being on the crossroads of the ancient routes through the Highlands. Excellent fishing, golf and walking nearby.

🏛🏛🏛 MONESS HOUSE HOTEL

Crieff Road, Aberfeldy, Perthshire PH15 2DY
📞 (01887) 820446 FAX (01887) 820062
GRAHAM BOYLE

🛏 12, 12 en-suite, from £35.00 per person, double occ.
Non-residents welcome. Open all year.
✕ £15.95, last orders 9pm.
🍴 Daily changing menus featuring fresh Scottish produce including Roast Loin of Scottish Hill Lamb crowned with a Mushroom Pate and served with Haggis Dumplings. Angus Beef, Sirloin stuffed with Dunsyre Cheese wrapped in Bacon. Fresh venison and salmon always available.

A country house dating from 1753 with every modern amenity, including the recent inclusion of its own leisure centre, offering swimming, squash, snooker etc. Regular live-entertainment including weekly Highland Dinner Dances.

⚜ From the crossroads in town, the hotel is half a mile south on the Crieff road.
VISA 🔲 💷 AmEx ↘ ✓ 🕸 Ⓢ ⬥ A

ABERFOYLE, Stirlingshire

A good base for visiting the Trossachs and lochs. The Rob Roy visitor centre is 20 minutes drive away and Stirling Caslte only 35 minutes. *See also Port of Menteith.*

🏛🏛 ALTSKEITH HOTEL

Kinlochard, Aberfoyle, Trossachs FK8 3TL
📞 (01877) 387266 FAX (01877) 387223
MALCOLM & MARGARET CAMPBELL

🛏 5, 5 en-suite, from £25.00 per person, double occ.
Lunch served. Non-residents welcome. Closed Christmas.
✕ from £15.00 a la carte, last orders 9pm.
🍴 Fresh regional produce. Venison Rob Ruadh with Wild Mushrooms, Red Wine and Juniper Berries. Fillet of Scottish Salmon with a Butter, Lemon, Dill and Pink Peppercorn Sauce.

A family run hotel overlooking the loch, with stunning views of Ben Lomond and Queen Elizabeth Forest. Parts of the white walled building date back to the eighteenth century. 'Rob Roy' is reputed to have visited the premises, even hiding in the cellar once to evade the redcoats.

VISA 🔲 💷 ♿ ✓ 🕸 B

ABOYNE, Aberdeenshire

A small village on the banks of the Dee River, ten miles east of Ballater. An ideal centre for visiting the many castles and historical sites on beautiful Royal Deeside. *See also Ballater.*

HAZLEHURST LODGE & RESTAURANT

Ballater Road, Aboyne, Aberdeenshire AB34 5HY
*(013398) 86921
ANNE STRACHAN

3, 3 en-suite, from £28.50 per person, double occ.
Non-residents welcome. Closed January.
from £14.00 a la carte, last orders 9.30pm.
Taste of Scotland menu using the best of local produce. Aberdeen Angus beef, fresh fish from the sea and river, game from the ancient Caledonian forests of Deeside, wild mushrooms and fruit. Generous use of herbs and vegetables.

Hazlehurst, the former coachman's lodge to Aboyne Castle, retains the intimate charm of a Victorian Highland home, while the interior shows a continuation of the Scottish art and craft movement. Lunch available by prior arrangement.

VISA AmEx A B

ALTNAHARRA, Sutherland

A small hamlet 20 miles north of Lairg on the road to Tongue, renowned for its fishing. Walking, stalking and shooting are all possible within the immediate surrounding area. *See also Tongue, Lairg.*

ALTNAHARRA HOTEL

Altnaharra, By Lairg, Sutherland IV27 4UE
*(01549) 411222 FAX (01549) 411222
P. PANCHAUD

18, 17 en-suite, from £39.50 per person, double occ.
Non-residents welcome. Closed mid October to 1st March.
£17.00, last orders 8.30pm.
Freshly caught salmon, local lamb and beef.

This hotel is one of Scotland's best known fishing centres. Originally built as a coaching inn, the hotel has been fully refurbished and decorated to provide a high quality standard of accommodation. The Altnaharra enjoys a completely isolated situation with beautiful views of the surrounding countryside, and is the perfect place to relax and unwind.

VISA B

ANSTRUTHER, Fife

Picturesque fishing village, in the East Neuk of Fife, with easy access for many Golf Courses, "Scotland's Secret Bunker", St Andrews and Local Mansion Houses & Gardens.

🏠 THE SPINDRIFT

Pittenweem Road, Anstruther, Fife KY10 3DT
☎ (01333) 310573
ERIC & MOYRA MCFARLANE

🛏 8, 8 en-suite, from £25.00 per person, double occ.
Closed 10th January to 3rd February.
✗ £11.50, last orders 8pm.
🍴 Orkney Herring. Chicken Liver Pate with Cointreau. Pittenweem Prawns and Cottage Cheese. Griddled Spring Lamb. Fresh Peaches poached in Wine and served in a Brandy Basket. Toffee Fudge Pie. Anstruther Coffee Cake. Artic Lemon Slice.

A stone built Victorian house with a wealth of original features. All bedrooms are individually and tastefully furnished. The hotel offers a friendly relaxed atmosphere. A totally non-smoking hotel.

⚐ On the A917, first building on the left approaching from Pittenweem.

VISA 🖃 ⊗ ✓ 🏊 A

APPIN, Argyll

A small village. The hotel is actually situated in Kentallen, a loch-side hamlet between Appin and Ballachulish, near the top of Loch Linnhe. Good base for walking, climbing, fishing, pony riding or touring the Western Highlands.

🏠🏠🏠 THE HOLLY TREE HOTEL

Kentallen, By Appin, Argyll PA38 4BY
☎ (01631) 740292 FAX (01631) 740345
KEITH & GILLIAN BANYARD

🛏 10, 10 en-suite, from £37.50 per person, double occ.
Lunch served. Non-residents welcome. Closed two weeks in November.
✗ £23.50, last orders 9.30pm.
🍴 Saddle of Venison with Oatmeal and Malt Whisky. Local Prawns, baked in Ginger and White Wine Sauce. Fillet of Wild Salmon with Hazlenuts and Creme Fraiche.

A turn of the century converted railway station in a quiet and restful location at the very edge of loch Linnhe. Log fires welcome guests in the dining room and lounge. Comfortably furnished bedrooms, all enjoying a view of the loch. Friendly, welcoming hospitality.

VISA 🖃 ⊗ ♿ ✓ 🏊 C

AYR, Ayrshire

Town on the West Coast, known for its racecourse, surrounded by Burns country including his Cottage, Monument, Alloway Kirk and Auld Brig O'Doon.

PICKWICK HOTEL

19 Racecourse Road, Ayr, Ayrshire KA7 2TD
☎(01292) 260111 FAX (01292) 285348
ALEX MCKENZIE

⊨ 15, 15 en-suite, from £35.00 per person, double occ.
Lunch served. Non-residents welcome. Open all year.
✕£15.95, last orders 9.45pm.
🍴 Chicken & Mushroom Crepes. Prawn Cocktail. Grilled Rainbow Trout. Gammon Steak Hebridean. Meringue Parfait.

A friendly hotel situated just outside the town centre in its own grounds. The hotel has recently been completely refurbished and has two restaurants.

✢ From town centre (Burns Statue Square) follow road onto Miller Road and turn left.

VISA ⬛ AmEx ✓ 🌫 🏊 🐾 A

THE BURNS MONUMENT HOTEL

Alloway, Ayr, Ayrshire KA7 4PQ
☎(01292) 442466 FAX (01292) 443174
DAVID LOCHANS

⊨ 9, 8 en-suite, from £30.00 per person, double occ.
Lunch served. Non-residents welcome. Open all Year.
✕£12.00, last orders 9.45pm.
🍴 Button Mushrooms and Norwegian Prawns sauteed in Garlic Butter. Fresh Pork stuffed with mature Scottish Cheddar and Honey Roast Ham. Breast of Chicken, in a mild Cream and Curry Sauce.

A 19th century coaching inn situated in its own grounds with landscaped gardens running alongside the banks of the River Doon and bordered by the famous Auld Brig O'Doon and Burns Monument.

✢ Follow signage for Alloway, south of Ayr on the A77.

VISA ⬛ AmEx ✓ 🌫 🐾 A

BALLACHULISH, Argyll

A small village on the banks of Loch Leven, where Glencoe meets the sea, surrounded by beautiful highland scenery. Numerous sporting and outdoor activities.

⌂⌂⌂ THE ISLES OF GLENCOE HOTEL AND LEISURE CENTRE

Ballachulish, Fort William, Argyll PA39 4HL
☎ (0185) 5811602 FAX (0185) 5811770
LAURENCE YOUNG

🛏 39, 39 en-suite, from £37.00 per person, double occ.
Lunch served. Non-residents welcome. Open all year.
✕ £19.50, last orders 10pm.
🍴 Taste of Scotland and international cuisine menus.

A recently completed hotel and leisure centre which offers guests a high standard of service and cuisine. The centre is close to Glencoe for summer climbing or winter ski-ing and boasts two loch-side harbours and three kilometres of water frontage for those interested in water sports.

✛ Hotel lies adjacent to A82 Glasgow/Fort William road, 1 mile west of Glencoe.

VISA 🔳 ⊗ ⌇ ✓ 🕭 🆂 B

BALLANTRAE, Ayrshire

Close to Culzean Castle, Galloway forest and mountains, The Mull of Galloway and Burns' country.

⌂⌂ BALKISSOCK LODGE

Ballantrae, Ayrshire KA26 0LP
☎ (01465) 83537
JANET & ADRIAN BEALE

🛏 3, 3 en-suite, from £27.50 to £30.00 per person, double occ.
Lunch served. Non-residents welcome. Closed for two weeks in November or December.
✕ £18.00, last orders 9pm.
🍴 Taste of Scotland menu featuring vegetarian specialities. Vegetarian a la carte menu. Wee Chicken Parcels. Venison with Berries. Carrot Roulade with Ginger & Lemon Sauce. Ecclefechan Tart with Orange & Honey. Reservations essential for non-residents.

A stone built former shooting lodge, built in the 1830's to serve the Laggan Estate. Inside, the hotel has the feel of a comfortable rambling home, with bookcases full of maps, games, magazines and books.

VISA 🔳 ⊗ ♿ ✓ 🕭 A

BALLATER, Aberdeenshire

Picturesque town on the banks of the River Dee in the heart of the Grampian Mountains. Visit the Royal residence at Balmoral, many National Trust for Scotland properties, the Whisky Trail or simply enjoy the beautiful scenery. *See also Aboyne.*

DARROCH LEARG HOTEL

Braemar Road, Ballater, Aberdeenshire AB35 5UX
☎(013397) 55443 FAX (013397) 55443
NIGEL FRANKS

🛏 20, 20 en-suite, from £42.00 per person, double occ.
Lunch served. Non-residents welcome. Closed January.
✕£21.75, last orders 8.30pm.
🍴 Fillet of Scotch Lamb on a crisp Celeriac Pancake. Wild Dee Salmon with local Chanterelles. Aberdeen Angus and Highland Beef. Fresh game in Season. Selection of fine Scottish cheeses.

A finely appointed country house hotel set in 5 acre grounds on the wooded slopes of Craigendarroch, the rocky hill which stands above Ballater. The hotel is a 10 minute walk from the centre of town. A conservatory restaurant has a superb outlook across the Dee Valley towards the Grampian Hills.

✛ On the A93 at the western edge of Ballater.
VISA 🖾 💳 AmEx ⊗ ♿ ✓ 🐕 🐾 C

THE ALEXANDRA HOTEL

12 Bridge Square, Ballater, Aberdeenshire AB3 5QJ
☎(013397) 55376 FAX (013397) 55466
DONALD CHIDDICK

🛏 7, 7 en-suite, from £24.00 to £30.00 per person, double occ.
Lunch served. Non-residents welcome. Open all year.
✕£15.50, last orders 9pm.
🍴Scottish fresh produce, cooked with a French flavour. Dee salmon, venison, Scotch lamb, game in season, Aberdeen Angus steak.

A very comfortable, 150 year old, town centre hotel which has recently been completely refurbished. The atmosphere is very friendly and the cuisine under the direction of Alain is highly regarded.
VISA 🖾 💳 AmEx ✓ 🐕 A

THE GREEN INN

9 Victoria Road, Ballater, Aberdeenshire AB3 5QQ
☎(013397) 55701 FAX (013397) 55701
MR & MRS J. J. PURVES

🛏 3, 3 en-suite, from £25.00 per person, double occ.
Lunch served. Non-residents welcome. Closed November, first week of January, Sundays from December to February.
✕£19.50, last orders 9pm.
🍴 Local Ham and Haddie. Tweedie Kettlie. Crowdie Cake. Local and regional cheeseboard.

An excellent restaurant with three comfortable letting rooms. The granite house was formerly a temperance hotel, but now offers an interesting selection of traditional Scottish foods and a well balanced wine list.

✛ Take A93 to Ballater and Victoria Road is near the Church on the Green.
VISA 🖾 ♿ ✓ 🐕 🐾 A

BALLYGRANT, Isle of Islay

An ideal base from which to tour Islay, famous for the seven malt whisky distilleries bordering the islands shores. Good walking countryside and opportunities for fishing and bird watching.

BALLYGRANT INN

Ballygrant, Islay, Argyll PA45 7QR
☎ (01496) 840277 FAX (01496) 840277
DAVID & RUBY GRAHAM

🛏 3, 3 en-suite, from £25.00 per person, double occ.
Lunch served. Non-residents welcome. Open all year.
✖ £15.00, last orders 9.30pm.
🍴 Local game and fish, locally reared beef and lamb, shellfish Scallops in an Islay Cheese and Wine sauce. Roast leg of Islay Lamb in a Red Wine and Rowan Sauce. Sirloin steaks in whisky mushroom and cream. Home baked bread and sweets. "Taste of Islay" menu.

A traditional stone inn in two acres of grounds with comfortable furnishings and a friendly, welcoming atmosphere. Excellent food with wide use of local produce   Islay is the southern most Island of the Hebrides.

⊕ Ballygrant Inn is 3 miles south of Port Askrig ferry port.

VISA 🖸 ⊗ ⚹ ∿ ⌾ ⚐ A

BALQUHIDDER, Perthshire

This quiet, peaceful region of Scotland is within easy driving distance of all the major cities. Formerly the home village of Rob Roy, Balquhidder is set amongst spectacular scenery overlooking the lochs and glens. *See also Strathyre.*

MONACHYLE MHOR FARMHOUSE HOTEL

Balquhidder, Lochearnhead, Perthshire FK19 8PQ
☎ (01877) 384622 FAX (01877) 384305
ROB & JEAN LEWIS

🛏 5, 5 en-suite, from £25.00 per person, double occ.
Lunch served. Non-residents welcome. Open all year.
✖ £16.00 - £20.00, last orders 10pm.

🍴 Mousseline of Salmon and Fresh Herbs. Plate of Mixed Game served with a wild Raspberry Dressing. Marzipan, Chocolate and Brandy Wedge.

Small 18th century award winning farmhouse hotel set in its own two thousand acres with magnificent views over two lochs. The hotel is furnished with period furniture and fine pictures and has an open fire in the cosy Highland bar. Fishing and stalking can be organised in season. The farmhouse is six scenic miles from the A84 main road, with Glasgow/Edinburgh less than one hours drive away. A perfect retreat for those who simply want to 'get away from it all'.

VISA 🖸 ⚹ ∿ ⌾ A

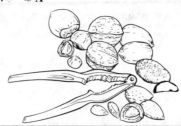

BEATTOCK, Dumfriesshire

Close to Moffat, set just off the A74 Glasgow to Carlisle road. This region of Scotland is often overlooked by visitors speeding north but is surrounded by spectacular scenery, lochs and fells. *See also Moffat, Tweedsmuir.*

AUCHEN CASTLE HOTEL

Beattock, Moffat, Dumfriesshire DG10 9SH
☎ (01683) 300407 FAX (01683) 300667
HAZEL BECKH

🛏 25, 25 en-suite, from £37.50 per person, double occ.
Lunch served. Non-residents welcome. Closed 3 weeks
Christmas & New Year.
✗ £13.50 - £18.00, last orders 9pm
🍴 Leg of Annandale Lamb with Rosemary and Coriander. Ayrshire
Duckling with Marjoram. Solway Salmon. Ayrshire Ham poached
in Bouillion and served with Madiera Sauce. Langoustines,
scallops and sea trout.

Set in 50 acres of grounds in a spectacular position on the hillside
above the upper Annandale valley, Auchen Castle was originally
built in 1849, and for many years was the home of the William
Younger family. The hotel enjoys its own attractive trout loch and
is an ideal spot for a short break or overnight stay on the way
further north or south. There is an especial collection of trees.

✤ Signposted direct from A74/M74, 1 mile north of Beattock Village.
VISA 💳 AmEx 🦷 〰 ⬦ **B**

BEITH, Ayrshire

Equidistant from the coast at Troon, with some of the most famous golf
courses in the world, and central Glasgow, this small town is ideally
situated for exploring Burns country, Ayrshire coast and Glasgow. Fifteen
miles from Glasgow Airport. *See also Cardross, Glasgow.*

MANOR FARM HOTEL

Burnhouse, Beith, Ayrshire KA15 1LT
☎ (01560) 484006
ROBERT & BETTY ROBERTSON & JOAN WILSON

🛏 9, 7 en-suite, from £24.00 per person, double occ.
Open all year.
✗ approx £10.00 a la carte, last orders 8pm.
🍴 Limited menu but all fresh home cooking.

An elegant, stone built, farmhouse which has been converted to a
friendly and informal hotel. The accommodation has recently been
completely refurbished to a high standard. A cosy lounge bar
doubles as a restaurant for evening dinners. Dogs allowed by prior
arrangement only. A putting green and childrens' soft play area
are planned for Spring 1995.

✤ M8 to Glasgow Airport, take A737 (to Beith Lirvine) by-pass
Beith and follow B706 (Dunlop Road) for 4 miles to Burnhouse.

VISA 💳 ⊗ 🦷 **A**

BRAE, Shetland

Busta is on the western coast of mainland Shetland, an island removed from the bustle of modern life, with an absence of noise and rush. Stunning scenery. Unwind and enjoy walking, birdwatching, fishing or archaeology.

BUSTA HOUSE HOTEL

Busta, Brae, Shetland ZE2 9QN
☎ (0180622) 506 FAX (0180622) 588
PETER & JUDITH JONES

🛏 20, 20 en-suite, from £42.00 per person, double occ.
Non-residents welcome. Closed 21st December to 3rd January.
✕ £21.50, last orders 9pm.
🍴 Daily changing menu, featuring fresh island produce. Shetland fish and shellfish, lamb, Orkney beef and ale. Home-made puddings. Restaurant open evenings only - an extensive bar meal menu available for lunches and suppers.

A 16th century former Lairds home, with its own friendly ghost. The hotel is decorated in comfortable yet elegant style. Busta House has its own little harbour and enjoys fabulous views over Busta Voe. The owners are happy to assist with travelling arrangements to the island. An ideal place to relax away from the hassles of modern life.

⊕ A970 north from Lerwick to Brae. After 1 mile, turn left for Muckle Roe and Busta House.

VISA 🔳 🔳 AmEx 🕲 🔄 C

CALLANDER, Perthshire

Small town, in the Trossachs, with good local shopping and a host of tourist attractions. Visit Loch Lomond, Loch Katrine or explore the surrounding nature trails and forest walks.

DALGAIR HOUSE HOTEL

Main Street, Callander, Perthshire FK17 8BQ
☎ (01877) 330283 FAX (01877) 331114
JIM, JENNIFER & LISA MCDONALD

🛏 8, 8 en-suite, from £27.00 per person, double occ.
Lunch served. Non-residents welcome. Open all year.
✕ from £12.00 a la carte, last orders 9pm.
🍴 Traditional Scottish cuisine prepared from fresh ingredients. Venison & salmon when in season.

A small, family run hotel offering caring, personal service. Dalgair House Hotel has both a bistro style cafe for light refreshments and a traditional restaurant. Simply but comfortably furnished.

⊕ From A 84, travelling north, enter Callander, turn right at the golf course then first left. Hotel car park is 200 yards down narrow road on the left.

VISA 🔳 🔳 AmEx 🖊 🕲 🔄 A

CARDROSS, Dunbartonshire

A village, 18 miles west of Glasgow, and north of the Clyde, midway between Dumbarton and Helensburgh. Only 14 miles from Glasgow airport, it is handy for Loch Lomond, the Trossachs and West Highlands. *See also Glasgow, Beith.*

🏠🏠 KIRKTON HOUSE

Darleith Road, Cardross, Dunbartonshire G82 5EZ
☎ (01389) 841951 FAX (01389) 841868
STEWART & GILLIAN MACDONALD

🛏 6, 6 en-suite, from £28.50 per person, double occ.
Lunch served. Closed 20th December to 10th January.
✗ £16.50, last orders 7.30pm.
🍲 Home cooking including salmon, venison, Dover sole and sirloin steak. Breakfast kippers or smoked haddock. Menu varied each day.

A converted 19th century farmhouse, which has superb views of the Clyde from a tranquil country location above the village. Kirkton House has a friendly, informal, unpretentious ambiance and a roaring open fire in the lounge on chilly evenings.

⊹ From A814 at west end of Cardross turn north up "Darleith Road". Kirkton House drive is 750 yards on the right.

VISA 💳 AmEx ✓ 🕲 ⊕ A

CARRBRIDGE, Inverness-shire

Carrbridge lies in Strathspey six miles north of Aviemore and within easy reach of the Cairngorms. Visit Distilleries, the Highland Wildlife Park, Clan Museums and the Landmark Visitors Centre.

🏠🏠 FAIRWINDS HOTEL

Carrbridge, Inverness-shire PH23 3AA
☎ (01479) 841240 FAX (01479) 841240
ROGER & ELIZABETH REED

🛏 5, 5 en-suite, from £26.00 per person, double occ.
Non-residents welcome. Closed 30th October to 19th December.
✗ £12.00, last orders 8.30pm.
🍲 Avocado with Prawns. Deep Fried Brie Wedges. Chicken in Lemon and Rosemary Sauce. Ragout of Venison. Breaded Plaice with Prawn and Mushroom filling. Pork in Cider. Toffee Pavlova. Peach Melba.

An early Victorian former manse which has been extensively modernised to afford guests every comfort yet retaining the character of the original. The lounge has welcoming log fire to keep out the winter chill and create a warm atmosphere.

VISA 💳 ✓ 🕲 ⊕ A

CRIANLARICH, Perthshire

Small Highland village close to the Northern tip of Loch Lomond, Glencoe, the Trossachs and the Falls of Dochart. Centrally situated for touring the Central Highlands by road or rail.

🏦🏦 ALLT CHAORIAN COUNTRY HOUSE

Crianlarich, Perthshire FK20 8RU
📞 (01838) 300283 FAX (01838) 300238
ROGER MCDONALD

🛏 8, 8 en-suite, from £33.00 per person, double occ.
Lunch served. Closed 1st November to 1st April.
✕ £15.00 - £18.00, last orders 7pm.
🍴 Taste of Scotland menu featuring local fresh produce, local venison and trout. Clootie Dumplings.

Situated in an elevated position, off the main road, Allt Chaorian House is a small residential hotel with all the comforts and atmosphere of one's own home. The log fire burns all year and the view from the conservatory toward Ben More is one of Scotland's finest.

✛ On the A82, 1 mile from Crianlarich on the road to Tyndrum.
VISA 🔳 ⊗ ♿ ✓ 🐕 ✈ A

🏠 THE LODGE HOUSE

Crianlarich, Perthshire FK20 8RU
📞 (01838) 300276
JIMMY & JEAN YOUNG

🛏 6, 6 en-suite, from £15.00 per person, double occ.
Open all year.
✕ £13.00 to £15.00, last orders 8pm.
🍴 Haggis Vol au Vents. Loch Tay Salmon Steak. Trout 'Rob Roy' Venison Chausseur. Delicately Smoked Ham with Peaches.

The Lodge is off the road with a panoramic outlook on all sides, offering a relaxed, informal atmosphere. All bedrooms are well appointed. A totally non-smoking hotel.

✛ 3/4 mile north of Crianlarich on A82.

VISA 🔳 ⊗ ♿ ✓ 🐕 A

CRIEFF, Perthshire

A pleasant town, seventeen miles west of Perth on the banks of the Strathearn river. The town is surrounded by beautiful scenery.

🏦🏦🏦 MURRAYPARK HOTEL

Connaught Terrace, Crieff, Perthshire PH7 3DJ
📞 (01764) 653731 FAX (01764) 655311
ANN & NOEL SCOTT

🛏 13, 13 en-suite, from £30.50 per person, double occ.
Lunch served. Non-residents welcome. Open all year.
✕ from £20.00, last orders 9.30pm.
🍴 Daily Taste of Scotland menu. Glenturret pigeon, trout and game in season. Scampi Pernod. Salmon with Dill Mayonnaise Venison Desmont.

Pink stoned, large Victorian house, standing in its own grounds in a residential area of the town. The comfortable restaurant has a calm atmosphere and overlooks a pleasant garden. Excellent accommodation standards.

VISA 🔳 💳 AmEx ✓ 🐕 ✈ A

CROMARTY, Ross-shire

Thirty miles north of Inverness at the tip of the Black Isle. Among the many local sites are Hugh Miller's Cottage and the town's courthouse museum.

🏨🏨 ## ROYAL HOTEL

Marine Terrace, Cromarty, Ross-shire IV11 8YN
☎ (01381) 600217
STEWART & YVONNE MORRISON

🛏 10, 10 en-suite, from £27.50 per person, double occ.
Lunch served. Non-residents welcome. Open all year.
✖ £16.50, last orders 9pm.
🍽 Popular fresh fish and grill dishes. Kiddies menu and special diets catered for.

Comfortable, friendly hotel overlooking the Firth, where guests are greeted by open fires and highland hospitality. The non-smoking conservatory/lounge has splendid views over the sea.

VISA 💳 💳 ⊗ ✓ 🛎 🏊 A

DUNBAR, East Lothian

A seaside town, 30 miles east of Edinburgh, with 14 golf courses within half an hour's drive. The surrounding Lammermuir Hills are good walking country.

🏨 ## REDHEUGH HOTEL

Bayswell Park, Dunbar, East Lothian EH42 1AE
☎ (01368) 862793 FAX (01368) 862793
JANETTE YOUNG

🛏 10, 10 en-suite, from £29.50 per person, double occ.
Closed 25th December to 3rd January.
✖ £16.50, last orders 8.30pm.
🍽 A popular, daily changing menu - predominantly British. Vegetarian dishes available.

A small hotel with personal attention to detail and home cooking. For children under 8 years, please contact the hotel direct. From town centre, follow road along cliff top.

✈ Take first right into Bayswell Park.

VISA 💳 💳 AmEx 🔍 ✓ 🛎 🏊 🐬 A

DUNDEE, Tayside

A former whaling port, now home to Captain Scott's ship S.S. Discovery. Visit the McManus art gallery, Jute Mill Museum and Glamis Castle. Central base for exploring The Trossachs, Edinburgh and Perth.

THE SHAFTESBURY HOTEL

1 Hyndford Street, Dundee, Tayside DD2 1HQ
☎ (01382) 669216 FAX (01382) 641598
DENNIS SMITH

🛏 12, 12 en-suite, from £34.00 per person, double occ.
Non-residents welcome. Closed Christmas & New Year.
✗ from £12.50, last orders 9pm.
🍴 Game Pies. Home-made pate, marmalade, jams and rowan jelly. Scottish beef and lamb. Vegetarian menu. No smoking permitted in the restaurant. Tiger Prawns in Filo Pastry, with a Lemon and Ginger dip. Poached Tay Salmon. Banana and Toffee Cheesecake.

An imposing Victorian mansion, once the home of a Jute Baron, that has been carefully converted into a fine town house hotel. Close to the town centre but in a quiet location. Comfortably furnished offering good value and excellent individual care. There is a coffee bar, a restaurant and a room for private dinners.

VISA 🔲 ⚖ ⊗ ✓ ⚐ A

DUNDONNELL, Ross-shire

Set amidst the spectacular scenery of Wester Ross, Dundonnell is a small hamlet at the southern tip of Little Loch Broom. Visit the nearby Inverewe Gardens and Gruinard Bay. The coast road south from Dundonnell is stunning.

DUNDONNELL HOTEL

Dundonnell, By Garve, Ross-shire IV23 2QR
☎ (01854) 633204 FAX (01854) 633366
SELBIE & FLORA FLORENCE

🛏 24, 24 en-suite, from £42.50 per person, double occ.
Lunch served. Non-residents welcome. Closed November to mid March.
✗ £19.75, last orders 8.30pm.
🍴 Local seafood, prawns and lobster. Lamb, beef, home-made soups and imaginative desserts.

A former highland drovers inn, the Dundonnell Hotel has now been fully modernised to a high standard of decor and facilities, yet it still remains a popular focus point for the surrounding farming and fishing community. The hotel has been in the Florence family for over 30 years.

⊹ From A832 between Ullapool and Gairloch. A9 from Inverness to Tore, then A835 to Braemore. Take A835 to Dundonnell.

VISA 🔲 ⊗ ⚓ ⚐ B

DUNKELD, Perthshire

Historic market town on the banks of the Tay, equidistant between Pitlochry and Perth. *See also Pitlochry.*

ROYAL DUNKELD HOTEL

Atholl Street, Dunkeld, Perthshire PH8 0AR
✆ (01350) 727322 FAX (01350) 728989
GRAHAM & ANN REES

🛏 35, 35 en-suite, from £30.00 per person, double occ.
Lunch served. Non-residents welcome. Open all year.
✕ £14.00, last orders 9.30pm.
🍴 Carvery restaurant with local salmon, haggis and vegetarian meals.

Formerly an 18th century coaching inn, the Royal Dunkeld is now a fully modernised and well appointed family run hotel.

VISA 🔳 💳 AmEx ♿ ✓ 🛇 ⚓ B

DUNOON, Argyll

This town is popularly known as 'The gateway to the Western Highlands' and lies on the Firth of Clyde. One hour from Glasgow airport, or two hours drive from Edinburgh. Visit Argyll Forest or enjoy walking and birdwatching.

ENMORE HOTEL

Marine Parade, Kirn, Dunoon, Argyll PA23 8HH
✆ (01369) 702230 FAX (01369) 702148
ANGELA & DAVID WILSON

🛏 10, 10 en-suite, from £40.00 per person, double occ.
Lunch served. Non-residents welcome. Open all year.
✕ £23.00, last orders 9pm.
🍴 Taste of Scotland menu, featuring home grown vegetables and herbs. Whole Prawns in Garlic Butter. Locally smoked venison. Curried Apple Soup. Roast Gigot of Lamb. Loch Fyne Scallops in Pernod. Creel caught Loch Fyne Crayfish.

A Georgian country house hotel with sea views and good food. The decor is elegant and formal. Many thoughtful individual touches create a luxury environment; fresh flower arrangements and open fires in the public rooms. Luxury bedrooms with four posters, water beds and jacuzzi baths are available. The hotel has two squash courts, one with video playback facility. Dogs by prior arrangement only.

✛ On coastal route between 2 ferries, 1 mile north of Dunoon.

VISA 🔳 ⊗ ♿ ✓ 🛇 ⚓ A

ABBOT'S BRAE HOTEL

West Bay, Dunoon, Argyll PA23 7QJ
✆ (01369) 705021 FAX (01369) 705021
CAROLE & DUNCAN NAIRN

🛏 7, 7 en-suite, from £26.00 per person, double occ.
Closed 1st November to end of February.
✕ £13.50, last orders 8.30.
🍴 Home-made Scotch Broth. Crispy coated Camembert with Tomato Chutney. Breaded King Prawns and Curry Sauce. Venison in Red Wine. Fresh Poached Scottish Salmon with Parsley Sauce.

A Victorian country house situated in secluded woodland with magnificent sea views. All bedrooms are attractively furnished.

VISA 🔳 💳 ⊗ ✓ 🛇 ⚓ A

ROYAL MARINE HOTEL

Hunters Quay, Dunoon, Argyll PA23 8HJ
☎ (01369) 705810 FAX (01369) 702329
MR M. J. GREIG & MR P. M. ARNOLD

🛏 35, 35 en-suite, from £29.00 per person, double occ.
Lunch served. Non-residents welcome. Open all year.
✕ from £16.00, last orders 9pm.
🍴 Traditional Scottish and international cooking.

The Royal Marine is a large Tudor style hotel, occupying the former home of the Royal Clyde yacht club. The hotel has retained much of its nautical past and enjoys splendid views across the bay. All the bedrooms, ten of which are situated in an adjacent lodge, are comfortably furnished.

⚓ Off the A815 on the seafront opposite Western Ferries.

VISA 🖃 ⚓ 🖊 🕭 🌊 🐟 A

EDINBURGH, Lothian

Scotland's artistic capital, full of historical interest and dominated by the ancient castle fortress. August sees the Festival when Edinburgh becomes a magnate for actors, comics, singers and dancers.

A HAVEN IN EDINBURGH

180 Ferry Road, Edinburgh, Lothian EH6 4NS
☎ (0131) 554 6559 FAX (0131) 554 5252
RONALD & MOIRA MURDOCH

🛏 10, 10 en-suite, from £27.00 per person, double occ.
Closed Christmas.
✕ £12.50, last orders 8pm.
🍴 Hearty Highland breakfasts.

A Victorian town house, close to the city centre. The owners offer a personal, warm, family welcome and residents are invited to make use of the hotel's secure car park free of charge.

⚓ From the East, A1-A119-A902 Ferry Road or from the West, M8/A8-A902-A90 City Centre - Blackhall fork left to A902 Crewe Toll Ferry Road.

VISA 🖃 AmEx A B

TEVIOTDALE HOUSE

53 Grange Loan, Edinburgh, Lothian EH9 2ER
☎ (0131) 667 4376 FAX (0131) 667 4376
JOHN & JANE COVILLE

🛏 7, 5 en-suite, from £33.00 per person, double occ.
Open all year.
✕ Evening meals by prior arranagement only.
🍴 Traditional Scottish breakfasts.

An elegant Victorian gentleman's town house situated in a quiet conservation area of the city. All rooms are spacious and light. Magnificent cedar doors and panelling have been restored to their original splendour.

⚓ 1 mile south from city centre on A7, 500 yards west Newington & Grange

VISA 🖃 AmEx ⊗ 🖊 A

ESKDALEMUIR, Dumfriesshire

An unspoilt backwater in the Borders region, close to Lockerbie and Langholm, in the heart of extensive forest and moorland. Excellent area for walking and fishing. *See also Moffat.*

HART MANOR HOTEL
Eskdalemuir, Dumfriesshire DG13 0QQ
☎ (013873) 73217
MARGARET & ANDREW BENNIE

🛏 7, 5 en-suite, from £25.00 per person, double occ.
Lunch served. Non-residents welcome. Closed Christmas Day.
✕ £16.50, last orders 8pm.
🍴 Traditional dishes, prepared from fresh produce. Lamb, venison, Aberdeen Angus beef, salmon, sea trout and fresh vegetables.

Originally an 18th century shooting lodge, Hart Manor is now a small traditional hotel with a homely interior. Open log fires and a relaxed informal atmosphere prevail.

⊹ On the B709
⊗ 🕭 ⅀ ⏊ A

FINTRY, Stirlingshire

Fintry is situated in the heart of the Campsie Fells, equidistant from Loch Lomond and Stirling, with easy acces north into the Trossachs, yet just 45 minutes from Glasgow or Edinburgh airport. *See also Port of Menteith.*

CULCREUCH CASTLE
Fintry, Stirlingshire G63 0LW
☎ (01360) 860228 FAX (01360) 860555
LAIRD ANDREW HASLAM

🛏 8, 8 en-suite, from £42.00 per person, double occ.
Lunch served. Non-residents welcome. Open all year.
✕ £17.00, last orders 8.30pm.
🍴 Local, national and international dishes, all prepared from fresh locally grown ingredients.

A magnificent, romantic, 13th century Clan castle, situated in acres of parkland grounds, which has been converted by its present owners into a very comfortable country house hotel. The hotel has a squash court and indoor bowling facilities.

VISA 🖃 ⚖ AmEx ✓ ⅀ ⏊ A

FORRES, Moray

A small town, 3 miles inland from the Moray Firth and 30 miles east of Inverness. As well as being situated on the Castle and Whisky trails; the town has many tourist attractions of its own.

PARKMOUNT HOUSE HOTEL
St Leonard's Road, Forres, Moray IV36 0DW
☎ (01309) 673312 FAX (01309) 673312
MRS VITA DE WAAL

🛏 4, 4 en-suite, from £30.00 per person, double occ.
Closed November to Easter.
✕ £14.95, last orders 8.30pm.
🍴 Fresh Scottish produce prepared with Continental influence.
A charming secluded Victorian town house, offering spacious individually decorated ensuite bedrooms. The hotel welcomes smoking guests although Parkmount House is mainly non-smoking.

VISA 🖃 ⊗ 🕭 ⚘ ✓ ⅀ S ⏊ A

FORT AUGUSTUS, Inverness-shire

Lovely village, surrounded by stunning scenery, on the edge of the Caledonian Canal.

🏛🏛 LOVAT ARMS HOTEL

Fort Augustus, Inverness-shire PH32 4DU
☎ (01320) 366206 FAX (01320) 366677
HECTOR & MARY MACLEAN

🛏 21, 21 en-suite, from £33.50 per person, double occ.
Lunch served. Non-residents welcome. Open all year.
✕ £16.50, last orders 9pm.
🍽 Taste of Scotland menu. Roast Aberdeen Angus Beef. Wild Scottish Salmon with Hollandaise and Watercress. Game when in season. Wild mushrooms. Home-made pates and terrines.

A traditional Victorian hotel set in several acres of grounds, overlooking Loch Ness and the Benedictine Monastery. The Lovat Arms is in the middle of the village, with easy access to local shops. Ample parking. Guests can expect to enjoy a relaxed, comfortable atmosphere and a warm welcome.

VISA 🔳 ⌖ 🕭 ⊕ B

GLASGOW, Strathclyde

A bustling city, the commercial centre of Scotland. Visit the Cathedral, Museum of Religion and The Barras (market). *See also Cardross, Beith.*

🏛🏛 BABBITY BOWSTER

16/18 Blackfriars St, Glasgow, Strathclyde G1 1PE
☎ (0141) 552 5055 FAX (0141) 552 5215
FRASER LAURIE

🛏 6, 6 en-suite, from £32.50 per person, double occ.
Lunch served. Non-residents welcome. Open all year.
✕ £11.50 & £14.50, last orders 11pm.
🍽 The hotel offers two styles of eating, with light snacks in the ground floor cafe/bar and full meals in the first floor restaurant. Fresh produce is prepared throughout. Haggis, fresh seafood and game.

The building housing Babity Bowster is attributed to Robert Adam. It now houses a cafe/bar/restaurant/hotel. The proprietors have a keen interest in traditional music, theatre and painting and this is reflected in a regular programme of events.

VISA 🔳 ⟐ B

🏛🏛 UPLAWMOOR HOTEL

66 Neilston Road, Uplawmoor, Glasgow, Strathclyde G78 4AF
☎ (01505) 850565 FAX (01505) 850565
STUART PEACOCK & PETER MULHOLLAND

🛏 14, 14 en-suite, from £25.00 per person, double occ.
Lunch served. Non-residents welcome. Closed 26th December & 1st January.
✕ £5.00 TO £12.50, last orders 9pm.
🍽 Chicken and Leek Pie. Medallions of Beef Bonnie Prince Charlie. Haggis in Malt Whisky Sauce.

Originally an 18th century coaching inn, the Uplawmoor has recently been completely refurbished and now offers very well appointed rooms, all with solid oak fitted furniture and luxurious en-suite facilities. A friendly and relaxed village atmosphere.

⚓ 10 miles from Glasgow, just off the A736 Irvine road.

VISA 🔳 ⊗ 🔍 ⌖ 🕭 A

GRANTOWN ON SPEY, Moray

The whisky capital of Scotland, surrounded by distilleries, rolling moors and forests. Follow the whisky trail toward the coast. Visit Cawdor and Brodie castles or enjoy the beauty of the Cairngorm mountains.

CULDEARN HOUSE

Woodlands Terrace, Grantown on Spey, Moray PH26 3JU
(01479) 872106 FAX (01479) 873641
ISOBEL & ALASDAIR LITTLE

9, 9 en-suite, from from £30.00 per person, double occ.
Closed 1st November to 28th February.
£18.00, last orders 7pm.
Local fresh produce. Home-made Soups. Smoked Haddock Pate. Roast Scotch Beef. Poached Wild Salmon. Culdearn Steak, Angus fillet, plain, pan-fried, or served with mushrooms, cream and Drambuie.

A quiet hotel, run from a Victorian family home. During winter, guests are greeted by roaring log and peat fires creating a friendly, informal atmosphere.

Entering Grantown on A95 from south west turn left at 30 MPH sign. Hotel faces you.

VISA B

SEAFIELD LODGE HOTEL

Grantown on Spey, Moray PH26 3JN
(01479) 872152 FAX (01479) 872340
ALASDAIR & KATHLEEN BUCHANAN

14, 14 en-suite, from £16.25 per person, double occ.
Lunch served. Non-residents welcome. Closed November & 4th to 31st January.
£17.50, last orders 8.30pm.
Haggis in Filo Pastry. Smoked Pheasant Breast with Apple Compote. Highland Venison in Red Wine. Rack of Moray Lamb with Wild Herbs. Spey Salmon en Croute. Home-made sweets and ice creams.

A former Victorian lodge, now fully modernised and refurbished but retaining its original charm and features. Open log fires. Comfortable accommodation. The hotel has a number of sporting and fishing connections and offers angling courses. Dogs are allowed only by prior arrangement.

VISA A

GREENLAW, Berwickshire

Small Borders market town, 8 miles north of Kelso. Visit the numerous surrounding ancient abbeys and monuments or Floors Castle or simply enjoy the beautiful scenery and walks.

THE CASTLE INN HOTEL

Greenlaw, Duns, Berwickshire TD6 1OUR
(01361) 810217 FAX (01361) 810500
ALISTAIR APPLETON

6, 3 en-suite, from £24.00 per person, double occ.
Lunch served. Non-residents welcome. Open all year.
£10.00-£12.00, last orders 10pm.
Local specialities in season. Tweed salmon.

A grand, but homely Georgian hotel, built in 1836, surrounded by history in the centre of this pleasant market town. Comfortable accommodation and a friendly personal touch from the owners.

Centre of the village on the A697 overlooking the green.

VISA AmEx ⊗ & / ⑤ ⇗ A

HAWICK, Roxburghshire

Borders town famous for it's Tweed manufacture and shops. Visit nearby Abbotsford, former home of Sir Walter Scott, Floors Castle, or the many surrounding ancient abbeys, stately homes and gardens. *See also Jedburgh.*

KIRKLANDS HOTEL

West Stewart Place, Hawick, Roxburghshire TD9 8BH
(01450) 372263 FAX (01450) 370404
BARRIE NEWLAND

12, 12 en-suite, from £37.50 per person, double occ.
Lunch served. Non-residents welcome. Closed 25th/26th December, 1st/2nd January.
£15.00, last orders 9.30pm.
Tournedos Queen O'Scots. Sirloin Teviotdale. Salmon Royal Scot.

This Victorian town house hotel is situated in a quiet residential area, just outside the town centre. The hotel is pleasantly furnished in period style and makes an ideal base for both leisure and business in the Borders region.

VISA AmEx / ⑤ ⇗ B

HUNTLY, Aberdeenshire

On the whisky trail, and close to the Aberdeenshire coast. Our member is in a small village, five miles north of Huntly, famous for its Salmon and Sea Trout fishing.

THE FORBES ARMS HOTEL

Miltown of Rothiemay, Huntly, Aberdeenshire AB45 5LT
☎ (01466) 81248 FAX (01466) 81328
MR & MRS HALKETT

⊨ 6, 6 en-suite, from £27.50 per person, double occ.
Non-residents welcome. Open all year.
✗ £15.00, last orders 9pm.
🍽 Deveron Salmon and Sea Trout (traditional Scottish cooking), Aberdeen Angus Steaks. Home-made soups, and puddings.

A salmon fishermans delight! This lodge has two private beats on the middle Deveron. The hotel is situated in the quiet village of Miltown on Rothiemay. Guests are assured of a warm, cheerful welcome and excellent hospitality. There are two bars, offering light food and a separate, more formal dining room.

⊹ A96 from Aberdeen to Huntly, then B9022 for 6 miles. B9118 to Milltown of Rothiemay.

VISA 💳 ⊗ ⌇ ⸰/ ⇙ A

INVERNESS, Inverness-shire

An ideal centre from which to tour the Highlands. The surrounding countryside is famous for its abundant wildlife and beautiful scenery. There are castles and forts to explore or cruises on Loch Ness to enjoy.

GLENDRUIDH HOUSE HOTEL

Old Edinburgh Road, Inverness, Inverness-shire IV1 2AA
☎ (01463) 226499 FAX (01463) 710745
MICHAEL & CHRISTINE SMITH

⊨ 7, 7 en-suite, from £36.00 per person, double occ.
Lunch served. Non-residents welcome. Open all year.
✗ £17.50, last orders 8pm.
🍽 A daily changing menu featuring traditional dishes, prepared from the best fresh local produce. Cullen Skink, Angus Beef, Highland lamb, wild salmon. Queen of Puddings. Raspberry Cranachan. Bramble and Apple Pie. Drambuie Spiced Peaches.

An attractive, mainly Victorian, white walled building at the edge of Inverness, set in pleasant grounds, yet only two miles from the town centre. This is a no smoking hotel. The owners are happy to cater for vegetarians and other special diets with advance notice. Ample parking available.

⊹ On entering Inverness follow signs to Hilton. Follow Old Edinburgh Road southwards to hotel.

VISA 💳 ⚵ AmEx ⅙ ⸰/ ⌇ B

IONA, Argyll

Historic island, abbey and nunnery, west of the Isle of Mull. A natural paradise with silver sands and blue green seas.

ARGYLL HOTEL

Isle of Iona, Argyll PA76 6SJ
☎(01681) 700334 FAX (01681) 700334
FIONA MENZIES

🛏 16, 15 en-suite, from £38.50 per person, double occ.
Lunch served. Non-residents welcome. Closed 8th October 1994 to March 31st 1995.
✕£17.50, last orders 7pm.
🍴Food prepared from fresh local ingredients. Home grown organic vegetables, local wild salmon. Vegetarian fare prepared from quality wholefoods.

A relaxed, friendly hotel, simply but comfortably furnished with antiques and some fine paintings. The inn dates from the 19th century.

VISA 🅫 ᕼ✓ 🍸🍴🍷 B

ISLE OF SEIL, Argyll

Dramatic scenery, and abundant wildlife. This area was the setting for the film 'A Ring of Bright Water'. Visit the nearby Isles of Easdale and Luing. *See also Oban.*

WILLOWBURN HOTEL

Isle of Seil, By Oban, Argyll PA34 4TJ
☎(01852) 300276
MAUREEN & ARCHIE TODD

🛏 6, 6 en-suite, from £30.00 per person, double occ.
Lunch served. Non-residents welcome. Closed January, February & March.
✕included in room rate, 8pm.
🍴 Locally caught fish and shellfish. Atlantic salmon, squat lobsters, prawns, mussels, and oysters. Scottish beef.

Modern hotel set in two acres of ground on the sheltered north eastern shore of the Isle of Seil, 11 miles south of Oban. The island is linked to the mainland by the only single span bridge to cross the Atlantic!

⊹ 11 miles South of Oban, via A816 and B844 (signposted Easdale), over Atlantic road bridge.

VISA 🅫 🚫ᕼ✓ 🍸🍷 B

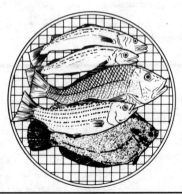

JEDBURGH, Roxburghshire

Small Borders market town. Visit the many surrounding historic abbeys and monuments, Floors Castle, Traquair or Abbotsford, the former home of Sir Walter Scott. *See also Hawick.*

☖☖ GLENFRIARS HOTEL

The Friars, Jedburgh, Roxburghshire TD8 6BN
✆ (01835) 862000 FAX (01835) 862000
C. J. BYWATER

🛏 6, 6 en-suite, from £29.00 per person, double occ.
Lunch served. Closed Christmas & New Year.
✕ £14.50, last orders 8pm.
🍴 Fresh local produce at all times. Borders beef and lamb.

A small Georgian country house set in its own garden, in a quiet situation above the town, affording pleasant views across the valley and Jedburgh. A very personal, friendly atmosphere.

✛ Travel down High Street, turn left at Fire Station. 300 yards left into the Friars.

VISA 💳 AmEx ⌇ 🕲 ⚷ A

KILLIECHRONAN, Isle of Mull

Mull is a naturalist's paradise with deer, otters and eagles.

☖☖☖ KILLIECHRONAN HOUSE

Killiechronan, Aros, Isle of Mull PA72 6JU
✆ (01680) 300463 FAX (01680) 300403
GABRIELLA WIJKER

🛏 5, 5 en-suite, from £20.00 per person, double occ.
Non-residents welcome. Closed 1st November to 1st March.
✕ £21.00, last orders 8pm.
🍴 Local seafood and shellfish. Venison.

Mid 19th century country house with comfortable accommodation and a personal welcome situated at the head of Loch Na Keal. The estate of over 5,000 acres offers fishing, pony-trekking and hill walking.

VISA 💳 ⊗ ⌇ 🕲 ⚷ C

KINGUSSIE, Inverness-shire

A small town in the heart of the Cairngorm Mountains 10 miles from Aviemore. Visit Loch Ness, Culloden Moor, the Highland Museum or follow the Strathspey whisky trail toward the coast.

☖☖ THE SCOT HOUSE HOTEL

Kingussie, Inverness-shire PH21 1HE
✆ (01540) 661351 FAX (01540) 661111
NIGEL MC CONACHIE & BILL GILBERT

🛏 9, 9 en-suite, from £30.00 per person, double occ.
Non-residents welcome. Open all year.
✕ £15.00, last orders 9pm.
🍴 Scottish fare, made from fresh local ingredients. Medallions of Beef. Wild Spey salmon, local Scotch lamb and venison in season. Home-made desserts.

A beautifully appointed country style hotel, offering superb cuisine and a warm welcome. All rooms are well equipped with many individual personal touches designed to ensure a relaxed comfortable stay.

VISA 💳 ♿ 🐾 ⌇ 🕲 ⚷ A

KINLOCHLEVEN, Argyll

Between Glencoe and Fort William, this is an ideal destination for long walks, slow scenic drives on quiet peaceful roads and touring the highlands of Scotland.

MACDONALD HOTEL

Wades Road, Kinlochleven, Argyll PA40 4QL
(018554) 539 FAX (018554) 539
PETER & SUSAN MACDONALD

10, 8 en-suite, from £30.00 per person, double occ.
Lunch served. Non-residents welcome. Closed 5th January to 5th March.
£18.00, last orders 9pm.
Sauteed Garlic Mushrooms finished with an Elderflower Wine and Cream Sauce. Melon Sorbet. Darne of Loch Lochy Salmon with a Lobster and Cream Dressing. Black Isle Lamb with Onich Honey and Rosemary.

A traditional style West Highland hotel built in 1991 offering modern facilities. The spectacular location offers splendid views of the mountains from every bedroom.

Travel on A82 Glasgow to Fort William Road, turn onto B863 at Glencoe Village.

VISA 🖃 ✓ 🕲 ⛽ A

KINROSS, Kinross-shire

Town on the side of Loch Leven, within easy reach of Glenrothes, St Andrews, the Fife peninsular, Perth and Edinburgh. The village of Kinnesswood is on the unspoilt, quiet side of the loch. *See also West Wemyss.*

LOMOND COUNTRY INN

Kinnesswood, Kinross-shire KY13 7HN
(01592) 840253 FAX (01592) 840693
DAVID ADAMS

12, 12 en-suite, from £27.50 per person, double occ.
Lunch served. Non-residents welcome. Open all year.
from £10.00 a la carte, last orders 9pm.
Fresh local produce depending on season, wholesome home-made soups, wild salmon, lobsters and Venison, tasty desserts using fresh local berries. "Scottish Menu".

A very friendly inn on the eastern shores of Loch Leven. Comfortable bedrooms, a pleasant restaurant and cosy bar which enjoys fine views across the loch from the Lomond Hills. Within easy travelling distance from Edinburgh, Perth and St. Andrews. There is a 9 hole golf course adjacent to the hotel.

Northbound M90 junction 5, following signs for Glenrothes/Scotlandwell. Southbound junction 7

VISA 🖃 🔛 AmEx ♿ ✓ 🕲 ⛽ A

THE GLENFARG HOTEL
Glenfarg, Nr Kinross, Kinross-shire PH2 9NU
📞 (01577) 830241 FAX (01577) 830665
PHIL ROSE

🛏 15, 12 en-suite, from £29.50 per person, double occ.
Lunch served. Non-residents welcome. Open all year.
✕ from £13.95, last orders 9pm.
🍴 Scottish cuisine using the best of fresh local produce. Venison and pheasant, in season. Haggis with Drambuie Cream. Extensive bar meal menu available.

A Victorian, turreted, castle-style hotel with a cosy, friendly and welcoming atmosphere, in a small village four miles north of Kinross. A popular base for golfing and other sporting breaks.

VISA 🔲 💳 AmEx⊗🔍 ✓ 🚭🐾 A

KINTAIL, Ross-shire
An area of interest to the historian and naturalist. Visit Eilean Donan Castle or the site of the battle at Glen Shiel, or take the ferry to Skye.

🔒🔒 **KINTAIL LODGE HOTEL**
Glenshiel, Kyle, Ross-shire IV40 8HL
📞 (0159) 981275 FAX (0159) 981 226
STUART & MARGARET HENDERSON

🛏 12, 10 en-suite, from £36.00 per person, double occ.
Non-residents welcome. Closed 23rd December to 3rd January.
✕ £17.00, last orders 8.30pm
🍴 Daily changing set menu prepared from fresh local produce. Scotch Broth. Home-made Ham and Broccoli Flan. Beef Olives with Herb and Oatmeal Stuffing. Poached Wild Loch Duich Salmon with Cucumber Sauce. Walnut Cream Flan.

A former Victorian shooting lodge. The hotel is surrounded by four acres of walled gardens, on the edge of Loch Duich and the Scottish National Trust Kintail estate. A magnificent centre for hill walking. Vegetarian and special diets catered for. From May to September only half board accommodation is available.

✛ On the A87, 17 miles east of Kyle of Lochalsh.

VISA 🔲 ♿ 🚭🐾 B

LAIRG, Sutherland
The market village of Lairg is situated on the shore of Loch Shin. See the Shin or Cassley Falls and Dunrobin Castle. An ideal location for exploring the completely unspoilt far northern highlands. *See also Altnaharra, Tongue.*

🔒🔒 **SUTHERLAND ARMS HOTEL**
Lairg, Sutherland IV27 4AT
📞 (01549) 402291 FAX (01549) 402261
H. SPENCER

🛏 24, 22 en-suite, from £40.00 per person, double occ.
Lunch served. Non-residents welcome. Closed November to April.
✕ £18.00, last orders 8.45pm.
🍴 Traditional Scottish fare. Grilled supreme of Sutherland Salmon 'Hollandaise'. Poached Rainbow Trout. Baked Ross-shire Gammon with Madeira Sauce. Queen of Puddings. Eve's Pudding.

The Sutherland Arms is in a central village location, overlooking the Loch. Open fires create a warm and friendly atmosphere. A fisherman's paradise.

VISA 🔲 💳 ⊗✓ 🚭🐾 C

LOCHCARNAN, South Uist

Tiny village on the east coast of the Hebridean island of South Uist. The islands are ideal for ornithology and archaeology. There are also many rare flowers to be seen on the Machair land on the west coast of the Uists.

⌂⌂ THE ORASAY INN

Lochcarnon, South Uist, Western Isles PA81 5PD
✆ (01870) 610298 FAX (01870) 610390
ALAN & ISOBEL GRAHAM

🛏 7, 7 en-suite, from £27.00 per person, double occ.
Lunch served. Non-residents welcome. Open all year.
✗ from £8.00 a la carte, last orders 10pm.
🍴 Hebridean and Scottish dishes prepared using locally caught seafood. A la carte menu with choice from 36 main courses including chicken, duck, steaks, lamb, vegetarian and seafood.

A modern house which has been extended and converted to form a small country hotel. The furnishings and decor are contemporary, whilst the restaurant is popular with both locals and visitors. A friendly and relaxed atmosphere prevails for those who simply want to get away from it all.

VISA 🔳 ⊗ ♿ ✓ 🚭 🐾 A

LOCHCARRON, Wester Ross

A picturesque west coast fishing hamlet close to Kyle and the Isle of Skye. Visit the nearby Applecross peninsula and Torridon mountains.

⌂⌂ LOCHCARRON HOTEL

Lochcarron, Wester Ross IV54 8YS
✆ (015202) 226 FAX (015202) 612
PAM & TONY WILKINSON

🛏 10, 10 en-suite, from £38.00 per person, double occ.
Lunch served. Non-residents welcome. Open all year.
✗ £15.50, last orders 8.30pm.
🍴 Table d'hote menu changes daily. Extensive a la carte available in restaurants and bars. Fresh local fish always available along with prime Scottish Steaks and Venison. Seafood Platter with 10 varieties of fish and shellfish.

An old established Lochside inn in one of Britain's most spectacularly beautiful regions. The panoramic restaurant enjoys wonderful views across the loch to the mountains beyond.

⚓ Right on the shore at east end of Lochcarron village.

VISA 🔳 ✓ 🚭 🐾 B

LOCHGILPHEAD, Argyll

A small fishing and market town at the head of Loch Fyne on the northern tip of the Kintyre peninsula. The coast road from Loch Lomond to Oban on leaving the village passes numerous ancient abbeys, castles and monuments. *See also Tarbert.*

🏨 THE CAIRNBAAN HOTEL

Cairnbaan, By Lochgilphead, Argyll PA31 8SJ
℡ (01546) 603668 FAX (01546) 606045
MR & MRS FERGUSON

🛏 7, 7 en-suite, from £45.00 per person, double occ.
Lunch served. Non-residents welcome. Closed 20th January to 17th February.
✗ £20.00, last orders 10pm.
🍴 Scottish cuisine, using fresh local produce. Venison. Loch Fyne fish and seafood.

Overlooking the Crinan canal, this traditional coaching inn has recently been refurbished to an extremely high standard. Sporting guests can enjoy golf at Lochgilphead whilst nearby fishing, pony trekking and trail riding can be arranged.

⊹3 miles north of Lochgilphead just off the A816 Lockgilphead to Oban road.

VISA 🔲 AmEx ⊗ ⌂ 🐾 **B**

LOCKERBIE, Dumfries-shire

Small market town, adjacent to the M6/A74 route north between Carlisle and Glasgow.

🏨 SOMERTON HOUSE HOTEL

Carlisle Road, Lockerbie, Dumfries-shire DG11 2DR
℡ (01576) 202583 FAX (01576) 204218
ALEC & JEAN ARTHUR

🛏 7, 7 en-suite, from £28.25 per person, double occ.
Lunch served. Non-residents welcome. Closed 25th December.
✗ £17.50, last orders 9.30pm.
🍴 Taste of Scotland menu featuring the best of regional fare. Galloway lamb, pork and beef. Local salmon and trout. Extensive bar snack menu also available.

A Victorian mansion, retaining many original features, but still offering all modern facilities in comfortable bedrooms. The hotel stands in its own grounds away from the road. Guests are assured of a warm family welcome.

VISA 🔲 🔳 AmEx ⌂ 🐾 🦮 **A**

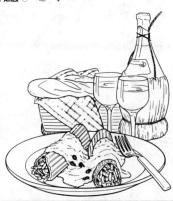

MELROSE, Borders

Town in the heart of the Scottish Borders. Melrose was the original venue for Rugby Sevens and still holds an event every April. Visit nearby Floors Castle, Mellerstain, Melrose Abbey, Manderston, or Dryburgh Abbey.

BON ACCORD HOTEL

Market Square, Melrose TD6 6PQ
✆ (01896) 822645 FAX (01896) 823474
BILL & BRENDA SPENCE

🛏 10, 10 en-suite, from £32.50 per person, double occ.
Lunch served. Non-residents welcome. Closed 25th December.
✗ £10.00, last orders 8.45pm.
🍽 Abundant use of fresh local produce.

A traditional style hotel which has been recently refurbished to a high standard. Guests are warmly welcomed. A four poster bridal suite is available. The Bon Accord can accommodate up to 100 guests for weddings or business meetings.

✛ In the central Market Square.

VISA 🖃 AmEx ✓ 💲 B

MELVICH, Sutherland

A quiet, friendly crofting village on Scotland's northern seaboard. Plenty of outdoor pursuits; trout fishing, sea fishing, surfing, deer stalking, bird watching, botanising, hill walking and golf. 15 minutes drive from the Orkney Ferry.

MELVICH HOTEL

Melvich, Thurso, Sutherland KW14 7YJ
✆ (016413) 206 FAX (016413) 347
PETER & MAUREEN SCHOONENBERG

🛏 14, 14 en-suite, from £30.00 per person, double occ.
Lunch served. Non-residents welcome. Closed 25th December & 1st January.
✗ £17.50, last orders 8.15pm.
🍽 Fresh local seafood and game. Lobster. Crab. Casserole of Venison in Red Wine. Poached Halladale Salmon Glenlivet. Home-made Apple Pie. Tipsy Laird. Bar food and packed lunches also available.

A country hotel, run by a friendly, helpful team who are keen that guests should enjoy their stay. Peat fires help to create a relaxed atmosphere and the hotel's collection of malt whiskies is worth sampling! The public rooms and almost all the guest bedrooms have stunning views. Special childrens rates are available. Dogs welcome.

✛ On the A836 from Thurso to Tongue. From the A9 by the A897 from Helmsdale.

VISA 🖃 ♿ ✓ 💲 🐕 A

MOFFAT, Dumfriesshire

A delightful small Dumfriesshire town set just off the A74 Glasgow to Carlisle road. Moffat, often overlooked by visitors speeding north, is surrounded by beautiful scenery including impressive fells, forests and lochs. *See also Beattock, Eskdalemuir, Tweedsmuir.*

♨♨♨ WELL VIEW HOTEL

Ballplay Road, Moffat, Dumfriesshire DG10 9JU
✆ (01683) 20184
J. & J. SCHUCKARDT

🛏 6, 6 en-suite, from £38.00 per person, double occ.
Lunch served. Non-residents welcome. Open all year.
✗ £22.00, last orders 8.30pm.
🍴 Scottish cuisine with a French influence. Mousseline of Chicken with Lanark Blue Butter and an Apple Hollandaise. Carrot and Apricot Soup. Medallions of Venison with an Elderberry and Thyme Sauce.

A lovely small hotel run by enthusiastic owners, who are both knowledgeable and adventurous with their food and wine. The hotel is set in half an acre of gardens in a quiet environment, and is furnished to immaculate standards. Lunch by prior arrangement.

⊹ Leave Moffat by Selkirk road A708 pass the Fire Station on the left, turn left into Ballplay Road, hotel is 300 yards on the right.
VISA 🖸 AmEx ⊘ ✓ 🗞 B

MUIR OF ORD, Ross-shire

Small town 16 miles north of Inverness at the head of the Beauty Firth. Visit the Orrin Falls, Loch Ness (18 miles), the castle at Dunrobin and Cawdor or enjoy a tasting at the Glen Ord Distillery.

♨♨ ORD HOUSE HOTEL

Muir of Ord, Ross-shire IV6 7UH
✆ (01463) 870492 FAX (01463) 870492
MR & MRS JOHN ALLEN

🛏 10, 10 en-suite, from £38.00 per person, double occ.
Lunch served. Non-residents welcome. Closed from mid October to the end of April.
✗ £19.00, last orders 9pm.
🍴 Wild Salmon with Whisky and Cream Sauce. Medaillons of Venison with Brandy and Cream. Queen Scallops served in their shells.

A 17th century country house hotel, set in sixty acres of garden and parkland. Antique furnishings and open log fires create a warm, relaxed atmosphere.

VISA 🖸 ⒉ AmEx ⅋ ✓ 🗞 ⊕ B

NEWTON STEWART, Wigtownshire

A town in southern Scotland, surrounded by beautiful scenery. Close to the ferry terminal at Stranraer.

CORSEMALZIE HOUSE HOTEL

Port William, Newton Stewart, Wigtownshire DG8 9RL
☎ (01988) 860254 FAX (01988) 860213
MR & MRS P. MC DOUGALL

🛏 14, 14 en-suite, from £43.00 per person, double occ.
Lunch served. Non-residents welcome. Closed 25th & 26th December, mid January to mid March.
✕ £17.50, last orders 9pm.
🍴 Taste of Scotland cuisine. Local fish and game. Entrecote Steak Balmoral. Local Pheasant with Orange and Chestnut Sauce. Braised Ox Tongue with Nectarine and Port Sauce. Grilled Fresh Trout Rob Roy.

A small, friendly country house, set in forty acres of garden and woodland. Open fires and good service. Outdoor activities include golf, walking, shooting, riding and pony trekking. Extensive salmon and trout fishing.

⊹ 8 miles from Newton Stewart on A714, over the bridge and turn right at 300 yards to Glenluce Hotel. Five miles along B7005.

VISA 🔳 ⌖ ⑤ ⊕ A

OBAN, Argyll

Oban harbour is the gateway to Mull, Colonsay, Tiree, Coll and the Western Hebridean islands of South Uist and Barra. The town itself is set amongst the spectacular scenery of Scotland's west coast. *See also Isle of Seil.*

MANOR HOUSE HOTEL

Gallanach Road, Oban, Argyll PA34 4LS
☎ (01631) 62087 FAX (01631) 63053
MARGARET & PATRICK FREYTAG

🛏 11, 11 en-suite, from £37.50 per person, double occ.
Lunch served. Non-residents welcome. Closed January.
✕ £21.50, last orders 8pm.
🍴 Scottish and French cuisine, prepared from fresh local ingredients. Fresh West Coast Oysters with Fennel and Honey. Scampi Laphroaig. Parfait Flora MacDonald.

An 18th century manor house overlooking the sea, with stunning views and furnishings to match. Guests are offered a friendly Highland atmosphere at this beautiful hotel. For children under 10 years, please contact the hotel directly. The rates quoted at this hotel are for dinner, bed and breakfast.

VISA 🔳 ⌖ ⑤ ⊕ C

🏠🏠 **DUNGALLAN COUNTRY HOUSE**

Gallanach Road, Oban, Argyll PA34 4PD
☎ (01631) 63799 FAX (01631) 66711
ELSPETH ALLAN

🛏 10, 9 en-suite, from £30.00 per person, double occ.
Lunch served. Non-residents welcome. Closed 23rd to 30th
December.
✕ £18.00, last orders 10pm.
🍴 Smoked Salmon Pate. Loch Fyne Queen Scallops. Poached
Supreme of West Coast Salmon. Trio of Scotch Lamb. Sirloin of
Black Angus Beef. Magret of Duck in a soft Peppercorn and Cream
Sauce.

Built in 1870 Dungallan is a Victorian house set in 5 acres of
wooded grounds. It lies high above Oban Bay with its own private
drive from the shore road. All bedrooms are cosy and welcoming.

VISA 📇 ♿ ⊘ ✓ 🕃 ⬅ 🐾 A

PERTH, Perthshire

Historic city on the banks of the Tay, approximately 45 minutes drive
north of Edinburgh. Visit Gleniturret Whisky Distillery, Glamis Castle,
Rait Antique Centre, Discovery Point Dundee and St Andrews Golf Course.

🏠🏠🏠 **NEWTON HOUSE HOTEL**

Glencarse, Nr Perth, Perthshire PH2 7LX
☎ (01738) 860250 FAX (01738) 860717
CHRISTOPHER & CAROL TALLIS

🛏 10, 10 en-suite, from £45.00 per person, double occ.
Lunch served. Non-residents welcome. Closed 24th to 26th
December.
✕ £13.00 to £23.00, last orders 9pm.
🍴 Scottish/French cuisine. Taste of Scotland menu. A full range
of lighter snacks and meals are available in Cawley's Bar.

A former dower house, built in 1840, which has been tastefully
decorated throughout. All bedrooms overlook the pretty gardens.

✈ 4 miles from Perth and 13 from Dundee, just off the A90.

VISA 📇 2 AmEx ♿ ✓ 🕃 🐾 C

PITLOCHRY, Perthshire

One of Scotland's most popular holiday destinations, in the centre of over
2,000 square miles of breathtaking scenery. There are many surrounding
castles and ruins to explore, distilleries to visit and the world famous
salmon ladders to see. *See also Dunkeld.*

🏠🏠🏠 **BIRCHWOOD HOTEL**

2 East Moulin Road, Pitlochry, Perthshire PH16 5DW
☎ (01796) 472477 FAX (01796) 473951
R. B. & O. S. HARMON

🛏 12, 12 en-suite, from £33.50 per person, double occ.
Lunch served. Non-residents welcome. Closed November to February.
✕ £17.00, last orders 8pm.
🍴 Highland beef, lamb, venison, salmon and trout using only fresh
local produce. Delicious home-made soups and desserts.

Popular family owned hotel set in four acres, offering a haven of
peace and tranquillity, yet only minutes away from the centre of
this bustling Highland town. All rooms are individually furnished
to a high standard with private facilities, hospitality trays.

VISA 📇 ♿ ✓ 🕃 🐾 B

GREEN PARK HOTEL

Clunie Bridge Road, Pitlochry, Perthshire PH16 5JY
✆ (01796) 473248 FAX (01796) 473520
GRAHAM & ANNE BROWN

🛏 37, 37 en-suite, from £40.00 per person, double occ.
Lunch served. Non-residents welcome. Closed 27th October to 2nd April.
✕ £17.50, last orders 8.30pm.
🍴 Taste of Scotland dinner, served on Friday evening, featuring local game in season, Tay salmon, highland bonnets and a Scottish cheeseboard.

A large Victorian house which has been extended to form a country hotel on the shores of Loch Faskally. Most bedrooms overlook the gardens and loch and enjoy wonderful views to the hills beyond.

VISA 🌐 ⊗ 🗞 ✓ C

WESTLANDS OF PITLOCHRY

160 Atholl Road, Pitlochry, Perthshire PH16 5AR
✆ (01796) 472266 FAX (01796) 473994
ANDREW & SUE MATHIESON

🛏 15, 15 en-suite, from £29.00 to £37.00 per person, double occ.
Lunch served. Non-residents welcome. Open all year.
✕ £15.00, last orders 9pm.
🍴 Daily taste of Scotland menu. Warm Salad of Wood Pigeon with Pine Kernels in a fresh Rosemary flavoured Butter. River Tay Salmon Mousse served with Cucumber Salad and Dill Mayonnaise.

Recently totally refurbished, this traditional stone building offers the highest standards in comfort, cuisine and hospitality.

VISA 🌐 ✓ 🗞 ⊕ B

PORT OF MENTEITH, Perthshire

A small lakeside village, set amongst spectacular scenery, five miles from Callender and the Trossachs, and within an hour of Loch Lomond, Glasgow or Stirling. *See also Aberfoyle, Fintry.*

LAKE HOTEL

Port of Menteith, Perthshire FK8 3RA
✆ (01877) 385258 FAX (01877) 385671
JOHN L. LEROY

🛏 12, 12 en-suite, from £37.50 per person, double occ.
Lunch served. Non-residents welcome. Open all year.
✕ £21.50, last orders 8.30pm.
🍴 Traditional Scottish fare. Fillet of West Coast Halibut baked in a Fresh Herb and Cream Sauce. Loin of Lamb pan-fried in a Cranberry and Port Sauce. Supreme of Chicken cooked in a Wild Mushroom and Red Wine Sauce.

Situated on the banks of the Lake of Menteith, in the Trossachs, with fabulous surrounding scenery. The hotel has been refurbished in an art deco style with a spectacular conservatory overlooking the lake. Guests are assured of a friendly Scottish welcome. For children under 12 years, please contact the hotel directly. The rates quoted at this hotel are for dinner, bed and breakfast.

VISA 🌐 ✓ 🗞 ⊕ C

SALEN, Isle of Mull

Mull is a naturalist's paradise with deer, otters and eagles.

THE GLENFORSA HOTEL

Salen, By Aros, Isle of Mull PA72 6JW
✆ (01680) 300377 FAX (01680) 300535
JEAN & PAUL PRICE

🛏 13, 13 en-suite, from £22.50 to £31.00 per person, double occ.
Lunch served. Open all year.
✗ £15.00, last orders 8.30pm.
🍽 Local seafood and shellfish. Prawns, fresh lobsters, Mull
oysters, Lorn lamb, Grampian fowl. Traditional Gaelic dishes.

Glenforsa is an attractive Scandinavian style log chalet, set in 6
acres of secluded grounds and enjoying magnificent views across
the Sound to Morven and Ardmurchan. All the rooms are well
appointed. A good centre for exploring the island, walking or
climbing.

VISA 🖃 ⚏ ⊗ ⠌ ⟍ ⚔ ⊲ A

SLEAT, Isle of Skye

Situated on the southern coast of the island, on the Sound of Sleat. Varied
local wildlife. Ten miles from the Skye airstrip and close to the Mallaig
ferry. Visit the Clan Donald Centre, Dunvegan Castle and The Talisker
Distillery. *See also Uig.*

HOTEL EILEAN IARMAIN

Sleat, Isle of Skye IV43 8QR
✆ (0147833) 332 FAX (0147833) 275
SIR IAIN & LADY NOBLE

🛏 12, 12 en-suite, from £43.00 per person, double occ.
Lunch served. Non-residents welcome. Open all year.
✗ £24.50, last orders 8.45pm.
🍽 The best of local fresh produce, prepared to order. Lobsters,
oysters and venison. Fresh Scallops in Ginger and Cream Breast
of Guinea Fowl with an Apple and Calvados Sauce. Fresh Whole
Sole with Hazelnut Butter. Cloutie Dumpling.

A white walled, traditional inn, set above the magnificent natural
local harbour. The hotel takes pride in offering a traditional
welcome, with blazing log fires and friendly local staff. Small
seminar groups of up to 25 can be catered for and during low
season the whole hotel can be booked for use as a house party.

VISA 🖃 AmEx ⊗ ♿ ⠌ ⟍ ⊲ C

SPEAN BRIDGE, Inverness-shire

Close to Fort William. Excellent location for hill walking, fishing, ski-ing or day trips to Skye, Mull and Ansaig and the small Isles Ardnamurchan, Glen Affric, Aviemore, the Spey Valley and Loch Ness.

🏠🏠 OLD PINES

Gairlochy Road, Spean Bridge, Inverness-shire PH34 4EG
☎ (01397) 712324 FAX (01397) 712433
BILL & SUKIE BARBER

🛏 7, 7 en-suite, from £30.00 per person, double occ.
Lunch served. Non-residents welcome. Closed two weeks November & Sunday lunch & dinner.
✗ £18.50, last orders 9pm
🍴 Taste of Scotland menus. Langoustine and Mussel Soup garnished with Leeks. Wild venison, pheasant and salmon. Lochy trout. Raspberry & Hazlenut Meringue Gateau. Scottish farmhouse cheeses & oatcakes. Home-smoked salmon and trout and home-made bread, preserves. FINALIST REPRESENTING SCOTLAND IN THE 1994 LOGIS REGIONAL CUISINE COMPETITION.

Old Pines is an informal relaxing Scandinavian style log and stone building with excellent access facilities for wheelchairs. Log fires, books, flowers, pine, pretty country fabrics and friendly welcome, conservatory dining room with spectacular views. The hotel is unlicensed; guests are welcome to arrive with their own wine, the hotel does not charge corkage.

✤ 1 mile north of Spean Bridge on A82 at Commando Memorial take B8004 to Gavlochy, hotel is 300 metres on the right.

VISA 📷 ⊗ ♿ ✓ 🐾 A

ST ABBS, Berwickshire

St Abbs is an unspoilt village in Scotland's beautiful Border country. There is a safe sandy beach nearby and birdwatching on St Abbs Head nature reserve.

🏠 CASTLE ROCK

Murrayfield, St Abbs, Berwickshire TD14 5PP
☎ (01890) 771715 FAX (01890) 771520
PETER & KATHRYN LUTAS

🛏 4, 4 en-suite, from £21.00 per person, double occ.
Closed November to Easter.
✗ £13.00, last orders 8pm.
🍴 Scotch Broth. Carrot and Cashew Nut Gratin. Mushrooms in Garlic. Local Smoked Salmon. Baked Gammon with Apricot. Chicken Breasts with Lemon. Pork and Cider Casserole. Home-made Ice Cream. Fudge Bananas.

An attractive Victorian house set in a lovely position on the cliffs. The hotel provides magnificent sea views from every room along with good food and comfort.

✤ From A1, A1107 to Coldingham, B6438 to St Abbs. First right, proceed to end of road.

VISA 📷 ✓ 🐾 🐚 ⟐ A

ST ANDREWS, Fife

Golfing capital of Scotland and the World. Visit the British Golf Museum, the St Andrews Sea Life Centre, one of the many nearby castles or the fabulous local sandy beaches

⌂⌂ ## THE PARKLAND HOTEL & RESTAURANT

Kinburn Castle, St Andrews, Fife KY16 9DS
☎ (01334) 473620 FAX (01334) 473620
BRIAN & ROSEMARY MAC LENNAN

🛏 15, 10 en-suite, from £32.00 per person, double occ.
Lunch served. Non-residents welcome. Closed 25th, 26th December & 1st January.
✗ from £15.00, last orders 8.30pm.
🍽 Gourmet dinners prepared, by the chef proprietor, from fresh local ingredients.

A Victorian castelated building, set in its own grounds opposite Kinburn park, a few minutes walk from the centre of town. Parkland is a comfortable, family run hotel where outstanding food is served in a relaxed environment.

VISA 🖃 ⚹ ✓ A

STRACHUR, Strathclyde

More than 400 years ago, Mary Queen of Scots landed at Creggans on her way through the Highlands. Today Creggans stands on the same headland, looking out across Loch Fyne. Visit Inveraray Castle, Cowal Peninsula, Isle of Bute.

⌂⌂⌂ ## THE CREGGANS INN

Strachur, Strathclyde PA27 8BX
☎ (0136 986) 279 FAX (0136 986) 637
SIR FITZROY & LADY VERONICA MACLEAN

🛏 17, 17 en-suite, from £25.50 per person, double occ.
Lunch served. Non-residents welcome. Open all year.
✗ £18.50, last orders 9pm.
🍽 Home-made Game Pate. Smoked Ham and Asparagus Platter. Magret of Duckling with a Green Peppercorn Sauce. Rack of Hillside Lamb. Grilled Oban Plaice. Medallions of Ardentinny Venison in a Port Sauce.

An old country inn with prettily decorated bedrooms, peaceful sitting-room, a cheerful split level restaurant and two attractive bars with log fires. The hotel offers good food and a warm welcome.

✛ From Glasgow via Loch Lomond, Arrochar and the A83 or, via Gourock, the car ferry across the Clyde to Dunoon, and the A815.

VISA 🖃 ⚹ AmEx ⊗ ⚹ ✓ 🛇 ⬦ A

STRATHYRE, Perthshire

A small village at the head of Loch Lubnaig. The area is noted for its beautiful scenery, a forms part of the Queen Elizabeth Forrest Park. *See also Balquhidder.*

🏠🏠 CREAGAN HOUSE RESTAURANT WITH ACCOMMODATION

Strathyre, Callander, Perthshire FK18 8ND
☎ (01877) 384638 FAX (01877) 384638
GORDON & CHERRY GUNN

🛏 5, 3 en-suite, from £30.50 per person, double occ.
Lunch served. Non-residents welcome. Closed February.
✗ £15.50 & £21.00, last orders 8.30pm.
🍴 Variations on classical French cuisine with strong Scottish influence, using fresh local produce.

A peaceful, family owned 17th century farmhouse with five charming bedrooms. The Baronial Hall, with its grand fireplace, provides a unique setting. Although "The Gunns" are well established at Creagan, they still gain great pleasure from welcoming guests to their home, and ideal retreat.

⊹ On A84, 500 metres north of Strathyre.

VISA 🅰 AmEx ⊘ ♿ ✎ ∿ 🌿 ⊕ A

STRONTIAN, Argyll

On the north bank of Loch Sunart in an area of outstanding unspoilt natural beauty. Ideal walking and fishing country, and within easy driving distance of Fort William, Ben Nevis, Glencoe and the surrounding Ardnamurchan peninsula.

🏠 LOCH SUNART HOTEL

Strontian, Argyll PH36 4HZ
☎ (01967) 402471
PETER & MILDRED RENTON

🛏 11, 10 en-suite, from £25.00 per person, double occ.
Non-residents welcome. Closed 1st November to 31st March.
✗ £18.00, last orders 7.30pm.
🍴 Seafood, salmon, local game and venison, all prepared t traditional Scottish recipes. Home-made soups, fruit ice cream and sticky puddings. Scottish cheese board.

An 18th century country house hotel set in its own grounds. Th bedrooms are all tastefully furnished and offer simple ye comfortable facilities. Many rooms enjoy splendid views across th loch and mountains.

♿ 🌿 ⊕ A

TARBERT, Argyll

Situated on the shores of Loch Fyne, Tarbert is an ideal base for touring the Islands of Argyll and the Kintyre peninsula. Outdoor pursuits include golf, yachting and fishing. There is an abundance of local wildlife. *See also Lochgilphead.*

THE COLUMBA HOTEL

Tarbert, Loch Fyne, Argyll PA29 6UF
✆ (01880) 820808
BOB & GINA CHICKEN

📧 11, 11 en-suite, from £27.95 per person, double occ.
Non-residents welcome. Open all year.
✗ £16.95, last orders 9pm.
🍴 Cullen Skink Seared. Loch Tarbert Scallops in a Scottish Cheese Sauce. Medallions of Scottish Beef with Dunsyre Blue Cheese and Madeira Sauce. Argyllshire Venison and Oyster Pudding.

A family run hotel situated in a peaceful lochside position with panoramic views over Loch Fyne. The hotel's facilities include a gym, sauna and solarium, cosy log fired bars and a restaurant serving only the best of Scottish food, imaginatively prepared.

⚓ Hotel is half a mile along Tarbert Harbour.
VISA 🔳 ᕗᚱ/ 🌊 Ⓢ ⊕A

TONGUE, Sutherland

On the northern Scottish coast. Stunning views towards Ben Loyal inland, and towards the sea over the Kyle of Tongue. Local wildlife includes red deer, otters, foxes, golden eagles, peregrine and ptarmigan. *See also Altnharra, Lairg.*

BEN LOYAL HOTEL

Main Street, Tongue, by Lairg, Sutherland IV27 4XE
✆ (0184755) 216
MEL & PAULINE COOK

📧 12, 9 en-suite, from £30.00 per person, double occ.
Lunch served. Non-residents welcome. Closed 1st January to 11th February.
✗ £18.50, last orders 8pm.
🍴 Pheasant Salad with Quail Eggs and Tarragon Dressing. Grilled Lamb Cutlets with Carmelized Pears and Red Wine Gravy. Pentland Firth Monkfish Tails poached with Baby Vegetables and a Chardonnay Sauce. Strawberry shortbread with Glayva Cream.

The Ben Loyal hotel is set in the quiet village of Tongue and decorated in pine and floral fabrics creating a warm relaxed atmosphere. Guests can expect personal, friendly service.

⚓ On the coast of Scotland, between John O' Groats and Cape Wrath, at the junction of A836 and A838.

VISA 🔳 ᕗᚱ/ 🌊 ⊕A

TWEEDSMUIR, Peeblesshire

Small village between Moffat and Peebles, close to the source of the Tweed. Excellent trout and salmon fishing, complemented by spectacular scenery, lochs and reservoirs, forests and fells. *See also Beattock, Moffat.*

🏛🏛 THE CROOK INN HOTEL

Tweedsmuir, Tweeddale, Peeblesshire ML12 6QN
☎ (0189) 97272 FAX (0189) 97294
STUART REID

🛏 7, 6 en-suite, from £26.00 per person, double occ.
Lunch served. Non-residents welcome. Open all year.
✗ £12.50, last orders 8.30pm.
🍴 Cruikett Egg. Local lamb. Fresh Tweed salmon and trout. Covenantors Cream. Dunsyre cheese.

The Crook Inn is Scotland's oldest licensed premises. It's flagstone bar is dominated by a huge central fireplace, complete with roaring log fire. More modern art deco additions to the accommodation have resulted in a unique and famous country inn. Guests may be interested to visit the glass blowing and glass making centre in the hotel's old stable block.

⊹ On A701 Moffat to Edinburgh road.

VISA 🔲 💳 AmEx ⋰ 🌑 🐾 A

UIG, Isle of Skye

Town on the western edge of the Trotternidge peninsula at the ferry terminal to Uist and South Harris. Skye enjoys over 900 miles of stunning unspoilt coastline and is rich in romantic history, reflected in its museums and historical sites. *See also Sleat.*

🏛🏛 UIG HOTEL

Uig, Isle of Skye IV51 9YE
☎ (01470) 542205 FAX (01470) 542308
GRACE GRAHAM & DAVID TAYLOR

🛏 16, 16 en-suite, from £30.00 to £43.00 per person, double occ.
Lunch served. Non-residents welcome. Closed mid October to mid April.
✗ £18.50, last orders 8.30pm.
🍴 Peat Smoked Salmon. Local Beef and Fish. Home-made sweets.

A delightful old coaching inn with a charming steading conversion in the grounds providing comfortable accommodation. The hotel stands on a hillside overlooking Uig Bay and enjoys spectacular views to the west. Pony trekking is arranged daily through the hotel's private stables, whilst day trips to Harris and Lewis are conducted twice per week. Dogs by arrangement only.

VISA 🔲 💳 AmEx ⊗ 🌑 C

WALKERBURN, Peebles

A village on the northern bank of the river Tweed, eight miles east of Peebles. There are a number of local craft shops and castles to be explored. Visit the town's Museum of Woollen Textiles.

TWEED VALLEY HOTEL

Walkerburn, Peebles, Peebleshire EH43 6AA
☎ (01896) 870636 FAX (01896) 870639
CHARLES, JOYCE & KEITH MILLER

🛏 16, 16 en-suite, from £40.00 per person, double occ.
Lunch served. Non-residents welcome. Closed 25th & 26th December.
✕ £23.00, last orders 8.30pm
🍽 Smoked salmon, trout, meats and smoked cheeses from the hotel's own smokehouse. Venison and game dishes in season. Scotch roast beef and lamb.

A family run Edwardian country house hotel set in its own grounds. The hotel has a walled kitchen garden where the herbs and vegetables for the restaurant are grown.

VISA 🖃 ♿ ✓ 🖹 🆂 🐾 C

WEST WEMYSS, Fife

Visit the Wemyss caves, Kirkcaldy Museum and Art Gallery. 30 minutes drive from Edinburgh, 20 minutes from St. Andrews. *See also Kinross.*

THE BELVEDERE HOTEL

Coxstool, West Wemyss, Fife KY1 4SL
☎ (01592) 654167 FAX (01592) 655279
GUY BERGER

🛏 20, 20 en-suite, from £30.00 per person, double occ.
Lunch served. Non-residents welcome. Open all year.
✕ £17.50, last orders 9.30pm.
🍽 Fresh local fare. Fresh fish from Pittenweem and best Scotch meats.

The Belvedere is made up of a large rambling collection of white walled buildings in a quiet seaside town. Excellent views out over the sea. The hotel has a bright, airy feel, good atmosphere and offers simple, comfortable accommodation.

✦ Follow A92 Kirkcaldy East. Follow A915 Kirkcaldy, St Andrews, turn at Coaltown of Wemyss follow signs for the

VISA 🖃 AmEx ⊗ ♿ 🆂 ✓ 🖹 🐾 A

WHITING BAY, Isle of Arran

Seaside village on the sheltered south east coast of Arran. Visit Brodick castle and the nearby stone circles.

GRANGE HOUSE HOTEL

Whiting Bay, Isle of Arran KA27 8QH
℆ (01770) 700263 FAX (01770) 700263
JANET & CLIVE HUGHES

🛏 9, 6 en-suite, from £30.00 per person, double occ.
Non-residents welcome. Closed November to February.
✗ £14.00, last orders 8.30pm.
🍴 Victorian, Scottish and French cuisine featuring local venison, seafood, salmon, beef and fresh vegetables. Home-made sweets & ice creams.

A Victorian country house, decorated in period style creating a pleasant environment. Guests dine using antique silver and there is a comprehensive selection of wines available. Many activities are arranged for guests to enjoy, including horse riding, golfing and hill & ridge walking. The hotel is totally non-smoking.

✝ From Brodick Ferry terminal turn left, through Lamlash to Whiting Bay. Buses meet the ferries.

VISA 🖃 ⊗ ♿ ✓ ➥ ⚓ Ⓢ A

IRELAND

ATHY, Co Kildare

At the centre of the famous plains of Kildare, an area rich in history and steeped in culture

TONLEGEE HOUSE & RESTAURANT

Athy, County Kildare
☎ (0507) 31473 FAX (0507) 31473
MARK & MARJORIE MOLLOY

🛏 5, 5 en-suite, from £30.00 per person, double occ.
Non-residents welcome. Closed 24th to 28th December & first two weeks of November.
✗£20.00-£25.00, last orders 9.30pm.
Fresh fish and game in season.

A magnificently restored Georgian house and restaurant standing in its own grounds. Antique furnishings and open fires throughout encourage a friendly and relaxed atmosphere.

VISA ☐ ✓ ☐ B

AUGHRIM, Co Wicklow

A picturesque village in the heart of the Wicklow Hills, less than one hour's drive from Dublin or Rosslare. National Disabled Anglers Park adjacent to the hotel. Trout fishing all year.

LAWLESS' HOTEL

Aughrim, County Wicklow
☎ (0402) 36146 FAX (0402) 36384
SEOIRSE & MAEVE O'TOOLE

🛏 10, 8 en-suite, from £26.00 to £28.50 per person, double occ.
Lunch served. Non-residents welcome. Closed 23rd to 26th December.
✗£17.00, last orders 9.15pm.
The best of local beef, Wicklow lamb, fresh local smoked fish including trout, wild venison, rabbit, pheasant and pigeon in season.

An 18th century village inn full of character which has been totally refurbished. Comfortable accommodation, good cuisine and a warm friendly welcome.

VISA ☐ 🔢 AmEx ✓ ☐ A

BALLINA, Co Mayo

Visit Ceide Fields, Ballycastle, North Mayo Heritage Centre, Foxford Woollen Mills

DEANWOOD HOTEL

Bury Street, Ballina, County Mayo
☎ (096) 21655 FAX (096) 21028
MOLL MCGUIRE

🛏 10, 10 en-suite, from £27.50 per person, double occ.
Lunch served. Non-residents welcome. Closed for Christmas.
✗£15.00, last orders 9.30pm.
Fresh seafood, steaks and Moy salmon in the Oyster Restaurant. Lunch and bar bites in Bloom's Bar.

An old world family run hotel adjacent to the town centre, offering comfortable accommodation and friendly personal service.

VISA ☐ ✓ ☐ ☐ ☐ B

BALLYBOFEY, Co Donegal

Visit Glenveagh National Park, the Donegal County Museum and Castle Grianan of Aileach.

🏠🏠🏠 ## KEE'S HOTEL ✗ ✗

Stranorlar, Ballybofey, County Donegal
☎ (074) 31018 FAX (074) 31917
ARTHUR KEE

🛏 37, 37 en-suite, from £32.50 per person, double occ.
Lunch served. Non-residents welcome. Open all year.
✗£16.00, last orders 9.15pm.
🍽 Fillet Steaks in Irish whiskey sauce. Fresh salmon. Chicken stuffed with crab. Local shellfish.

150 year old coaching inn tastefully refurbished to a high standard but retaining an old world atmosphere with open fires, comfortable lounges and professional, caring staff.

VISA 🔲 💳 AmEx 🏊 ✓ 🎿 S 🛁 B

BALLYBUNION, Co Kerry

Local amenities include two championship golf courses, the world famous Ballybunion golf club just 1 mile from the hotel, sea fishing, tennis courts, pitch & putt, swimming and boating.

🏠🏠 ## MARINE LINKS HOTEL & SEAFOOD RESTAURANT

Sandhill Road, Ballybunion, County Kerry
☎ (068) 27139 FAX (068) 27666
SANDRA WILLIAMSON & ROSALEEN RAFTER

🛏 11, 11 en-suite, from £26.00 to £35.00 per person, double occ.
Non-residents welcome. Closed November to March.
✗£20.00, last orders 9.30pm.
🍽 Oysters Fried in Guinness Batter. Pan fried Cashen Salmon. Roast Rack of Kerry Lamb.

A small homely hotel overlooking the Atlantic Ocean. The hotel is personally supervised by the owners.

VISA 🔲 💳 AmEx ✓ 🎿 🛁 B

BALLYLICKEY, Co Cork

An ideal centre for visiting and touring West Cork and Kerry peninsulas. Visit Bantry House & Gardens, Garnish Island, French Armada Centre & Glengarriff. Forest & mountain walks.

🏠🏠 ## REENDESERT HOTEL

Ballylickey, Bantry, County Cork
☎ (027) 50153 FAX (027) 50597
ANNE CRONIN

🛏 18, 18 en-suite, from £24.00 to £29.00 per person, double occ.
Non-residents welcome. Closed 1st November to mid March.
✗ from £16.00, last orders 9pm.
🍽 Fresh fish,lamb, West Cork farmhouse cheeses & locally grown vegetables. Extensive bar food menu. Restaurant specialises in seafood.

An owner managed hotel overlooking Bantry Bay offering a warm & friendly welcome, personalised service & quality cuisine.

VISA 🔲 💳 AmEx ✓ 🎿 🛁 A

BALLYSHANNON, Co Donegal

Visit Fermanagh Lakelands, Rossnowlagh Beach, Glenveagh National Park, Ardara Heritage Town, Florence Court House, Castlecoole House, Marble Arch Caves.

DORRIAN'S IMPERIAL HOTEL

Main Street, Ballyshannon, County Donegal
(072) 51147 FAX (072) 51102
BEN & MARY DORRIAN

26, 26 en-suite, from £36.50 to £39.00 per person, double occ. Lunch served. Non-residents welcome. Closed 23rd to 31st December.

from £17.60, last orders 9.15pm.

Traditional Irish home cooked food, prepared from quality ingredients.

Traditional town centre hotel, recently renovated in old world style with modern facilities. Managed by the Dorrian family for over 50 years. Warm & personal atmosphere with open fires.

VISA AmEx S B

BALLYVOURNEY, Co Cork

THE MILLS INN

Ballyvourney, Macroom, County Cork
(026) 45237 FAX (026) 45454
DONAL & MARY SCANNELL

10, 10 en-suite, from £25.00 per person, double occ. Lunch served. Non-residents welcome. Closed 25th December.

£12.00 to £18.00 last orders 9.30pm

Fish dishes. Fresh local produce.

A country inn dating back to 1755, surrounded by landscaped gardens. The hotel also has a vintage car museum in the courtyard.

VISA AmEx A

BALTIMORE, Co Cork

Ideal base for touring scenic West Cork and the Mizen Peninsula.

BALTIMORE HARBOUR HOTEL

Baltimore, West Cork, County Cork
(028) 20361 FAX (028) 33131
TERRI CULLINANE

35, 35 en-suite, from £29.00 per person, double occ. Lunch served. Non-residents welcome. Open all year.

£15.00.

Fresh local produce.

Recently refurbished, situated in a coastal fishing village.

VISA AmEx B

BANDON, Co Cork

Set in beautiful West Cork, an ideal base for touring Blarney, Cork City, Killarney and the Ring of Kerry.

MUNSTER ARMS HOTEL

Bandon, West Cork, County Cork
✆ (023) 41562 FAX (023) 41562
SEAMUS HEANEY

🛏 29, 29 en-suite, from £28.00 per person, double occ.
Lunch served. Non-residents welcome. Closed 25th December.
✗ £15.00, last orders 9.15pm.
🍴 Fresh cuisine using local ingredients.

Traditional hotel offering a homely atmosphere, quality cuisine, personalised service and comfortable facilities.

VISA 💳 💳 AmEx 🖊 A

BUNCRANA, Co Donegal

Set within the beautiful and scenic peninsula of Inishowen, visit Dunree Military Fort, Grianan of Aileach and Buncrana Castle.

LAKE OF SHADOWS HOTEL

Grianan Park, Buncrana, County Donegal
✆ (077) 61005 FAX (077) 62131
MR & MRS P DOHERTY

🛏 23, 23 en-suite, from £25.00 per person, double occ.
Lunch served. Non-residents welcome. Closed 25th December.
✗ £15.00, last orders 10pm.
🍴 Fine regional foods prepared from the freshest local ingredients.

The hotel is tastefully decorated with well appointed bedrooms, all of which enjoy scenic views. Nightly entertainment. A homely atmosphere prevails.

VISA 💳 💳 AmEx 🖊 🏊 A

CAHIR, Co Tipperary

Visit Cahir Castle, Swiss Cottage, Rock of Cashel, Mitchelstown Caves, Waterford and Tipperary Crystal Glass factories. Cork, Kilkenny, Waterford and Limerick are all within 1 hour.

CASTLE COURT HOTEL

Cahir, County Tipperary
✆ (052) 41210 FAX (052) 42333
FRANK & MARY NOLAN

🛏 10, 10 en-suite, from £26.00 per person, double occ.
Lunch served. Non-residents welcome. Closed 25th & 26th December.
✗ £10.00 to £14.00, last orders 9pm.
🍴 Irish Stew. Symphony of Seafood Mornay. Irish Spring Lamb.

Long established family run hotel where the accent is firmly on friendly service and a high standard of Irish cooking.

VISA 💳 🚫 🖊 🍷 B

CARAGH LAKE, Co Kerry

One mile from the famous "Ring of Kerry" and just a short drive from Ballybunion.

⌂⌂⌂ CARAGH LODGE

Caragh Lake, County Kerry
☎ (066) 69115 FAX (066) 69316
MARY GAUNT

🛏 10, 10 en-suite, from £44.00 to £52.25 per person, double occ.
Lunch served. Non-residents welcome. Closed mid October to Easter.
✕ £24.00, last orders 9pm.

🍴 Seafood, wild salmon, Kerry lamb. Fruit and vegetables from the hotel garden.

A mid Victorian house, originally built as a fishing lodge, on the shores of the lake. The Lodge is furnished throughout with antiques. Bedrooms are individually appointed to a high standard.

VISA 🖃 AmEx ⊗ ⅙ ⌁ 🔧 ✓ 🕭 ☇ C

CARLINGFORD, Co Louth

Ireland's best preserved medieval village set on the southern shore of the beautiful Carlingford Lough.

⌂⌂ MCKEVITTS VILLAGE HOTEL ✗ ✗

Market Square, Carlingford, County Louth
☎ (042) 73116 FAX (042) 73144
MR BRIAN MCKEVITT

🛏 3, 3 en-suite, from £22.00 per person, double occ.
Lunch served. Non-residents welcome. Open all year.
✕ from £15.00, last orders 9pm.

🍴 Traditional Irish dishes prepared from fresh local produce. Local oysters, mountain lamb.

Situated in the market square of Carlingford in the heart of the village. Easy walking access to the medieval remains, Heritage Centre and mountain and shore walks. A very comfortable, family run hotel.

VISA 🖃 AmEx ⊗ ✓ A

CASTLECONNELL, Co Limerick

Castleconnell is a picturesque village set on the banks of the Shannon. Visit the Clare Glens, the scenic Silvermines Mountains & the nearby heritage town of Killaloe.

⌂⌂⌂ CASTLE OAKS HOUSE HOTEL

Castleconnell, County Limerick
☎ (061) 377666 FAX (061) 377717
MICHAEL L. FAGAN

🛏 11, 11 en-suite, from £33.00 to £49.50 per person, double occ.
Lunch served. Non-residents welcome. Closed 24th & 25th December.
✕ £16.95, last orders 9.30pm.

🍴 The "Presidents Room" restaurant enjoys views over the River Shannon and beautiful Clare mountains and specialises in fresh local produce, particularly salmon and trout.

A Georgian mansion house set in 25 acres of mature grounds surrounded on three sides by the Shannon. The hotel has magnificent sports and leisure complex.

VISA 🖃 ⌁ AmEx ⅙ ⌁ ✓ 🕭 ♨ B

CASTLEDERMOT, Co Carlow

Within easy reach of Counties Dublin, Wicklow and Kilkenny. Golf, horse riding and fishing available nearby. Many local ancient historical sites.

DOYLE'S SCHOOLHOUSE COUNTRY INN & ACCOMMODATION

Main Street, Castledermot, County Carlow
☎ (0503) 44282 FAX (0503) 43653
J.W.A. DOYLE

🛏 4, 4 en-suite, from £22.50 per person, double occ.
Non-residents welcome. Open all year.
✕ £22.00, last orders 10pm.
🍴 Old world country cooking, including fish, poultry and game. A wide and varied menu.

Old school furnished with Georgian and Victorian antiques giving a genuine old world atmosphere.

✓ 🛇 ⊕ A

CELBRIDGE, Co Kildare

Visit Castletown House, River Liffey & Celbridge Abbey, National Stud & Japanese Gardens.

SETANTA HOUSE HOTEL & RESTAURANT

Clane Road, Celbridge, County Kildare
☎ (01) 627 1111 FAX (01) 627 3387
MR BERNARD LALOR

🛏 10, 10 en-suite, from £35.00 per person, double occ.
Non-residents welcome. Closed Christmas Day.
✕ £19.50, last orders 9.30pm.

🍴 Fresh Darne of Liffey Salmon, salmon poached in white wine with fine Julienne of vegetables and glazed in a light Hollandaise sauce. Mussels in white wine sauce. Roast Rack of Kildare Lamb.

An 18th century building set in beautiful grounds with modern en-suite bedrooms, twenty minutes from the city centre.

VISA 🖃 ᗑ AmEx ♿ ✓ 🛇 B

CLIFDEN, Co Galway

Beautiful scenery and a host of outdoor sporting activities including golf, horse riding, deep sea fishing and tennis.

FOYLE'S HOTEL ✗ ✗ ✗

Clifden, Connemara, County Galway
☎ (095) 21801 FAX (095) 21458
EDMUND P FOYLE

🛏 30, 30 en-suite, from £27.50 to £37.50 per person, double occ.
Lunch served. Non-residents welcome. Closed 1st November to 1st May.
✕ £18.00, last orders 9.30pm.
🍴 Lobster, wild salmon. Fillet of Steer Beef. Connemara Lamb.

Connemara's longest established hotel situated in the picturesque capital of Clifden. The hotel which has been managed by the Foyle family for nearly a century, has been recently redesigned to the highest standards yet retains its old world charm and atmosphere.

VISA 🖃 ᗑ AmEx ⊗ ♿ ✓ 🛇 ⊕ B

COBH, Co Cork

Visit the Fota Gardens and Wildlife Park, Harbour Cruises, try windsurfing or fishing. Visit Queenstown Heritage Centre, Cobh, or Jamestown Heritage Centre, Midleton.

THE COMMODORE HOTEL ✗

Cobh, County Cork
☎ (021) 811277 FAX (021) 811672
FRANK O'SHEA

🛏 36, 36 en-suite, from £25.00 to £30.00 per person, double occ. Lunch served. Non-residents welcome. Closed 25th to 27th December.
✗ from £15.00, last orders 9pm.
🍽 Fresh local ingredients and produce.

Overlooking Cork harbour, the hotel is being refurbished and enjoys an indoor heated swimming pool, sauna & snooker rooms. Five miles from Ringaskiddy car ferry via cross river ferry.

VISA 🔳 💳 AmEx 🔜 ✓ 🄢 A

COLERAINE, Co Antrim

The ideal base for touring the famous Causeway Coast and the Glens of Antrim.

BUSHTOWN HOUSE HOTEL AND COUNTRY CLUB

Coleraine, County Antrim
☎ (0265) 58367 FAX (0265) 320909
MR ROBERT MC COOK

🛏 21, 21 en-suite, from £34.00 to £36.00 per person, double occ. Lunch served. Non-residents welcome. Closed 26th December.
✗ £15.00, last orders 9.30pm.
🍽 Wholesome food prepared from fresh local ingredients. Chicken Bushtown. Salmon.

This brand new hotel has much to offer with extensive leisure facilities, well appointed bedrooms and an elegant restaurant.

VISA 🔳 💳 AmEx ⊗ ♿ 🔜 🎱 ✓ 🄢 🅂 B

COLLOONEY, Co Sligo

Visit Sligo Castle, Yeat's Country, Parkes Castle, Lough Key Forest Park & Carrowmore megalithic remains.

MARKREE CASTLE

Collooney, County Sligo
☎ (071) 67800 FAX (071) 67840
CHARLES & MARY COOPER

🛏 14, 14 en-suite, from £43.50 (low season) per person, double occ. Lunch served. Non-residents welcome. Closed for the month of February.
✗ £19.50 to £22.50, last orders 9.30.
🍽 Trout and Eels from the hotel's own fishery. Deer from the adjoining woods.

A spectacular castle with magnificent interiors which has been the home of the Cooper family for 350 years. Markree retains the atmosphere of a family home with all the facilities of a modern hotel.

VISA 🔳 💳 AmEx ✓ 🄢 ⚓ C

CORK CITY, Co Cork

Visit Blarney Castle House and Stone, Cobh Heritage Centre, Fota Wildlife Park, Middleton Distillery and the Cork City Tourist Trails. Close proximity to local golf course, ferries and airport.

🏠🏠🏠 FLEMINGS RESTAURANT & ACCOMMODATION ✗ ✗

Silvergrange House, Tivoli, Cork City, County Cork
☎ (021) 821621 FAX (021) 821800
MICHAEL & EILEEN FLEMING

🛏 4, 4 en-suite, from £32.00 per person, double occ.
Lunch served. Non-residents welcome. Closed 23rd to 26th December.
✗ £20.00, last orders 10.30pm.
🍴 Classic regional dishes from France and Ireland using organically grown vegetables and fruit from the kitchen garden, locally caught fish and game in season. Traditional home smoked bacon and cabbage. Home-made breads baked daily.

A Georgian House, circa 1820, set in five acres of grounds on the edges of the city. All rooms are furnished with period antiques, open fires and a wonderful homely atmosphere.

VISA 💳 💳 AmEx ⊗ ♿ ✓ B

DELPHI, Co Galway

Visit nearby Connemara, Westport or Kylemore Abbey.

🏠🏠🏠 DELPHI LODGE ✗

Delphi, Leenane, County Galway
☎ (095) 42211 FAX (095) 42296
PETER MANTLE

🛏 11, 11 en-suite, from £37.50 per person, double occ.
Lunch served. Closed 1st November to 31st January.
✗ £25.00. Last orders 8.00pm.
🍴 Fish and shellfish.

A country house surrounded by mountains and overlooking the famous salmon lake.

VISA 💳 ✓ 🍴 ♿ ✓ 🍴

DINGLE, Co Kerry

Dingle is unrivaled in its beauty, with seaviews, coves & inlets. Rich in historic beginnings, this quaint area has within it more antiquities & historic sites than any part of the country.

🏠🏠 BENNERS HOTEL ✗ ✗ ✗ ✗

Main Street, Dingle, County Kerry
☎ (066) 51638 FAX (066) 51412
DANNO O'KEEFE

🛏 24, 24 en-suite, from £30.00 per person, double occ.
Lunch served. Non-residents welcome. Closed 23rd to 26th December.
✗ £18.00, last orders 9.30pm.
🍴 A menu with a strong emphasis on regional dishes & seafood prepared from fresh local ingredients.

A gem within the Emerald Isle. This 250 year old inn has undergone a transformation which while maintaining its historical facade can also offer all modern appointments inside. The best of old world charm, tradition and hospitality.

VISA 💳 💳 AmEx ✓ 🍴 B

Dingle continued overleaf...

DUN AN OIR GOLF HOTEL

Ballyferriter, Dingle, County Kerry
☎ (066) 56133 FAX (066) 56153
JOHN & CELESTE SLYE

🛏 21, 21 en-suite, from £23.30 per person, double occ.
Lunch served. Non-residents welcome. Closed November to
Easter.
✗ £15.00 - £18.50, last orders 9.30pm.
🍽 Local seafood and shellfish. Kerry lamb. Home-made breads.

20 years old, the most westerly hotel in Europe situated on an
eighteen hole links course overlooking the Atlantic Ocean.

VISA 🔲 ⊗ 🔜 🥄 ✓ 🕭 🔱 A

DUBLIN
Ireland's capital city with everything a capital city should offer. Shopping
on Grafton Street, the National Concert Hall, theatres, top golf courses,
horse racing and sport.

ABERDEEN LODGE

53/55 Park Avenue, Ballsbridge, Dublin 4
☎ (01) 283 8155 FAX (01) 283 7877
PAT HALPIN

🛏 16, 16 en-suite, from £36.00 to £48.00 per person, double occ.
Non-residents welcome. Open all year.
✗ from £19.50, 9pm.
🍽 Finest Irish ingredients cooked with care and attention,
including fish, poultry and game. An extensive wine list.

Aberdeen Lodge is located in the heart of Dublin 4's Embassy Belt.
Combination of early Edwardian grace and every modern comfort,
including suites with jacuzzi. Private gardens, parking,
convenient to Dart, City Centre and Airport.

VISA 🔲 ◖ AmEx ⊗ ✓ 🕭 🔱 Ⓢ C

FINNSTOWN COUNTRY HOUSE HOTEL & RESTAURANT

Newcastle Road, Lucan, County Dublin
☎ (01) 628 0644 FAX (01) 628 1088
EOIN HICKEY

🛏 35, 35 en-suite, from £37.50 per person, double occ.
Lunch served. Non-residents welcome. Open all year.
✗ £18.00, last orders 9.30pm.
🍽 All produce local and fresh with a good selection of meats,
poultry and fresh fish daily.

An 18th century country house hotel standing in 52 acres of
mature woodlands, 8 miles from the city centre. Ornate ceilings,
turf fires and modern bedrooms.

VISA 🔲 ◖ AmEx ⊗ 🔜 🥄 ✓ 🕭 Ⓢ C

THE GREY DOOR RESTAURANT & RESIDENCE

22/23 Upper Pembroke St, Dublin 2
☎ (01) 676 3286 FAX (01) 676 3287
BARRY WYSE & P J DALY

🛏 7, 7 en-suite, from £49.45 per person, double occ.
Non-residents welcome. Closed Sunday & all bank holidays.
✕ £22.50, last orders 10.45pm.
🍽 The Grey Door Restaurant specialises in classic Russian/Scandinavian cuisine. Pier 32, is a traditional Irish restaurant & bar specialising in seafood & live music most nights.

Beautifully restored Georgian town house located near St Stephens Green. The hotel has seven deluxe bedrooms en-suite and elegant private dining rooms with warm, professional and friendly service.

VISA 💳 AmEx ✓ C

DUNGARVAN, Co Waterford
Dungarvan and it's surrounding areas can provide white sandy beaches, exhilarating hill walking or visiting the numerous sites of architectural or historical interest. Visit Ardmore, Clonea Strand, Nire Valley.

THE PARK HOTEL ⚲

Dungarvan, County Waterford
☎ (058) 42899 FAX (058) 42969
DONAL FLYNN

🛏 39, 39 en-suite, from £31.00 per person, double occ.
Lunch served. Non-residents welcome. Open all year.
✕ £16.00, last orders 9.30pm.
🍽 Freshly caught seafood.

A new hotel with indoor leisure centre, yet remaining firmly family run with a warm welcome. The hotel overlooks the Colligan River Estuary and is just five minutes from the town centre.

VISA 💳 AmEx ♿ ≈ ✓ 🚭 Ⓢ B

DUNMANWAY, Co Cork
Situated in the heart of scenic west Cork, Dunmanway has a lot to offer with its proximity to the touring areas of Cork and Kerry. Visit Gougane Barra, Clonakilty Model Village.

DUN MHUIRE HOUSE & RESTAURANT

Kilgarry Road, Dunmanway, County Cork
☎ (023) 45162
LIAM & CARMEL HAYES

🛏 5, 5 en-suite, from £25.00 per person, double occ.
Non-residents welcome. Restaurant closed to non-residents Sunday, Monday & Tuesday in winter.
✕ £17.00, 9.30pm.
🍽 Traditional Irish cuisine using fresh local ingredients. Trolley home-made desserts.

A small, exclusive family-run guesthouse with an award wining restaurant, well appointed bedrooms and a relaxed cosy atmosphere.

VISA 💳 ⊗ ♿ ✓ 🚭 A

ENNISKERRY, Co Wicklow

In the heart of the Wicklow mountains, surrounded by stunning scenery and walks.Visit Powerscourt House Gardens, Glendalough ancient monastic site. Dublin city is 15 miles north.

ENNISCREE LODGE & RESTAURANT ✕

Glencree Valley, Enniskerry, County Wicklow
☎ (01) 286 3542 FAX (01) 286 6037
PAUL JOHNSON & LYNDA FOX

🛏 10, 10 en-suite, from £33.50 per person, double occ.
Lunch served. Non-residents welcome. Open all year.
✕ From £18.00, last orders 9.30pm.
🍴 Modern Irish Cuisine. Wicklow lamb. Smoked Wicklow trout. Wild mushrooms.

Country inn and hunting lodge which enjoys spectacular mountain views. Log fires throughout and fully furnished in antiques to provide a very special ambiance.

VISA 💳 💳 AmEx ♿ ✓ 🚭 ⌖ C

GALWAY, Co Galway

Oranmore is a small village located just outside Galway City, surrounded by the beautiful scenery of Galway Bay.

ORANMORE LODGE HOTEL

Oranmore, County Galway
☎ (091) 94400 FAX (091) 90227
BRIAN O'HIGGINS

🛏 10, 10 en-suite, from £30.00 to £40.00 per person, double occ.
Lunch served. Non-residents welcome. Closed 24th to 26th December.
✕ £17.50, last orders 10pm.
🍴 Fresh seafood daily from Galway Bay. The best of Irish meats.

An Old World House which carries a crest with the motto, "comme je trouve" meaning "as you find you find us" the best tradition in Irish hospitality.

VISA 💳 💳 AmEx ✓ 🚭 ⌖ B

GLENBEIGH, Co Kerry

Picturesque seaside village, situated on the Ring of Kerry, amidst mountains, lakes and rivers.

TOWERS HOTEL

Glenbeigh, County Kerry
☎ (066) 68212 FAX (066) 68260
DOLORES SWEENEY

🛏 34, 34 en-suite, from £34.00 per person, double occ.
Lunch served. Non-residents welcome. Closed January to Easter.
✕ £20.25, last orders 9.00pm.
🍴 Seafood caught locally in Dingle Bay. Fresh Caragh Salmon.

An old style country hotel with a unique friendly atmosphere. The emphasis is firmly on the internationally famous seafood restaurant.

VISA 💳 💳 AmEx ✓ 🚭 ⌖ B

GLENGARRIFF, County Cork

In the heart of historic West Cork. Visit Bantry Bay. Hill walking, cycling.

CASEY'S HOTEL

Glengarriff, County Cork
✆ (027) 63010 FAX (027) 63010
SINEAD DEASY

🛏 19, 19 en-suite, from £20.00 per person, double occ.
Lunch served. Non-residents welcome. Closed 1st December to 16th March.
✕ £14.00 to £15.00.
🍴 Fresh fish dishes. Fresh local produce.

A country hotel with all bedrooms newly refurbished.

VISA AmEx A

GREYSTONES, Co Wicklow

With easy access to central Dublin, this traditional seaside town is a paradise for walkers, horse riding and fishing.

LA TOUCHE HOTEL

Trafalgar Road, Greystones, County Wicklow
✆ (01) 287 4401 FAX (01) 287 4504
NIALL KENNY & GERRY CARRON

🛏 32, 31 en-suite, from £35.00 per person, double occ.
Lunch served. Non-residents welcome. Closed 24th December.
✕ from £9.00.
🍴 Fresh fish and fresh local produce.
100 year old mansion style building with a warm, homely atmosphere.

VISA B

KILKEE, Co Clare

Visit the Cliffs of Moher, the Burren, Aillwee Caves, the Loop Head Drive, Bunratty and Dromoland Castles.

HALPINS HOTEL

Erin Street, Kilkee, County Clare
✆ (065) 56032 FAX (065) 56317
PAT HALPIN

🛏 12, 12 en-suite, from £26.00 to £35.00 per person, double occ.
Lunch served. Non-residents welcome. Closed 10th January to 15th March.
✕ £18.00, last orders 9.00pm.
🍴 Fine selection of seafood, meat and vegetarian dishes using fresh local ingredients. Extensive wine list. Old world atmosphere, modern comforts, fine food and good wines are all part of this cosy hotel.

Located in the Victorian resort of Kilkee. Close to the cliffs of Moher, Connemara and the Ring of Kerry (via Shannon car ferry).

VISA AmEx B

KILKENNY, Co Kilkenny

An ideal centre for touring the south east of Ireland. There is a wide choice of leisure activities for all the family. Visit Kilkenny Castle, medieval Kilkenny city, Bothe House, Dunmore Caves, picturesque villages such as Inistoique, Nore & Barrow River Valley & forests.

LACKEN HOUSE RESTAURANT & GUESTHOUSE

Dublin Road, Kilkenny, County Kilkenny
☎ (056) 61085 FAX (056) 62435
EUGENE & BREDA MCSWEENEY

🛏 8, 8 en-suite, from £25.00 to £32.00 per person, double occ.
Non-residents welcome. Closed for Christmas.
✕ £22.00, last orders 10.00pm.
🍴 Eugene specialises in using local raw ingredients to show that modern progressive Irish cooking is at the cutting edge of international cuisine.

This delightful Victorian Dower House, built in 1850, is now a friendly, family run guesthouse & award winning restaurant. Eugene appears regularly on national television with his cookery programme.

VISA AmEx B

KILLARNEY, Co Kerry

Visit Ross Castle, St Mary's Cathedral, Muckross House and Gardens, Ring of Kerry & Lakes of Killarney.

RANDLES COURT HOTEL

Muckross Road, Killarney, County Kerry
☎ (064) 35333 FAX (064) 35206
KAY RANDLES

🛏 37, 37 en-suite, from £45.00 to £60.00 per person, double occ.
Non-residents welcome. Closed January to February.
✕ £15.00 to £22.00, last orders 9.30pm.
🍴 The Court Restaurant serves both A La Carte and Table D'Hote menus which feature seafood as a speciality.

Originally built in 1906 as a family residence, we would like to think that the warmth and friendliness that one would associate with a a family home has been maintained through to the present day.

VISA AmEx C

KILLEEN HOUSE HOTEL

Aghadoe, Lakes of Killarney, County Kerry
☎ (064) 31711 FAX (064) 31811
MICHAEL & GERALDINE ROSNEY

🛏 15, 15 on suite, from £32.50 to £37.50 per person, double occ.
Non-residents welcome. Closed January to March.
✕ from £21.50, last orders 9.30pm.
🍴 Irish & International cuisine using the best of local produce.

A charming little hotel, formerly a Victorian rectory, set in 1.5 acres of beautifully manicured gardens. It enjoys the charm and elegance of the 19th century combined with the comfort and convenience of the 20th.

VISA AmEx C

KINGSCOURT, Co Cavan

Visit Carlingford Lough, medieval village, the tombs of New Grange, the Boyne Drive.

CABRA CASTLE HOTEL

Kingscourt, County Cavan
☎ (042) 67030 FAX (042) 67039
THE CORSCADDEN FAMILY

🛏 35, 35 en-suite, from £35.00 per person, double occ.
Lunch served. Non-residents welcome. Closed 25th December.
✗ £19.75, last orders 9.00pm.
🍴 Elegant restaurant serving traditional Irish dishes. Salmon, lamb.

A family run 14th century castle located in 88 acres of gardens and parkland within Dun Na Ri National Park. The hotel enjoys delightful views over the Cavan countryside and is surrounded by its own 9 hole golf course.

VISA 💳 💷 AmEx ♿ 🔍 ✓ 🐕 🐾 C

KINSALE, Co Cork

The town of Kinsale is one of Ireland's leading tourist destinations. The French, Spanish and English influences can still be seen in the many interesting historic buildings and narrow streets. Visit Charles Fort, Desmond Castle, Fota Island, Cobh Heritage Centre, Midleton Heritage Centre, Lismore Heritage town.

KIERAN'S FOLK HOUSE & RESTAURANT

Guardwell, Kinsale, County Cork
☎ (021) 772382 FAX (021) 774085
DENIS & GERALDINE KIERAN

🛏 19, 19 en-suite, from £20.00 to £25.00 per person, double occ.
Lunch served. Non-residents welcome. Closed 25th December.
✗ £13.00, last orders 10.15pm.
🍴 An imaginative and modestly priced menu featuring locally caught fish, shellfish and prime Irish steaks.

Kieran's Folkhouse is a 250 year old inn of immense charm situated in the heart of Kinsale, one of Ireland's historic & picturesque towns. The rooms are finished to a high standard in cottage style. Music is featured nightly in one of the popular bars.

VISA 💳 ♿ ✓ 🐕 A

LISDOONVARNA, Co Clare

Visit the Cliffs of Moher, Aillwee Caves, The Burren and the nearby Aran Islands.

CARRIGANN HOTEL

Lisdoonvarna, County Clare
☎ (065) 74036 FAX (065) 74567
GERRY & MARY HOWARD

🛏 18, 18 en-suite, from £22.00 to £30.00 per person, double occ.
Lunch served. Non-residents welcome. Closed 1st November to 28th February.
✗ £15.00, last orders 9pm.
🍴 Fresh smoked fish, local cheeses, Carrigann Farm organic beef and lamb, prepared by the chef patron.

A quiet, friendly & relaxing hotel set in its own landscap grounds. The lounge and restaurant enjoy views of the gardens. Open fires in winter. Walking tours arranged.

VISA 💳 ✓ 🐕 🐾 A

LOUGHREA, Co Galway

Twenty miles from Galway City, visit Thoor Ballylee (Yeat's sumer home)

🏨 ## O' DEAS HOTEL
Loughrea, County Galway
✆ (091) 41611 FAX (091) 42635
MARY O'NEILL

🛏 15, 14 en-suite, from £25.00 per person, double occ.
Lunch served. Non-residents welcome. Open all year.
✕ £15.00 to £20.00. Last orders 9.00pm.
🍽 Fresh local produce, lamb, beef, fresh fish.

A Georgian town house built in 1830 with traditional furnishings.
A friendly family run hotel with a warm atmosphere.

VISA 💳 AmEx 👌 ✓ 🚭 A

MACROOM, Co Cork

Quaint town, situated in the Lee Valley. See Macroom Castle grounds and the many lovely walks. Blarney Castle and Stone within easy reach.

🏨 ## VICTORIA HOTEL
Macroom, County Cork
✆ (026) 41082 FAX (026) 42148
MARY & TIM O'LEARY

🛏 16, 16 en-suite, from £22.00 per person, double occ.
Lunch served. Non-residents welcome. Closed 24th to 28th December.
✕ £9.00 to £14.00, last orders 9.30pm.

🍽 Traditional Irish fare, combined with some modern dishes.
Macroom Oatmeal. Bacon and Cabbage. Tripe and Onions.

Small, friendly family run hotel dating from the 17th century which has recently been completely refurbished. Comfortable furnishings and a warm atmosphere.

VISA 💳 AmEx ✓ 🚭 🐕 A

MALLOW, Co Cork

Within easy reach of Cork City, Blarney and Killarney.

🏨 ## HIBERNIAN HOTEL
Main Street, Mallow, County Cork
✆ (022) 21588 FAX (022) 22632
JOHN MCMAHON

🛏 40, 40 en-suite, from £25.00 per person, double occ.
Lunch served. Non-residents welcome. Closed Christmas Day & Good Friday.
✕ £12.75, last orders 9.30pm.
🍽 Traditional Irish cooking. Blackwater Trout.

Old world style town centre hotel which was originally built in 1770 but was totally refurbished in 1990 to provide an excellent standard of accommodation and good value. The hotel enjoys exclusive fishing rights on the Blackwater River.

VISA 💳 💷 AmEx ⊗ 👌 ✓ 🚭 🐕 A

MOHILL, Co Leitrim
Visit Lough Rynn Gardens, Strokestown House, Florencecourt House, Marble Arch Caves, Shannon Erne Waterway Cruising.

🏠🏠 **GLEBE HOUSE**
Ballinamore Road (R202 North), Mohill, County Leitrim
✆ (078) 31086 FAX (078) 31886
MARION & JOHN MALONEY

🛏 7, 7 en-suite, from £22.00 to £29.00 per person, double occ.
Lunch served. Closed December & January.
✗ £12.00, last orders 9pm.
🍴 Home cooking with fresh locally produced ingredients.

Lovely 19th century Georgian house in over 40 acres of woods & farmland. Ideal base from which to tour the scenic northwest. Itineraries suggested. Close to many activities which include golf, horseriding, trekking & fishing.

VISA 💳 AmEx ⊗ ✓ 🛏 🐾 A

MOVILLE, Co Donegal
Set in the scenic Innishowen peninsula on the main tourist route for Malin Head.

🏠 **MCNAMARA'S HOTEL**
Moville, County Donegal
✆ (077) 82010 FAX (077) 82564
BILLY TIGHE

🛏 50, 50 en-suite, from £23.00 per person, double occ.
Lunch served. Non-residents welcome. Open all year.
✗ £15.00, last orders 10pm
🍴 Local fresh farm produce and daily fresh fish.

Recently refurbished and extended 18th century hotel of comfortable and good value accommodation.

VISA 💳 💳 AmEx ⊗ ♿ ✓ 🛏 🏊 A

NENAGH, Co Tipperary

Visit Nenagh Heritage Centre, Historical sights, Lake walks, cycles and drives with beautiful views, Dromineer Harbour where barges and steamboats docked 150 years ago.

🏠🏠 **DROMINEER BAY HOTEL**
Dromineer, Nenagh, County Tipperary
✆ (067) 24114 FAX (067) 24288
DENIS & LILY COLLISON

🛏 10, 10 en-suite, from £29.00 to £45.00 per person, double occ.
Lunch served. Non-residents welcome. Closed 25th December.
✗ £17.00, last orders 9pm.
🍴 "Moorings Restaurant" boasts fine cuisine at reasonable prices. Bar food menu in the "Captain Deck" overlooking the Lake.

A magnificent lakeshore hotel over 100 years old. Steeped in the tradition of barges and steamboats which moored in Dromineer. Panoramic lake views from the restaurant bar and bedrooms, modern comfortable facilities together with warm friendly services provided by the owners and staff.

VISA 💳 AmEx ♿ 🔌 ✓ 🛏 🏊 B

NEW ROSS, Co Wexford

Many local forest walks, golf, horse riding. J.F. Kennedy and Heritage Park within easy driving distance.

CEDAR LODGE HOTEL

Carrigbyrne, Newbawn, New Ross, County Wexford
☎ (051) 28386 FAX (051) 28222
THOMAS MARTIN

🛏 18, 18 en-suite, from £35.00 per person, double occ.
Lunch served. Non-residents welcome. Closed 20th December to 20th January.
✕ £20.00 Last orders 9.00pm.
🍴 Wexford scallops, crab & lobster, local lamb, beef and cheese. Wild salmon when in season.

A country hotel located in a picturesque setting offering a relaxed friendly atmosphere. 30 minutes drive from Rosslare port.

VISA 💳 ⊗ ✓ B

OUGHTERARD, Co Galway

Visit Lough Corrib and it's islands or Aughnanure Castle. The area enjoys many fine walks.

SWEENEY'S OUGHTERARD HOUSE

Oughterard, Connemara, County Galway
☎ (091) 82207 FAX (091) 82161
PATRIC & MAIRE HIGGINS

🛏 20, 20 en-suite, from £47.00 to £54.00 per person, double occ.
Lunch served. Non-residents welcome. Closed mid December to mid January.
✕ £20.00, last orders 9pm.
🍴 Seafish, freshwater fish, shellfish and Connemara lamb.

Long established family run Georgian country house hotel.
VISA 💳 AmEx ✓ 🦢 ⚓ C

PORTBALLINTRAE, Co Antrim

Nearby is Bushmills Distillery and the world famous Giant's Causeway and 2 miles east of Dunluce Castle ruins. Seven golf courses nearby including Royal Portrush Championship Course. Miles of scenic coastal drives.

BEACH HOUSE HOTEL ✗✗

The Seafront, 61 Beach Road, Portballintrae, County Antrim
☎ (02657) 31214 FAX (02657) 31664
MARTIN & JANETTE MC CLAINE

🛏 32, 32 en-suite, from £32.00 to £34.00 per person, double occ.
Lunch served. Non-residents welcome. Open all year.
✕ £16.00, last orders 9pm.
🍴 Fresh local produce. Wild Atlantic Salmon (in Season), Extensive salad buffet and bar meal menu. Local fish and beef. "Beach" speciality - Butterscotch Fudge Sundae.

One of the last truly family hotels, started in 1924 by Martin's grandparents. The hotel combines traditional values with modern comforts. The original hotel has been extended and modernised to provide the comfort and facilities expected in the 90's. Above a sandy beach and safe bathing and rock fishing, it is the ideal base from which to explore the famous Causeway.

VISA 💳 AmEx 🔍 ✓ 🦢 ⚓ A

RENVYLE, Co Galway

Visit Connemara National Park, Kylemore Abbey and Clifden, "Twelve Bens". Beautiful beaches and boat trips to Inishboffin Island.

🏛 RENVYLE HOUSE HOTEL

Renvyle, Connemara, County Galway
✆ (095) 43511 FAX (095) 43515
VINCENT FLANNERY

🛏 65, 65 en-suite, from £33.00 to £60.00 per person, double occ.
Lunch served. Non-residents welcome. Closed 3rd January to 15th March.
✗ £21.00, last orders 9pm.
🍴 Fresh Seafood and vegetables produced locally feature on the daily menu.

An historic coastal hotel situated on the edge of the Atlantic Ocean. Turf fires, comfort and fine fare - a place in which to relax and feel at home. The hotel has many facilities and there are excellent walking routes within the area.

VISA 💳 💳 AmEx ♿ ⚓ 🎣 ✓ 🏊 ⛳ ♜ C

ROSCOMMON, Co Roscommon

Visit Strokestown Heritage Centre, Clonalis House, Knock Shrine and the River Shannon.

🏛 ABBEY HOTEL   ✗ ✗

Roscommon, County Roscommon
✆ (0903) 26240 FAX (0903) 26021
TOM & ANYA GREALY

🛏 25, 25 en-suite, from £32.50 per person, double occ.
Lunch served. Non-residents welcome. Closed 25th December.
✗ £18.50, last orders 9.30pm.
🍴 Local lamb, steaks and fresh produce.

An 18th century manor house with a fine restaurant and comfortable accommodation. Ideally located in the Heart of Ireland.

VISA 💳 💳 AmEx ✓ 🏊 ♜ B

ROUNDSTONE, Co Galway

Set in the heart of Connemara. Visit the famous Roundstone Bogs, Alcock & Brown memorial and the Aran Islands National Park.

🏛 ELDON'S HOTEL

Roundstone, Connemara, County Galway
✆ (095) 35933 FAX (095) 35921
MRS ANN CONNEELY

🛏 13, 13 en-suite, from £25.00 per person, double occ.
Lunch served. Non-residents welcome. Closed December 25th, January & February.
✗ £17.50, last orders 9.30pm.
🍴 Lobster, fresh fish delivered daily. Steaks, chicken and vegetarian dishes cooked by the chef patron.

A new hotel, designed in comfortable old style, overlooking the harbour in this small village. All the bedrooms are fully appointed with many enjoying views to the surrounding mountains.

VISA 💳 💳 AmEx ✓ ⛳ 🏊 A

SLIGO, Co Sligo

Vist Sligo Castle, Yeats Country, Parkes Castle, Lough Key Forest Park and Carrowmore megalithic remains.

🏨 **HOTEL SILVER SWAN**

Hyde Bridge, Sligo, County Sligo
☎ (071) 43231 FAX (071) 42232
MICHAEL HIGGINS

🛏 29, 29 en-suite, from £35.00 per person, double occ.
Lunch served. Non-residents welcome. Closed 25th & 26th December.
✕ £17.00, last orders 9.15pm.
🍽 The Cygnet Restaurant offers traditional Irish fare. Seafood, lobster, shellfish and desserts.

Town centre hotel which has recently been refurbished. Over looking the river, the bedrooms are modern and large. Popular restaurant and bars frequently featuring traditional Irish music.

VISA ⬛ 💳 AmEx ✓ ⑤ B

TERRYGLASS, Co Tipperary

Area rich in historical interests. Visit Clonmacnoise, Birr Gardens and Damer House, Roscrea, Loug Derg Drive, Rock of Cashel.

🏨 **GURTHALOUGHA HOUSE**

Ballinderry, Nenagh, County Tipperary
☎ (067) 22080 FAX (067) 22154
BESSIE & MICHAEL WILKINSON

🛏 8, 8 en-suite, from £34.00 to £40.00 per person, double occ.
Non-residents welcome. Closed 23rd to 29th December & the month of February.
✕ £23.00, last orders 8.30pm.
🍽 Use of own garden vegetables and fruit. Pike and smoked eel.

A 19th century country home standing on the banks of a lake and comfortably furnished with antiques.

VISA ⬛ 💳 AmEx 🔍 ✓ ⑤ ⑭ B

TRAMORE, Co Waterford

Popular seaside resort with numerous family leisure activities. Waterford Glass and Reginalds Tower and Celt World are closeby.

🏨 **MAJESTIC HOTEL**

Tramore, County Waterford
☎ (051) 381761 FAX (051) 381766
ANNETTE DEVINE

🛏 60, 60 en-suite, from £24.50 to £29.50 per person, double occ.
Lunch served. Non-residents welcome. Open all year.
✕ £14.95, last orders 9.30pm.
🍽 Varied menu featuring local fresh seafood and steaks.

Modern family run seaside hotel overlooking Tramore Bay. The restaurant enjoys panoramic views and the large lounge bar provides entertainment in season.

VISA ⬛ AmEx ♿ 🏊 ✓ 🎾 A

WESTPORT, Co Mayo

Historic west coast town. An ideal base for walking and golf. Visit Westport House.

GRAND CENTRAL HOTEL
The Octagon, Westport, County Mayo
☎ (098) 25027 FAX (098) 26316
FINOLA HUGHES

🛏 14, 14 en-suite, from £30.00 per person, double occ.
Lunch served. Non-residents welcome. Closed 25th & 26th December.
✕ £15.00 Last orders 9.00pm.
🍲 Fresh local produce.

A 200 year old hotel which has recently been refurbished. The hotel offers a warm welcome.

VISA 🔷 AmEx ✓ 🔖 ⏦ B

WEXFORD, Co Wexford

The Irish National Heritage Park is only 400 metres from Slaney Manor. Visit Johnstown Castle, the Ring of Hook and Enniscorthy Castle and Museum, "and the John F Kennedy Memorial Park".

SLANEY MANOR
Ferrycarrig, Wexford, County Wexford
☎ (053) 45751 FAX (053) 46510
ESTHER CAULFIELD

🛏 8, 8 en-suite, from £30.00 to £35.00 per person, double occ.
Lunch served. Closed December to January.
✕ £18.00, last orders 5.00pm.
🍲 Wild salmon and prime Irish beef.

A traditional manor house, 1820's, standing in 30 heactares of woods and farmland overlooking the Slaney River. Retains the characteristics of affluent country living. A non smoking hotel.

VISA 🔷 ⚙ AmEx ⊗ ♿ ✓ 🔖 B

WICKLOW, Co Wicklow

Visit Mount Usher Gardens, Powerscourt House Gardens, Glendalough and Avondale House. Horse riding, fishing and several good walks are nearby.

HUNTER'S HOTEL
Newrathbridge, Rathnew, County Wicklow
☎ (0404) 40106 FAX (0404) 40338
THE GELLETLIE FAMILY

🛏 17, 17 en-suite, from £42.50 per person, double occ.
Lunch served. Non-residents welcome. Closed 24th to 26th December.
✕ £20.00, last orders 9pm.
🍲 Wicklow lamb and beef. Locally caught fish and shellfish. Game in season.

A 270 year old coaching inn retaining all it's original character and charm. Furnished entirely in antiques, Hunter's is set in peaceful, delightful gardens.

VISA 🔷 ⚙ AmEx ✓ ⏦ C

YOUGHAL, Co Cork

An "Historic Walled Port" nestling at the mouth of the magnificent Blackwater River. Visit Youghal Heritage Centre, Cobh Heritage Centre and Jameson Heritage Centre.

DEVONSHIRE ARMS HOTEL

Pearse Square, Youghal, County Cork
☎ (024) 92827 FAX (024) 92900
MR & MRS S O'SULLIVAN

🛏 10, 10 en-suite, from £25.00 per person, double occ.
Lunch served. Non-residents welcome. Open all year.
✗ £17.00 Last orders 9.45pm.
🍽 Seafood dishes. The restaurant offers locally cut fresh seafood and a wide range of dishes to suit all tastes.

Old world family run hotel. All bedrooms individually decorated.

VISA 💳 💳 AmEx ⊗ ✓ 🚫 🏊 🐟 A

INDEX BY TOWN

INDEX BY TOWN

INDEX BY TOWN

INDEX BY TOWN

Use Logis for all your accommodation needs!

Use the Logis Central Reservations System to answer all your accommodation needs.

We can search among the 500 member hotels listed in this guide on our reservations computer to find the particular hotel that will suit you and your requirements. Selection can be made using any or all of the following criteria:-

> *Location*
> *Building style*
> *Facilities (swimming pool, golf nearby,*
> *   fishing, tennis etc.)*
> *Cuisine specialities*
> *Non-smoking rooms*
> *Pets welcome*
> *Local tourist attractions*
> *Pricing level*

And, if you are a business person why not join our Corporate Club? Members are offered preferential single room rates at many Logis hotels, automatic upgrade to a double or twin room at no extra charge (when available) and a free morning newspaper. To enroll simply complete the form at the end of this guide and return it to the Oxford office.

LOGIS CENTRAL RESERVATIONS

TEL 01865 875888
FAX 01865 875777

INDEX BY HOTEL

INDEX BY HOTEL

INDEX BY HOTEL

INDEX BY HOTEL

INDEX BY HOTEL

INDEX BY HOTEL

INDEX BY HOTEL

INDEX BY HOTEL

Logis
of
Great Britain

The Logis Corporate Club

Offering regular business users of Logis hotels a range of benefits which we hope will make your corporate travel enjoyable. **E**very member will receive...
• Access to a special 'corporate rate' at hundreds of independent Logis hotels around Britain and Ireland. This rate will include: A single room with en-suite bath or shower, full English, Welsh, Scottish, or Irish breakfast, early morning newspaper (where available), VAT and all service charges.
• Automatic free upgrade to double or twin room if available.
• Guaranteed reservation to 6pm on day of arrival.
• Regular promotions, offers and incentives.
• A numbered membership card.
• Free touring map(s), listing all Logis hotels.

All reservations and enquiries can be placed through our central reservations office, on **01865 875888,** or by fax on **01865 875777.**

How much does membership cost?
Membership of the Logis Corporate Club is absolutely free to bona fide business travellers who have completed the application form overleaf in full.

How do I join?
Simply fill out the form on the reverse and post it to: Logis of Great Britain, 20 Church Road, Horspath, Oxford OX9 1RU. (Please allow 28 days for the delivery of your card and map).

Logis
of
Great Britain

Logis Corporate Card
Membership Application Form

About you:

Name _____

Address _____

_____

_____

Home Tel No. _____

Car Phone or Mobile Phone No _____

About your company:

Name _____

Business Address _____

_____

_____

_____

Business Tel. No. _____

Business Fax No. _____

How many employees are there at this

address? _____

Please specify your regular requirements:

Vegetarian meals Yes ☐ No ☐

Special diet (please specify) _____

A non-smoking room (where available)

Yes ☐ No ☐

Your morning newspaper _____

Do you normally settle your account by

credit card? Yes ☐ No ☐

If yes, which one? _____

Who normally places hotel reservations on your behalf?

Name _____

Title _____

Contact Tel. No. _____

How many nights per year do you spend
away from home on average?

1. In the UK _____

Scotland _____ Wales _____

Ireland _____ England _____

2. Abroad _____

Please specify countries _____

Your other business needs:

Do you often entertain non-resident clients/

colleagues while on business: Yes ☐ No ☐

Do you organise conferences or meetings?

Yes ☐ No ☐

If yes, on average how many delegate places

do you require? _____

Your holidays:

Do you take short break holidays in the UK

or Ireland? Yes ☐ No ☐

How many per year? _____

In which regions? _____

What are your sporting/leisure interests?

_____

Do you have any children? Yes ☐ No ☐

If yes, please list their ages _____

Your Logis Corporate Club Card and map will
be posted to your business address within 28
days.

Which map do you require?

England & Wales ☐ Scotland ☐ Ireland ☐

Under the terms of the Data Protection Act, the
above information will be treated in the strict-
est confidence.
If you do not wish us to include you in any
mailings or offers from member hotels, or re-
lated supply companies, please tick this box. ☐

For office use:

Date card issued _____

Card No. _____

Logis
of
Great Britain

The Logis Corporate Club

Offering regular business users of Logis hotels a range of benefits which we hope will make your corporate travel enjoyable. **E**very member will receive...

• Access to a special 'corporate rate' at hundreds of independent Logis hotels around Britain and Ireland. This rate will include: A single room with en-suite bath or shower, full English, Welsh, Scottish, or Irish breakfast, early morning newspaper (where available), VAT and all service charges.

• Automatic free upgrade to double or twin room if available.

• Guaranteed reservation to 6pm on day of arrival.

• Regular promotions, offers and incentives.

• A numbered membership card.

• Free touring map(s), listing all Logis hotels.

All reservations and enquiries can be placed through our central reservations office, on **01865 875888,** or by fax on **01865 875777.**

How much does membership cost?
Membership of the Logis Corporate Club is absolutely free to bona fide business travellers who have completed the application form overleaf in full.

How do I join?
Simply fill out the form on the reverse and post it to: Logis of Great Britain, 20 Church Road, Horspath, Oxford OX9 lRU. (Please allow 28 days for the delivery of your card and map).

Logis
of
Great Britain

Logis Corporate Card
Membership Application Form

About you:

Name _____

Address _____

_____

_____

Home Tel No. _____

Car Phone or Mobile Phone No _____

About your company:

Name _____

Business Address _____

_____

_____

Business Tel. No. _____

Business Fax No. _____

How many employees are there at this

address? _____

Please specify your regular requirements:

Vegetarian meals Yes ☐ No ☐

Special diet (please specify) _____

A non-smoking room (where available\

Yes ☐ No ☐

Your morning newspaper _____

Do you normally settle your account by

credit card? Yes ☐ No ☐

If yes, which one? _____

Who normally places hotel reservations on your behalf?

Name _____

Title _____

Contact Tel. No. _____

How many nights per year do you spend

away from home on average?

1. In the UK _____

Scotland _____ Wales _____

Ireland _____ England _____

2. Abroad _____

Please specify countries _____

Your other business needs:

Do you often entertain non-resident clients/

colleagues while on business: Yes ☐ No ☐

Do you organise conferences or meetings?

Yes ☐ No ☐

If yes, on average how many delegate places

do you require? _____

Your holidays:

Do you take short break holidays in the UK

or Ireland? Yes ☐ No ☐

How many per year? _____

In which regions? _____

What are your sporting/leisure interests?

_____

Do you have any children? Yes ☐ No ☐

If yes, please list their ages _____

Your Logis Corporate Club Card and map will
be posted to your business address within 28
days.

Which map do you require?

England & Wales ☐ Scotland ☐ Ireland ☐

Under the terms of the Data Protection Act, the
above information will be treated in the strict-
est confidence.

If you do not wish us to include you in any
mailings or offers from member hotels, or re-
lated supply companies, please tick this box. ☐

For office use:

Date card issued _____

Card No. _____

Logis
of
Great Britain

The Logis Corporate Club

Offering regular business users of Logis hotels a range of benefits which we hope will make your corporate travel enjoyable. Every member will receive...

- Access to a special 'corporate rate' at hundreds of independent Logis hotels around Britain and Ireland. This rate will include: A single room with en-suite bath or shower, full English, Welsh, Scottish, or Irish breakfast, early morning newspaper (where available), VAT and all service charges.
- Automatic free upgrade to double or twin room if available.
- Guaranteed reservation to 6pm on day of arrival.
  Regular promotions, offers and incentives.
- A numbered membership card.
- Free touring map(s), listing all Logis hotels.

All reservations and enquiries can be placed through our central reservations office, on **01865 875888,** or by fax on **01865 875777.**

How much does membership cost?
Membership of the Logis Corporate Club is absolutely free to bona fide business travellers who have completed the application form overleaf in full.

How do I join?
Simply fill out the form on the reverse and post it to: Logis of Great Britain, 20 Church Road, Horspath, Oxford OX9 1RU. (Please allow 28 days for the delivery of your card and map).

Logis
of
Great Britain

Logis Corporate Card
Membership Application Form

About you:

Name _____

Address _____

_____

_____

Home Tel No. _____

Car Phone or Mobile Phone No _____

About your company:

Name _____

Business Address _____

_____

_____

_____

Business Tel. No. _____

Business Fax No. _____

How many employees are there at this

address? _____

Please specify your regular requirements:

Vegetarian meals Yes ☐ No ☐

Special diet (please specify) _____

A non-smoking room (where available)

Yes ☐ No ☐

Your morning newspaper _____

Do you normally settle your account by

credit card? Yes ☐ No ☐

If yes, which one? _____

Who normally places hotel reservations on your behalf?

Name _____

Title _____

Contact Tel. No. _____

How many nights per year do you spend

away from home on average?

1. In the UK _____

Scotland _____ Wales _____

Ireland _____ England _____

2. Abroad _____

Please specify countries _____

Your other business needs:

Do you often entertain non-resident clients/

colleagues while on business: Yes ☐ No ☐

Do you organise conferences or meetings?

Yes ☐ No ☐

If yes, on average how many delegate places

do you require? _____

Your holidays:

Do you take short break holidays in the UK

or Ireland? Yes ☐ No ☐

How many per year? _____

In which regions? _____

What are your sporting/leisure interests?

_____

Do you have any children? Yes ☐ No ☐

If yes, please list their ages _____

Your Logis Corporate Club Card and map will
be posted to your business address within 28
days.

Which map do you require?

England & Wales ☐ Scotland ☐ Ireland ☐

Under the terms of the Data Protection Act, t
above information will be treated in the stri
est confidence.
If you do not wish us to include you in a
mailings or offers from member hotels, or
lated supply companies, please tick this box.

For office use:

Date card issued _____

Card No. _____

Logis
of
Great Britain

The Logis Corporate Club

Offering regular business users of Logis hotels a range of benefits which we hope will make your corporate travel enjoyable. Every member will receive...

- Access to a special 'corporate rate' at hundreds of independent Logis hotels around Britain and Ireland. This rate will include: A single room with en-suite bath or shower, full English, Welsh, Scottish, or Irish breakfast, early morning newspaper (where available), VAT and all service charges.
- Automatic free upgrade to double or twin room if available.
- Guaranteed reservation to 6pm on day of arrival.
  Regular promotions, offers and incentives.
- A numbered membership card.
- Free touring map(s), listing all Logis hotels.

All reservations and enquiries can be placed through our central reservations office, on **01865 875888,** or by fax on **01865 875777.**

How much does membership cost?
Membership of the Logis Corporate Club is absolutely free to bona fide business travellers who have completed the application form overleaf in full.

How do I join?
Simply fill out the form on the reverse and post it to: Logis of Great Britain, 20 Church Road, Horspath, Oxford OX9 1RU. (Please allow 28 days for the delivery of your card and map).

Logis
of
Great Britain

Logis Corporate Card
Membership Application Form

About you:

Name _____

Address _____

_____

_____

Home Tel No. _____

Car Phone or Mobile Phone No _____

About your company:

Name _____

Business Address _____

_____

_____

.

Business Tel. No. _____

Business Fax No. _____

How many employees are there at this

address? _____

**Please specify your regular
requirements:**

Vegetarian meals Yes ☐ No ☐

Special diet (please specify) _____

A non-smoking room (where available)

Yes ☐ No ☐

Your morning newspaper _____

Do you normally settle your account by

credit card? Yes ☐ No ☐

If yes, which one? _____

**Who normally places hotel
reservations on your behalf?**

Name _____

Title _____

Contact Tel. No. _____

How many nights per year do you spend

away from home on average?

1. In the UK _____

Scotland _____ Wales _____

Ireland _____ England _____

2. Abroad _____

Please specify countries _____

Your other business needs:

Do you often entertain non-resident clients/

colleagues while on business: Yes ☐ No ☐

Do you organise conferences or meetings?

Yes ☐ No ☐

If yes, on average how many delegate places

do you require? _____

Your holidays:

Do you take short break holidays in the UK

or Ireland? Yes ☐ No ☐

How many per year? _____

In which regions? _____

What are your sporting/leisure interests?

_____

Do you have any children? Yes ☐ No ☐

If yes, please list their ages _____

Your Logis Corporate Club Card and map will
be posted to your business address within 28
days.

Which map do you require?

England & Wales ☐ Scotland ☐ Ireland ☐

Under the terms of the Data Protection Act, t'
above information will be treated in the stric
est confidence.
If you do not wish us to include you in a
mailings or offers from member hotels, or r
lated supply companies, please tick this box.☐

For office use:

Date card issued _____

Card No. _____

Logis
of
Great Britain

The Logis Corporate Club

Offering regular business users of Logis hotels a range of benefits which we hope will make your corporate travel enjoyable. Every member will receive...

• Access to a special 'corporate rate' at hundreds of independent Logis hotels around Britain and Ireland. This rate will include: A single room with en-suite bath or shower, full English, Welsh, Scottish, or Irish breakfast, early morning newspaper (where available), VAT and all service charges.

 Automatic free upgrade to double or twin room if available.
• Guaranteed reservation to 6pm on day of arrival.
• Regular promotions, offers and incentives.
 A numbered membership card.
• Free touring map(s), listing all Logis hotels.

All reservations and enquiries can be placed through our central reservations office, on **01865 875888,** or by fax on **01865 875777.**

How much does membership cost?
Membership of the Logis Corporate Club is absolutely free to bona fide business travellers who have completed the application form overleaf in full.

How do I join?
Simply fill out the form on the reverse and post it to: Logis of Great Britain, 20 Church Road, Horspath, Oxford OX9 lRU. (Please allow 28 days for the delivery of your card and map).

Logis
of
Great Britain

Logis Corporate Card
Membership Application Form

About you:

Name _____

Address _____

_____

_____

Home Tel No. _____

Car Phone or Mobile Phone No _____

About your company:

Name _____

Business Address _____

_____

_____

_____

Business Tel. No. _____

Business Fax No. _____

How many employees are there at this

address? _____

**Please specify your regular
requirements:**

Vegetarian meals Yes ☐ No ☐

Special diet (please specify) _____

A non-smoking room (where available)

Yes ☐ No ☐

Your morning newspaper _____

Do you normally settle your account by

credit card? Yes ☐ No ☐

If yes, which one? _____

**Who normally places hotel
reservations on your behalf?**

Name _____

Title _____

Contact Tel. No. _____

How many nights per year do you spend

away from home on average?

1. In the UK _____

Scotland _____ Wales _____

Ireland _____ England

2. Abroad _____

Please specify countries _____

Your other business needs:

Do you often entertain non-resident clients/

colleagues while on business: Yes ☐ No ☐

Do you organise conferences or meetings?

Yes ☐ No ☐

If yes, on average how many delegate places

do you require? _____

Your holidays:

Do you take short break holidays in the UK

or Ireland? Yes ☐ No ☐

How many per year? _____

In which regions? _____

What are your sporting/leisure interests?

_____

Do you have any children? Yes ☐ No ☐

If yes, please list their ages _____

Your Logis Corporate Club Card and map will
be posted to your business address within 28
days.

Which map do you require?

England & Wales ☐ Scotland ☐ Ireland ☐

Under the terms of the Data Protection Act, the
above information will be treated in the strict-
est confidence.
If you do not wish us to include you in any
mailings or offers from member hotels, or re-
lated supply companies, please tick this box. ☐

For office use:

Date card issued _____

Card No. _____

Guest Report Form

While every hotel listed in this directory is carefully inspected to the European Logis standard, any business can vary; staff may change, decor be damaged or the surrounding country be altered by development work. In the interests of keeping up the standards of Logis membership and the accuracy of this guide, we would therefore like to hear from you, the most important person in the Logis chain, the Logis customer. Simply complete and return this report form to us at the address listed below.

Name _____

Address _____

_____ Post code _____

Name of hotel visited_____

Main town reference (as listed in the guide) _____

Date of visit_____

Nature and purpose of visit (please tick as applicable)
□ Overnight stay □ Meal □ Holiday □ Business □ Both

Is this hotel a possible candidate for our national regional cuisine award?
(please tick) □ Yes □ No

Your comments. (Please continue your comments on an additional sheet of paper if you wish to.)

_____

We would also like to hear of other hotels, not presently listed in this directory, that offer a 'Logis' standard of service, so that we can ask them whether they would like to be included in future editions of this directory:

Hotel name _____

Address _____

_____ Tel. no. _____

Owner's name _____

Signed _____ Date _____

Thank you for taking the time to complete this form.

Return to: Logis of Great Britain, 20 Church Road, Horspath, Oxford OX9 1RU.

Half Price Logis Guides

The 1996 edition of the Logis of Great Britain guide will be printed in February 1996, available through all good bookshops, Logis member hotels and our offices, priced at £7.50. We expect the 1996 edition to feature even more hotels that have passed the European Logis inspection and are proud to display the yellow and green fireplace.

To reward our loyal readers, we are offering the opportunity to place an advanced order for the 1996 edition for £3.75 (including postage in the UK), half the final published price.

Simply fill in the form below and post it, together with cheque/postal order or details of your Access/Visa number, to arrive in our offices before January 31st 1996. We will then rush you a copy of the new Logis of Great Britain guide as soon as it is 'off the press'.

For orders outside the UK add £1 for postage to Europe, £2 for the rest of the world.

Order form

☐ I enclose a cheque for £3.75 made payable to LGB

☐ I enclose my order on company letterhead, please invoice me (UK registered companies only)

☐ Please debit my credit Access/Visa card account

Card number _____ Expiry Date _____

Name as shown on the card _____

Signature _____

Send an advance copy of the 1996 Logis of Great Britain directory to:

Name _____

Address _____

_____

_____ Post code _____

Return this form to: Logis of Great Britain, 20 Church Road, Horspath, Oxford OX9 1RU.

Only orders received before 31st January 1996 will be supplied at this special discounted price.

Guest Report Form

While every hotel listed in this directory is carefully inspected to the European Logis standard, any business can vary; staff may change, decor be damaged or the surrounding country be altered by development work. In the interests of keeping up the standards of Logis membership and the accuracy of this guide, we would therefore like to hear from you, the most important person in the Logis chain, the Logis customer. Simply complete and return this report form to us at the address listed below.

Name _____

Address _____

_____ Post code _____

Name of hotel visited _____

Main town reference (as listed in the guide) _____

Date of visit _____

Nature and purpose of visit (please tick as applicable)
☐ Overnight stay ☐ Meal ☐ Holiday ☐ Business ☐ Both

Is this hotel a possible candidate for our national regional cuisine award?
(please tick) ☐ Yes ☐ No

Your comments. (Please continue your comments on an additional sheet of paper if you wish to.)

_____

We would also like to hear of other hotels, not presently listed in this directory, that offer a Logis' standard of service, so that we can ask them whether they would like to be included in future editions of this directory:

Hotel name _____

Address _____

_____ Tel. no. _____

Owner's name _____

Signed _____ Date _____

Thank you for taking the time to complete this form.

Return to: Logis of Great Britain, 20 Church Road, Horspath, Oxford OX9 1RU.

Half Price Logis Guides

The 1996 edition of the Logis of Great Britain guide will be printed in February 1996, available through all good bookshops, Logis member hotels and our offices, priced at £7.50. We expect the 1996 edition to feature even more hotels that have passed the European Logis inspection and are proud to display the yellow and green fireplace.

To reward our loyal readers, we are offering the opportunity to place an advanced order for the 1996 edition for £3.75 (including postage in the UK), half the final published price.

Simply fill in the form below and post it, together with cheque/postal order or details of your Access/Visa number, to arrive in our offices before January 31st 1996. We will then rush you a copy of the new Logis of Great Britain guide as soon as it is 'off the press'.

For orders outside the UK add £1 for postage to Europe, £2 for the rest of the world.

Order form

☐ I enclose a cheque for £3.75 made payable to LGB

☐ I enclose my order on company letterhead, please invoice me (UK registered companies only)

☐ Please debit my credit Access/Visa card account

Card number _____   Expiry Date _____

Name as shown on the card _____

Signature _____

Send an advance copy of the 1996 Logis of Great Britain directory to:

Name _____

Address _____

_____

_____ Post code _____

Return this form to: Logis of Great Britain, 20 Church Road, Horspath, Oxford OX9 1RU.

Only orders received before 31st January 1996 will be supplied at this special discounted price.

Guest Report Form

While every hotel listed in this directory is carefully inspected to the European Logis standard, any business can vary; staff may change, decor be damaged or the surrounding country be altered by development work. In the interests of keeping up the standards of Logis membership and the accuracy of this guide, we would therefore like to hear from you, the most important person in the Logis chain, the Logis customer. Simply complete and return this report form to us at the address listed below.

Name _____

Address _____

_____ Post code _____

Name of hotel visited_____

Main town reference (as listed in the guide) _____

Date of visit_____

Nature and purpose of visit (please tick as applicable)
☐ Overnight stay ☐ Meal ☐ Holiday ☐ Business ☐ Both

Is this hotel a possible candidate for our national regional cuisine award?
(please tick) ☐ Yes ☐ No

Your comments. (Please continue your comments on an additional sheet of paper if you wish to.)

_____

We would also like to hear of other hotels, not presently listed in this directory, that offer a Logis' standard of service, so that we can ask them whether they would like to be included in future editions of this directory:

Hotel name _____

Address _____

_____ Tel. no. _____

Owner's name _____

Signed _____ Date _____

Thank you for taking the time to complete this form.

Return to: Logis of Great Britain, 20 Church Road, Horspath, Oxford OX9 1RU.

Half Price Logis Guides

The 1996 edition of the Logis of Great Britain guide will be printed in February 1996, available through all good bookshops, Logis member hotels and our offices, priced at £7.50. We expect the 1996 edition to feature even more hotels that have passed the European Logis inspection and are proud to display the yellow and green fireplace.

To reward our loyal readers, we are offering the opportunity to place an advanced order for the 1996 edition for £3.75 (including postage in the UK), half the final published price.

Simply fill in the form below and post it, together with cheque/postal order or details of your Access/Visa number, to arrive in our offices before January 31st 1996. We will then rush you a copy of the new Logis of Great Britain guide as soon as it is 'off the press'.

For orders outside the UK add £1 for postage to Europe, £2 for the rest of the world.

Order form

☐ I enclose a cheque for £3.75 made payable to LGB

☐ I enclose my order on company letterhead, please invoice me (UK registered companies only)

☐ Please debit my credit Access/Visa card account

Card number _____   Expiry Date _____

Name as shown on the card _____

Signature _____

Send an advance copy of the 1996 Logis of Great Britain directory to:

Name _____

Address _____

_____

_____ Post code _____

Return this form to: Logis of Great Britain, 20 Church Road, Horspath, Oxford OX9 1RU.

Only orders received before 31st January 1996 will be supplied at this special discounted price.

Guest Report Form

While every hotel listed in this directory is carefully inspected to the European Logis standard, any business can vary; staff may change, decor be damaged or the surrounding country be altered by development work. In the interests of keeping up the standards of Logis membership and the accuracy of this guide, we would therefore like to hear from you, the most important person in the Logis chain, the Logis customer. Simply complete and return this report form to us at the address listed below.

Name _____

Address _____

_____ Post code _____

Name of hotel visited_____

Main town reference (as listed in the guide) _____

Date of visit_____

Nature and purpose of visit (please tick as applicable)

☐ Overnight stay ☐ Meal   ☐ Holiday ☐ Business ☐ Both

Is this hotel a possible candidate for our national regional cuisine award?
(please tick) ☐ Yes   ☐ No

Your comments. (Please continue your comments on an additional sheet of paper if you wish to.)

_____

We would also like to hear of other hotels, not presently listed in this directory, that offer a Logis' standard of service, so that we can ask them whether they would like to be included in future editions of this directory:

Hotel name _____

Address _____

_____ Tel. no. _____

Owner's name _____

Signed _____ Date _____

Thank you for taking the time to complete this form.

Return to: Logis of Great Britain, 20 Church Road, Horspath, Oxford OX9 1RU.

Half Price Logis Guides

The 1996 edition of the Logis of Great Britain guide will be printed in February 1996, available through all good bookshops, Logis member hotels and our offices, priced at £7.50. We expect the 1996 edition to feature even more hotels that have passed the European Logis inspection and are proud to display the yellow and green fireplace.

To reward our loyal readers, we are offering the opportunity to place an advanced order for the 1996 edition for £3.75 (including postage in the UK), half the final published price.

Simply fill in the form below and post it, together with cheque/postal order or details of your Access/Visa number, to arrive in our offices before January 31st 1996. We will then rush you a copy of the new Logis of Great Britain guide as soon as it is 'off the press'.

For orders outside the UK add £1 for postage to Europe, £2 for the rest of the world.

Order form

☐ I enclose a cheque for £3.75 made payable to LGB

☐ I enclose my order on company letterhead, please invoice me (UK registered companies only)

☐ Please debit my credit Access/Visa card account

Card number _____ Expiry Date _____

Name as shown on the card _____

Signature _____

Send an advance copy of the 1996 Logis of Great Britain directory to:

Name _____

Address _____

_____

_____ Post code _____

Return this form to: Logis of Great Britain, 20 Church Road, Horspath, Oxford OX9 1RU.

Only orders received before 31st January 1996 will be supplied at this special discounted price.

Guest Report Form

While every hotel listed in this directory is carefully inspected to the European Logis standard, any business can vary; staff may change, decor be damaged or the surrounding country be altered by development work. In the interests of keeping up the standards of Logis membership and the accuracy of this guide, we would therefore like to hear from you, the most important person in the Logis chain, the Logis customer. Simply complete and return this report form to us at the address listed below.

Name _____

Address _____

_____ Post code _____

Name of hotel visited_____

Main town reference (as listed in the guide) _____

Date of visit_____

Nature and purpose of visit (please tick as applicable)
☐ Overnight stay ☐ Meal   ☐ Holiday ☐ Business ☐ Both

Is this hotel a possible candidate for our national regional cuisine award?
(please tick) ☐ Yes ☐ No

Your comments. (Please continue your comments on an additional sheet of paper if you wish to.)

_____

We would also like to hear of other hotels, not presently listed in this directory, that offer a Logis' standard of service, so that we can ask them whether they would like to be included in future editions of this directory:

Hotel name _____

Address _____

_____ Tel. no. _____

Owner's name _____

Signed _____ Date _____

Thank you for taking the time to complete this form.

Return to: Logis of Great Britain, 20 Church Road, Horspath, Oxford OX9 1RU.

Half Price Logis Guides

The 1996 edition of the Logis of Great Britain guide will be printed in February 1996, available through all good bookshops, Logis member hotels and our offices, priced at £7.50. We expect the 1996 edition to feature even more hotels that have passed the European Logis inspection and are proud to display the yellow and green fireplace.

To reward our loyal readers, we are offering the opportunity to place an advanced order for the 1996 edition for £3.75 (including postage in the UK), half the final published price.

Simply fill in the form below and post it, together with cheque/postal order or details of your Access/Visa number, to arrive in our offices before January 31st 1996. We will then rush you a copy of the new Logis of Great Britain guide as soon as it is 'off the press'.

For orders outside the UK add £1 for postage to Europe, £2 for the rest of the world.

Order form

☐ I enclose a cheque for £3.75 made payable to LGB

☐ I enclose my order on company letterhead, please invoice me (UK registered companies only)

☐ Please debit my credit Access/Visa card account

Card number _____ Expiry Date _____

Name as shown on the card _____

Signature _____

Send an advance copy of the 1996 Logis of Great Britain directory to:

Name _____

Address _____

_____

_____ Post code _____

Return this form to: Logis of Great Britain, 20 Church Road, Horspath, Oxford OX9 1RU.

Only orders received before 31st January 1996 will be supplied at this special discounted price.